GHOST TOWNS

Colorado Style

VOLUME ONE
NORTHERN REGION

KENNETH JESSEN

J. V. Publications

2212 Flora Ct.
Loveland, Colorado 80537

Ghost Towns, Colorado Style
Volume One - Northern Region
Copyright © 1998 by Kenneth Jessen

Published by J. V. Publications, 2212 Flora Ct., Loveland, CO 80537

First Edition

1 2 3 4 5 6 7 8 9

Library of Congress Catalog Card Number: 98-66536
ISBN 0-9611662-8-2 (pbk.)

Printed in the United States of America

Front Cover: Eldora, Boulder County
Back Cover: Apex, Gilpin County

Design by LaVonne Ewing; Production by LaVonne Ewing and Candace Harron; Illustrations by Julia McMillan; Maps drawn by Kenneth Jessen; Contemporary photography by Kenneth and Sonje Jessen; Photo processing by Custom Darkroom and Superior One Hour Photo.

To my wonderful family,
Sonje, Todd, April, Chris, and Ben Jessen
and Dusty Arnold

Schoolhouse in Lake Gulch *(Drawing by Julia McMillan)*

Acknowledgements

Many thanks goes to the patient staff at the Colorado Historical Society and the Denver Public Library. Also thanks go to my readers Lee Gregory, Beth Nobles, Russ Livingston, Larry Jones, Sonje Jessen, Larry Glass, Joe Bolesta, Christine Skellett and Mary Edelmaier.

For information on Northwest Colorado, many thanks go to Dan Davidson, Director of the Museum of Northwest Colorado.

For her fine illustrations, I would like to thank Julia McMillan. And my appreciation goes to LaVonne Ewing and her sister, Candace Harron for their design and production of this book.

About The Author

This is Kenneth Jessen's ninth book; other works include *Railroads of Northern Colorado, Thompson Valley Tales, Eccentric Colorado, Colorado Gunsmoke, Bizarre Colorado, Estes Park - A Quick History, Georgetown - A Quick History and An Ear in His Pocket.* Ken is also the author of well over 500 published articles plus several booklets. He is a life member of the Colorado Railroad Museum, a longtime member of the Rocky Mountain Railroad Club, a member of the Colorado Historical Society and one of the founders of the Western Outlaw-Lawman History Association. He also belongs to the San Luis Valley Historical Society.

Sonje Jessen, Ken's wife, was a major contributor to this book and acted as editorial consultant. She was also instrumental in locating and photographing many of the ghost towns on various field trips.

Currently Ken owns and operates J. V. Publications, after spending thirty-three years working as an engineer for Hewlett-Packard. Ken and Sonje live in Loveland, Colorado, and have three grown sons and one daughter-in-law.

THE AREAS OF

GHOST TOWNS

Colorado style

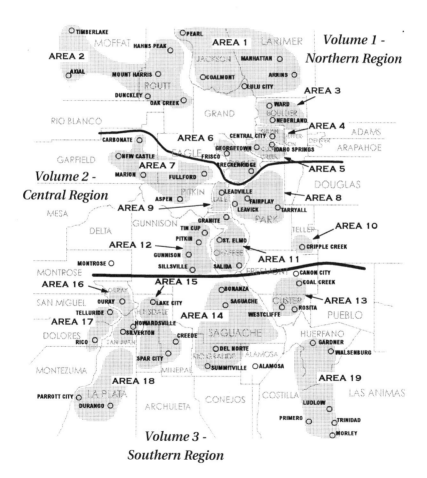

Volume 1 -
Northern Region

Volume 2 -
Central Region

Volume 3 -
Southern Region

THE THREE VOLUMES OF

GHOST TOWNS

Colorado Style

Volume One - Northern Region
ISBN: 0-9611662-8-2

Includes the following counties:

Boulder, Clear Creek, Gilpin, Grand, Jackson, Larimer,
Moffat, Routt and Summit

Volume Two - Central Region
ISBN: 0-9611662-9-0

Includes the following counties:

Chaffee, Eagle, Garfield, Gunnison, Lake, Park, Pitkin and Teller

Volume Three - Southern Region
ISBN: 0-9611662-4-x

Includes the following counties:

Conejos, Costilla, Custer, Dolores, Fremont, Hindsdale,
Huerfano, Las Animas, La Plata, Mineral, Ouray, Rio Grande,
Saguache, San Juan and San Miguel

Volume One - Northern Region

Table of Contents

Organization Of This Book

This three-volume book is broken into areas, an area being similar to a chapter. An area consists of ten to thirty ghost towns, abandoned mining camps plus occupied towns. Most of the sites in an area can be visited in one or two days. Contemporary and historic photographs are combined to provide a perspective of how it once appeared.

An overall map plus a table of contents is presented at the beginning of an area. Each area has its own introduction with short stories about people and events that shaped that area's history. After the introduction, the story of each town is presented in alphabetical order.

Each town history starts with a summary of its general location, accessibility, and if any historic structures are still standing. Within the text are facts on how the town was named, when it was founded, and if it had its own post office. The text may also include the peak population, an estimate of the number of structures, and a general description of the businesses and schools. For a town which has vanished, a chronology of its disappearance may be included, based on the observations of other historians. For towns which are difficult to locate, maps are included to guide the adventurous.

For some readers, it is important to know where the information on an individual town came from, and end notes present the source material for each story.

Research For This Project

Every possible reliable source of information, which added to the knowledge about a particular town, was consulted. Some sources, where the research was not performed well, were intentionally ignored, while others were used to distill the history of a particular site. In some cases, newspaper articles were used, however, reliable secondary sources of information dominate the material. To provide some insight as to which sites remain physically, the author and his wife visited most of the sites included in this work.

The basis for the maps are field trips combined with United States Geological Survey topographic maps. In some cases, Trails West maps were consulted to verify road locations.

INTRODUCTION

This book, presented in three volumes, concentrates on towns and mining camps in the Colorado mountains. The first volume covers the northern region, the second volume covers the central region, and the third volume covers the southern region of the state. Special emphasis is placed on towns which are completely or partially abandoned.

What's A Ghost Town?

Just the mention of a ghost town seems to pique the interest of many people. It is among the most romantic historical topics Colorado has to offer. How could a once thriving boom town be abandoned and fall to ruin? Many have disappeared leaving hardly a trace. What happened to the tens of thousands of people? Some towns were abandoned only to be re-populated, then abandoned again. There are well over 300 ghost town sites in Colorado, most associated with the mining industry. Their varied and interesting history is covered in these volumes.

The term "ghost town" is applied liberally to describe practically any mountain town, mining camp or even random collection of shanties which, at some point in time, was abandoned. Even the use of the word "town" is misleading since many of these places did not have the structure normally associated with a town such as a post office, stores, hotels, schools and some type of government. A ghost town could also be a town which was a ghost of its former self. Some ghost towns could better be referred to as camps, since they were never anything more than a collection of cabins and tents scattered near a mine. Despite arguments over definitions, there are interesting stories behind these locations.

Many towns and camps were never officially surveyed or registered, much less incorporated. Their existence may yet be verified. "New" ghost towns have been found during recent years in some of the more remote areas of the state. Real estate developers have been around for a long time, and there are sites which were surveyed, promoted, given names and even presented on maps, even though not a single structure was ever built. In many cases, a group of nameless cabins high on a mountainside will remain anonymous. Some smaller, less important camp will appear in numerous ghost town books because it has a name.

Changes in the mountain economy, especially after World War II, have drastically altered the fate of many abandoned towns. Breckenridge, Frisco and Keystone, with brand new buildings and nearly a 100% occupancy rate, hardly seem like former ghost towns. At one time, however, they were nearly abandoned. The old cabins in Gold Hill and Platoro have been restored to meet the demand for mountain property. This book deals with traditional ghost towns as well as those rejuvenated by the economy.

Most town sites were withdrawn from public lands long ago. This is called "preemption," meaning that the right to purchase a specific piece of government land is given ahead of others. Where a plat or drawing for a town was filed, the preemption took effect. Title to individual lots were sold, and through generations of owners, most remain private property. Within the information on a given town, this book delineates those accessible by the public from those where access is limited by private property designation.

Most mining towns and camps are directly associated with gold and silver. There were also important Colorado towns which were based on mining coal, uranium, copper, iron, molybdenum, gypsum, stone and other minerals. There are other towns which acted as supply points to the mining towns where freighting was important to the economy. Although not covered in these books, there is a whole category of ghost towns based on failed attempts at agricultural colonies.

The mental picture of a ghost town is a group of ramshackle

abandoned cabins set in a deep, forested valley high in the mountains where the only noise is the wind. There are certainly picturesque places like this, but one disappointment is that few traces remain of most of Colorado's true ghost towns. Some were destroyed by fire never to be rebuilt, others were built in an avalanche track and were eventually leveled, and still others fell victim to vandals. Wooden buildings are biodegradable, and a century of high winds and heavy snow claimed the majority of structures. Large trees have grown in the middle of many an old cabin, and the forest has hidden others from view. There are several cases where buildings from one town were simply moved a short distance to form a new town. Even heavy two story log buildings were skidded to another site.

At the rate structures are vanishing, precious little will be left of Colorado's ghost towns for the next generation, and it is a case of ashes to ashes and dust to dust. Where once destructive mining practices stripped the land barren of vegetation, the natural healing process is restoring the land. After the passage of another century, the land will look once again like it did prior to human invasion.

A simplification of the early demographic history of Colorado goes something like this: gold or silver was discovered, thousands of prospectors poured into the area, towns were established and gained instant population. When the ore was exhausted, the prospectors moved, on abandoning the town just like in the musical *Paint Your Wagon.* If a new strike was made, the once abandoned town would be repopulated. Sometimes the mines closed because of the difficulty processing the ore. If a new smelting process was introduced, then a once abandoned site may again flourish. Colorado society during the 1860s through the 1880s was very mobile, and the majority of people were willing to pick up and move on a moment's notice. There was little loyalty to a particular town.

Surprising reversal of fortune include the town of Nevadaville, which was at one time larger than Denver or its neighbor, Central City. Nevadaville is almost a ghost town today, and a very small fraction of its original buildings are left standing. It is a challenge to find any remains, dilapidated or not, of Parkville. At one time, it was the Summit County Seat and the largest town in the region. It had three theaters and its own mint for gold coins. There is little left of the Garfield County Seat of Carbonate. Oro City, the forerunner to Leadville, had a population of 10,000, yet hardly a stick of wood remains. A single rusted metal sign marks its location. Dayton was the Lake County Seat, and when the ore was exhausted in the area mines, it was abandoned. Dayton was discovered by tourists wanting a peaceful place to relax and was reborn as Twin Lakes. The town sites of Ruedi, Montgomery and old Dillon are under reservoirs. Victims of avalanches, Masontown, Tomichie and Woodstock were never rebuilt.

Unusual names are pervasive among Colorado's ghost towns, such as Sky City and Spook City near Del Norte or Royal Flush, northeast of Hahns Peak. Near Hahns Peak, a town nicknamed "Bugtown" was founded. West of Boulder there was a camp called Puzzler, and not too far away in Gilpin County, Wideawake was named by alert miners. Mosquito got its name when the flattened remains of that insect were found on the blank line where the name of the town was to have been filled in by its settlers. Orient was located in the northeast corner of the San Luis Valley, and Bachelor City sat in a flat above Creede. The remains of Pieplant are located north of the Taylor Reservoir. Stringtown, located near Leadville, still shows up on contemporary maps. It was located between Jacktown and Bucktown, but well below Stumptown.

It is the sincere hope of the author that you find this book entertaining and yet informative.

Kenneth Jessen
2212 Flora Court
Loveland, CO 80537

AREA ONE

Larimer, Jackson and Grand Counties

AREA 1: Larimer, Jackson and Grand Counties
Selected Towns

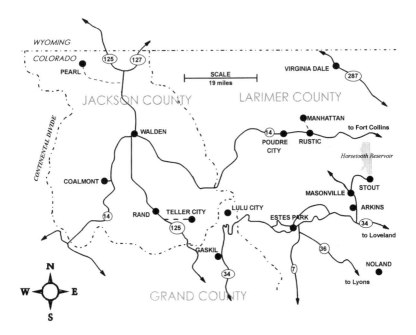

Introduction to Larimer, Jackson and Grand Counties

L arimer County, Jackson County and the northern portion of
Grand County encompass an enormous land area. North Park
occupies most of Jackson County, and this expanse of relatively
flat area is flanked to the west by the Continental Divide in the
Mount Zirkel Wilderness Area and on the east by the Front Range
within Rocky Mountain National Park. The high mountains of the
Front Range make up the western half of Larimer County while to
the east are the plains.

The mining towns founded in this area are spread out, and
what little mineralization existed containing precious metals

failed to sustain any long-lasting economy. At the far northwestern corner of North Park were the copper deposits at Pearl. On the south-central end, west of the Continental Divide, the short-lived camps of Tyner, Crescent, Park City and Teller City blossomed, based on silver ore. Within what is now Rocky Mountain National Park the mining camps of Gaskil, Dutchtown and Lulu City once existed. West of Fort Collins, the gold mining towns of Poudre City, Manhattan and Masonville grew. Coalmont was supported by a large coal deposit in the south-central part of North Park.

The area's most sustained form of mining was the rock quarry industry, satisfying the needs of the growing cities along the Front Range. Quarry towns along the eastern base of the Front Range included Noland, located north of Lyons in Boulder County, Arkins, west of Loveland, and Stout, west of Fort Collins. Gypsum was mined until 1965 west of Loveland at Wilds.

Mining continues to this day with new discoveries of diamonds, both industrial and gem quality, northwest of Fort Collins. The largest gem quality diamond ever recovered in Colorado came from the Kelsey Lake deposit in 1997.

As for ghost towns, Coalmont, Tyner, Crescent, Park City, Teller City, Gaskil, Dutchtown, Lulu City, Poudre City, and Manhattan are devoid of human inhabitants. The high demand for land along the Front Range has resulted in new housing at Noland and Arkins. A combined bar and restaurant sits on the Stout site at the south end of Horsetooth Reservoir. Pearl is now a ranching community, and new homes have been built in the vicinity of Wilds. Masonville was never abandoned and many new homes have been built in the area.

ARKINS

Supported By Stone Industry

- *Larimer County, Big Thompson drainage*
- *Site accessible by paved road*
- *Town had a post office; number of original structures unknown*

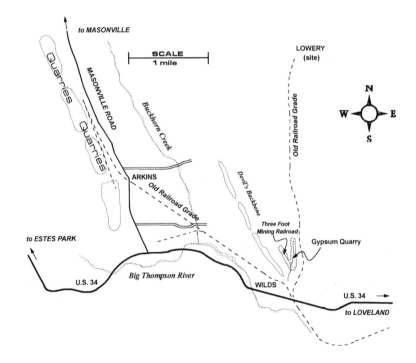

The quarry town of Arkins was served by the Greeley, Salt Lake & Pacific from Loveland. The railroad passed through Wilds diagonally across to Arkins, then using a switchback, climbed up to the quarries. There are now modern homes at Arkins.

A t one time, a vast stone industry existed along the foothills between Lyons and Fort Collins. One of the most active quarries was located seven miles west of Loveland on the ridge which parallels the Masonville Road. These were known as the Buckhorn or Arkins quarries and were developed in 1886 by the Union Pacific Railroad in an effort to increase its freight business.

A large order was needed to get the quarries off to a good start. One potential customer was Kansas City, and samples of stone were shown to town officials. A contract was signed to supply all of the paving stone and curbing for the entire city. This single order amounted to 2,500 carloads of stone.

The Union Pacific, however, put the cart before the horse. At the time the contract was signed, there wasn't any rail service from Loveland to the quarries. Work began on the railroad in early 1887, and at the same time, men were sent to the quarries to begin extracting stone to fill the Kansas City order.

The rail line to the Arkins Quarries above the Masonville Road climbed the hillside then doubled back on itself. This photo was made between 1901 and 1903 and shows a loading area with several pole derricks on the lower level of track. A man is dumping waste rock from a wheelbarrow in the right center of the photo. *(Jim Wild collection)*

To break off a large slab of rock, holes were first drilled, then long steel wedges were driven into the drill holes to fracture the rock. After the slab was free from the quarry face, it would be lifted onto a railroad car by a pole derrick. *(Jim Wild collection)*

The number of men working at the quarry soon exceeded 100, and a post office was established that year at the base of the ridge at a place named Arkins. A large frame boarding house, complete with a kitchen and dining hall, was constructed by the Union Pacific. The kitchen had a spacious brick oven able to bake seventy loaves at a time. The dining hall could seat 280 men, and as the number of quarry workers reached that number, six cooks were kept busy full time.

There were bunkhouses for the workers, but supervisors were provided with a separate bunkhouse connected to the boarding house by a covered passageway. A company store was added to one end of the kitchen and carried overalls, hats, shoes, groceries and a few medicines. A second store, known as the Charles & Smith, soon opened at Arkins.

Building the rail line west of Loveland to serve the quarries was relatively easy. The railroad ran west out of Loveland, past Alfred Wild's property, then turned north at the Masonville Road where it passed the small Arkins Depot. The railroad angled up the ridge and, after a mile, reached the halfway point. A switchback was used to reverse direction and gain the remainder of the distance to the quarries. By using this zig-zag technique, the railroad could maintain a reasonable grade. The old railroad grade can still be seen stretching across the hillside, and the stone abutments for both the upper and lower trestles across a small ravine are quite evident.

The railroad made its first shipment of eleven cars of stone to Kansas City on April 7, 1887. Business picked up to fifteen cars of stone per day. The Loveland depot agent soon reported that overall business had doubled both in passengers and freight service over the previous year.

There were a number of different types of stone shipped from the Arkins Quarries. Paving stones, flagging and curbing for streets and sidewalks were the primary products. Large foundation stones, weighing many tons, were also shipped.

Each aspect of removing stone and shaping it was specialized. Some men worked at drilling and used wedges to break large slabs of stone free from the quarry face. At the bottom of the face, other quarry workers used wheelbarrows to carry the smaller pieces of stone across the tracks to the block cutters. Quarry workers were also required to operate the numerous pole derricks used to lift large foundation stones onto the railroad cars.

Some forty-five skilled block cutters were brought in from Missouri. Most were Swedes and were highly skilled at their trade. A block cutter used a set of three hammers, all stored within easy reach with the heads down. The first step in block cutting was to score the stone with one of the hammers then flip it over and tap it with a sledge hammer. If done correctly, the slab would break along the score. The third hammer was used to even up the edges. The finished stone was stacked neatly along the railroad track for shipment.

Back in the 1880s, the brake system on the railroad cars was crude and the quarries were plagued with a constant series of accidents. One of the worst accidents occurred in June of 1887 at the upper quarry. Three fully loaded cars began to slip down the hill towards the switch. A worker jumped on one of the cars and began cranking on the brakes. They were defective. When the worker tried the brakes on the next car, they too were defective. The cars began to pick up speed, and all the worker could do was jump. At the bottom of the upper grade near the switch, the speeding cars struck another loaded car and wrecked it where it stood. The cars went through the switch, off the end of the track, into a gully, and were totally demolished.

Even with these problems, the contract for Kansas City was filled in March of 1888. The four quarry openings used to fill this order were abandoned and the men laid off. However, by May of 1889, a stone crusher was installed and the quarries were back to capacity shipping a dozen cars a day. Employment returned to one hundred men.

In 1904, stone from the Arkins Quarries was selected for the new Denver Mint along with Tennessee and Vermont marble. Many other important structures in Denver, including the entrance to the City Park, the Tabor Grand Opera House and even the State Capital, were built from Arkins stone.

The stone industry was not to last. The use of concrete as a structural material replaced stone foundations. Asphalt began to replace the paving stone business and the industry dwindled to the supply of ornamental stone and some flagging. The Arkins post office closed in 1906, and in 1926, the railroad tracks were taken up. A few independent quarries have remained in operation over the years, but none on the grand scale of the Arkins Quarries.

In a shallow valley running north from the Devil's Backbone north toward Stout were other quarries. A small town or camp called Lowery was located at the end of the railroad spur serving these quarries. Little is known about Lowery, its size and number of structures. Nothing remains at the site today.

Ansel Watrous, *History of Larimer County*, Colorado, The Courier Printing & Publishing Company, Fort Collins, Colorado, 1911, pp. 152, 205, 393.

Kenneth C. Jessen, *Railroads of Northern Colorado*, Pruett Publishing Company, 1982, (based on newspaper articles published at the time), pp. 57, 59-61, 164-165.

Loveland Reporter. August 5, 1885; May 27, 1886; November 4, 1886; February 1, 1887; March 3, 1887; March 10, 1887; March 17, 1887; April 28, 1887; May 12, 1887; July 28, 1887; November 17, 1887; January 5, 1885; March 1, 1888.

William H. Bauer, James L. Ozment, John H. Willard, *Colorado Post Offices*, Colorado Railroad Museum, Golden, Colorado, 1990, p. 13.

ARROW
Overlooking Middle Park

- *Grand County, Ranch Creek drainage*
- *Accessible by graded dirt road*
- *Town had a post office; no standing structures remain*

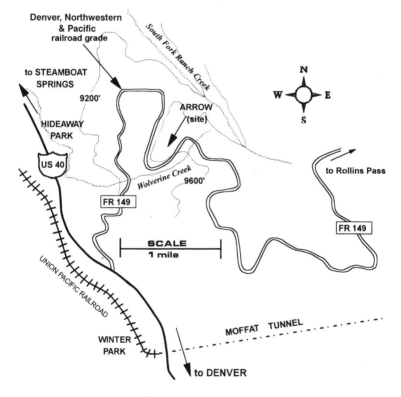

Arrow is located along Moffat Road (FR149) 3.7 miles from its intersection with U.S. 40.

The town or Arrow (or Arrowhead as it was sometimes called) was many things. It was initially a logging camp, then a construction camp for the Denver, Northwestern & Pacific Railway (also called "The Moffat Road"), and finally a place where train crews and track maintenance workers lived. The town was situated between switchbacks on the railroad at an elevation of 9,585 feet, over one thousand feet above the floor of Middle Park.

The rails of the Denver, Northwestern & Pacific climbed from Tolland over Rollins Pass and headed down toward Middle Park reaching Arrow in the fall of 1904. The railroad constructed a fine, sturdy log depot. After the first winter storm, the agent discovered drifted snow inside the structure. The space between the logs had not been chinked.

Initially, tents were the prevailing structure in Arrow until sawmills could supply lumber. Liquor was sold from tent saloons, and Forest Rangers monitored the town, hoping for an arrest since it was illegal to sell liquor within a national forest. Before the end of 1904, the town was incorporated to make liquor sales legal. Arrow was the first incorporated town in Grand County.

This overview of Arrow was taken in 1910 by well-known Denver photographer Louis C. McClure. *(Denver Public Library, Western History Department MCC-755)*

As permanent structures began to appear, the dominant business in Arrow was its saloons. At first, there were seven saloons, and this number grew to over a dozen. Owners had to pay $500 apiece for their license to operate. Most were located at the top of a hill where saloon keepers could toss out unruly customers. During the spring, some customers would end up tumbling down the hill into a mud hole. The saloon keepers brought in "girls" for entertaining its male patrons. As the girls began to show up at public dances, the wives of the railroad employees threw the girls out, sending them back to the saloons.

Prominent among businesses were the Grahams. They ran a saloon and restaurant called Graham's Silver Brick. They built one of the first permanent structures in Arrow, and at the time, the main street was still a dense forest full of trees yet to be harvested. The Grahams offered meals for twenty-five cents. In front of their establishment, a stump was carved like a beer bottle.

Arrow purchased two street lights, which used white gasoline. They were located at the town's only two intersections. To add to the sense of permanency, a post office was established in March, 1905, and it remained opened for a decade. Although there were only two hundred people living in Arrow during its early years, the post office served two thousand patrons spread out over a large area.

There are a number of stories connected with life in Arrow. An impromptu rodeo was held inside the wye formed by the rails of the Denver, Northwestern & Pacific. This was the only flat place in town. One of the potato race's outcomes was in dispute. This led to a battle where potatoes were thrown at full force by the contestants at each other.

One of the merchants kept his Bible handy and read whenever he could. After the death of a boy whose body went unclaimed, the merchant took down his Bible. He gathered a small crowd and walked to the top of the hill overlooking the town. Here he read selected passages from the Bible as his own way of providing some sort of funeral service.

Looking down Aspen Street, Arrow's residents had a spectacular view of Middle Park. Graham's Silver Brick is on the right with an advertisement for meals at twenty-five cents. *(Denver Public Library, Western History Department MCC-344)*

Eventually, Arrow became a stopping place for tourists, and a fine, frame dining hall was constructed. Special summer trips were sponsored by the railroad just to Arrow. Deluxe dinners were served for fifty cents, and in the town, passengers could buy a chicken dinner for forty cents.

Most of the town was destroyed by a fire, and by 1920, only the depot, the dining hall and a couple of other structures remained. Nothing was left of the once flourishing business district. The site, now vacant, located 3.7 miles from the intersection of the Moffat Road (FR149) and U. S. 40.

Edward T. Bollinger and Frederick Bauer, *The Moffat Road*, Sage Books, Denver, 1962, pp. 40-42, 51.

Edward T. Bollinger and William C. Jones, *Rails that Climb*, Colorado Railroad Museum, Golden, Colorado, 1979, pp. 117-189.

Robert L. Brown, *Colorado Ghost Towns - Past and Present*, Caxton Printers, Caldwell, Idaho, 1977, pp. 21-26.

William H. Bauer, James L. Ozment, John H. Willard, *Colorado Post Offices*, Colorado Railroad Museum, Golden, Colorado, 1990, p. 14.

BISMUTH

- *Larimer County, on the divide between the North Fork of the Big Thompson River and Buckhorn Creek*
- *Site not accessible; private property*
- *Town did not have a post office; remains of several cabins*

In search of gold, prospectors founded a small mining community called Bismuth on the east side of Crystal Mountain in 1882. Mining claims were staked, and a mine owned by J. A. Brown seemed to have the most promise. At one point, Brown was offered $50,000 for his claim, which he foolishly declined. Several years later, he accepted just $600 for his property. After a while, the new owner gave up on finding any riches, and the mine was abandoned along with the town of Bismuth.

In 1884, a fire spread over the forest to the west of Fort Collins including Crystal Mountain. This forced the temporary evacuation of Bismuth. Residents buried their belongings, then fled from the area. A light rain slowed the fire and the following day, it was extinguished by a heavy downpour. Bismuth was saved from destruction.

Today, the Bismuth site is marked by one partially standing log cabin and a row of foundations. The site is on private property and along a privately owned road not open to the public. At an elevation of 8400 feet, the town site is located about two miles southeast of Crystal Mountain in a small park near Boiler Hill. The United States Geological Survey map shows a number of mines in the general area.

Harold Marion Dunning, *Over Hill and Vale*, Vol. II, Johnson Publishing Company, Boulder, Colorado, 1962, pp. 202-203.
Interview with Ron Denton, property owner, February 14, 1998.

COALMONT

At The End Of The Hahns Peak Line

- *Jackson County, North Platte River drainage*
- *Accessible by graded dirt road*
- *Town had a post office; several standing structures remain*

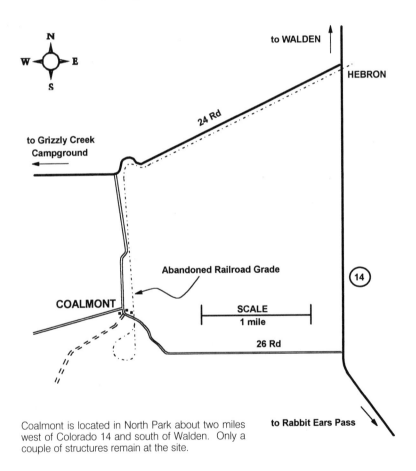

Coalmont is located in North Park about two miles west of Colorado 14 and south of Walden. Only a couple of structures remain at the site.

Coalmont was the end of the line for the Laramie, Hahns Peak & Pacific. The railroad originally planned to build to Hahns Peak north of Steamboat Springs, but Coalmont, reached in 1911, was its furthest point. The town was located 111 miles by rail from the railroad's terminus in Laramie, Wyoming.

The coal deposit, from which the town got its name, was discovered accidently by coyote hunters. After one animal escaped into a hole, the brothers began digging. They struck some of the coal in this vast deposit which was near the surface. It was known as the Riach Coal Field and contained an estimated 400 million tons of high quality coal. The name came from the Riach brothers who sold coal directly out of the vein to local ranchers, but the deposit was not extensively mined until it changed ownership and fell into the hands of the Northern Colorado Coal Company in 1909. The company was financially linked to the railroad as part of a coordinated development of the natural resources in Colorado and the southern region of Wyoming.

The Northern Colorado Coal Company owned a little over 4,000 acres in North Park. The coal deposit itself was covered by only a dozen or so feet of overburden, and the vein was 65 to 75

A distant view of the Northern Colorado Coal Company's facilities at Coalmont in North Park. Some of the homes can be seen to the left of the cluster of buildings. *(Walden Pioneer Museum, John Gresham collection WAL27)*

The former schoolhouse at Coalmont, located in North Park, has been converted into a community center as shown in this 1983 photograph. Other buildings were probably sold and moved. *(Kenneth Jessen 072A14)*

feet thick. Below the first vein was a second vein approximately 10 feet thick. The coal was mined through an inclined tunnel, which allowed mining cars to be loaded at the bottom of the pit and hoisted to the surface using a cable. After the coal was screened and sorted, it was loaded directly into LHP&P cars for shipment.

The coal company constructed twenty homes through 1910. A post office opened in 1912. By 1929, Coalmont had about sixty homes plus the post office, a store, warehouse, bath house, doctor's office, stables and a schoolhouse. Early photographs show a row of identical company houses spread across the treeless expanse of North Park. The population reached about 200 during the winter months when the demand for coal was high and less during the summer months.

By 1970, the coal deposit was exhausted, and the rails of the Laramie, Hahns Peak & Pacific were removed some time afterward. The post office closed in 1983.

At the Coalmont site today are several structures. One of them is the schoolhouse, which is used as a community center.

Kenneth C. Jessen, *Railroads of Northern Colorado*, Pruett Publishing Company, 1982, p. 258.
Hazel Gresham, *North Park*, The Steamboat Pilot, 1975, p. 197.

CRESCENT, TYNER
and PARK CITY
Satellites Of Teller City

- *Jackson County, Jack Creek drainage*
- *Sites not accessible, private property*
- *Two towns had post offices*

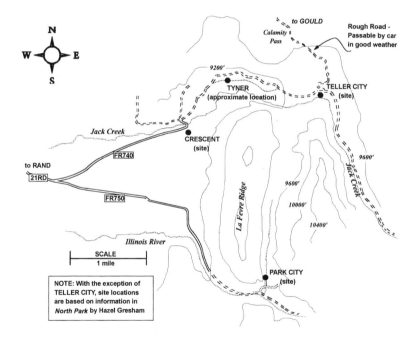

Other towns in the general vicinity of Teller City included Tyner and Cresent to the west and Park City to the south.

There were two towns in the vicinity of Teller City, Tyner and Crescent. Both had their own post offices. The Tyner post office opened in 1879 and closed after only two years. The Crescent post office lasted a little over seven months.

Tyner amounted to nothing more than two log cabins. One cabin was a store of sorts with miner's clothing and equipment plus the post office. The other cabin was the mess hall for a nearby mine. Crescent consisted of just a mess hall for the miners. A survey of these town sites failed to located any ruins or foundations.

There was a third town in this area called Park City. It was located south of Teller City on the Illinois River and did not have a post office. There are two partially collapsed cabins at the site.

One of two collapsed cabins at the Park City site, south of Teller City in Jackson County. *(Kenneth Jessen 109D9)*

Hazel Gresham, *North Park,* The Steamboat Pilot, 1975, pp. 352-353.

William H. Bauer, James L. Ozment, John H. Willard, *Colorado Post Offices,* Colorado Railroad Museum, Golden, Colorado, 1990, pp. 39, 144.

DUTCHTOWN

Founded By Expelled Germans

- *Grand County, Colorado River drainage*
- *Accessible by foot only*
- *Town did not have a post office; no standing structures remain*

A couple of German prospectors came into the Lulu City area looking for the mother lode. They stopped in a saloon and drank too much, then proceeded to shoot up the town, thus shattering its tranquility. Residents valued their peace and quiet and promptly ran the errant "Dutchmen" out of town. The Germans headed up the gulch to the west of Lulu City and founded their own community of cabins. In just two years, however, what little mineral wealth they found was exhausted, and Dutchtown was abandoned. The harsh weather may also have played a role.

The site for this satellite of Lulu City sits at 11,000 feet, high up Big Dutch Creek, also called Hitchens Gulch. It is located just east of 12,797-foot Mount Cirrus. The mountains in which it sits are aptly called the Never Summer Range because of their extended snow season.

Muriel Sibell Wolle, in her book *Stampede to Timberline*, describes her trip during the 1940s. Using the Grand Ditch as access, she rode on horseback to Hitchen's Gulch. Immediately above the ditch she noted Hitchen's Camp, which was established during the 1890s. The shaft house and several buildings were standing at the time. Traveling farther up Hitchen's Gulch for about a mile, she reached Dutchtown. At that time, the remains of five or six cabins could be found at the edge of a dried mud-hollow, which once held a shallow lake. Dutchtown was built in the very last stand of trees below timberline.

This is how Dutchtown looked in 1938. Very little was left of this remote camp at the time, and the site is difficult to located today. *(National Park Service 572)*

Today, to reach Dutchtown requires a hike up to Big Dutch Creek using the Colorado River Trail, all within Rocky Mountain National Park. The trail begins at the western foot of Trail Ridge Road.

A detailed map can be found in the story, "Lulu City."

Mary Lyons Cairns, *Grand Lake in the Olden Days*, The World Press, Denver, 1971, pp. 152-153.

Robert Black III, *Island in the Rockies*, Grand County Pioneer Society, Grand Lake, Colorado, 1969, p. 154.

Muriel Sibell Wolle, *Stampede to Timberline*, Sage Books, Chicago, 1949, 1974, pp. 268-269.

EUGENIA MINE

- *Larimer County, Fish Creek drainage*
- *Site accessible by foot trail*
- *No standing structures remain*

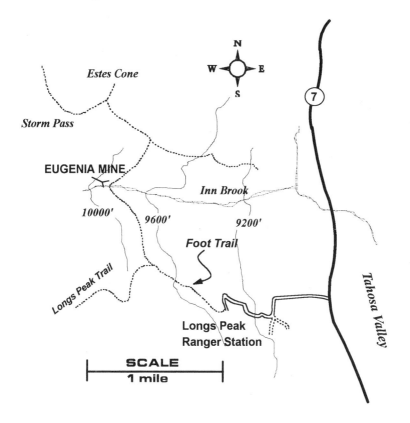

The Eugenia Mine is located on a branch off of the Longs Peak Trail on the way to Estes Cone and Storm Pass. It is a relatively easy hike from the Longs Peak Ranger Station.

The Eugenia claim was made by Carl Norwall and Edward Cudahy in 1905. In hopes of discovering valuable mineralization, they drove a tunnel approximately 1000 feet long.

Norwall, his wife and two daughters, lived at the mine in a comfortable cabin; they even had a piano. The walls of this cabin are partially standing. The mine has a considerable tailings pile, and a boiler sits up near the portal.

There is no record of paying ore being shipped from the mine, but the site is certainly in a scenic location.

The mine is totally isolated from any other mines or mining district and sits on the east side of Longs Peak a short distance north of the Longs Peak trail on a trail leading to Estes Cone. It is located within Rocky Mountain National Park and is easy to find.

Harold Marion Dunning, *Over Hill and Vale*, Vol. I., Johnson Publishing Company, Boulder, Colorado, 1956, pp 241-242.

Doris B. Osterwald, *Rocky Mountain Splendor*, Western Guideways, Ltd., Lakewood, Colorado, 1989, p. 175.

GASKIL
Short Lived

- *Grand County, Colorado River drainage*
- *Site accessible from Trail Ridge Road*
- *Town did not have a post office; no standing structures remain*

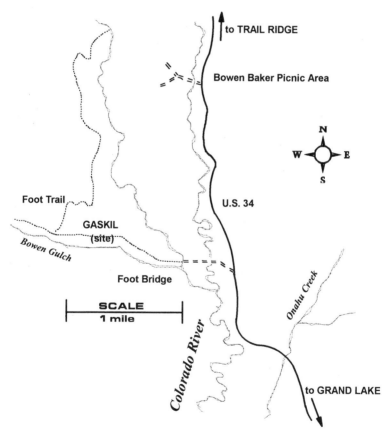

The Gaskil site is located across a foot bridge over the Colorado River on the way west to Bowen Gulch. Little remains to even indicate its presence.

Gaskil got its start when Al Warner put up a small cabin in 1880 at the foot of Bowen Gulch and started to sell liquor and other provisions. John Mowery was next to arrive, with a stock of flour and more liquor. A general store was built, and by 1882, buildings at Gaskil were scattered over sixty acres. The town's name came from the manager of the nearby Wolverine Mine, Lewis D. C. Gaskill, but for some reason, the second "l" was dropped from the town's name.

The Grand Lake Mining & Smelting Company drew up a town plat for a city called Auburn, which contained many blocks and a public square. The site encompassed Gaskil. Within Auburn, there were to be 11 numbered avenues and 15 named streets. The name came from Auburn, New York, the home of mine manager Lewis Gaskill. Auburn never got beyond the planning stage.

The Wolverine was a silver mine that was worked through two levels connected by a shaft. A mill to process its ore was to have been built in Gaskil, but never materialized.

Gaskil had a store, hotel, restaurant and mine offices. The hotel was called the Rogerson House and was run by Joseph Rogerson. Ads for the hotel appeared in the Grand Lake newspaper, *The Prospector.* By 1882, an estimated 100 people called Gaskil home. A second saloon was opened along with another mercantile business. The town also had a boarding house. Gaskil lasted about six years, then was abandoned.

By 1945, only one small log structure remained standing, with its roof, doors and windows missing. The walls of an old wine cellar, made of cobblestone, were still visible. It was constructed to keep the wine cool for one of the saloons. Today, nothing remains at the site, and the town is no longer indicated on topographic maps making its exact location even more difficult to find.

Mary Lyons Cairns, *Grand Lake in the Olden Days*, The World Press, Denver, 1971, pp. 149-152.
Robert Black III, *Island in the Rockies*, Grand County Pioneer Society, Grand Lake, Colorado, 1969, pp. 152-153.

HOMESTEAD MEADOWS

- *Larimer County, Little Thompson River drainage*
- *Site accessible by foot only*
- *No post office or school; a number of standing structures remain consisting of homestead buildings*

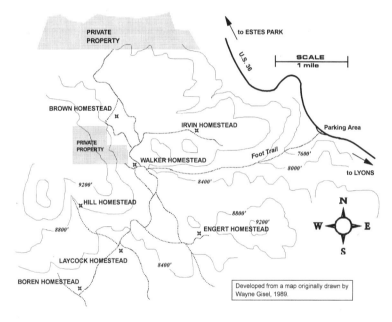

To reach Homestead Meadows requires a two and a half mile hike with a gain in elevation of a little over eight hundred feet. The Lion Gulch trail head is located along U.S. 36.

Homestead Meadows is not a ghost town or abandoned mining camp, but it is a ghostly place unique in Colorado. Contained within Forest Service land are a number of picturesque abandoned homestead buildings well worth visiting.

The Homestead Act of 1862 was used by the United States

For many years, the Engert family vacationed at their homestead in this secluded meadow. Charles Engert was the Lyons postmaster while his wife lived alone on the homestead to meet the five year requirement for title. *(Kenneth Jessen 011C7)*

government to encourage western expansion. It was a land giveaway of unprecedented proportions, providing more than a million families with acreage. A person could file for 160 acres and, within five years, receive title to the land. The homesteader was required to construct a home and live on the land at least half the time. Some of the land had to be under cultivation, and some attempt had to be made to make a living off of the land. All of this investment in money and time was called "proving up," and afterwards, the homesteader could file for title for a fee of just $15.

By the turn of the century, virtually all of the good land had been taken. An area overlooked initially was located about six miles southeast of Estes Park at the head of Lion Gulch. It was here that a number of families filed for land with most receiving title well after the turn of the century. The area had little water, but good grazing land. Timber was the main source of income.

The Great Depression of the 1930s forced many to sell their property. Declining cattle prices after World War II forced others to give up on the area. Eventually, most of the homesteads became part of the Holnholz Ranch. In 1978, the U.S. Forest Service purchased 2,240 acres for winter range for migrating elk. A foot trail up Lion Gulch provides access, and the homesteads are connected via a network of trails.

The first homesteader in the area was William Laycock. His patent was issued in 1889, but he stayed only a few months. The property was purchased by William Turner House who lived on the homestead from 1933 to 1952, the longest continuous stay of any resident. Over the years, he purchased five other homesteads and consolidated the land for ranching. He also operated a saw mill, which supplied milled lumber to Estes Park and Longmont. Laycock dammed Deer Creek and stocked the pond formed by the dam. Hay was cut during the summer for winter feed. Unfortunately for visitors, the original homestead house was dismantled by a subsequent owner.

Robert Boren's wife passed away in 1898, and the following year, the widower moved his family to Lyons. He filed for a homestead in Homestead Meadows receiving his patent in 1906. With his youngest children, he moved his homestead and engaged in ranching and the lumber industry.

An interesting characteristic of Robert Boren was befriending tourists and even inviting them to stay at his ranch. Many of the tourists were in Colorado to recuperate from tuberculosis. Eventually Boren constructed a large two story house with six bedrooms for his guests. A fire destroyed the structure in 1914.

The only woman to homestead in this area was Sarah Walker. After separating from her husband, she came to Homestead Meadows and received her patent in 1914. There was a spring on the property, and she raised dairy cows as well as

Sarah Walker was the only woman to homestead in Homestead Meadows, and she earned title to her property in 1914. She lived here for fifteen years and outlived her ex-husband and both of her children. *(Kenneth Jessen 011C4)*

chickens. The spring allowed her to have a garden. She sold her produce in Lyons.

The Irwin homestead still has a number of its original structures intact including a bathhouse with a sunken tub. Frank Irwin received his patent in 1917 for 320 acres. He died a short time later, and the property changed hands many times. One owner, R. J. Nettleton, developed an active logging business. Most of what he cut was virgin timber consisting of large logs. He used Percheron horses to drag the logs through the forest to his mill. Nettleton raised hay, oats, potatoes and other produce to feed his family.

The old Brown homestead remains standing along the road through the general area. Brothers Harry and Cloyd Boren received titles in 1917 and 1919. The family held on to the land for almost forty years, longer than any other homesteader in Homestead Meadows.

After Harry got married and had children, the family moved to Lyons during the school year. During the summers, the family lived along U.S. 34 and traveled up Lion Gulch to work their land. Al Rose and his family were probably the last to occupy the old Brown homestead. They decorated its interior walls with a written record of their lives.

The old single room home at the Engert homestead is still standing and is located near the end of a wagon road that winds its way through the forest. In 1921, Charles Engert received his title for 320 acres. He was postmaster in Lyons, and while he delivered the mail, his wife stayed up at the cabin. She spent six months at a time on the property to "prove up" the land.

Clayton Hill filed on this homestead in 1916 and received his patent five years later. The property was sold to Daisy Baber, author of *Injun Summer* and *The Longest Rope.*

Homestead Meadows, *A Hike into History,* United States Forest Service (no date), pp 6-18.

LULU CITY
Named For A Beautiful Girl

- *Grand County, Colorado River drainage*
- *Site accessible by foot only*
- *Town had a post office; no standing structures remain*

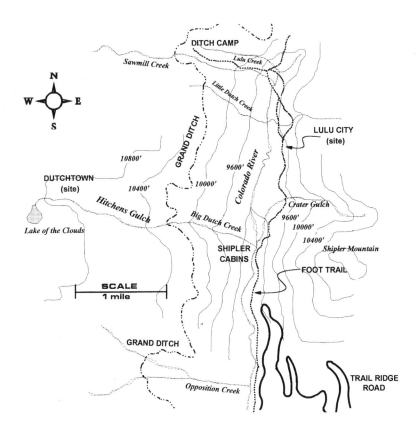

Benjamin Burnett was a Fort Collins merchant involved with several Larimer County mining towns and founded Lulu City.

Benjamin Burnett's life was closely associated with mining in several areas west of Fort Collins. Burnett and his family moved to Fort Collins in 1879 from their home town of Peoria, Illinois. In Fort Collins, he opened a mercantile business and began prospecting; he held claims in Lulu City and in Manhattan. Burnett and his family spent their summers at a cottage near Manhattan on the banks of the Cache la Poudre River. They called the place "Laughalot."

When Burnett found some promising silver ore in the upper Colorado River drainage, in what is now Rocky Mountain National Park, he founded the town of Lulu City in 1879. He named it for his eldest daughter, Lulu, a beautiful girl with jet black hair, black eyes, and very pale skin. Her rosy red lips required no makeup.

Ambitious in its concept, Lulu City enclosed one hundred blocks with sixteen lots per block. The streets were numbered, but the avenues were called Mountain, Trout, Riverside and Ward. Lulu City was close to timberline at an elevation of 9,400 feet and winters were very difficult. On July 25, 1882, the town plat was officially entered into the records. For those who wished for isolation, lots could be purchased in Lulu City.

The best mines in the area were the Wolverine, Rustic, Ruby, Southern Cross, North Star and P. Wimple. At one time, a smelter was to have been built near the town by the Grand Lake Mining & Smelting Company, but in reality, there was not enough ore to make the smelter profitable. This left the mines near Lulu City with extremely high transportation costs to the smelters in Georgetown, Colorado. Ore had to be hauled through Grand Lake and over Berthoud Pass. Lulu City, however, was served by a toll

road, which came over Cameron Pass and Lulu Pass and down
the Colorado River.

The hotel was the largest structure in Lulu City and had a
cellar dug into the rocky ground under the kitchen. It was run by
Parker and Godsmark and began as a long tent. The log structure,
which replaced the tent, measured 25 feet by 50 feet. Dances
were held there and the tables were covered with fine linen table-
cloths. Place settings included crystal and silverware. Godsmark
& Company was the name of the general store and the saloon was
called the Hally Saloon after its owner, J. S. Hally. William Dugnay
ran the drug store. The proprietors of the supply store were
Buxton and Playter, and Snell and Larosh operated a grocery
store. Keeping residents looking trim, Gleason and Meyers ran a
barber shop.

From 1879 to 1883, with a peak population of several hundred, Lulu City experienced its best years. It was reported that in
December, 1881, the town contained forty buildings. A post office
was established in 1880, and closed a half dozen years later. Soon

By the time this photograph was taken in 1889, Lulu City had already reached its peak
and was in a state of decline. *(National Park Service 651)*

after, the stage coach over Thunder Pass to Grand Lake no longer stopped at Lulu City.

The Wolverine, supervised by E. P. Weber, was the most active mine in the area with thirty-five men employed. Hope faded when construction of the smelter was cancelled. Merchants began to leave Lulu City, and the mines in the area began to close. In February, 1883, the Wolverine closed after an avalanche killed Jules C. Harmon. The last news to come from Lulu City appeared in a Georgetown newspaper in September, 1884.

Like so many other Colorado mining towns, Lulu City was founded on the dreams and hopes of prospectors. The small amount of placer gold was hardly worth mining, and the silver ore was of low grade. One discouraged prospector, about ready to leave for good, prophesied that some day there would be nothing but a foot trail along Lulu City's main street and that raspberry bushes would grow through the roof of the town's only hotel. His predictions came to pass.

A Lulu City cabin in 1938. Today there are a few foundations, scattered logs and piles of rock to mark the location of fireplaces, but little else to identify Lulu City. *(National Park Service 668)*

These are the Shipler Cabins near the Shipler Mine in 1938. They were is good condition at the time, but only a few rotting logs remain today. *(National Park Service 692)*

With the prospectors gone, the abandoned town began to crumble and slowly yield to the forces of nature. Today there are a few foundations, scattered logs and a few piles of rock to mark the location of fireplaces, but little else to identify Lulu City.

On the way to Lulu City, the trail passes the ore dump of the Joseph Shipler Mine. At one time there were cabins, referred to as Shipler Cabins, located near the mine. Shipler himself was a Civil War veteran, and constructed his first cabin in 1876. He was reported still living there in 1914.

As a sidelight to the story of Lulu City, a group of German prospectors came to Lulu City and were apparently not well behaved. After being expelled, they founded a suburb of sorts called Dutchtown on the mountainside high above Lulu City.

Ansel Watrous, *History of Larimer County, Colorado*, The Courier Printing & Publishing Company, Fort Collins, Colorado, 1911, pp. 206, 243, 461-462.

Colorado Georgetown Miner: April 29, 1882; September 16, 1882; September 18, 1880; June 11, 1881; July 21, 1881.

Kenneth C. Jessen, *Thompson Valley Tales*, Century One Press, Colorado Springs, Colorado, 1984, pp. 55-58.

Mary Lyons Cairns, *Grand Lake in the Olden Days*, The World Press, Denver, 1971, pp. 143-149.

Robert Black III, *Island in the Rockies*, Grand County Pioneer Society, Grand Lake, Colorado, 1969, pp. 153-154.

William H. Bauer, James L. Ozment, John H. Willard, *Colorado Post Offices*, Colorado Railroad Museum, Golden, Colorado, 1990, p. 152.

MANHATTAN

Colorado

- *Larimer County, Manhattan Creek drainage*
- *Site accessible by car over graded dirt road*
- *Town had a post office; no standing structures remain*

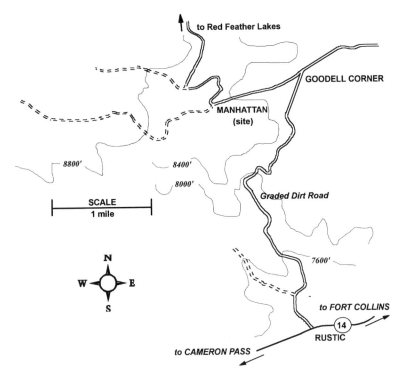

Manhattan is relatively easy to reach from Colorado 14 running up the Poudre Canyon.
A graded, but steep, road leaves the highway at Rustic, and leads to the Manhattan site.

L ike so many Colorado mining towns, Manhattan vanished leaving hardly a trace. A lush meadow, a few grave markers, and some bits of wood and glass are all that is left of this once thriving town located about forty-five miles west of Fort Collins.

In 1886, a number of prominent Fort Collins citizens put together an organization to systematically search for precious metals in the hills west of town. The group hired three experienced prospectors. In September, these men reported finding gold ore on the divide between Seven Mile and Elkhorn creeks. The prospectors boasted that gold could be panned from almost any piece of crushed rock. This immediately caused a gold rush, and in the process, over 300 claims were filed.

A town was started and given the unlikely name of Manhattan. It had a hotel, stores, a post office and even a newspaper called *The Manhattan Prospector.* Incidentally, the newspaper lasted less than a year. Its saloon, the Ace of Clubs, was located at the corner of the two main streets, Chestnut and Manhattan. The Ace of Clubs had a central two-story portion with three shed-like structures attached to its sides. Even for a Colorado mining town, the structure had a unique architectural appearance.

There are over forty structures in this distant shot of Manhattan taken in the 1880s when the town was at its peak. Nothing remains today of this once thriving town west of Fort Collins. *(Fort Collins Public Library FC2000)*

Population estimates for Manhattan vary considerably according to the source, with some placing it at well over 1000. Based on the size of the town and published estimates made by the newspaper, a more realistic figure is 100 to 200. Photographs show that the town did have over forty structures.

In a mine explosion at the Black Hawk tunnel in 1892, two Manhattan miners were killed. A cemetery was established, and they were buried north of the present day road through the town site. Later, another miner was killed and buried in the cemetery. It is possible that others who died in Manhattan were also buried there.

Manhattan had a one room schoolhouse, which featured a school year of only four months, but later expanded to six months. The school included eight grades, and on cold days, the younger children got first choice in seating. After the population of Manhattan began to decline, the school building was moved to Elkhorn about four and a half miles to the east.

This 1888 view of Manhattan clearly shows the nature of the buildings. On the right is a log structure under construction with its roof partially complete. Some structures were made entirely of logs while others appear to be made of milled lumber. *(Fort Collins Public Library FC984)*

A number of companies sold stock in the mines at Manhattan. Among these was the French Creek Mining & Milling Company. Another was the Robertson Gold Mining Company with a Fort Collins druggist, A. W. Scott, as its president. The Missouri Mining & Milling Company had three mines in the area. The Democratic Mining Company was run by prominent Fort Collins residents Abner Loomis and Frank Stover.

In 1888, construction of a mill was financed by Fort Collins businessmen and built on Seven Mile Creek. It never operated properly and was eventually dismantled. The Zimmerman brothers built a five-stamp mill and reduction works at a placed called Poudre City along the Poudre River about three miles above Rustic. Hoping for big returns, a lot of ore was crushed, and the concentrate was shipped to St. Louis for refining. The results were so poor the mill was abandoned.

In 1890, Fort Collins butcher shop owner Benjamin Burnett proudly displayed ore from the district. Burnett owned the general store in Manhattan and was involved with the mining towns of Teller City and Lulu City.

F. C. Goodell was born in Manhattan and tells of a trip he took when he was twelve years old. He drove one of two wagons loaded with ore from Manhattan to Denver to be milled. The mine's owner drove the other wagon. When the owner received payment for the gold content, he figured he had been working his mine for a dollar a day.

As late as 1898, mines in the area were being patented, but Manhattan was all but abandoned. The post office was closed and moved to Elkhorn; some of the buildings were moved to other locations. For reasons known only to the Forest Service, those cabins that remained were burned by the Forest Service during the 1930s.

Evadene Burris Swanson, "Where's Manhattan?", *Colorado Magazine*, XLVIII No. 2, Colorado Historical Society, Denver, 1971, pp. 148-158.

Ansel Watrous, *History of Larimer County, Colorado*, The Courier Printing & Publishing Company, Fort Collins, Colorado, 1911, Ansel Watrous, pp. 159-160.

MASONVILLE
Gold Rush

- *Larimer County, Buckhorn Creek drainage*
- *Accessible via paved road*
- *Town has a post office; original structures unknown*

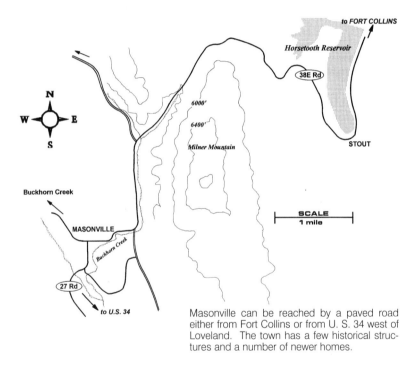

Masonville can be reached by a paved road either from Fort Collins or from U. S. 34 west of Loveland. The town has a few historical structures and a number of newer homes.

The search for gold is a fundamental part of Colorado history and, to a great extent, was what initially attracted settlers to the state. Such adventures were so common place during the late 1800s that practically every man in the state could have boasted of time spent prospecting.

50

Masonville, like so many other Colorado towns, was founded on a gold rush. It began sometime in the early 1890s when
news broke that a man named Thomas Llewellyn shipped one ton
of ore from his Red Elephant Mine on Redstone Creek west of
present day Horsetooth Reservoir. The ore was sent to Omaha for
processing and showed promising results.

The big gold strikes had already taken place decades before,
but new discoveries of gold ore, precipitated a gold rush.
Numerous claims were filed in and around the Redstone Creek—
Buckhorn Creek area. Mining camps sprang up with names and
locations which have long since been forgotten, such as Camp
Rickert with its 125 claims, Quigleyville which boasted of fine ore
at the depth of 85 feet, and Camp Callahan with assay values at
$75 per ton.

The mining activity continued to grow, and by 1896, the
area was said to be another Cripple Creek. *The Loveland Reporter*
announced that $8,000 in outside capital from the Globe Smelter
in Denver would be used to develop the Longview claim at a place
called Camp Carter. Camp Carter was the location of Cal Carter's
claim; he would turn out to be the very last miner to give up on
finding gold in the Masonville area.

In anticipation of the arrival of many prospectors, a town
was strategically located in the center of all of the activity. It was
formed on 80 acres of land donated by local pioneer James R.
Mason. At first, the name "Mason City" was used for the new
town, but the post office warned of confusion with Mason City,
Iowa. The name was changed to Masonville.

Today, Masonville takes but a blink of the eye to drive
through, but it was originally laid out with 800 building lots.
News of very few improvements to the town itself appear in newspaper articles, but the town company raised $5,000 to begin
drilling a tunnel to undercut six of the major claims to insure a
steady flow of good gold ore.

This flurry of activity drew the attention of the Union Pacific
Railroad. They responded by sending in a mining expert to see if

it was worth extending its Arkins branch all the way into the new town. The existing rails stopped just two and a half miles south of Masonville. The railroad elected to wait and see if any substantial mining developed.

During this time, Loveland had an assay office opened by George Clarke. He immediately began to advertise his services. Clarke would frequently leave his office, head west to the mines, poke around, and drum up business. He was always optimistic about how much gold was contained in the Masonville ore. The assays, incidentally, were based on a very small amount of ore selected directly from a promising vein. When the results of an assay were converted to dollars per ton, the mine in question would appear to hold untold riches. Cal Carter, for example, hit a pocket of good ore which assayed at an astonishing $50,000 per ton. To reap the rewards of his hard labor, Cal optimistically shipped a load of his ore to a Denver smelter. It yielded only $12 per ton, half the amount of a typical Cripple Creek mine.

Practically every issue of the Loveland newspaper was filled with stories of new strikes, and the figures on gold content were always included. The Masonville gold rush even spread to Greeley. Evidence of this comes from the following story which ran in *The Loveland Reporter*, "It is stated for fact that immediately after his sermon, one of Greeley's clergymen pulled from his pocket an assay certificate, looked it over and remarked, 'Brothers and sisters, I have here an assay report showing a vast amount of gold laying west of Loveland. In these days of depression, particularly in the price of spuds, I feel that I should be lax in my duty did I fail to advise you to hunt your honey early Monday morning. My team is a trifle slow and I shall start this afternoon!'"

In the old Opera House located over Loveland's W. & T. Pharmacy, a meeting was held to organize the Loveland Mining & Development Company. Each of the share holders agreed to pay $2.00 a month to the company for developing mining property. To prevent a possible monopoly, only one share could be held by each person. Failure to pay one of the monthly assessments would cost the shareholder his entire interest in the company. Naturally, the assayor George Clarke was the chairman, but much to Loveland's surprise, the editor of the newspaper became the secretary, adding some respectability to the gold rush.

A small stamp mill was constructed above Redstone Creek, but was not successful in processing the low-grade ore found in the area. Its ruins can still be seen east of Masonville on the road to Horsetooth Reservoir just above the Hansen Feeder Canal.

The interest in gold mining died off as suddenly as it began since no one struck any kind of mother lode. Cal Carter, however, hung on to become the area's last miner. He worked alone, forcing him to climb down the mine shaft, load the ore, then climb back to the surface to hoist up the ore. He passed away in 1936 at the age of 91, still searching for the mother lode. Cal's lonely grave is located on a small ridge to the west of Masonville Road. The remains of many mines dot the hills as a reminder of Masonville's gold rush days.

1887 Masonville School, Morning Glories Extension Homemaker Club, Masonville, Colorado, 1986, p. 43.

Ansel Watrous, *History of Larimer County*, Colorado, The Courier Printing & Publishing Company, Fort Collins, Colorado, 1911, p. 160, p. 199.

Harold Marion Dunning, *Over Hill and Vale*, Vol. II., Johnson Publishing Company, Boulder, Colorado, 1962, p. 235.

Harold Marion Dunning, *Over Hill and Vale*, Vol. III., Johnson Publishing Company, Boulder, Colorado, 1971, p. 214.

Loveland - Big Thompson Valley, Clara Ball, editor, Big Thompson Valley Centennial Commission, Loveland, Colorado, 1975, pp. 42-43.

NOLAND

Stone Canyon Town

- *Boulder County, St. Vrain Creek drainage*
- *Site not accessible; private property*
- *Town had a post office; no standing structures remain*

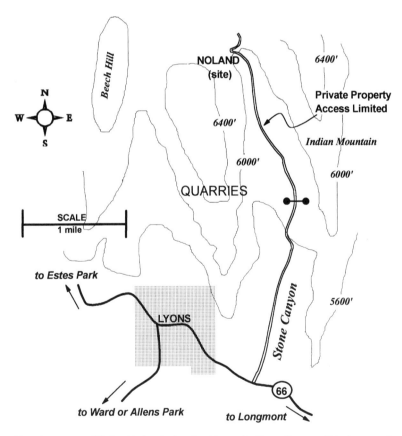

The ghost town of Noland is located north of Lyons in Stone Canyon. Private property prevents access to the area.

The Denver, Utah & Pacific, a narrow gauge railroad, laid 10.8 miles of track from Longmont west to Lyons in 1885. The purpose was to develop the stone quarry business. Abundant was fine-grained sandstone of exceptional quality which varied in color from pink to almost white. From a point about a mile east of Lyons, a branch was constructed in 1887 north 3.7 miles up Stone Canyon to a company quarry town called Tower. Tower served the quarry workers needs with dormitories, a bakery and a company store.

The problem with the narrow gauge Denver, Utah & Pacific was that stone had to be transferred to standard gauge cars for shipment to points outside of the railroad's immediate territory. In 1889, the line was converted to standard gauge and ownership taken over by the Burlington & Missouri Railroad (a subsidiary of the Chicago, Burlington & Quincy). It was about this time that the name Tower was changed to Noland.

A year later, the Stone Mountain Railroad & Quarry Company extended the railroad beyond Noland, around Beech Hill, and another four miles to higher quarries. The railroad gained altitude by using a set of switchbacks and followed the

The quarries above Noland were served by this steep railroad which required the use of geared locomotives to negotiate the grades. *(Harold Dunning Over Hill and Vale)*

contour of Beech Hill into the next valley. The railroad purchased a geared Shay locomotive to handle the steep grades. A small depot was built at the end of the track. The Stone Mountain Railroad operated over all of its own track as well as the track belonging to the Burlington & Missouri down to the main line.

For two decades, hundreds of cities received the high quality sandstone from these quarries. Some of the stone was used to construct buildings at the 1893 Chicago World's Fair.

Noland grew to become the largest quarry town in northern Colorado. A post office was established in 1890, discontinued in 1895, re-established in 1899, and then discontinued for the last time in 1901. As the number of individuals living in Noland grew, the town gained several stores, including a general merchandise store, a butcher shop, a feed and grain store and a blacksmith shop. Noland also had five saloons and its own school. A dozen homes were constructed, bringing the total number of structures to well over two dozen. The most spectacular structures were the great stone boarding houses, the Matthew House and the Nebraska House, one of them two stories high. Dances were held

Noland had a small, but substantial downtown area, with the general store in the center and the post office to the left. *(Harold Dunning Over Hill and Vale)*

The ruins of one of two large stone boarding houses in Noland. These structures were razed years ago and the stone removed for other purposes. *(Harold Dunning Over Hill and Vale)*

in the upper story on weekends. Although little information exists on Noland's exact population, it was probably several hundred.

As with other quarry railroads, the Stone Mountain Railroad was vulnerable to accidents. On August 29, 1890, three men were killed near Noland when seven fully loaded cars got out of control on the steep grade.

When concrete began to replace stone as a building material, the stone industry began a steady decline. After the railroad was abandoned and dismantled in 1918, the roadbed was converted into a gravel road and quarry work continued on a limited basis. The town of Noland began to slowly disappear, and little is left to mark its location today.

Harold Marion Dunning, *Over Hill and Vale*, Vol. I., Johnson Publishing Company, Boulder, Colorado, 1956, pp. 166-174.

Lyons and Surrounding Area, Lyons Centennial - Bicentennial Commission, Lyons, Colorado, 1977, p. 29.

Robert A. LeMassena, *Colorado Mountain Railroads*, Sundance Publications, Ltd., Denver, 1984, p. 323.

Tivis Wilkins, *Colorado Railroads*, Pruett Publishing Company, Boulder, Colorado, 1974, pp. 87, 141, 198.

PEARL

Had Luster

- *Jackson County, Big Creek drainage*
- *Accessible by graded dirt road*
- *Town had a post office; several original structures remain*

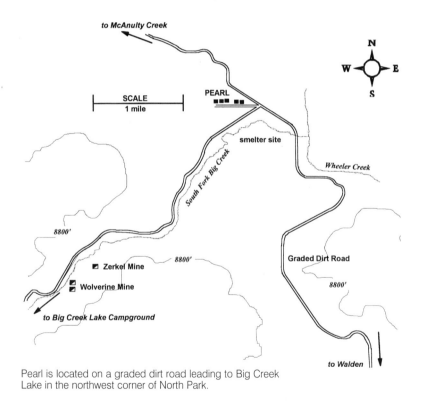

Pearl is located on a graded dirt road leading to Big Creek
Lake in the northwest corner of North Park.

One of Colorado's least known mining camps is Pearl, located in the extreme northwest part of North Park, nineteen miles from Cowdrey over a good graded dirt road. In 1901, the town of Pearl was taking its first steps toward incorporation with a town election. A city government was in place by 1902. At the time, Pearl had twenty-three structures covering fourteen city blocks, including a smelter for locally mined copper ore. There were two saloons, three stores, a meat market, three hotels, a town hall, a post office, and a schoolhouse. A couple of Dutchmen operated a general store in competition with the Smith Store and a store owned by the mining company.

The Wheeler brothers were the first settlers in the Big Creek area. Copper ore was discovered in 1894-95, but at the time, copper had little market value. After five years, Charles Knapp purchased the deposit and formed the Pearl Mining and Smelting Company.

Pearl Wheeler became the first postmistress in 1889, and the town was named for her. She remained in her position until 1890. The post office was closed for good in 1919.

Pearl's main street sees little traffic today and is posted as private. *(Sonje Jessen SJ105)*

The copper smelter, south of the Pearl town site, collapsed years ago, but the smoke stack looks almost new. *(Sonje Jessen SJ104)*

The Wolverine Mine was located in 1900 and an 85-foot shaft was sunk with a 200-foot crosscut into the hillside. Other Pearl mines included the Grand Republic, the Lizzie and the Copper King. The most famous mine in the area was the Zirkel; a large vein of silver was discovered there in 1903.

Analysis of the ore found in the Pearl area was encouraging enough to construct a smelter in 1901. The last piece of machinery was installed in 1905. A power plant, possibly associated with the mill, provided Pearl with electricity. *The Pearl Mining Times,* a weekly newspaper, was published for a while.

When Muriel Sibell Wolle visited Pearl in the 1940s, she found the remains of the smelter, one home which had been remodeled, and a barn. A short distance away, she found three or four other structures, with the remains of a wooden sidewalk running in front of them. When noted ghost town historian Robert Brown visited Pearl in the 1970s, he reported that only four original structures were still standing.

Many of the buildings, which show clearly in a historic photograph along Pearl's main street, have completely vanished, but there are a number of original structures remaining today. These have been restored and some appear to be seasonally occupied. Even though the town site is on private property, it is possible to photograph Pearl from the public road. The smelter chimney sits off to the south of the town site and is fenced and posted.

In the extreme northwest portion of North Park, the economy of Pearl was based on copper mining. There are a number of homes on the site. *(Kenneth Jessen 110A11)*

Hazel Gresham, *North Park*, The Steamboat Pilot, 1975, pp. 240-243.

Robert L. Brown, *Colorado Ghost Towns - Past and Present*, Caxton Printers, Caldwell, Idaho, 1977, pp. 197-200.

William H. Bauer, James L. Ozment, John H. Willard, *Colorado Post Offices*, Colorado Railroad Museum, Golden, Colorado, 1990, p. 111.

POUDRE CITY
Didn't Last Long

- *Larimer County, Cache la Poudre drainage*
- *Site accessible by car*
- *Town did not have a post office; no standing structures remain*

Approximately three miles upstream from Rustic was the mining camp of Poudre City, founded by John Zimmerman and his brother Michael. They discovered surface mineralization and began digging into the north side of the canyon in 1888. The Zimmerman brothers hit some promising gold ore. Realizing the cost of transporting ore out of the Poudre Canyon was potentially more than the ore was worth, they set about building a mill. John used his previous experience gained in Austin, Nevada.

The mill consisted of a battery of five stamps to grind the ore. A trio of amalgamation tables were installed using mercury to recover the metallic gold. A large square chimney, constructed for the retort furnace, was used to drive off the mercury in the form of mercury vapor, leaving behind what the Zimmermans thought was nearly pure gold. The retort condensed the mercury so that it could be reused. The mill, completed in 1890, was powered by a twelve foot high water wheel and a steam engine. It began processing ore in October from Zimmerman's Elkhorn Mine a short distance away and up the hillside from the mill.

After running his mill for four days, John Zimmerman went down to Fort Collins and proudly displayed his "gold." Soon, prospectors were combing the hills around the mill, digging holes over a three mile wide area.

Zimmerman shut the mill down for the winter and sold the mine to the Cash Mining Company. The new owners changed the name to Cash No. 4. After the sale, the mining company had the concentrate from the mill analyzed, and the results showed that it contained a lot of copper but not much gold.

John sold the mill the following year, and it was a good thing he did. The 1891 winter was severe and spring rains combined with the melt water to weaken the Chambers Lake dam. On June 10, it broke, sending a wall of water down the Cache la Poudre River right through Poudre City. John Zimmerman heard the wall of water and was able to warn the thirteen people living at the camp prior to the flood. Except for the stout chimney, the mill was wiped out. Poudre City lasted less than a year, but it was a bold attempt to capitalize on the mineralization in the area. In 1923, a plaque was placed on the chimney by the Colorado Historical Society providing visitors with a brief history of Poudre City.

Only the chimney for the smelter at Poudre City remains, and a bronze plaque at its base tells of its significance to the area's history. *(Kenneth Jessen 109D6)*

Stanley R. Case, *The Poudre - A Photo History*, self-published, Bellvue, Colorado, 1995, pp. 38-39.

STOUT

- *Larimer County, Cache la Poudre drainage*
- *Site on private property at the south end of Horsetooth Reservoir*
- *Town had a post office; original structures unknown*

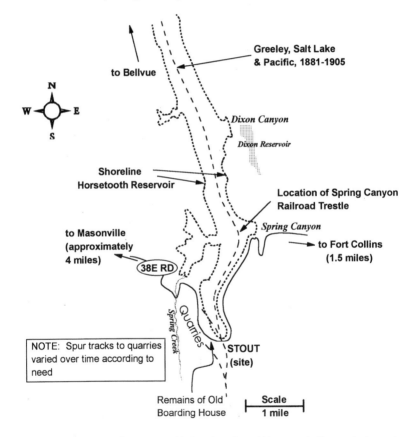

This map shows the Stout area with the shoreline of Horsetooth Reservoir shown in heavy dotted lines. The Highland School was located just south of the Spring Canyon dam. A network of track served the quarries and was moved as new quarries opened.

A s boaters skim over the surface of Horsetooth Reservoir, few
realize that they are passing over the route of a railroad which
once led to the quarry town of Stout. And when boaters relax at
the inn at the south end of Horsetooth Reservoir, few realize they
are in the old town of Stout.

As early as 1873, the sandstone found in this valley was
quarried and used in Fort Collins buildings. Frank Avery, in fact,
used some of the red sandstone in 1879 to trim his show-place
home on Mountain Avenue.

In 1880, the quarry business began with fifty men at Spring
Canyon. Stone was hauled east down to the Colorado Central
Railroad main line four miles away. Some of this stone was used
by the Union Pacific for their Denver depot.

The most prominent early stone quarry operator was
William Bachelder. He moved to Spring Canyon in 1871 to raise

An overview of Stout shows what was once a thriving town built to serve the stone quarries. The depot can be seen to the left-center and the boarding house off to the right. Horsetooth Reservoir would be to the right of this photograph and the present-day paved road passes to the right of the boarding house. *(Fort Collins Public Library)*

sheep, and a decade later, he installed a tramway to bring flagstone down from the top of the ridge above his property. By June,
1882, he was shipping as much as $8,000 in stone a month. His
land became filled with a tent-town of quarry workers. Bachelder
was interested in a more permanent settlement and founded the
town of Petra. He became its first postmaster. Petra also had a
large store.

The Highland School was built to serve the growing population of families moving into the area. The first school building
was of frame construction, but in 1883, a substantial stone schoolhouse was erected. The school remained in use for more than six
decades. The stone mason, M. Thomas, was so proud of his work
on the school that he left his name carved into one of the stones.

During the summer of 1881, a new railroad called the
Greeley, Salt Lake & Pacific was formed as a subsidiary of the
Union Pacific to build a line from Greeley, through Fort Collins,
and over Cameron Pass. The plans also called for construction of a
branch running south from Bellvue, up the valley now occupied by
Horsetooth Reservoir, to the Union Pacific-owned stone quarries.

Enticed by the prospects of being put on a transcontinental
railroad, the citizens of Fort Collins gladly agreed to give the
Union Pacific the right-of-way through the city, just as they had in
1877 for the Colorado Central. Businessmen guaranteed to pay all
damages and legal fees to secure the right-of-way. The town
board let the railroad's surveyors pick a location for the line, then
the city created a dummy street to allow it to condemn the property. Once the right-of-way for the street was secured, the City of
Fort Collins simply turned it over to the railroad.

The most expensive work on the Greeley, Salt Lake & Pacific
was above Pleasant Valley. It cost the Union Pacific $200,000 to
construct this portion of the line because of the heavy rock work
and grading. This branch was a little over fifteen miles long as
measured from Fort Collins. In that short distance, there were
thirty-two trestles, with the largest across Spring Canyon.

Nebraska stone contractor William B. Stout leased the

Union Pacific quarries, and in 1882, a new post office was established called Stout. Although only a short distance from the pioneer town of Petra in Spring Canyon, the Stout post office replaced the Petra post office.

The Stout family name dominated the area. William B. Stout purchased Bachelder's entire flagstone quarry and became the primary stone contractor in the valley. The boarding house was run by R. M. Stout, one of William B. Stout's cousins. Half-brother Homer D. Stout took over as postmaster. The paymaster was yet another cousin, E. L. Stout.

William Stout erected a boarding house near the quarries for his workers. It measured 52 feet by 60 feet and was two stories high, with a full basement. It had twenty one rooms with a dining hall and kitchen. A spring located above the boarding house provided running water. Workers claimed that Stout's boarding house was constructed more like a prison. There may have been some truth to this, since before leaving Nebraska, William Stout constructed the Nebraska State Penitentiary. The remains of this boarding house are still visible along the road to the southwest of Horsetooth Reservoir.

The death of Homer Stout in August, 1883, prompted the entire family to return to Nebraska, and all of the property was transferred to the Union Pacific.

What became known as the Stout Branch of the Greeley, Salt Lake & Pacific was plagued by a rapid succession of accidents during its first months of operation. The railroad cars of the day had crude, difficult to control braking systems, using compressed air applied directly to the brakes. The couplers were nothing more than large links held to the cars by removable pins. Just days after the first shipment of stone was made, a car loaded with flagging got away on the steep grade. The brakeman rode the rapidly accelerating car for a mile and a half, attempting to stop it by cranking on the hand brake. At the time the brakeman jumped, the car was moving towards Bellvue at a terrific speed. The brakeman was knocked unconscious by his fall, but was not seriously

This attractive 20-by-48-foot frame depot was constructed in July, 1882, by the Greeley, Salt Lake & Pacific to serve the Stout stone quarries. A telegraph line connected this depot with the Colorado Central depot in Fort Collins. *(Greeley Municipal Museum)*

injured. The runaway car collided with explosive force with another car standing on the track. Broken stone fragments and car parts were sent high into the air in all directions.

Two months later, an engine had just pulled a string of empty cars up to Stout and was switching them into a siding. The rest of the train began to move down grade. Again, a brave brakeman rode the cars, desperately cranking on the brakes, attempting to stop the train. The moving cars collided with a second string of cars on the main line, causing three of them to start down grade. A second chain reaction ended the incident when the three cars telescoped into another string of cars. Many of the cars were totally destroyed, and it took weeks for the railroad to clear the debris from the track.

Business at the quarries was brisk with twenty carloads of stone shipped per day during the early part of 1882. Stone shipments continued to grow and soon doubled. An extra locomotive had to be brought in to handle the business, and three to four trains per day made the steep climb up to Stout. For workers commuting to Stout, the round trip fare from Fort Collins was fifty cents. A wood frame depot was erected at Stout along with a water tower, and a telegraph line was run up to it from the depot in Fort Collins.

During the summer of 1882, many ties were floated down the Poudre to LaPorte from tie camps near Chambers Lake. There was a siding at LaPorte on the Stout Branch where flat cars could be loaded. After the ties were pulled from the water, they were stacked and dried before being loaded on the flat cars. Some careless man had uncoupled a string of cars to allow them to be loaded more easily. When the job was done, the locomotive backed down to couple the cars, accidentally bumping the first car which, in turn, coasted into the second and so on. When the last car was hit, it began to coast down grade. Once again, a brakeman rode the car, trying to stop it, only to find the brake broken.

Below in Fort Collins, an old man was walking along the tracks near the depot. The morning passenger train, with its bell clanging, was just pulling out, and the sound of the rapidly approaching runaway car was obscured by the noise. The car struck the old man, and as its wheels passed over his body, he was virtually cut in half, much to the horror of an eye witness. The car eventually hit a switch, left the track and came to a halt.

Stout continued to grow as a community with blacksmith shops, a livery stable, several saloons, stores and a number of homes. The use of stone as a building material, however, dropped off as concrete gained favor after the turn of the century, and in 1905, three miles of the Stout branch were taken up and the frame depot abandoned. Another four miles were removed in 1909, and in 1918, only a short siding was left at Bellvue. For many years and into the 1980s, trains continued to operate over the old Greeley, Salt Lake & Pacific from Fort Collins to Rex (near Owl Canyon), hauling limestone to the Great Western sugar factories. Even this portion of the line has now been dismantled.

Edith Bucco, "Founded on Rock: Colorado's Stout Stone Industry," *Colorado Magazine*, LI/4, 1974, pp. 317-335.

TELLER CITY
Founded By Old Cush

- *Grand County, Jack Creek drainage*
- *Site accessible by car over rough dirt road*
- *Town had a post office; many partially standing structures and foundation logs*

During the late 1800s, mining activity in Colorado was at an all time high, and prospectors picked over virtually every square inch of the state looking for quick riches. On Jack Creek in North Park, prospects of a rich silver strike looked good, and in 1879, Madore Cushman, locally known as "Old Cush," founded Teller City. Located southwest of Cameron Pass, Cushman's deed to the town site was the first such deed recorded in Grand County. Old Cush named his town after Colorado U.S. Senator Henry M. Teller, who tried to keep the country on the silver standard.

Old Cush had an interesting history of his own. He had left his wife and daughter in 1861 to join the Pikes Peak gold rush. He was bitter about his broken marriage and the child he left behind. After wandering through various Colorado mining camps for years, he started prospecting in North Park.

After Old Cush founded Teller City, he remained there for a couple of years, then like so many other prospectors, moved on. He ended up at the copper strike at Encampment, Wyoming, but what happened to him in later years is unknown.

When Old Cush passed away in 1908, the attorney handling the estate tried to locate his wife and daughter only to find that they too had passed away. The daughter, however, had married and left two children. The daughter's husband died, leaving the two children orphans; the children were raised by a guardian.

When the attorney finally tracked them down, they were surprised to discover that they were heirs to a handsome estate from a grandfather they never knew.

As news of the silver strike on Jack Creek spread, more prospectors and miners came to Teller City. In 1881, the population reached 300, and a year later, it topped at 1,300.

The town had a mayor, four trustees, two city judges, a recorder and a town marshal. It also had four saloons within its 300 acres, a meat market, assay office, hardware store, and a forty room, two-story hotel called the Yates House.

When the editor of the newspaper first arrived, he soon discovered that it wasn't all that easy setting up his press in such a remote location. The only space available was a crude cabin with a dirt floor. The editor could not even purchase a can of lye or a scrub brush to clean the type, and he was unable to get oil for his press. Nevertheless, *The North Park Miner* was the first newspaper in Grand County and had a subscription price of $2.50 a year.

Mines in the area had names like the End-O-Mile, Legal Tender, Josephine, Rainbow, Gaslight, Ironclad, and Annie. In September, 1882, the North Park and Vandalia Mining and Smelting Company began to issue stock.

At Teller City, the remains of at least seventeen log cabins can be found among the lodge pole pines. By 1885, the town was all but deserted with only a handful of hardy souls hanging on to nothing more than hope. *(Kenneth Jessen 109D8)*

The first regular stage coach service to reach Teller City originated in Laramie, Wyoming, some one hundred miles away over primitive roads through North Park. By the fall of 1881, a Fort Collins resident, Samuel B. Stewart, opened a toll road from Rustic in the Poudre Canyon, over Cameron Pass, to Teller City.

Although such stories are impossible to verify, Teller City may have been the site of a swindle where an eastern company hired two men to sink a one hundred foot shaft. The men dug down fifty feet and struck a good flow of water, which soon made it impossible to keep digging. The men then sunk a second fifty foot shaft with the same result. Putting the two holes together, they figured they had met their contract and collected on the one hundred foot shaft.

In 1884, the price of silver dipped, and the residents of Teller City were attracted to the new Cripple Creek gold rush. It is said that some cabins were abandoned so quickly that dirty dishes were left behind on the tables. By 1885, Teller City was all but deserted, with only a handful of hardy souls hanging on to nothing more than hope. The post office closed, the stage coach service terminated, and the town crumbled into history.

Today, the remains of at least seventeen log cabins can be found among the trees on both side of the road. Teller City once had buildings made of milled lumber, but hardly any trace of these structures are left. A grill covers an old stone-lined well in the center of town. No longer is there any sound of human activity, only the wind whispering through the trees. A parking lot and trail to some of the cabins has been constructed for visitors.

For a map of where Teller City is located, see "Crescent, Tyner and Park City."

Robert Black III, *Island in the Rockies*, Grand County Pioneer Society, Grand Lake, Colorado, 1969, pp. 155, 226-228.

Mary Lyons Cairns, *Grand Lake in the Olden Days*, The World Press, Denver, 1971, pp. 153-161.

Hazel Gresham, *North Park,* The Steamboat Pilot, 1975, pp. 50-54.

VIRGINIA DALE

Established By Jack Slade

- *Larimer County, Dale Creek drainage*
- *Accessible via graded dirt road; limited by private property*
- *Town did have a post office; several standing structures remain*

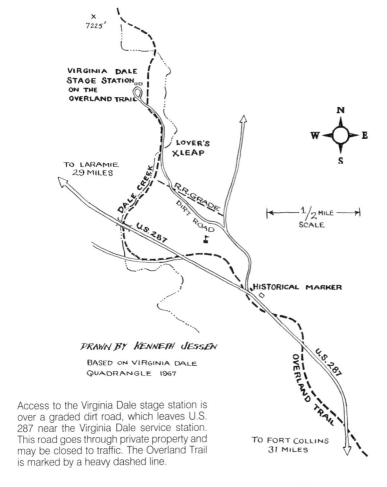

DRAWN BY KENNETH JESSEN

BASED ON VIRGINIA DALE
QUADRANGLE 1967

Access to the Virginia Dale stage station is over a graded dirt road, which leaves U.S. 287 near the Virginia Dale service station. This road goes through private property and may be closed to traffic. The Overland Trail is marked by a heavy dashed line.

Mining did not dominate the founding of Virginia Dale. Instead, it was founded as a division point along the Overland, a stage coach route across the Western United States.

The story of Virginia Dale begins when the famed express company of Russell, Majors & Waddell was in financial difficulty. Western business tycoon, Ben Holladay, bought it in 1862 and made it a success as part of the Central Overland California & Pikes Peak Express Company, or Overland for short.

Starting with several terminals on the Missouri River, the stage route followed the Platte River Trail all the way to Salt Lake City, Utah, then crossed the desert and over the Sierra Nevada Mountains. It also boasted of a busy branch line diverging from the main route at Julesburg in the northeastern corner of Colorado to Denver.

When Ben Holladay took over, the Civil War had drained all but a half dozen companies of regular troops from the posts along the Platte River Trail. Only small garrisons remained, which weakened military strength. This was an open invitation to Indian tribes who were resentful of the white man's destructive invasion of their territory. During

The Virginia Dale stage station was established by Jack Slade in 1862 and is one of the oldest structures in northern Colorado. A great deal of effort and money has been put into its restoration. *(Kenneth Jessen 051A34)*

1862, they raided stage stations at various points along the line from North Platte Bridge (present site of Casper, Wyoming) to Green River, Wyoming. They ran off the stock and killed several employees.

The attacks not only interrupted schedules and caused mail to pile up, but left the agents hard pressed to replace stolen stock and keep the exposed stations manned. These depredations and other raids farther west caused travel on the Overland to cease. Coaches stopped running and stations were temporarily abandoned. West bound mail piled up at the Julesburg station.

In the last of May, 1862, Superintendent Jack Slade received word to remain at Horseshoe Creek (near Glendo, Wyoming) and to wait for the arrival of his new employer, Ben Holladay. Holladay wanted to view the damage done by the Indians himself. Slade joined them at Horseshoe Creek and was informed by Holladay that he was considering moving the line south to establish a more direct route. He was thinking of a route either due west of Denver or one along the so-called Cherokee Trail to the northwest of Denver through LaPorte.

As Holladay's party continued westward, they found the line deserted and only a few occupied stations. The abandoned stations and ranches had been ransacked by the Indians and some burned to the ground. Mail sacks were cut open and their contents strewn over the prairie. Valuable letters, bills, and drafts were left exposed to the harsh Wyoming weather. The party came upon the two abandoned coaches near Split Rock that served as barriers against the attacks and found them riddled with bullets and arrows.

Hardly had the line been restored to operation than an order came on July 8, 1862, from Holladay himself. The North Platte River route was to be abandoned in favor of the Cherokee Trail to the south. Slade was told to move the stage stock and equipment to the Cherokee Trail as quickly as possible.

The new route, instead of crossing the South Platte River at Julesburg, followed the south bank of the river to a point opposite the mouth of the Cache la Poudre River where Cherokee City was established. The name was changed later to Latham. From Latham, the route ran southwest to Denver, then from Denver north to Laporte using a route along the base of the Front Range. From the Laporte station, it followed a route northwest around the north side of Elk Mountain, Wyoming and over Bridger's Pass.

Slade was given the responsibility of Division Agent to operate the portion of the line running from Denver to the crossing of the North Platte River just beyond Elk Mountain, a distance of 226 miles. For his headquarters, he selected a station located almost in the middle of the division. Its setting was one of the most beautiful on the entire line, situated in a small valley near Dale Creek. Jack Slade named the place Virginia Dale in honor of his wife, Maria Virginia. The station was constructed in June, 1862, and is still standing, about thirty-five miles northwest of Fort Collins not far from U. S. 287. It remained a division point on the Overland route until the Union Pacific Railway completed its line to Cheyenne in 1867. At that time, the station was abandoned.

Since the original road from Fort Collins to Laramie ran by the old station, it was used for many years as a store and also served as a post office for the region. It has also been used as a community center, and at one time, a large addition was built on the south side to expand its use for dances. Through community effort, the foundation at the east end was stabilized and reinforced. The old structure also received a new cedar shingle roof. In 1996, more work was done to stabilize the foundation and to prevent rot of the lower layer of hand-hewn logs. Virginia Dale is one of the few stage stations still at its original location, and it was placed on the National Register of Historic Places in 1985.

To visit Virginia Dale, a graded dirt road leaves U.S. 287 just northwest of the Virginia Dale service station. The Colorado Historical Society has a marker at this point. The dirt road forks with the left branch going over a small pass and down into the valley were the Virginia Dale station is located. Next to it is a homestead house. Access to the site is through private property which, at times, may be closed to traffic. Only a few people lived in Virginia Dale, although it did have its own school.

Jack Slade was fired by the Overland for drinking episodes. He was an exceptionally competent division agent and a considerate gentleman, but only when sober. His drinking binges continued after he moved to Virginia City, Montana. He was hanged by vigilantes in 1864 as a public nuisance.

A contemporary photograph of the Virginia Dale stage station, once the division headquarters for the Overland. The Overland Trail runs directly in front of the old station. *(Kenneth Jessen 008B)*

Ansel Watrous, *History of Larimer County*, Colorado, The Courier Printing & Publishing Company, Fort Collins, Colorado, 1911, p. 189.

Edward Bliss, "Denver to Salt Lake by Overland Stage in 1862," *The Colorado Magazine*, Vol. VIII. No. 5, September, 1931 pp. 190-191.

Forbes Parkhill, *The Law Goes West*, Sage Books, Denver, 1956, pp. 56-57.

John S. Gray, *Cavalry & Coaches*, Fort Collins Corral of Westerners, Publication No. 1, Old Army Press, Fort Collins, Colorado, 1978, p. 13.

William H. Bauer, James L. Ozment, John H. Willard, *Colorado Post Offices*, Colorado Railroad Museum, Golden, Colorado, 1990, p. 152.

Zethyl Gates, *Mariano Medina, Colorado Mountain Man*, Johnson Publishing Company, Boulder, Colorado, 1981, pp. 67-68.

WILDS

- *Larimer County, Buckhorn Creek drainage*
- *Accessible by paved road*
- *Site has several original structures including the Wild Mansion*

Alfred Wild pioneered a number of businesses, including a plaster business using gypsum found on his property west of Loveland. He was first to raise hops commercially in Colorado, and also had a brick business. *(Jim Wild collection 033C24)*

The town of Wilds is closely linked to its remarkable founder, Alfred Wild, who came to the Loveland area in the early 1880s to manage his brother's homestead. Alfred filed for his own homestead and eventually began to experiment with fruit trees. By 1894, he had succeeded in raising 2,000 trees covering some thirty-two acres.

His homestead was in an unusual location, sitting at the south end of a long series of vertical fins. This formation was known as the Devil's Backbone. Buckhorn Creek ran through his property and emptied into the Big Thompson River.

Wild recognized that the growing Colorado beer industry had to purchase

78

hops from other states. This led Wild to begin experimenting with a hop crop, something horticulturists deemed impossible in Colorado's dry climate. Nevertheless, Wild forged ahead and became a pioneer in the cultivation of hops. The P. H. Zang Brewing Company of Denver was his biggest customer.

During the years of hard work it took to establish his homestead, Alfred Wild was forced to take odd jobs. One job was to the south in Cripple Creek where he worked as a carpenter. He also learned about mining. So that he could experiment with various ideas, he built his own machine shop along the Big Thompson River powered by a water wheel.

An irrigation company started building a ditch from the Big Thompson River around the southern end of the Devil's Backbone through Wild's property. The workers struck some soft, white material and continued excavating. Nothing much was thought of the material until the time came to run water through the ditch. The water could not get by the white material for weeks. It was able to absorb large quantities of water.

Wild watched the ditch being built and the problems with water flow. He became curious about the material and sent a sample to Brown University in Rhode Island for analysis. It turned out to be gypsum of the purest form.

Using his wife's pots and pans, Alfred Wild began experimenting with the gypsum, hoping to discover how to convert the material into plaster. He pulverized it into a fine powder, then heated it in a kettle over an open fire, and dumped the block of material out on the ground. After it cooled, Wild pulverized the block of material to form plaster. The heating process, incidentally, drives off a water molecule, thus converting gypsum into plaster. When water is mixed with plaster, the water molecule is returned, and it hardens into its original chemical state.

Wild continued his experimentation until he perfected the process. People passing by on the road to Estes Park believed Alfred had gone mad as they watched him grind and heat the gypsum, ignoring his fruit trees and his hops.

Just like the hops, all of Colorado's plaster was shipped in from other states. As a result, plastered walls were a luxury and reserved for the rich. Wild planned to change this and make plaster affordable. He met a man who loaned him the money to purchase a carload of sacks. By using an old threshing machine engine, Wild constructed a crude crusher for his plaster mill. A large iron kettle was used to heat the crushed gypsum over an open coal fire. Regrinding it produced plaster.

Wild's success was immediate, as Denver contractors clamored for as much plaster as he could produce from what he called his Buckhorn Plaster Company. An enclosed mill was constructed and began operating in 1887.

The house once used to dry hops was converted into the plaster company's office and boardinghouse for its employees. It was two stories high and included a large dining hall.

Above the gypsum deposit, Alfred Wild discovered some fire clay suitable for making brick. He did not want to take on the additional burden of running a brick factory so he tried for years to attract investors. Finally, in 1924, a company built kilns just north of present-day U.S. 34. The fire clay was hauled by a two foot gauge railroad known as the Buckhorn Northern. It ran from the east side of the Devil's Backbone, through a tunnel, then down to the kilns. The brick factory went bankrupt, and Wild was forced to take over its management. The brick kilns continued to operate until the end of World War II.

The Buckhorn Plaster Company was eventually purchased by the United States Gypsum Company and continued to operate until 1965 when a flood damaged the mill. The company decided not to repair the mill since the supply of gypsum was nearly exhausted.

Alfred Wild was on the board of directors for the First National Bank of Loveland. As a board member, he was personally responsible for the bank's assets. During the Great Depression, starting in 1929, this bank, like thousands of others throughout the United States, was on the verge of collapse. Alfred Wild used his own wealth to keep the bank open. He was forced to liquidate his stock and even took out a note secured on his own home.

The bank eventually went into voluntary liquidation in 1932. Wild, along with all the other directors, used their own wealth to keep the bank solvent and thus lost all their money. The Loveland First National Bank took over all the obligations of the old bank, and none of the depositors lost a cent.

Alfred Wild founded the town of Wilds in 1926 at the south end of the Devil's Backbone. His 26 room mansion overlooked the town. A post office opened in Wilds in 1926 and remained opened until 1934. The town had rail service from Loveland. Alfred Wild died in 1933 as a result of an injury received while backing his car down the driveway from his mansion.

During recent years, Alfred Wild's twenty-six room mansion has been converted into a bed and breakfast and overlooks the

This was Alfred Wild's barn and combination machine shop along the Big Thompson River to the south of Wilds. Just visible in the central portion of the rock foundation is a water wheel which powered his tools. *(Jim Wild collection 048D19)*

town site. During its early years, only a few individuals built homes in Wilds. Today, it is the site of a housing development stretching up the valley from the original town site.

The remains of the brick kilns can be seen north of U.S. 34 just past the south end of the Devil's Backbone. There is nothing left of the plaster mill, but the railroad grade can be seen passing under U.S. 34.

"Arkins" includes a map showing the location of Wilds.

Alfred Wild constructed a large mansion overlooking the town of Wilds. He called his property "Peep O Day Park" presumably for the peep hole in the Devil's Backbone, east of his mansion. *(Kenneth Jessen 035C)*

Kenneth C. Jessen, *Thompson Valley Tales*, Century One Press, Colorado Springs, Colorado, 1984, pp. 55-58.

William H. Bauer, James L. Ozment, John H. Willard, *Colorado Post Offices*, Colorado Railroad Museum, Golden, Colorado, 1990, p. 152.

AREA TWO **2**

Moffat and Routt Counties

AREA 2: Moffat and Routt Counties
Selected Towns

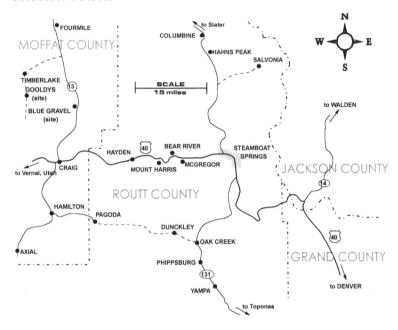

An old log home at Dunckley. *(Drawing by Julia McMillan)*

Introduction to Moffat and Routt Counties

Routt County contains very little in the way of precious metal deposits, and for this reason, few mining towns were formed. Gold was discovered in the Hahns Peak area during the 1860s, which

Gooldys was a small mining camp located south of the ghost town of Timberlake. *(Sonje Jessen SJ109)*

led to the founding of Poverty Bar, later named Hahns Peak, International Camp and Columbine. Vast coal fields, still active today, were found and developed in the region from Oak Creek to the west and south of Craig into Moffat County.

An unusual, remote mining area was located in Moffat County north of Craig in a vast area of little population. Placer deposits, consisting of gold found in sand and soil, were discovered. Limited dredging took place for a period of years, but not enough mineralization was discovered to fuel the formation of permanent towns. Among the towns formed were Timberlake, Fourmile, Goodlys and Blue Gravel.

Summit County, one of the seventeen original Colorado counties, was established in 1861. Its area embraced what is now Routt County. Out of Summit County, Grand County was formed in 1874, and three years later, part of its area was renamed Routt County. It extended west to the Utah border and included all of the northwest portion of the state. In 1911, the western portion of Routt County became Moffat County, establishing the present-day Routt County borders.

BEAR RIVER and McGREGOR

- *Routt County, Yampa River drainage*
- *Accessible via paved road and gravel side roads; access to sites limited by private property*
- *Town had a post office; several standing structures remain*

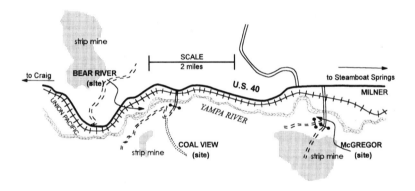

Established in 1915, Bear River at the mouth of Coal View Gulch on the Yampa River, was supported by a single mine. Its hoist house stood east of a small draw with the mine portal on the opposite side. Mine cars were pulled across a trestle prior to unloading. Bear River's peak years were 1935 to 1940, with a population of 150 families.

Bear River had a general store, school, boarding house, hotel and a post office which opened in 1914. The coal company constructed a three-story structure for its supply warehouse and offices. This building also had baths, pool hall and a dance hall.

The town had its own water system and electrical supply. Bear River was characterized by a row of tin garages facing U.S. 40.

When the coal deposit was exhausted during the early 1940s, the town of Bear River died, and the post office closed.

McGregor was located about six and a half mile east of Bear River and was owned by the McGregor Coal Company. The bachelors lived in a large two story boarding house in town. It had indoor plumbing and was heated by a coal fired furnace. A kitchen took up one end of the building, and small bedrooms filled the other end, with a large dining hall in the center. More bedrooms were located on the second floor.

Married miners could live in the nearly identical company houses with either two bedrooms or three bedrooms. By each house was a coal shed and an outhouse. All automobiles had to be parked in a common garage. The coal company provided water, electricity and coal to its workers free of charge. Inside the homes, only cold water plumbing existed. To produce hot water, a reservoir by the coal stove could be filled.

The McGregor branch of Cameo Mercantile was the only store in McGregor, and it sold gasoline and groceries. The store

There are only two structures left in the ghost town of McGregor. They sit up on a hill above the mine and are on private property. *(Sonje Jessen SJ107)*

included the post office which opened in 1915 and remained in operation until 1942 when the mine closed. Also, the store included a meat locker with a big butcher block out front. Sawdust, confined by boards nailed in the floor, covered this portion of the floor. On one side of the store's central aisle were clothes and on the other side food. Other merchandise could be found in the basement with the furnace. Like most coal mining towns, the miners were paid in scrip issued by the coal company. The store accepted this and scrip from other area towns.

Social life centered around the McGregor Amusement Hall, constructed in 1916, and included billiard and pool tables. To discourage drunkenness so common in other mining towns, only soft drinks were served. The hall was also used for dances and community events. A stage for live performances took up one end of the hall, and the building could be converted into a movie theater. Movies cost adults thirty cents and children a dime.

History of Hayden & West Routt County 1876-1989, Curtis Media Corp., Dallas, Texas, 1990, pp. 21-22.

The Historical Guide to Routt County, The Tread of the Pioneers Museum, 1979, p. 55.

William H. Bauer, James L. Ozment, John H. Willard, *Colorado Post Offices*, Colorado Railroad Museum, Golden, Colorado, 1990, p. 96.

COLUMBINE
Gold Camp

- *Routt County, Willow Creek drainage*
- *Accessible via graded dirt road; private property*
- *Town had a post office; numerous original structures*

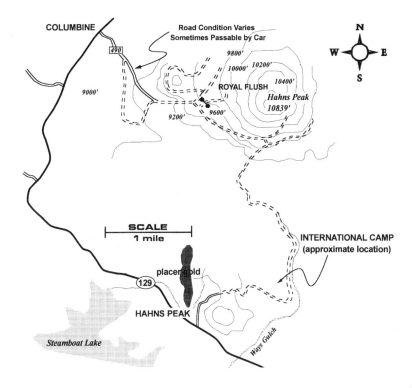

The "Columbine Stampede" took place in 1881, and was fueled by gold ore discovered to the east on the slopes of Hahns Peak. The richest mines were the Royal Flush and the Tom Thumb. The Columbine area lacked the placer deposits found to the south near the town of Hahns Peak, but rather was supported by lode mining.

In 1880, a general store was constructed along with a few cabins. Columbine was laid out officially in 1897 by James Caron on eleven acres. It had already gained its own post office a year before, and by this time, a dozen cabins occupied the site. The camp also had a school. Columbine was the stopover for the stage run between Laramie and Steamboat Springs.

James Caron became the town's civic leader as well as official founder. He held a variety of public positions including justice of the peace, postmaster and coroner. One of the most brutal murders in Routt County had its ties to Columbine. In the town's only saloon, sheep herder Joe Belardi got drunk. He gambled away all of his wages and the wages of two Mexican sheep herders. When he returned to the sheep camp, he murdered the two Mexican sheep herders, then burned their bodies in the campfire. The location is now called Dead Mexican Park.

Columbine is very much intact with a number of original structures. The town was purchased and operated as a resort

after the mining died, and the present owners have remodeled many of the cabins for guests.

This old cabin at Columbine has collapsed since being photographed in 1983, but the majority of the original structures have been fully restored as guest cabins. *(Kenneth Jessen 072A19)*

Thelma V. Stevenson, *Historic Hahns Peak*, Robinson Press, Fort Collins, Colorado, 1976, pp. 31-32.

DUNCKLEY

- *Routt County, Yoast Creek drainage*
- *Site on private property*
- *Town had a post office; several standing structures remain*

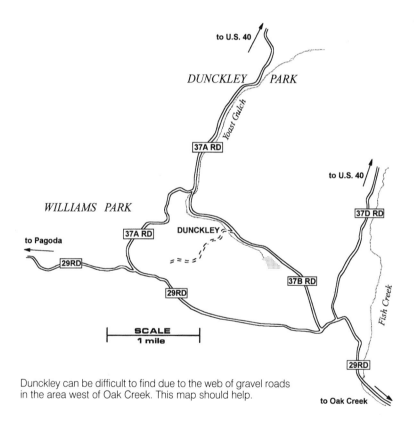

Dunckley can be difficult to find due to the web of gravel roads in the area west of Oak Creek. This map should help.

Dunckley (also spelled Dunkley) was not founded on mining, but rather was a ranching community. It did have a school and post office. The post office opened in 1892 and remained opened for fifty years. The filing was originally made under the name "Argo," however, there already was an Argo, Colorado post office. Dunckley was the family that settled the area in the 1880s and was the logical second choice. The Dunckley's raised cattle in the area west of Oak Creek, now known as Dunckley Park.

It is tricky to reach Dunckley in the web of irregular roads west of Oak Creek. Good maps are essential for travel in the area. Dunckley is located along 37B RD, and its dominant structure is an old two story log house, which looks out of place in Colorado. There are a number of other structures on the site, most of them barns and stables.

The back of the old log home at Dunckley looks more like a house found in the hills of West Virginia. *(Kenneth Jessen 110A8)*

History of Hayden & West Routt County 1876-1989, Hayden Historical Society, Hayden, Colorado, pp. 168-171.

William H. Bauer, James L. Ozment, John H. Willard, *Colorado Post Offices*, Colorado Railroad Museum, Golden, Colorado, 1990, p. 48.

HAHNS PEAK
Named For Joseph Hahn

- *Routt County, Willow Creek drainage*
- *Accessible by paved road; private property*
- *Town had a post office; numerous original structures remain*

Joseph Hahn (originally spelled "Henn") and his companions are credited with the discovery of gold in northwestern Colorado in 1862. This discovery sparked the beginning of the development of the region. Gold was not, however, found in large quantities, and the region eventually grew around agriculture.

Hahn and his two companions were from Germany and were impressed by this vast, unpopulated area. This was in stark contrast to the densely populated region of Europe where they were raised.

This is a log hotel which once stood in the mining town of Hahns Peak along with numerous other log structures. *(Colorado Historical Society F31690)*

93

For weeks, they explored Middle Park and North Park without finding any gold. Crossing over the range, they reached low lying mountains and large expanses of native grass. As autumn approached, they reached the base of a conical gray volcanic mountain. They found "color" in their pans. The gold did not come in great quantity, but it was sufficient to merit further exploration. Winter was approaching, with ice forming during the cold nights, and the party headed back to Clear Creek.

It is not known what became of Hahn's companions. Possibly the trip was a little too exciting and a bit too demanding. Joseph Hahn confided in two other men, William A. Doyle and Captain George Way. Doyle was a miner living in Black Hawk, and Way lived in Empire. He told them of his discovery, and the trio made secret plans to return to the area of the discovery.

The Civil War interrupted their plans. Doyle enlisted in the Third Colorado Cavalry and fought on the side of the Union.

In 1865, the trio of men invited other men to join them in an expedition back to the gold fields originally discovered by Hahn and his German companions. The trip took place in the fall, too late to explore the county, but a sufficient amount of gold was recovered to lead them to believe they had made a significant discovery. Only a modest amount of gold was brought back, but it caused a great deal of excitement among the mining men in the Clear Creek area.

During this trip, William Doyle and Captain Way left camp and climbed the gray peak. Doyle

Hahns Peak has a number of neat summer cabins dating back a century or more. On the side of this home there is a sign that reads, "1893-1993." *(Kenneth Jessen 103D5)*

brought an empty yeast or baking can with a screw top. At the 10,839-foot summit, he placed a note in the can relating details of the trip. In the note, he said the following, "This is named Hahn's Peak by his friend and comrade, William A. Doyle, August 27, 1865."

After returning to the Clear Creek area, Doyle and Way returned to their homes while Hahn stayed the winter in Kansas.

A new expedition was organized, and it was agreed that the three men should have the first choice on any mining claims. In July, 1866, the snow had apparently melted enough to get over Berthoud Pass. There were about fifty men in this party, and they soon found, after leaving Empire, that they had to shovel their way over the pass.

A noted prospector, hunter and trapper named Charlie Utter joined the party at his home in Middle Park. The men camped at Hot Sulphur Springs and crossed the headwaters of Muddy Creek. They gained access to the area near the present-day Steamboat Springs using a pass north of Rabbit Ears previously discovered by Joseph Hahn.

Late in August, 1866, the men established a camp on the gravel beds south of Hahns Peak. Some prospected while others constructed cabins. They named the gulches in the area and called the camp Poverty Bar.

As a side note, historian Frank Hall, in his monumental work, *History of Colorado*, refutes this story of the first discovery of gold in the Hahns Peak area. He credits Captain Way with reaching the base of the peak first and finding gold.

None of the party struck it rich, at least compared to the initial discoveries made at Gregory Gulch near Central City or Jackson's Diggings along Clear Creek. Doyle seemed to do the best with $5 to $10 per pan at one spot. Nevertheless, the group formed a mining district based on the principals laid down for Central City.

The Ute Indians regarded the party as an invasion into their territory. Under Chief Colorow, a party approached the camp and demanded to know why the white men were there. Utter spoke the Ute language, and this may have been why he was included in the party. He explained what they were doing and this apparently satisfied Colorow.

As winter approached, claims were staked, and the prospectors began the long trip back to civilization. Hahn, Way and Doyle elected to stick it out and made plans to begin mining when spring arrived. On October 2, Captain Way was sent to get supplies for his companions. He took the gold dust with him to purchase what was needed, telling his companions that he would be back on the 14th. Now Hahn and Doyle were left alone to whipsaw wood and put up a substantial cabin. It was built near Way Gulch, but Captain Way never returned. He abandoned his companions and lived out his life in New Mexico.

Heavy snow began to fall and Hahn and Doyle realized that their survival was up to themselves. The wild game, which had been the camp's source of food, began to disappear. Beginning on November 24 through December 31, it snowed every day until the accumulation reached twelve feet. Starvation forced the pair to abandon their cabin, and on April 22, 1867, the two tried to make it back to civilization on snowshoes.

On April 29, the pair reached the Muddy River in Middle Park and rested. When it came time to move on, Hahn was too weak and exhausted. Doyle spread out blankets, and using his own body warmth, kept Hahn warm during the night. Doyle set out in the morning for help in the vast, unoccupied land. He wandered about all day, and when he returned, he found Hahn dead.

The following morning, Doyle set out once again to find human population. At the time, John Sumner and Ashely Franklin were living in William Newton Byers' house in Hot Sulphur Springs. They had gone out looking for some stray cattle and spotted Doyle floundering in the snow. They took the then snow blind Doyle to the closest cabin where he was fed and nursed back to health. Sumner and Franklin tried in vain to find Hahns' body, based on Doyle's directions.

Editor and founder of the *Rocky Mountain News*, William

Newton Byers, joined Jack Sumner in November to find the body and give it a proper burial. The body had been seen by a fisherman during the summer, and he guided them to the site. The grave was marked by a pile of rock with a snowshoe placed at the head of the grave. A greater monument to this pioneer is Hahns Peak.

The Poverty Bar camp was rediscovered by Bibleback Brown in 1868. He told Bill Slater of the placer gold. In the spring of 1870, Brown and Slater began sluicing gold out of the Willow Creek gravel.

A second mining district was formed replacing the original Hahns Peak Mining District as an increasing number of prospectors arrived. It is possible that the new wave of prospectors knew nothing about the original mining district or that the records were lost.

For years, individual prospectors washed gravel along Willow Creek, then a large mining company arrived. The company began consolidating various small claims and mining began on a much larger scale using hydraulic techniques. Water was brought in via a flume which was originally constructed to supply the nearby International Camp. The flume was extended to Poverty Bar making it nearly thirty miles long.

A post office was opened under the name Hahns Peak in 1877 and remained an active office until 1941.

Fully restored, the District 34 school house in Hahns Peak stands as a monument to pioneer effort. *(Kenneth Jessen 072A18A)*

The Routt County Seat was located at Hayden for the years 1877 and 1878, but then in an election, Hahns Peak cast 12 votes and International Camp cast an additional 47 votes, enough to move the county seat. Even though located about a mile apart, a lawsuit determined that these two places were one and the same. The county seat was moved in 1879, along with its records, to International Camp. A year later, the records were moved again, but this time to a log house at the south end of Hahns Peak. In 1901, a two-story courthouse was built on the north end of town to house the county records. Hahns Peak remained the Routt County seat until 1912 when Steamboat Springs out-voted Hahns Peak for the title.

By 1912, Hahns Peak was dying. The big hydraulic nozzles used to tear away the gravel along Willow Creek failed to produce enough gold to justify the expense. Hard rock miners on the slopes of Hahns Peak didn't strike any rich lodes. A dredge near International Camp, capable of processing tons of gravel per day, also failed to yield enough gold to make a profit.

Poor roads into the area hindered development. A new railroad, the Laramie, Hahns Peak & Pacific, was to solve these problems with a line from Laramie, across the mountains, to Hahns Peak. In 1911, the railroad turned south at Centennial, west of Laramie, instead of heading west across the mountains to Hahns Peak.

Despite its economic failure as a mining camp, Hahns Peak never quite became a ghost town. The majority of its buildings, however, were abandoned before World War I after the placer gold played out. Some of the original cabins were maintained by seasonal residents, and there was enough population in the area to keep the post office open. Today, the town has moved into the resort era and maintains a small museum. The Hahns Peak schoolhouse, located on the museum grounds, is on the National Register of Historic Places.

As a side note to Hahns Peak history, the town was the scene of a famous jail break by David Lant and Harry Tracy in

1898. Tracy was a member of the Wild Bunch headed by Butch Cassidy. The pair were captured in Brown's Park, which was then part of Routt County, by Routt County Sheriff Neiman. He took personal responsibility for standing guard by the Hahns Peak jail.

Somehow, Lant was able to get into an unlocked cell, and when Sheriff Neiman least expected it, he was attacked. To prevent being killed, Neiman faked being unconscious. Meanwhile, Tracy and Lant escaped on the only pair of horses in the entire town. Once the outlaws were gone, Neiman traveled to the nearest ranch on the Elk River were he was able to get a horse.

He had overheard the outlaws discuss going to the stage coach stop just outside Steamboat Springs. Neiman rode directly to Steamboat Springs, and he and an armed deputy boarded the stage. When it arrived at the stage station outside of town, Tracy and Lant were waiting and were promptly arrested. The outlaws were taken all the way south to the Pitkin County jail in Aspen to await trial for the murder of a deputy. Tracy later killed Lant, and when Tracy was cornered in eastern Washington, he killed himself rather than be captured.

For a map showing the location of Hahns Peak, the town and the mountain, see "Columbine."

Al Wiggins, *Hahns Peak and the Beautiful Basin*, Rilla Wiggins Family Collection, 1993.

Charles H. Leckenby, *The Tread of the Pioneers*, Steamboat Pilot, Steamboat Springs, Colorado, 1945, pp. 21-24.

Douglas W. Ellison, *David Lant, The Vanished Outlaw*, Midstates Printing, Aberdeen, South Dakota, 1988, pp. 137-150.

Frank Hall, *History of Colorado*, Vol. IV, The Blakely Printing Company, Chicago, 1895, pp. 300-301.

The Historical Guide to Routt County, The Tread of the Pioneers Museum, 1979, pp. 38-44.

Thelma V. Stevenson, *Historic Hahns Peak*, Robinson Press, Fort Collins, Colorado, 1976, pp. 1-16.

Thomas J. Noel, Paul F. Mahoney and Richard E. Stevens, *Historical Atlas of Colorado*, University of Oklahoma Press, Norman, Oklahoma, 1993,, pp. 15-16.

William H. Bauer, James L. Ozment, John H. Willard, *Colorado Post Offices*, Colorado Railroad Museum, Golden, Colorado, 1990, p. 67.

INTERNATIONAL CAMP
Called "Bugtown"

- *Routt County, Willow Creek drainage*
- *Site not accessible, private property*
- *Believed to have no standing structures*

On the gravel beds south of Hahns Peak, the mountain, a place called International Camp was formed next to String Ridge in 1874. By 1876, the place had a population of 75. The Purdy Mining Company, headed by John Farwell, began operations at International Camp. The company built a boarding house, and Farwell, being a religious man, had a chapel constructed. He allowed no saloons in International Camp.

The camp sprawled along a low ridge near Way's Gulch and north toward Hahns Peak. Because mine officials lived at the camp, the miners nicknamed the place "Bugtown." The humor in this name is lost to history. Possibly the miners referred to management as "bugs." The nearest town was Hahns Peak, just a mile to the west. Hahns Peak was popular with the miners because, unlike International Camp, it had saloons!

For John Farwell, the operation at International Camp was a financial disaster. He failed to find enough gold in the gravel to make any money. He sold his $200,000 investment in 1879 for $32,000, which was the value of the merchandise in the company store. "Bugtown" was abandoned by 1881, and many of its buildings were moved to Hahns Peak. A forest fire took care of the rest. Among the buildings which were moved was a three gabled log structure which served as the county courthouse in Hahns Peak.

When Hahns Peak historian Thelma Stevenson visited the Bugtown site in 1974, she could not find a trace of the place.

Today, access is restricted by private property.

The exact location of International Camp varies according to the historical source, *but for a map which shows its approximate location, see "Columbine."*

The Historical Guide to Routt County, The Tread of the Pioneers Museum, 1979, p. 89.

Thelma V. Stevenson, *Historic Hahns Peak*, Robinson Press, Fort Collins, Colorado, 1976, pp. 1-16.

MOUNT HARRIS

And Its Over-Under Gas Station

- *Routt County; Yampa River drainage*
- *Accessible by paved road*
- *Town had a post office; no standing structures remain*

Mount Harris was a company town with rows of identical cottages for the miners and their families, as shown in this 1915 photograph. *(Colorado Historical Society F32067)*

There is nothing left to remind people that Mount Harris along U.S. 40 even existed, except for a parking area and a sign which describes its history.

In June, 1914, a coal mine was opened at the mouth of the Bear River Canyon by George and Byron Harris. The area had gained rail service just a few years before, making coal shipments economical. The mine was purchased by the Colorado-Utah Coal Company. Located on the south side of the Yampa River, the coal was brought over to a coal tipple along the tracks by a conveyor.

The coal company built a small town on the north side of

A 1915 photograph shows the combination general store - drug store in Mount Harris. *(Colorado Historical Society F32066)*

the Yampa River for its workers and called it Harris. Confusion with another post office of the same name caused the name to be changed to Mount Harris. The post office opened in 1915 and remained opened until the town's abandonment in 1958.

In the center of town, a sandstone building housed the company offices, a general store, post office, drug store, barber shop and pool hall. There were also three boarding houses and the Colburn Hotel. Mount Harris had a church, two doctors, a fire department and a community center. The most unique business, however, was an over-under filling station with the upper level serving travelers along U.S. 40 and the lower level for Mount Harris residents.

In the residential area, four long rows of identical company houses were constructed for the miners. They were painted white with gray trim and had spacious yards. Residents had access to several barns built below town next to the Yampa River for their livestock.

Minorities were relegated to an area west of town with some of their homes located across the river from Mount Harris. They had their own church.

The coal company gave free movie tickets to local children in exchange for cleaning the side walks which ran the length of the company houses. The result was a very clean town.

Mount Harris was sports-minded and had a two-story grandstand for various sporting events. Boxing, however, took center stage. "Rattlesnake" Jack Carson was a boxing champion from Mount Harris.

By 1920, Mount Harris became the largest town in Routt County with 1,295 residents. In the late 1950s, the mine closed, spelling the end to Mount Harris. No structures remain standing on the site. The Mount Harris site is west of Steamboat Springs along U.S. 40. There is a parking area, with an interpretative sign giving a brief history of the town.

The Historical Guide to Routt County, The Tread of the Pioneers Museum, 1979, pp. 53-55.

OAK CREEK

Originally Belltown

- *Routt County, Yampa River drainage*
- *Accessible via paved road*
- *Town has a post office; occupied town with many original structures*

Coal was called "Routt County Gold," and towns like Oak Creek depended almost entirely on coal mining. Originally named Belltown for the Bell brothers, Sam and Ed, Oak Creek came into its own in 1907. This was also the year the post office opened. By the end of the following year, the town had a store and fifty residents. *The Oak Creek Times* published its first issue and continued to publish under its original name and as *The Miner* for 40 years. By 1910, five mines were in full production in the Oak Creek area.

Coal mining, however, dates back to the 1880s when "wagon mines" were in operation. Coal seams were opened up, then ranchers came to the mine and purchased coal on the spot using their wagons to haul it back to their homes. A couple of Cripple Creek businessmen arrived in

Oak Creek is not a ghost town nor has it ever been completely abandoned. This is an example of one of the fine homes in the town. *(Kenneth Jessen 110A9)*

1907 and purchased a ranch in upper Oak Creek for a town site. Sam Perry opened the first high production coal mine in 1905, and joined the Cripple Creek men in forming the Oak Creek Town, Land and Mining Company. A town plat was filed, and the town of Oak Creek was incorporated.

On the northern edge of Oak Creek was a place called Cowboy Hill where ranchers and farmers lived. The valley above Oak Creek became a vegetable producing area.

The coming of the Denver, Northwestern & Pacific (The Moffat Road) in 1909 produced a small population explosion to 200 residents. Oak Creek grew to include two stores, a restaurant, the Pacific Hotel, a lumber yard, barber shops, a couple of saloons, a pool hall, laundry, livery stable, drug store and a dairy. In addition, it had a school and a church.

The town continued to grow as the demand for coal increased. By 1915, Oak Creek was a town of 2,000 residents with three churches, more than 30 businesses, an elementary school and a high school. Oak Creek also had its own hospital. It gained economic status to the point where it made a serious bid for county seat, but lost to Steamboat Springs.

During the 1920s, Oak Creek's coal production was hampered by labor trouble and strikes. Following the strikes, the town prospered until the Great Depression. During this time, the Bell Building was constructed and housed stores on the ground floor and a boarding house, dance hall and fraternal lodges on its second floor. A state bank opened, and a red light district developed on Hickory Flats.

During the 1940s, mine closures began, and by 1952, only one mine remained in operation. Oak Creek is located south of Steamboat Springs on Colorado Highway 131 and is still occupied by a number of permanent residents.

The Historical Guide to Routt County, The Tread of the Pioneers Museum, 1979, p. 57.

ROYAL FLUSH

Best Hand In The House

- *Routt County, Willow Creek drainage*
- *Access near site over rough dirt road; on private property*
- *Town did not have a post office; there may be several original standing structures*

One of the cabins distributed about the slopes of Hahns Peak in the vicinity of the mining camp of Royal Flush. *(Kenneth Jessen 103D10)*

After placer gold was found at Poverty Bar (renamed Hahns Peak) to the south, it was reasoned that the origin of the gold was Hahns Peak itself. It was only after the free gold in the gravel beds was exhausted that any serious effort was made to find its origin. Hard rock mining, after all, required capital, where as placer mining was simple and could be accomplished with a pan or sluice box.

The Royal Flush mine on the flanks of Hahns Peak was developed sometime around 1897, and after three miles of tunnels were cut into the peak, the mine was abandoned. At the mine, there was a blacksmith shop, assay office, mine office and a bunk house. The camp became known as Royal Flush. After World War I was over, Royal Flush reopened and was worked until 1920. As recent as 1955, new timbering was put into place. Today, access is limited by private property, and the current status of the mine and the camp is unknown.

Some miners working at Royal Flush may have lived in the camp, but Columbine, not too far away, probably offered more comfort.

The route to Royal Flush is simple. Across the road from Columbine, on the southeast side, a narrow dirt road FR490 heads towards Hahns Peak and crosses Independence Creek practically within sight of Columbine. In the spring, this crossing may require the use of a four-wheel drive vehicle. At the first fork in the road, stay to the left, and at the second fork in the road, stay left again. Beyond this second fork, the road becomes quite steep and rough. It may not be suitable for a regular car.

At the top of the grade, the road to the left goes to Royal Flush, while straight ahead, the road leads to a beautiful meadow and continues around Hahns Peak to other mines. There are several cabins overlooking this meadow, now privately owned. These cabins might have been part of the Royal Flush camp, but private property limits exploration. Farther to the east in a second meadow, there is a foundation, water supply pipe, and garbage pit
indicating where a building once stood.

It should be noted that there are other cabins scattered about the south side of Hahns Peak, indicating a distributed population. *For a map showing Royal Flush, see "Columbine."*

Thelma V. Stevenson, *Historic Hahns Peak*, Robinson Press, Fort Collins, Colorado, 1976, pp. 37-40.

SLAVONIA

- *Routt County, Middle Fork of the Elk River drainage*
- *Accessible via graded dirt road*
- *Town did not have a post office; no standing structures remain*

At the Slavonia site, there are no standing structures; in fact, hardly a trace shows that a camp once existed. This site is occupied by a parking lot for those wishing to hike into the Mount Zirkel Wilderness Area. The camp stood where Gilpin Creek and Gold Creek join to form the Middle Fork of the Elk River. The Slavonia site is still indicated on topographic maps, and the mine, which supported it, is a short distance up Gilpin Creek. To reach the site, take the Seedhouse Road east from Clark to its very end.

Perry Eberhart, *Guide to the Colorado Ghost Towns and Mining Camps*, Sage Books, Chicago, 1959, p. 117.

TIMBERLAKE, FOURMILE, GOODLYS and BLUE GRAVEL

- *Moffat County, Timberlake Creek and Fourmile Creek drainages*
- *Accessible either by graded gravel road or paved road*
- *Fourmile had a post office; Timberlake has standing structures*

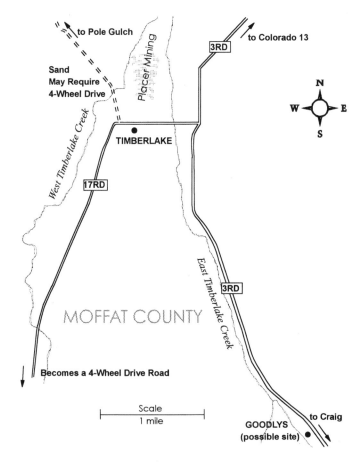

North of Craig, placer deposits were discovered along the Iron Springs Divide. On the north slope of the divide, where the gulches drain into the Little Snake River, gold was discovered in the sand along Fourmile, Timberlake and Housel creeks. The southernmost and earliest placer gold mining town was Blue Gravel. The site is a short distance from the confluence of Blue Gravel Creek and Fortification Creek. Moffat County pioneer Val Fitzpatrick reported that the town had a hotel with a restaurant, a livery barn, a blacksmith shop, a saloon and a store. By the 1870s, however, the town had been abandoned and only two structures remained. Today, the site is difficult to locate, and nothing remains to indicate the presence of a town.

Other accounts claim that the first discovery was made in 1882 along Fortification Creek, much later than Blue Gravel. Hugh Morrison, an Aspen prospector, found gold on Fourmile Creek in 1891. He returned the following year to stake out claims and construct a cabin at Fourmile Creek. In 1893, hydraulic mining began, and between 1895 and 1903, several ditches were constructed to bring water into the dry area. The longest ditch began near Dixon, Wyoming and ran for 38 miles.

The town of Fourmile was founded in 1894 and began with Morrison's cabin and a store. A small restaurant opened followed by a second store run by the J. W. Hugus Company. This store included a bank where gold could be exchanged for cash. J. W. Hugus also operated stores in Rawlings, Baggs, Dixon, Craig, Meeker, Steamboat Springs and several other towns. A post office opened at Fourmile in 1895 and remained opened for four years. Historical photographs show many tents and dugouts where the prospectors lived. They were more in a hurry to mine than to construct cabins. As time passed, a number of frame homes were built, and the town gained a two-story hotel. Fourmile reached an estimated population of 400. By 1898, people began leaving Fourmile having realized that the gold-bearing sands were not especially rich. Today, the Colorado Department of Highways maintenance shop occupies the Fourmile site.

A small dredge was built on Timberlake Creek by B. L. Law in 1900. The dredge burned in 1904, but its tailings can still be seen in the creek bottom. During 1937 and 1938, a dry plant was used to recover gold from the sand bars above Timberlake Creek, and some lode mining was done at the head of Housel Gulch nearby. Today, Timberlake has five standing structures and was probably abandoned around 1904 when the dredge burned.

Approximately three miles south of Timberlake was a place called Goodlys, at least based on a 1912 Clason map. It is difficult to determine the size of this town since only the collapsed remains of two cabins mark the Goodlys site.

This same 1912 Clason map also shows a place called Housels at a point five miles south of Goodlys, but on Housel Creek. Examination of the area failed to find evidence of any

settlement. Nothing in the vast area was of enough economic importance to fuel the construction of any extensive towns.

One of five structures standing at Timberlake, north of Craig. The town was founded on nearby gold placer deposits and worked for a few years after the turn of the century. *(Kenneth Jessen 110A3)*

Ben H. Parker Jr., *Gold Panning and Placering in Colorado*, Colorado Geological Survey, Denver, Colorado, 1992, pp. 72-73.

Harold Babcock, "Moffat County's Extinct Town of Blue Gravel," *The Frontier Magazine*, December 1995/January 1996.

Harold Babcock, "Fourmile: The Gold Mining Town that was," *The Frontier Magazine*, February, 1996.

Terry Hankins, "The Town of Fourmile, Moffat Co., Colo," a paper prepared in collaboration with Jean Russel and the Northwest Colorado Historical Commission, March 27, 1987.

William H. Bauer, James L. Ozment, John H. Willard, *Colorado Post Offices*, Colorado Railroad Museum, Golden, Colorado, 1990, p. 57.

AREA THREE

3

Boulder County

continued

AREA 3: Boulder County
Selected Towns

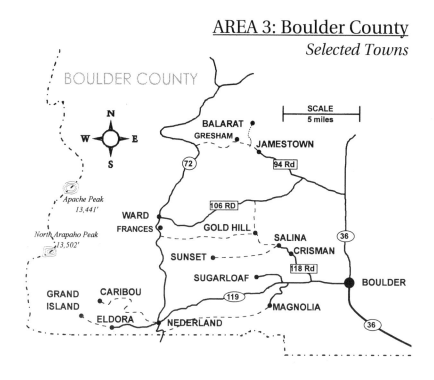

Introduction to Boulder County

Boulder County has one of the highest concentrations of old mining towns and camps in the state of Colorado. Its mining economy was founded on a variety of minerals including gold, silver, and tungsten. Mining activity, although sporadic today, lasted well over a century.

Boulder County has several worthwhile ghost towns and mining camps, and they are all within a one day drive of the Denver-Boulder area. Gold Hill, the earliest mountain mining town in the state, is in a wonderful state of preservation and a good place to begin. Most of its structures are privately owned and seasonally occupied, but there is also a year-round resident population. The Blue Bird Casey's Table Inn and the Gold Hill Inn

are on the National Register of Historic Places. Eldora's main
street is lined with abandoned stores, and although many of the
cabins are still occupied, the town is a ghost of its former self. The
ruin of the great Gold Extraction Company's mill at Wall Street is
likened to some old Roman fortress. A few authentic shanties, of
the kind which the ordinary miner could afford, can be found in
the towns of Sunshine and Summerville. A once substantial town
with over eighty structures is the ghost town of Caribou. Its high
altitude, severe weather and strong winds hindered its development. It has practically vanished, and the stone walls of a couple
of stores plus the collapsed remains of a cabin are all that mark
the site today. Ward is a typical mining town; it is strung out in a
disorderly fashion in a small valley. Its community church still
stands along with its schoolhouse and the Columbia Hotel. Above
the town is the railroad depot for the Colorado & Northwestern.
One of the most interesting driving experiences is to follow the old
railroad grade from Sunset up to the Peak-to-Peak Highway via
Glacier Lake or in the other direction to Gold Hill.

Boulder County Mineral Deposits

The mineral deposits in Boulder County covered a wide area.
The mines, with their associated mining towns, were dispersed
over much of the mountainous portion of the county. The gold-
bearing alluvial deposits were discovered first in 1859 by prospectors using panning as a means of discovery. These deposits were
quickly worked out. At the same time, gold ore was found in Gold
Run. This was followed a decade later by the discovery of silver
ore. Telluride, an ore rich in both gold and silver, was found in
extensive deposits over a wide area in Boulder County and created
a second mining boom. Another important mineral was coal,
found to the south of Boulder in the Marshall coal field. The
"black iron," which hindered milling, was identified as tungsten at
the turn of the century. The high demand for tungsten during
World War I produced another mining boom during which ore

This is a Boulder County mine at about the turn of the century, location unknown. *(Kenneth Jessen collection)*

valued at tens of million of dollars was removed from the county.

Mining is never straightforward, and by its very nature, produces many ups and downs. As lode mines got progressively deeper toward the mid to late 1860s, the decomposed gold ore was depleted. In its place were more complex ores containing sulfides and other minerals. The ores could no longer be simply ground to a powder and exposed to mercury to amalgamate the precious metal. Mining fell to a low ebb, and mines began to close. The mills stopped running, and towns were quickly abandoned.

Professor Alden Smith and others began testing the more complex ores and found a strange mineral not common to other Western states. He identified this as tellurium at his Central City laboratory. It has no intrinsic market value itself, but is often combined with gold and silver. Until this discovery, it was passed over as worthless and fooled many prospectors because its physical appearance was so different from gold or silver ore. It was first discovered near Gold Hill in 1873.

Telluride ore had to be smelted, but yielded well. Its discovery led to extensive prospecting in Boulder County, and many new mines were opened. The telluride belt is about twenty miles long and a couple of miles wide. Telluride ore formed the economic base for Sunshine, Salina, Camp Providence, Balarat and Magnolia. The Smuggler Mine at Balarat was on the northernmost part of the telluride belt and Eldora at the southern tip. Telluride caused the return of population growth to mining communities like Gold Hill and Jamestown.

For the first twenty years of precious metal production, ore worth well over fifty million dollars in today's currency was removed from Boulder County mines. Of the production, about sixty percent was gold. The biggest producing mines were the Columbia lode near Ward, the Horsfal Mine near Gold Hill, the Caribou silver mine, and the silver mine near Eldora.

As for the smelters, half of the ore was shipped to the Boston & Colorado Smelter in Black Hawk. After it closed, the ore was sent to Argo, just outside of Denver. Next in size was Boyd's Smelting Works in Boulder followed by the New Jersey Smelter at Caribou. Some ore was also processed in Golden and at the Washington Avenue Smelter in Sugarloaf.

Early Roads

Roads in the newly developed mining areas in Boulder County were essential. The first pioneer road was to Gold Run and serviced the mines in the Gold Hill area. It had steep grades and wound its way between the trees directly up the foothills. A better road was needed, and the St. Vrain, Altona, Gold Hill and Gregory Road Company was formed. It selected a route up Left Hand Canyon to Lickskillet Gulch, then straight up the gulch to Gold Hill.

The Colorado Territorial Legislature granted a charter for another toll road called the Boulder Valley and Central City Wagon Road. It was constructed up Boulder Canyon with work starting in 1865 under the direction of James P. Maxwell. In three months, the graders reached the mouth of Four Mile Canyon.

Within this first section was the Maxwell Pitch so named for the supervisor, James Maxwell. The road clung to the north wall of the canyon, around a point, then dropped down to Boulder Creek. Today, there is a parking lot at the Maxwell Pitch, and the old railroad grade of the Colorado & Northwestern has been converted into a bicycle trail. Above the trail are the remains of this pioneer toll road, which charged $1.00 for a wagon pulled by a brace of draft animals.

After silver was discovered at Caribou in 1871, the road up Boulder Canyon was extended to Nederland (then called Dayton). Wells Fargo promised service over this road but failed to follow through. Another stage coach company initiated daily service from Boulder to Nederland then south to Black Hawk. A branch line used the newly constructed ore haulage road to provide Caribou with stage coach service.

In 1872, the Left Hand and Jamestown Wagon Road Company was incorporated to provide a reliable road up Left Hand Creek. Other toll roads were built, and as the charters for all of these roads expired, the county took over the maintenance and title. These pioneer roads served the mining towns until the early 1880s when a Union Pacific subsidiary constructed the first mountain railroad in Boulder County.

Pioneer Prospector Samuel Conger

Although Samuel Conger was one of the best known prospectors, explorers, hunters and mine owners in Colorado, most of his work was done in Boulder County. He started prospecting in Wisconsin at the age of seventeen, then moved to California. It was like Samuel Conger was born for no other purpose. When news of gold discoveries in what was to become the state of Colorado reached him, he was off to Gregory Diggings in late 1859 or early 1860. He prospected while earning a living hunting wild game for the meat markets of Black Hawk and Central City. He was first to explore the high altitude ridges near Arapahoe Peak, and in 1860, he found some float, which turned out to be a large silver lode. The town of Caribou grew up below Conger's discovery.

He was grubstaked in 1873 to explore Middle Park. This was supposed to have uncovered rich minerals in the area, and when Conger came back with the news that he ran across nothing of value, the men who grubstaked him put a rope around his neck. While the men were discussing what to do next, Conger wisely slipped away.

In Summit County, not far from Breckenridge, he founded Conger's Camp near a silver lode. By 1879, the camp grew to thirty or forty houses. Under the name Conger, it gained its own post office in 1880. For some reason, the name was changed to Argentine the following year. Conger named his silver mine the Dianthe in honor of his wife, and in the process, picked up the title "Colonel."

The most important discovery Conger made was not gold or silver, however, but correctly identifying tungsten ore in the Nederland area. Conger's tungsten mine north of Nederland kept the mining district alive well past the turn of the century.

Samuel Conger passed away at his Denver home in 1925 at the age of 92.

Boulder County Railroads

Without improved transportation, Boulder County mines could not have continued to develop. From Ward, for example, the charge per ton by wagon was $3.50. Only high grade ore could be mined economically and sent to distant smelters. Initially in the history of the area, lower grade ore was discarded. By constructing a railroad to Ward, the haulage price could be dropped in half. The economics were simple, and the railroad was the only answer to economic survival as reserves of high grade ore were depleted.

Another problem quite evident in historic photographs was the issue of fuel. Virtually all the forests were clear cut during the mining boom either for mining timbers, buildings or to fuel the boilers. Steam power was used extensively at the mines to run drills, to hoist the ore and to crush ore. A railroad meant that coal

Clearing snow from the tracks of the Colorado & Northwestern was a constant task as shown in this photograph taken near Ward. *(Denver Public Library, Western History Department MCC-1064)*

could be hauled from distant coal fields up to the mines at an economical price.

The first attempt to build a railroad to serve Boulder County mines was financed by the Union Pacific and constructed under the name Greeley, Salt Lake & Pacific. It began grading in 1881 and used a route up Boulder Canyon to enter Four Mile Canyon. The gauge was 3 feet as opposed to the more common standard gauge of 4 feet 8.5 inches. This allowed the Greeley, Salt Lake & Pacific to use sharper curves and less expensive, lighter equipment. So tight were the curves, in fact, that one of the stock locomotives had to be modified to keep from derailing. The grade was only a few feet above Boulder Creek and Four Mile Creek, leaving it vulnerable to flooding.

Construction of the railroad was difficult, however. The line was 14.43 miles long with grades of 4.5%, far greater than almost any standard gauge railroad. In that distance, there were sixty-six bridges and trestles. Within just one mile above Orodell, the railroad had to install fifteen bridges and trestles.

The line followed Four Mile Creek and terminated at Sunset, which at that time was known as Penn Gulch. The first train steamed into Sunset in April, 1883.

A network of wagon roads fed ore to the railroad. A good road was constructed down Gold Run through Summerville to Salina, where the railroad had a side track. Another road ran from Ward to Sunset using Pennsylvania Gulch. It also connected to a wagon road to Nederland.

A modest but reliable ore haulage business developed. The real money was in the tourist business. The railroad charged $1 for each passenger from Boulder to Sunset and back.

In May 1894, sixty hours of continuous, heavy rain produced a flood, which virtually destroyed the Greeley, Salt Lake & Pacific. Trestles were washed away leaving the rails and ties dangling in the air. In other places, the roadbed was undercut causing the track to slide into the stream. It was clearly uneconomical to rebuild the line, and the ties and track were removed.

The need for rail transportation did not go away. In 1897, a proposal for a 22-inch tram was tendered to connect Boulder to Ward. This was replaced with a more practical narrow gauge railroad incorporated as the Colorado & Northwestern Railway Company.

A great deal of the financing hinged on the Big Five, a company founded by Robert and John Duncan. It represented the consolidation of five of the largest mines and mills in the Ward area. The idea was to drill more than five miles of tunnels under the existing mines to drain them. In addition, the tunnel was to have a double track to allow continuous ore haulage. Promises were made to supply the railroad with a continuous 500 tons of concentrates per day to be hauled to Boulder mills. With extensive financial backing, work began on the Dew Drop Tunnel below Camp Frances.

Learning from past lessons, the Colorado & Northwestern selected a grade well above the old Greeley, Salt Lake & Pacific, and the new railroad reached Sunset in February, 1898. By June, 26 miles of line was completed to Ward. In that distance, the longest piece of straight track measured only 1,100 feet. To reach Ward, the railroad followed the contours of the hills climbing 4,115 vertical feet in the process. Not a single tunnel was necessary.

When the first train steamed into Ward, its arrival was celebrated with dynamite explosions and the sounds of a band from Boulder. Governor Adams was on board, for he felt this to be a significant event in the area's development.

Tourists played a significant role in the railroad's business, and it became known as the "Switzerland Trail." The railroad constructed Mont Alto Park above Sunset, selected for its spectacular view of the high mountains along the Continental Divide. Mont Alto Park included picnic tables, a fountain made of chunks of white quartz and fed by a spring, and a generous dance pavilion. The railroad transported as many at 2,500 individuals in a single day to and from Mont Alto Park.

The railroad had an effect on the demographics of the area

as towns grew up along the tracks. Beyond Mont Alto Park was Culbertson Pass where the line crossed over from the Four Mile Creek drainage to Left Hand Creek. This was the point where the track came the closest to Gold Hill. Gold Hill didn't move, but a station was constructed at that point with a side track to allow cars to be loaded with concentrate. Beyond Gold Hill station, the grade leveled off, and at a point above Camp Talcott, another station was constructed called Brainerd. A steep wagon road led down to Camp Talcott. Puzzler was the next station on the line, and it was located right at track level. Bloomerville was also built at track level, but did not have any facilities. It was located where the rails made a loop around the head of a small creek. Rail service during many winters ended at Bloomerville, beyond which the railroad crossed the treeless expanse of Grassy Mountain and a deep rock cut that frequently became clogged with drifted snow.

The Colorado & Northwestern constructed this beautiful pavilion at Glacier Lake for the benefit of its patrons. Glacier Lake is now on private property, and the pavilion is no longer standing. *(Denver Public Library, Western History Department MCC-323)*

A 0.7 mile long spur tack was built down a gentle grade to the Big Five and the adit of the Dew Drop Tunnel. The small community of Frances (also called Camp Frances) was located on the mainline above the Dew Drop Tunnel. Cabins were scattered from Frances down the gulch to the Big Five. The next town along the railroad was Ward. The tracks did not drop down into the town itself but were located above Ward.

During the late 1890s, the Mogul Tunnel was drilled at Eldora. Railroad officials reasoned that if the line was extended to the south, more tonnage would be carried from Eldora. Work began on a twenty-two mile extension to Eldora along the south wall of Four Mile Canyon, directly opposite the grade along the north wall to Ward. This branch was quite isolated and served very few towns. When crossing from the Four Mile Creek drainage, the tracks passed a mile west of Sugarloaf and provided this mining camp with rail service.

Glacier Lake was the next stop, and it replaced Mont Alto Park as the Colorado & Northwestern's premier scenic attraction. The pavilion was moved from Mont Alto Park to Glacier Lake, and a spur tack was laid from the main line down to the water's edge. Round trips cost $0.75 to Sugarloaf station, $1 to Glacier Lake and $1.25 to Eldora. During one day in August, 1908, 2,700 people were taken to Glacier Lake and back.

Cardinal, originally located several miles east of Caribou on Coon Creek, moved down to the railroad's trestle over Coon Creek. The new town of Cardinal was built around the trestle.

Operation of the narrow gauge Colorado & Northwestern was not profitable. The tonnage in ore promised by the mines never materialized. The tourist business could not make up for the losses, and the railroad went into receivership in 1907.

One project which did help sustain the railroad was the construction of Barker Dam below Nederland. Work began on the footings in July, 1908. To haul material to the dam, a spur track about three miles long was laid from a switch at Sulphide Flats, along the north side of Nederland and down Barker Meadow to the construction site. The contractor used small saddle tank locomotives to shuttle supplies.

The small narrow gauge line was reorganized as the Denver, Boulder & Western in 1909. This was at a time when tungsten shipments were on the rise with high demand for tool steel. Some 80% of the United State's entire output of tungsten came from Boulder County, and in 1915, during World War I, the county's output exceeded $16 million adjusted for inflation in today's currency. This figure rose the $50 million the following year.

The years of 1917 and 1918 were great for tourists. In 1917, the railroad reported that it carried 10,000 passengers, and for one picnic on July 18, 1918, the railroad used 18 trains to haul people to and from Glacier Lake. What helped business was a third rail between Boulder and Denver to allow Colorado & Southern narrow gauge trains, originating in Denver, to travel directly into the mountains above Boulder.

Despite this level of business, the railroad was unable to cover its expenses. Flooding closed the line in July, 1919, and the Colorado Public Utilities Commission granted permission to abandon service. The last rail was removed from the Denver, Boulder & Western in October, 1920.

The Switzerland Trail can still be enjoyed today since much of the old grade had been converted for use by automobiles. The most spectacular sections begin at Sunset. The first portion of the Eldora Branch can be driven up to Glacier Lake ending on the Peak-to-Peak highway. The first portion of the Ward Branch can be driven past Mont Alto Park, where the Forest Service built a picnic area, to the road running west of Gold Hill. Other sections of this old railroad are open to pleasant walks including the section from Bloomerville, around Grassy Mountain and toward Ward. The Eldora depot still stands and is used as a home. The Ward depot is also standing near its original location above the town. No. 30, one of the original locomotives used on the Switzerland Trail, sits in a park along Canyon Boulevard in Boulder.

The initial gold deposits found in Gold Run near Gold Hill were worked by prospectors using pans and sluice boxes. This primitive form of mining was backbreaking work. *(sketch from The Story of Colorado by Arthur Chapman)*

Donald C, Kemp, *Silver, Gold and Black Iron,* Sage Books, Denver, 1960, pp. 78-82.

Forest Crossen, *The Switzerland Trail of America*, Pruett Press, Boulder, 1962

Frank Fossett, *Colorado, its Gold and Silver Mines*, C. G. Crawford, New York, 1879, pp. 253-263.

BALARAT

Hindered By Isolation

- *Boulder County, South St. Vrain drainage*
- *Accessible by foot on a four wheel drive road; road blocked by windfall*
- *Town had no post office; no standing structures remain*

The Balarat site is located in Long Gulch.
The road leading to the site from the top of
Balarat Hill was blocked by windfall in 1995.

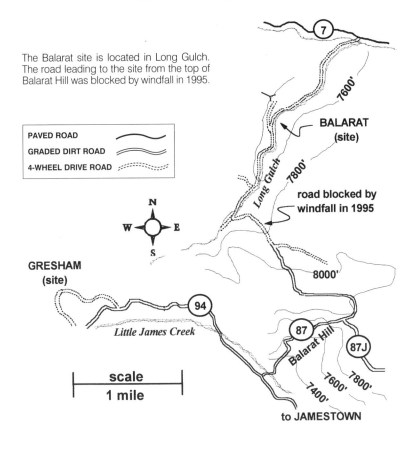

PAVED ROAD

GRADED DIRT ROAD

4-WHEEL DRIVE ROAD

N
W   E
S

BALARAT
(site)

road blocked by
windfall in 1995

GRESHAM
(site)

Little James Creek

7600'
7800'
8000'

94

87

87J

Balarat Hill

7400' 7600' 7800'

to JAMESTOWN

scale
1 mile

The big mine which kept the town of Balarat alive was the Smuggler, discovered in 1876 by Charles Mullen. Assay values topped $1,000 a ton in gold alone. Adjusted for inflation, the initial yield from the Smuggler, after the ore was processed, would be $18,000 a ton at today's gold prices. A great deal of ore was removed the same year as the discovery. Despite these returns, Mullen soon sold his claim.

The mining camp of Balarat grew up in the bottom of the creek in Long Gulch below the Smuggler Mine. It was the kind of mining camp that was strung out over a distance of several blocks. This open gravel area, by the way, was the only flat place in the canyon. By 1879, forty men worked at the Smuggler.

The year after the initial discovery, other lodes were located including Bindago and Eldorado. A mining district was formed in this remote location to regulate and protect the various claims.

The Smuggler was eventually consolidated with other lodes including the Wamego, Careless Boy, and Sweetheart so that the mining company owned the entire hillside. In 1877, the Smuggler Mining Company built a road from Jamestown over Balarat Hill,

Photographs of Balarat are rare, and this one of the "Chipmonk Store" (note the spelling) is the only one at the Colorado Historical Society. *(Colorado Historical Society F6135)*

down Long Gulch, to the town. It would have been far easier to construct a road from Balarat north down Long Gulch to the St. Vrain River, but there were no mills or smelters to process the ore in that direction. The road getting up over the Balarat Hill was (and still is) narrow, steep and exposed, then very steep with sharp switchbacks coming down the Jamestown side.

The mining company constructed fifty log houses as well as two large boarding houses to accommodate the miners. The town had a saloon, meat market and small company store. Employment at the Smuggler reached about sixty men, and the town of Balarat probably had a population of around one hundred. Virtually everyone who worked at the mine had to live in the town; there simply wasn't any other place to live.

Due to its remote location and rough road, transportation costs from Balarat were high. It was only practical to transport the highest grade ore. As a result, a stamp mill was constructed a short distance north of Balarat to concentrate the ore. During its life, the total output from the Smuggler was about two million dollars. In 1918, a new company took over the operation, and mining continued for several additional years.

The town of Balarat disappeared many years ago. Its location on the creek bottom made it vulnerable to floods, and most of the buildings were washed away in 1894; time and weather have taken care of the rest. The collapsed remains of one building and a tipped over outhouse sitting in a stand of trees is all that is left. The concrete foundation of the stamp mill is a short distance north of the town site, and high above the mill is a road angling across the hillside to the Smuggler Mine. Part way up this road, the powder house is intact, while at the Smuggler only the timbers from the collapsed head frame remain.

Muriel Sibell Wolle, *Stampede to Timberline*, Sage Books, Chicago, 1949, 1974, p. 511.
Frank Fossett, *Colorado, its Gold and Silver Mines*, C. G. Crawford, New York, 1879, pp. 278-279.

BIG FIVE MINE

- *Boulder County, Left Hand Canyon drainage*
- *Accessible by foot; private property but not posted*
- *One standing structure remains*

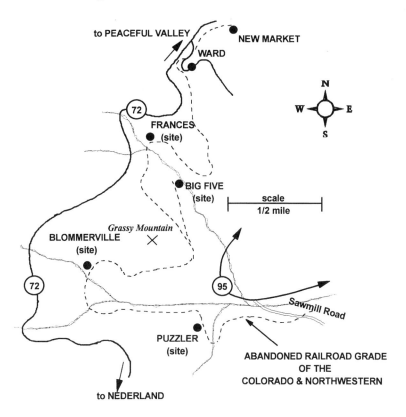

The Big Five Mine is located below Frances on a spur on the abandoned Colorado & Northwestern Railroad. It can be reached by hiking down from Colorado 72.

The Colorado & Northwestern Railroad constructed a spur track, seven tenths of a mile long, around Grassy Mountain one mile from Frances (also called Camp Frances or Francis) on the main line to Ward. The spur ran to the Big Five Mill and the Dew Drop Tunnel while the main line continued its steady climb up to Ward.

The Big Five, as the name suggests, was the combination of five separate mining properties. These properties were brought under one ownership in 1897 by Robert and John Duncan. They worked out the details for a tunnel, called the Dew Drop, connecting the five major mines in the Ward area. This provided drainage and transportation so that loaded ore cars could be brought directly into the concentration mill located only yards from the portal. It was estimated that gold production would amount to five million dollars a year. The railroad depended on this estimate and expected a steady flow of 500 tons per day of concentrate down Boulder Canyon and tons of freight up to the mine. The operation did not live up to expectations and contributed to the Colorado & Northwestern's eventual financial failure.

Some 200 men worked at the Dew Drop and its large mill. There were several cabins above the mine, but the constant noise from stationary steam engines and the loud clang of falling stamps must have made living near the mill far less than tranquil. The stamps were made of iron, were lifted by a cam and allowed to fall onto an iron ore-filled mortar. This may explain why the mining camp of Frances was formed at a comfortable distance above the mill.

During the 1940s, when Muriel Sibell Wolle visited the property, a number of buildings were still standing at the Big Five. The mill was still intact and contained all of its heavy machinery. Since her visit, the mill has been completely removed, and only the massive stone foundation remains. The iron clad mine office building, located near the tunnel, is the only standing structure at the Big Five. Some of the curved steel supports, used inside the tunnel, sit on the ground near the portal. There are even pieces of rail from the Colorado & Northwestern. The large flat area just outside of the portal was once the railroad yard and has now been taken over by a stand of aspen trees. Several collapsed log cabins above the mine suggest that a number of miners were willing to put up with the noise and preferred living close by rather than walking to and from Frances. The Big Five, however, was not really a town, but rather more of a mining camp.

In April, 1910, a powerful avalanche swept two Colorado & Northwestern locomotives off the main line down Grassy Mountain to the Big Five spur, killing one engineer, both firemen and one conductor. The avalanche was touched off when the crew was attempting to clear the line of heavy snow with a plow.

The mine office at the Big Five Mine is the only standing structure, but there are several collapsed cabins in the small gully above the mine. *(Kenneth Jessen 101B3)*

Forest Crossen, *The Switzerland Trail of America*, Pruett Press, Boulder, 1962 pp. 324-329.
Muriel Sibell Wolle, *Stampede to Timberline*, Sage Books, Chicago, 1949, 1974, p. 516.

BLOOMERVILLE
Founded By Bill Bloomer

- *Boulder County; Left Hand Canyon drainage*
- *Accessible by foot*
- *Town did not have a post office; no standing structures remain*

Bill Bloomer founded Bloomerville after he discovered rich gold ore. At the Bloomerville site, the narrow gauge Colorado & Northwestern made a complete loop across a wide gulch to begin its climb around Grassy Mountain to Ward. The railroad installed a water tank next to the small trestle, but did not build a depot.

Bloomerville was noted for its snowball specials where trains brought tourists to have summer snowball fights. It was also the point at which trains were forced to stop during severe winters when drifting snow clogged the long cut in Grassy Mountain immediately ahead of the town. Knowledge is limited on what structures once stood at Bloomerville.

Today, access is limited to travel by foot. The old wagon road leading down to Bloomerville is blocked by a gate as part of a reforestation project. All that is left today are the large timbers, which once supported the water tank by the creek. Over in the meadow are the faint outlines of several foundations.

From Bloomerville, a pleasant walk along the old railroad grade leads to Big Five Junction where the spur to the Big Five mining properties dropped down from the main line. From there the grade continues to climb around Grassy Mountain on its way to Ward.

For a map showing the location of Bloomerville, see "Big Five Mine."

Forest Crossen, *The Switzerland Trail of America*, Pruett Press, Boulder, 1962, pp. 324.

CAMP TALCOTT

Just A Memory

- *Boulder County, Left Hand Canyon drainage*
- *Accessible by paved road*
- *Town did not have a post office; no standing structures remain*

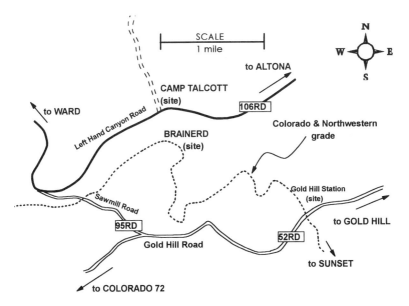

Camp Talcott was located along the Left Hand Canyon Road. The Colorado & Northwestern passed high above and served Camp Talcott via a steep wagon road from Brainerd. Exact location of this road is not known.

Camp Talcott is gone; only a meadow surrounded by second growth trees remain. The small camp was founded by Colonel Wesley Brainard, who came to Colorado during the 1870s to seek his fortune. He wandered about Left Hand Canyon for more than two decades before he struck pay dirt near Hanging Rock in the late 1890s. By this time, he knew practically every side canyon and gulch in the area.

Brainard got his financial backing to develop his mine from Lyman L. Gage. Gage was a personal friend of U. S. President William McKinley. This friendship led to Gage's appointment as Secretary of Treasury. On occasion, Gage visited Camp Talcott to relax and determine how his investment was doing. After President McKinley was assassinated, Gage returned to Camp Talcott in 1901 for an extended visit presumably to recover from the shock and grief over the loss of his friend.

Lyman Gage spent upwards to $700,000 on the Brainard Mine. Development work for the rich ore body was through a series of tunnels and cross cuts. A power plant supplied the mine and the camp with its own electricity, unique among Boulder County mining camps. Camp Talcott was lit up by arc lamps at night. The tram used to haul ore from the mine to the mill was electrically powered. Colonel Brainard functioned as mine super-intendent and had his home in the small camp.

Since the Colorado & Northwestern's line was high above Camp Talcott, a wagon road was constructed to get the concen-trates from Camp Talcott to market. The railroad built a small frame station covered with sheet iron at the end of a rock cut where the wagon road intersected the railroad. The railroad named the station "Brainerd" after Colonel Brainard (note the difference in spelling).

Forest Crossen, *The Switzerland Trail of America*, Pruett Press, Boulder, 1962, p. 324.

Robert L. Brown, *Colorado Ghost Towns - Past and Present*, Caxton Printers, Caldwell, Idaho, 1977, pp. 71-74.

CARDINAL

And Its Sinners

- *Boulder County, Coon Creek drainage*
- *Accessible over graded dirt road*
- *Town had post office; no standing structures remain*

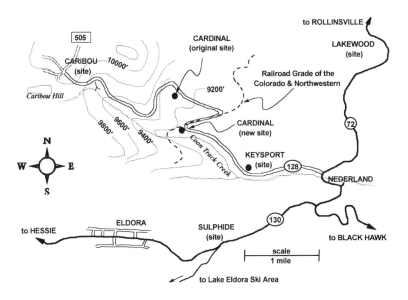

The "new" town of Cardinal is located at the first switchback on the road from Nederland to Caribou which follows Coon Track Creek.

The graded dirt road leading up from Nederland to Caribou followed Coon Creek and was locally known as the Coon Trail. Located in a high meadow, Cardinal was situated two miles east of Caribou along the Coon Trail. It consisted of structures centered around the Boulder County Mine.

137

Muriel Sibell Wolle, ghost town historian and author, took this photograph of Cardinal in 1942. *(Denver Public Library, Western History Department X-3598)*

Cardinal had its beginning in 1870, when Samuel Conger and a partner located silver ore at the site. Though dominated by the large mill, the town consisted of a compressor house, blacksmith shop, machine shop, mine office, assay laboratory, boarding house, and several log homes for mine personnel.

The original town plot sat on both sides of the Coon Trail. The town had a North Second Street and a South Second Street with the Coon Trail designated as First Street. Population statistics show that Cardinal grew to 200 people in 1872 and during its boom years between 1878 and 1883, its population soared to 1,500. Cardinal was almost deserted in 1893 when the U.S. stopped its purchase of silver, and the bottom fell out of silver prices.

The Eldora Branch of the Colorado & Northwestern, built in 1904, cut across the Boulder County Hill below the old town of Cardinal. This brought new life into the area, and a new town, also named Cardinal, formed near the trestle over Coon Creek. Until this time, the area lacked sufficient population to merit a post office. Reflecting the boom to bust to boom cycles typical of so many mining towns, a post office opened in 1905 at the new Cardinal site only to close in 1910, reopen in 1911, close again in

1913, reopen for a third time in 1915, and close for good in 1919.

A station was built at Cardinal on the Colorado & Northwestern to serve both Nederland and Caribou. The station stood west of the track at the north end of the trestle across Coon Creek. A spur track was used for freight cars.

Today, the meadow at the original town site is empty. This meadow is located above the switchbacks on the way to Caribou and is the only open area along the road. Nothing remains on the south side of the road, but there is a foundation on the north side in the trees. Below at new Cardinal, there are several summer homes. Part of the old railroad grade has become a section of the road between Nederland and Caribou. As a point of reference, the new town of Cardinal is located at the base of the first switch back above Nederland.

Robert Brown, in his *Colorado Ghost Towns - Past and Present*, tells that Cardinal gained a portion of its population when Caribou expelled all of its "ladies of the evening." The Caribou town fathers made it illegal for what they felt was a sinful practice, and as a result, these "brides of the multitude" relocated in Cardinal, only two miles away.

This is one of the homes in "new" Cardinal located about a mile below the original town site. *(Kenneth Jessen 110B13)*

Donald Kemp, *Silver, Gold and Black Iron*, Sage Books, Denver, 1960, p. 83.

Forest Crossen, *The Switzerland Trail of America*, Pruett Press, Boulder, Colorado, 1962, 1978, p. 334.

Robert Brown, *Colorado Ghost Towns - Past and Present*, The Caxton Printers, Caldwell, Idaho, 1977, pp. 75-78.

William H. Bauer, James L. Ozment, John H. Willard, *Colorado Post Offices*, Colorado Railroad Museum, Golden, Colorado, 1990, p. 30.

CARIBOU

A Windy Ghost Town

- *Boulder County, Coon Creek drainage*
- *Accessible over a graded dirt road*
- *Town had a post office; remains of one cabin and the stone walls of two other structures still standing*

This 1873 William H. Jackson photograph of Caribou shows the size of this high altitude town. With the exception of the remains of one cabin, hardly a stick of wood is left of Caribou. *(Colorado Historical Society WHJ3303)*

Of all the major mining towns in Colorado, Caribou is one of the few which has vanished leaving hardly a trace. A collapsed log cabin sitting in a high meadow and the crumbling rock walls of two other structures at the meadow's edge are all the physical evidence that this once important town ever existed. At its peak, Caribou had over eighty structures, including homes, a central business district with a row of two-story, false front stores, and even a three story hotel.

140

There are a variety of stories of how the rich silver deposit at Caribou was discovered, but possibly the most credible account involved William J. Martin. He learned about mining at Virginia City, Nevada. Later he was robbed of his investment by an evil partner who he decided to track down. After following him from town to town, Martin finally confronted his old partner at Central City. The man begged Martin not to turn him into the authorities, and Martin let the man go since the money was long gone anyway.

In the process of rebuilding his life, Martin became friends with a number of area residents. One was Samuel Mishler, who owned a ranch near Black Hawk and was in the business of furnishing area mines with timbers and cord wood. William Martin joined Mishler and several others in a business relationship. Among these men was Samuel Conger, who later gained notoriety for his many silver discoveries in Boulder County.

One day in July, 1869, Samuel Conger and another man returned from a hunting trip on the south side of Arapahoe Peak. They showed Martin some of the minerals they picked up along the way, which they were unable to identify. When Martin saw the samples, he recognized them as being very similar to the silver ore from the Comstock Mine in Nevada. George Lytle was the only other man in the group with any mining experience, having spent time in the Caribou Mountains of Alberta, Canada. Martin and Lytle agreed to return after finding the outcropping based on Conger's direction and with the understanding they would share the claim. They set out in August with a cart pulled by oxen and traveled from Black Hawk to Dayton (Nederland). There wasn't even a trail into this area, and the men were forced to hack their way through the dense forest.

It took Martin and Lytle six days to reach a small meadow located at 10,000 feet, immediately to the south of which was a round hill void of any trees. This was the landmark Conger described, and soon the pair found the outcropping of rich silver ore. Each man dug a prospect hole and filled a canvas sac with samples. They discussed what to do next. The area reminded

Lytle of the Caribou Mountains in Canada and suggested that Martin's claim be named the Caribou. As for his own claim, Lytle called it the Poor Man.

Upon their return, the men filed claims for the Caribou and the Poor Man, with Martin, Lytle and their partners named on the claims. The two lodes were developed during the rest of 1869 and into the following year. The first ore was shipped to New Jersey and brought $400 a ton. A primitive road, known as the Coon Trail, was built along Coon Creek into Caribou Park. Ore shipments were then made on a regular basis down to Dayton, then to the large Boston & Colorado Smelter in Black Hawk.

The story presented by historian Frank Fossett places Conger's discovery in 1864. Fossett says that Conger recruited some Gilpin County men to accompany him on a prospecting trip to an area north of Arapahoe Peak during the summer of 1869. Conger discovered the vein of silver ore, according to Fossett, and Conger gave it the name Poor Man. William Martin and George Lytle found the Caribou Lode. Mishler, McCammon and Pickel were brought in as partners to help supply the new camp, which formed near the mines. Martin and Lytle were credited with constructing the first cabin at the town of Caribou.

Once the news of the strike got out, there was a stampede into the area, and by the fall of 1870, several hundred claims had been filed. The Caribou Lode was sold to Abel Breed of Cincinnati, Ohio, and Martin was retained as mine superintendent. Under Breed's ownership, a mill was constructed in 1871 at Dayton, saving the expense to hauling ore to Black Hawk. In 1873, Breed sold the Caribou to the Mining Company of Nederland, Holland. This company managed the mine poorly, allowing Coloradoans Jerome Chaffee and to purchase the Caribou at a sheriff's sale in 1876, presumably for back taxes. Just three years later the mine had its biggest year with shipments of over a million dollars in silver. The mine was then expanded to seven shafts serving thirteen levels.

Caribou City sprang up in the meadow, and a town plat was

Caribou had been abandoned for many years by the time this 1920 photograph was taken. The walls of this old stone-concrete building remain standing along the road into the town site. *(Denver Public Library, Western History Department L-338)*

filed in September, 1870 to make the place official, and those included on the filing were Mishler, Lytle, Martin and Conger.

In the fall of 1870, 460 people lived in Caribou, and by the summer of 1872, over one hundred houses stood in the town. A glass plate negative taken in 1873 by William Henry Jackson shows the large, three-story Sherman House plus Caribou's row of stores. There are well over eighty structures in this photograph, illustrating that Caribou was a town of substantial size. The town had a bakery and even a brewery, a number of grocery stores, meat market, billiard parlor and several saloons. Hotels included the Colorado House, Sherman House, and Caribou House. The Methodists constructed a church, and the town built a school. A cemetery was established to the north of town.

The owners of the *Central City Register* opened a newspaper, the *Caribou Post*, in 1871. Reporters sent their stories to the Central City where they were edited and published. The newspaper was then sent out to its subscribers. The paper folded the following year, and a column was published in the *Central City Register* covering life in Caribou.

There were two stage coach routes which served the town. One ran three times a week from Boulder via Nederland, and the other came from Central City.

When mining in and around Caribou started its decline, the town was partially abandoned, though a few residents remained by the turn of the century.

Located at 10,000 feet, weather played a role in the departure of many of Caribou's citizens since it was not an easy place to live. The orientation of North and South Arapahoe Peaks, which tower over 13,000 feet, caused Caribou's wind to be fierce. Based on measurements taken in similar areas such as the Colorado Mines Peak and the Niwot Ridge, wind velocity could easily have exceed 100 miles per hour. Buildings had to be reinforced, and when the wind combined with snow, just getting to and from work could prove fatal. For this reason, one end of a thick hemp rope was fastened to a point near the center of town. The other end led to the Caribou shaft house so during a blizzard, miners could hang on to the rope to and from work. So dangerous was the winter that the school year began on May 1 and lasted only until November 1. Heavy wooden props were used to brace the sides of the schoolhouse. One story tells of a bull elk that used

The Sherman House was Caribou's largest structure. This is how this old hotel looked well after the town's abandonment. *(Colorado Historical Society F2824)*

Because of the dangers of getting to and from school during the winter, school children began their school year in May. Note the log pole braces on the side of the schoolhouse to support the structure against the relentless high winds coming over the Continental Divide. *(Denver Public Library, Western History Department K-122)*

one of the props to scratch his back. The prop was knocked down, and when the next high wind came, the school was lifted off of its foundation.

The snow usually stops falling in June, although there are light snow storms in July. Winter snows begin again in mid-September. The local joke had one Caribou resident saying that he enjoyed summer...both days of it!

Even though the silver boom came to an end in 1893, the Caribou post office, which opened in 1871, did not close its doors until 1917.

For a map showing the location of Caribou, see "Cardinal."

Donald Kemp, *Silver, Gold and Black Iron*, Sage Books, Denver, 1960, pp. 31-32, 52-60.

Frank Fossett, *Colorado, its Gold and Silver Mines*, C. G. Crawford, New York, 1879, pp. 261-263.

Isabel M. Becker, *Nederland - A Trip to Cloudland*, 2nd ed. Self-Published, 1989, p. 29.

William H. Bauer, James L. Ozment, John H. Willard, *Colorado Post Offices*, Colorado Railroad Museum, Golden, Colorado, 1990, p. 30.

CRISMAN

Ore Goes Directly To The Mint

- *Boulder County, Four Mile Creek drainage*
- *Accessible over a paved road; access limited by private property*
- *Town had a post office; occupied site*

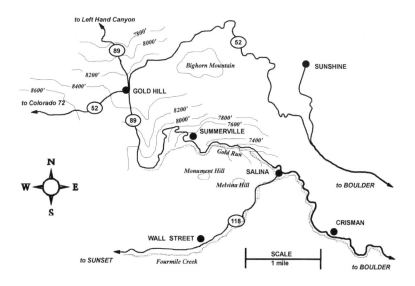

Crisman is located along the paved road from Boulder Canyon to Salina.

The mining town of Crisman, now filled with summer homes, is located between Boulder and Salina in Four Mile Canyon. It got its start in 1874 and was named for Obed Crisman, the owner of a local mill. A post office opened in 1874 only to close in 1894, then reopen in 1898 and finally close in 1918. The first closing was after a flood destroyed the narrow gauge Greeley, Salt Lake & Pacific resulting in termination of rail service. The year the post

146

office reopened was when rail service was re-established by the Colorado & Northwestern.

The best mine in the Crisman area was the Logan, discovered by General John Logan in 1874. So rich was some of the ore that it was put in a strong box and taken directly to the Denver Mint.

After the rich ore was exhausted, a tunnel more than two thousand feet long was drilled in 1908, in hopes of locating some new ore bodies. No worthwhile ore was discovered. When the mine's manager saw little hope of discovering ore, he offered to lease the Logan Mine to A. S. Coan, the mine's superintendent. Coan apparently did not take the manager up on his offer, but had one more blast fired at the end of the tunnel. As luck would have it, it exposed a rich vein of ore, and the offer of a lease was immediately withdrawn.

In 1875, Crisman's population stood at only thirty-five, and the town probably never grew much beyond one hundred.

The Colorado & Northwestern showed Crisman at milepost 6.2 as measured from Boulder and at an elevation of 6,200 feet. The railroad built a siding, but used part of the general store as a depot.

Crisman's combination store, post office and railroad depot. *(Colorado Historical Society F3064)*

Early photographs of Crisman show several homes and the general store. In a distant view, a total of eight structures can been seen. Due to limited access through private property, it is not known if any of the original structures are still standing, but there are a number of contemporary homes on the site.

Silvia Pettem, *Red Rocks to Riches*, Stonehenge Books, Boulder, Colorado, 1980, p. 45.

William H. Bauer, James L. Ozment, John H. Willard, *Colorado Post Offices*, Colorado Railroad Museum, Golden, Colorado, 1990, p. 40.

Muriel Sibell Wolle, *Stampede to Timberline*, Sage Books, Denver, 1949, 1974, p. 487.

Forest Crossen, *The Switzerland Trail of America*, Pruett Press, Boulder, Colorado, 1962, p. 309.

Delores S. Bailey, *God's Country U.S.A.*, Robinson Press, Fort Collins, 1982, p. 11.

COPPER ROCK

- *Boulder County, Four Mile Creek drainage*
- *Accessible by paved road*
- *Town had a post office; no standing structures remain*

Copper Rock was located about three miles above (west) of Wall Street in Four Mile Canyon. Gold ore was mined at this camp during the 1890s. The Orphan Boy Mine, high on the mountainside to the south, produced for years. The name of the settlement comes from a greenish outcropping of copper ore on the cliff above town. The railroad constructed a small frame station and siding at Copper Rock.

Historic photographs of Copper Rock show quite a little settlement, including a neat, two-story hotel, a small mill and an accumulation of about twenty other structures. Most of the town's structures were tents, however.

Beginning in 1892 through 1903, Copper Rock had a post office. It was reopened in 1915, but just for a few months before closing permanently.

See "Sunset" for a map showing the location of Copper Rock.

Forest Crossen, *The Switzerland Trail of America*, Pruett Press, Boulder, Colorado, 1962, p. 48.

Muriel Sibell Wolle, *Stampede to Timberline*, Sage Books, Denver, 1949, 1974, pp. 489-490.

William H. Bauer, James L. Ozment, John H. Willard, *Colorado Post Offices*, Colorado Railroad Museum, Golden, Colorado, 1990, p. 37.

ELDORA
Where Teenage Boys Learned To Dance

- *Boulder County, Middle Boulder Creek drainage*
- *Accessible by paved road*
- *Town had a post office and school; numerous original structures remain; seasonally occupied*

Eldora's Arcade Saloon stood along the main street as shown in this 1898 Sturtevant photograph. *(Colorado Historical Society F43209)*

It was the summer of 1889 when John A. "Jack" Gilfillan traveled over the mountains from Caribou searching for gold. On Spencer Mountain, near today's Lake Eldora Ski Area, Jack built a cabin and staked out a claim he called the Clara. He and his partner began mining, and soon a log shaft house was built. For some reason Jack moved to the base of Spencer Mountain along Middle Boulder Creek, where he built a second cabin thus becoming the first resident of the future town of Eldora. Located on the Happy

Valley placer claim, Eldora exploded in population, and Jack soon decided it was too crowded. He carefully numbered each of his cabin logs, dismantled it and moved it up on the side of Eldorado Mountain to the north. From his veranda, Jack could watch the developments below. The next cabin was built by mining expert John Kemp.

The Gold Miner Hotel, as it looks today, is the only surviving hotel from among many built in Eldora a century ago. Eldora bloomed late among Colorado mining towns and reached its peak around 1898. *(Kenneth Jessen 096A2)*

He methodically explored the entire area and finally settled on the Happy Valley placer claim. He was instrumental in forming the Grand Island Mining District in 1892. Hydraulic mining began the following year washing tons of gold-bearing gravel down into long sluice boxes for the recovery of free gold. As more cabins were constructed, a saw mill opened and began to supply milled lumber for the new town.

In 1897, the district got its own post office and was originally named "Eldorado." By this time, there were fifteen or more mining claims, and the population of Eldorado was about 300. The tents gave way to more permanent structures, and several business were built. Stage coaches, containing potential new residents, arrived daily from Boulder. By January, 1898, with a population of about 1,300 and 500 mining claims on file, residents decided to lay out a 320-acre town site.

The high volume of mail created storage and distribution problems, but worst of all, mail began to turn up missing. The payroll for the Terror Mine was one example. While investigating the situation, the postmaster started to find letters addressed to parties unknown in the camp. The destination was marked "Eldorado, CAL." not "Eldorado, COL." The town had somehow

In addition to business buildings, Eldora also has a number of attractive restored cabins converted for seasonal use. *(Kenneth Jessen 094B4)*

managed to pick a name already in use by another mining camp in California. The solution was quick and simple; drop the "do" and call the place Eldora.

So many people arrived that housing shortages developed. A flimsy bunkhouse was banged together out of green lumber while a saloon keeper added an extra layer of sawdust to his floor for over night guests. In the morning, the saloon keeper would wake up his guests, try to sell them a shot of whiskey, and dismiss them into the cold morning air.

Robert Little arrived in Eldora on a crowded stage coach and was told that there was absolutely no place to stay. It was a bitter cold January morning in 1898 and, as he searched for a place to survive the night, he was directed to a cabin with a loft. He paid Marion Rogers one dollar to sleep in a very small space with nine other men. The son of the owner was last to climb the steep stairs and accidentally dropped his kerosene lantern. Upon impact, the kerosene burst into flames, filling the loft with smoke. The window in the loft was nailed shut, and the only exit was blocked by flames. Though the owner quickly smothered the flames with a wet blanket, four of the men decided to sleep on the sawdust in the saloon, probably figuring the worst that could happen is they would be stepped on.

The Monte Carlo "Casino" presented a problem for the parents of inquisitive teenage sons. The Monte Carlo advertised its "hostesses" with an oversize sign showing a well rounded, scantily clad female with the proclamation, "This is the Monte Carlo - Fourteen Beautiful Girls to Serve You." Based on their popularity, they "served" quite well, day and night. The parents learned that their sons had visited this off-limits establishment supposedly to take ballroom dancing lessons. The lessons were, of course, given under the excellent guidance of female experts on the ways of men. The parents were unsuccessful in getting the place closed; in fact, within the town government, there was a move to make Eldora even more wide open.

Two men were spotted entering a saloon, not unusual for a mining town. However, each had a thinly dressed female over their shoulders, giving them a piggyback ride. An alert town marshal knew they were up to something and quietly entered the rear door of the saloon. He not only caught the couples in the act, but got a bonus of a third pair. One fleet-footed fellow was able to outrun the police while the others were booked. The next day, in front of the local judge, the men pleaded guilty while the females denied any guilt. The judge then questioned each girl asking their occupation. The first two responded "dressmaker," while the third said she was a "chippie." Not knowing just what a chippie was, the judge asked her, "... how's business?"

Quick of wit, the girl replied, "Poor, your Honor, very poor. There's too damn many dressmakers in this town!"

The mines in the Eldora area showed promise, but failed to

The citizens of Eldora are out in number at the post office when the mail arrives. Notice the women and children in what was, at the time, an isolated mining camp. *(Colorado Historical Society F40744)*

produce any consistent rich ore. Mining was a marginal industry with many properties failing to meet expenses. The most ambitious project was the Mogul Tunnel started by Jack Gilfillan, Eldora's first resident. His idea was to undercut all of the major veins on Spencer Mountain and also to drain the various mines. The tunnel would provide transportation using mine cars out to ore bins. The bins were served by the railroad so that the low grade ore could be hauled directly to outside smelters. In 1897, work began on the tunnel eight feet in height and ten feet wide just south of the downtown area. Double tracks were laid into the tunnel to allow two-way passage of ore trains. After six thousand feet of tunnel had been drilled, thirty veins of ore were intersected and worked. Most of the ore, however, was uneconomical to process.

The Greeley, Salt Lake & Pacific built a narrow gauge railroad from Boulder to Sunset in 1883. The railroad was washed out several years later and was replaced by the Colorado & Northwestern. In 1905, a branch was completed from Sunset to Eldora, bringing with it high hopes that the mine's low grade ore could be hauled to Denver, a task impossible at any volume for horse-drawn ore wagons. But this did not save the area economically. The ore was simply insufficient in precious metal content to merit shipping, and the rails were removed in 1919.

As the years passed, one mine after another closed. Eldora found it difficult to continue to operate as a town, and from April, 1915, to the present day, there has been no town election. The town also was never able to muster enough money to build a water system. Eldora was almost completely abandoned at one point, but after World War II, a revitalization occurred as the cabins were purchased for use as summer homes. Some of the residents are descendants of the original pioneers who settled Eldora.

For a map showing the location of Eldora, see "Cardinal."

Donald Kemp, *Silver, Gold and Black Iron, Sage Books*, Denver, 1960, pp. 134, 142, 144, 185.

FOURTH OF JULY MINE

- *Boulder County, Middle Boulder Creek drainage*
- *Accessible by foot*
- *Town did not have a post office; no standing structures remain*

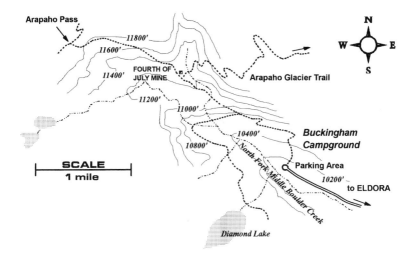

Getting to the Fourth of July mine involves a high altitude hike of about two miles. The site is located above 11,200 feet.

At about 11,300 feet, above timberline and just east of Arapahoe Pass, was the Fourth of July mine. A foot trail leads to the site today, but there was once a corduroy road (a road made of logs laid in the soil at right angles to the direction of travel). Only mining machinery remains at the site, including a boiler and two cable drums. It is amazing that this heavy equipment could be hauled into such a remote location. There are also the collapsed remains of a small cabin below timberline along the trail to the mine.

155

In 1875, C. C. Alvord discovered silver ore at this site, but the ore was uneconomical to mine. The property was deserted until 1900 when the ore was found to contain copper ore. The mine was reopened, but due to underground water, was expensive to work. At one time, a shaft house constructed of heavy logs stood at the mine. By 1947, it had collapsed.

To get to the Fourth of July mine requires a two-mile walk up the Arapahoe Pass trail through beautiful alpine scenery.

KENNETH JESSEN

John K. Aldrich, *Ghosts of Boulder County*, Centennial Graphics, Lakewood, 1990, p. 19.
Muriel Sibell Wolle, *Stampede to Timberline*, Sage Books, Denver, 1949, 1974, p. 502

FRANCES

- *Boulder County, Four Mile Creek drainage*
- *Access limited; site on private property*
- *No original standing structures remain*

A great deal of confusion exists over the location of Frances (also called Camp Frances and sometimes spelled Francis) relative to the Big Five mining properties. However, Frances was located at the head of a small gulch on the main line of the Colorado & Northwestern and higher than the Big Five. The confusion is possibly due to the fact that the camp was originally called Dew Drop, named for the Dew Drop Tunnel at the Big Five properties. The name was later changed to Frances for the daughter of the Big Five president.

Frances was located in a peaceful little valley, partially forested, which sloped down to the portal of the Dew Drop Tunnel. A log post office stood below the sweeping turn the railroad tracks made at the head of the gulch. An 1898 photograph reveals two false-front stores sitting along a block-long main street below the tracks. One structure was a general store. Several cabins and shanties, situated primarily below the tracks, made up the rest of the town. The railroad constructed a small frame station with a platform and siding. Frances also had a schoolhouse. Population estimates for Frances place it at 35 families.

When Muriel Sibell Wolle visited Frances during the 1940s, many of the weathered buildings were still standing, although the town was completely abandoned. She related in her book, *Stampede to Timberline*, that she had a short hike down to the town and that the buildings stood on either side of the road; some were in good repair while others had collapsed. She confirms that the Big Five was located farther down the gulch and not at Frances as some historians believe. Today, the town site is privately owned and only one small structure sits on the site. The entire area is covered with a dense aspen forest making field exploration difficult.

For a map which shows the location of Frances, see "Big Five Mine."

Forest Crossen, *The Switzerland Trail of America*, Pruett Press, Boulder, 1962, pp. 325, 329.
Muriel Sibell Wolle, *Stampede to Timberline*, Sage Books, Denver, 1949, 1974, pp. 514-516.

GLENDALE

- *Boulder County, Left Hand Creek drainage*
- *Accessible via a paved road*
- *Town did not have a post office; no original structures remain*

A fter the turnoff to Jamestown (going west), the first mining camp in Left Hand Canyon was Glendale, a site still occupied by homes today. Glendale was connected to Sunshine by a shelf road cut into the south wall of the canyon. It is not known when the town was established, but it was in existence by 1881. Although marked on contemporary topographic maps of the area, little has been written about Glendale, including its size and how long it lasted as a mining camp.

For a map showing its location, see "Springdale."

Muriel Sibell Wolle, *Stampede to Timberline*, Sage Books, Denver, 1949, 1974, p. 513.

GOLD HILL

First Mountain Mining Town

- *Boulder County, on the divide between Four Mile Creek and Left Hand Creek drainages*
- *Accessible by car*
- *Town had a post office and school; numerous original structures remain, most privately owned and restored*

Gold Hill is a most unusual town; it was the first permanent mining town in the Colorado mountains, and it sits up on top of a divide instead of nestled in a canyon like most other mining towns. It can be reached by any of four different roads coming

This hotel was constructed in 1873 and went by several names including the Grand Mountain Hotel, the Wentworth House and the Kinney House. After noted poet Eugene Field stayed here and wrote the poem, "Casey's Table d'Hote," it became known as the Blue Bird Casey's Table Inn. *(Kenneth Jessen 096A5)*

from all points of the compass. One road comes up from Boulder through Sunshine Canyon, and another road comes into Gold Hill via Four Mile Canyon past Summerville. There is also an excellent graded road coming down to Gold Hill from the Peak-to-Peak Highway, and finally the ultra steep, primitive Lickskillet road that comes straight up from Left Hand Canyon.

The first gold discovery in the area was made on January 15, 1859 by Charles Clouser, James Aiken and three others. They found large quantities of rich ore in decomposed quartz. They used what little water there was to pan over $70,000 in ore by August. The gold was laced among the quartz crystals and was free milling. Since the ore was naturally decomposed, amalgamation with mercury was all that was necessary to capture the gold flakes. A quartz mill was constructed the following spring, but primitive arrastras were also used to grind the ore.

The best lode was the Horsfal, discovered by William Blore, M. L. McCaslin and David Horsfal on June 13, 1859. It yielded $100,000 in gold, as adjusted in today's dollars, during its first few seasons and over three million dollars during its life.

Due the claim jumpers and the various abuses with earlier mining districts in California and elsewhere, the Gold Hill area decided to organize early in its history. On July 23, 1859, "Mountain District No. 1, Nebraska" was formed, and within a thirty-seven page book, the Gold Hill District laws were listed. It might be well to point out that Baseline Road in Boulder marks the fortieth parallel, which at the time, was the boundary between Nebraska Territory and Kansas Territory. The state of Colorado was still a distant seventeen years in the future.

A formal constitution governing the mining laws on Gold Hill was drafted by a committee. Since the miners were in a hurry to get back to work, the constitution was simple and to the point, and set the standard for many other mining districts. When the time came to elect a committee or to vote on some law, the rules were quite liberal. Any male or female sixteen years or older could vote, and as for residency, a person had to be living in the district for at least ten days! The government which evolved consisted of a president, a justice of the peace, and a constable. The government also recorded new claims and heard disputes. A standard practice was established for making a claim and investing in its improvements. After a specific time and number of improvements, the claim holder could patent the claim and be granted title.

Substantial discoveries of gold were made in the area during 1859 and 1860. Many prospectors returned to their homes in Nebraska, Kansas and other states to bring their families to Gold Hill. The town grew rapidly with upwards of 1,500 residents living in cabins and tents, and primitive hotels. An attempt to dig a town well was a failure, therefore, residents had to carry their water up from Left Hand Canyon.

The first Fourth of July celebration was held in Gold Hill in 1860. The ladies, what few there were, did the cooking. People gathered in a small grove of trees with the American flag flying in the clear mountain air to hear various speakers. Ceremonies began with a prayer by Reverend Steele. Dinner followed the speeches. Many toasts were directed at the ladies and to dearly departed relatives. The evening concluded with dancing.

The town was rebuilt after being partially destroyed by a forest fire. By 1861, the decomposed oxidized ore in surface deposits was exhausted, and many miners began to leave. The ore at deeper levels was complex and required smelting. Many promising discoveries being made in other parts of Colorado prompted an exodus. The few who stayed dug beyond the surface deposits and began hard rock mining.

During the Civil War, the U.S. dollar began to depreciate relative to the price of gold, causing investors in the Eastern part of the United States to invest in gold mines. This inflated the price of gold resulting in a resurgence in mining activity. By 1864, the mines in Boulder County were being purchased as investments. Over two hundred outside companies were represented. Eventually as speculation ended, the bottom dropped out of the inflated prices for gold mines. A ditch was later dug from Left Hand Canyon to Gold Hill to allow the resumption of placer mining in Gold Run.

Again, Gold Hill faltered as ore reserves were exhausted. By 1870, only one mine was left operating, and the town had a population of only six. Hope stirred with silver strikes at Caribou, and Professor Nathaniel Hill built a smelter in Black Hawk to economically treat low grade ore.

One such ore which required smelting was tellurium, containing both gold and silver (tellurite is one of the few metals which naturally combines with gold). In May, 1872, two prospectors found an outcropping of tellurium near Gold Hill in an old prospect hole. The two men, fearing that the owner would return to his claim and make the same discovery, transplanted a pine tree in the hole. Safely outside the claim, they staked their own claim and began tunneling back towards the outcropping. An assay of the tellurium proved favorable and the lode was dubbed the Red Cloud. From the first five tons removed, two hundred

The Gold Hill Inn is one of Gold Hill's historic structures and is listed on the National Register of Historic Places. *(Kenneth Jessen 096B3)*

dollars per ton was extracted in precious metal. The second shipment of six tons yielded four hundred dollars per ton, which was
very rich ore by any count.

Upon hearing the news of the discovery of tellurium, many
original claim-holders returned to reoccupy the town of Gold Hill.
The largest mine was the Slide, which produced over two million
dollars in gold by 1910. It had a thousand-foot shaft intersected
by a tunnel of nearly the same length. All in all, the Gold Hill
District produced twelve and a half million dollars in gold
between 1869 and 1909.

Development of the district was always limited by transportation. A succession of ill-fated toll road attempts were made,
and it wasn't until 1873 that a road up Gold Run past Summerville
to Gold Hill was completed. It typically took about two hours to
travel by wagon from Gold Hill down to Boulder; for the uphill
return trip, it took up to six hours. Wagon loads of heavy mining
machinery would require as many as twenty-four horses and a
week to reach Gold Hill. Passengers were carried in Concord stage
coaches, which maintained a regular schedule into Gold Hill. A

One of the many restored and privately owned cabins in Gold Hill. *(Kenneth Jessen 096B2)*

constant flow of ore wagons and stagecoaches coming and going characterized this road.

In 1898, the narrow gauge Colorado & Northwestern extended it tracks from Sunset to Ward, passing about two and a half miles to the west of Gold Hill. This gave residents a direct connection to Boulder and eased the transportation problems considerably. The location was known as Gold Hill Station and was the transfer point for freight and passengers. The railroad built a small 12 x 12 frame station and constructed a short siding for cars. In 1919, the narrow gauge railroad, also called "The Switzerland Trail," was abandoned. No structures remain at the Gold Hill Station site.

Gold Hill mines had very few accidents relative to other mining towns. In January, 1878, however, a couple of miners were working at the bottom of a seventy-two foot shaft. The hoist operator signaled for the men to return to the surface for their dinner. When there was no response to repeated signals the mine superintendent climbed down the shaft on a ladder and understood why the men failed to respond when his foot got wet well before he reached the bottom of the shaft. The mine had suddenly flooded, a constant danger to nearly all mines, and the men at the bottom did not have a chance. All activity in Gold Hill stopped as miners worked to pump the shaft dry. It took nine days to recover the bodies.

Some Gold Hill families gave up on the tenuous occupation of mining and moved to other areas. Gold Hill miners founded Valmont (east of Boulder) while others were involved in founding Berthoud (between Loveland and Longmont). Nederland's first permanent resident came from Gold Hill, while Jamestown was founded by an ex-Gold Hill miner. E. H. N. Patterson (known as "Sniktau") got his education in mining at Gold Hill and later became editor of *The Colorado Miner* in Georgetown.

Gold Hill is noted for visits by the famous writer, Eugene Field. He spent time in the town at the Blue Bird Casey's Table Inn and among his poems is "Casey's Table d'Horte." The setting for this poem was the inn, and its Irish owner was the principal character in the poem. This structure is on the National Register of Historic Places and still remains open for business.

A number of fires partially destroyed Gold Hill over the years. One of the worst was a forest fire in November, 1894. It started near Ward and spread quickly across the ridges toward Gold Hill. All of the residents gathered their possessions and headed away from town. The town's only piano was burned. Just as Gold Hill was about to be consumed, the wind died down and it began to snow, putting out the fire.

The ore was eventually exhausted, and the mines began to close in the 1930s. Gold Hill was partially abandoned. Cool summer evenings combined with the incredible view from the top of the mountain attracted summer residents. Today, nearly all of the old buildings in the town have been repaired and are occupied. Visitors get a genuine feel for what a Colorado mining town once looked like since few new structures have been built among the original buildings. Take your pick of routes; there are plenty of ways to reach this town.

For a map showing Gold Hill, see "Crisman."

Correspondence to *The Golden Western Mountaineer*, July 12, 1860.

Correspondence to *The Weekly Rocky Mountain News*, April 8, 1874.

Frank Hall, *History of Colorado*, Vol. III. The Blakely Printing Company, Chicago, 1895, pp. 290-291.

Robert Balsley, *Early Gold Hill*, Storyteller Images, Boulder, Colorado, 1992, pp. 5-48.

The Boulder County News, July 14, 1876.

GOLD LAKE and CAMP PROVIDENCE

- *Boulder County, Gold Lake is in the Left Hand Creek drainage and Camp Providence is in the James Creek drainage*
- *Gold Lake accessible by graded dirt road; Camp Providence accessible by four-wheel drive*
- *No original structures remain at either site*

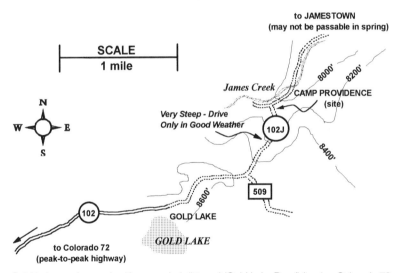

Gold Lake can be reached by a graded dirt road (Gold Lake Road) leaving Colorado 72 (the Peak-to-Peak Highway). Camp Providence is below Gold Lake and accessible in dry weather by four-wheel drive vehicles.

Gold Lake didn't amount to much as a mining camp, but is included in this book for the sake of completeness. Although some of the mines in the general area were worked for a while, the gold ore was soon exhausted. The mineral deposit was located at the north end of the Boulder County's gold belt. Only one house

167

was constructed at Gold Lake, and it was gone by the 1950s. Today, modern seasonal homes and a lodge occupy the old town site.

Camp Providence got its start in 1875, and was also called John Jay Camp. Veins of telluride ore, containing gold and silver, were discovered in the James Creek area. The camp was named by J. J. Van Deren of Boulder who apparently believed it was an act of Providence that led to the discovery.

High on the hillside above the Camp Providence site is the mine, which supported the camp's economy. The tailings are unusually light in color. *(Kenneth Jessen 107A4)*

Camp Providence is about a mile and a half to the northeast of Gold Lake, but on the floor of the canyon formed by James Creek. Forest Service Road 102 begins by the lodge in Gold Lake and heads down hill after passing Forest Service Road 509. The last half mile to the Camp Providence site is very steep and rough and it may require some driving skill to successfully negotiate. The road continues to Jamestown, but may be impassable during spring runoff. At any time of the year, the road requires high ground clearance and four-wheel drive.

The mine above the Camp Providence site has a very light colored tailings pile. In the meadow where Camp Providence was located, large rocks have been placed by the Forest Service to prevent people from driving into the meadow. There is nothing left of Camp Providence, not even foundations.

John K. Aldrich, *Ghosts of Boulder County*, Centennial Graphics, 1990, pp. 10-11.
Perry Eberhart, *Guide to the Colorado Ghost Towns and Mining Camps*, Sage Books, Chicago, 1959, p. 99.

GRAND ISLAND

- *Boulder County, North Fork of Middle Boulder Creek drainage*
- *Accessible over a graded dirt road*
- *Town had no post office; no standing structures remain*

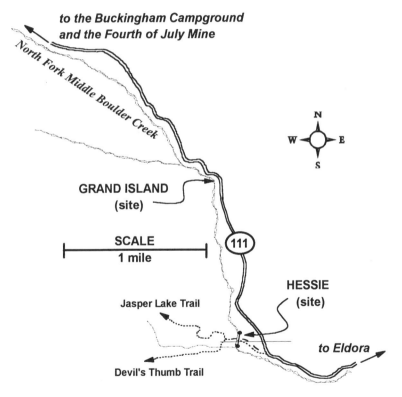

The Grand Island town site is on the road leading through Eldora, past Hessie on the way to the Buckingham Campground.

About three and a half miles west of Eldora along the North Fork of Middle Boulder Creek was the town of Grand Island. This was also the name of the mining district. Grand Island still shows up on topographic maps, although the town never amounted to much. It was a haphazard collection of log buildings. Very little is known about the town, who built it or how many people lived at the location. It did have a two-story hotel of sorts. The town was located on the east side of the creek between Chitten Mountain to the south and Klondike Mountain to the north. The town plat was in the shape of a quadrilateral with three streets running west to east and four streets dividing what remained of the town site.

According to mining historian Donald Kemp, Grand Island was abandoned by 1906, and a decade later the cabins had collapsed or been hauled off. Only the foundations remained. Today, the area is completely overgrown with jack pines and one would never know there was a town at the site. Near the site, there are a number of log structures on private property.

Donald Kemp, *Silver, Gold and Black Iron*, Sage Books, Denver, 1960, pp. 210-211.

GRESHAM

- *Boulder County, James Creek drainage*
- *Accessible by graded dirt road*
- *Town had a post office; one original structure remains*

One very old cabin sits in a meadow at the Gresham town site below the graded dirt road from Jamestown up to the Peak-to-Peak Highway (Colorado 72). The remainder of the site is filled with numerous modern mountain homes. In the 1940s, only the

post office was left standing and this may very well be the structure that one can see today. The Gresham post office opened in 1895 and closed in 1912.

The town site still appears on topographic maps. *For a map showing the location of the site, see "Balarat."*

This old cabin sits near the graded dirt road which runs by the Gresham town site. It could have been the old post office. *(Kenneth Jessen 101B1)*

Muriel Sibell Wolle, *Stampede to Timberline*, Sage Books, Chicago, 1949, 1974, p. 510.

HESSIE
Site Of A Murder Mystery

- *Boulder County, North Fork of Middle Boulder Creek drainage*
- *Accessible by graded dirt road; requires driving through a stream*
- *Town had a post office; no standing structures at the town site*

The town of Hessie was located just below the road leading up to the Fourth of July Mine and a little over a mile west of Eldora. It is necessary to turn left off the main graded road down into the town site. This requires driving through a stream that can be rather deep during the spring run-off.

The Hessie post office was established in 1898 and remained open until 1902. Captain J.H. Davis laid out the town at the confluence of the North Fork and Middle Boulder Creeks, naming the place after his wife. It was located in a beautiful, lush meadow with high mountains visible in the distance. There were one or two stores, a school, a boarding house and some cabins. The Colorado State Business Directory gave Hessie a population of eighty people for the years 1901 and 1902. Estimates placed the number of cabins in Hessie at a dozen.

A sawmill provided the town with a local industry, but there were also a number of mines in the immediate area. An early photograph of Hessie shows three buildings facing the road which ran to the Lost Lake trail head.

Hessie has its own murder mystery. A bachelor in his fifties, Champ Smith had prospected and mined in the Eldora region since 1897. On a June day in 1914, Champ was working in his mine on Bryan Mountain (the present day location for one of the ski lifts at Lake Eldora). G. W. Orear climbed up to the mine to deliver some mail, which had arrived for Champ. Not hearing any activity, Orear entered the tunnel only to find the dismembered remains of Champ Smith near the portal. Champ's left leg and trunk were in one place, the other leg and an arm in another, and Smith's head had been severed and was practically unrecognizable. Champ had obviously been blown to bits. The force of the blast blew Champ's watch into three pieces. Orear ran from this horrifying scene down the mountain to Eldora to notify the coroner in Boulder.

It looked like a mining accident caused by dynamite going off unexpectedly. Good detective work, however, revealed a bullet hole in Smith's hat and a trail of blood leading from a mine car deep inside the tunnel out to the point of the explosion. It looked like Smith had been killed first, then pulled out to a point where dynamite was placed under the corpse and set off. The investigator also found a .22 caliber slug. When Smith's skull was pieced

This meadow is located at the Hessie town site. There are a couple of cabins to the west of the site, which could have been considered part of Hessie. The Lost Lake trail head is located beyond the town site. *(Kenneth Jessen 103D1)*

back together and examined in a Boulder laboratory, it indicated he had been shot in the head.

The motive for the crime was less clear. However, Champ Smith, who had been appointed the local game warden, had put all of his friends on notice that he planned to enforce the law when it came to poaching. This led to some bad blood between the residents who depended on wild game to survive the winter months. Poaching was a generally accepted way of life in the Colorado Rockies. The investigator arrested three likely suspects, but lack of evidence hampered any hope of a conviction, and the men were released.

Today, a Forest Service sign marks the town site, which sits in a small meadow below the road between Eldora and the Buckingham Campground. There are, however, a couple of cabins on private land to the west, which may have been part of the town's original structures. Beyond the Hessie town site, the road ends in a dead end at the Jasper Lake trail head.

For a map showing the Hessie site, see "Grand Island."

Donald Kemp, *Silver, Gold and Black Iron*, Sage Books, Denver, 1960, p. 207-209.

Robert L. Brown, *Colorado Ghost Towns - Past and Present*, Caxton Printers, Caldwell, Idaho, 1977, p. 128.

William H. Bauer, James L. Ozment, John H. Willard, *Colorado Post Offices*, Colorado Railroad Museum, Golden, Colorado, 1990, p. 71.

JAMESTOWN
Was Jimtown

- *Boulder County, James Creek drainage*
- *Accessible by paved road*
- *Town has active post office; occupied site; several original structures remain*

This historic photograph of Jamestown was taken by Boulder photographer Joe Sturtevant. Successive floods have destroyed most of these structures in this photograph. *(Colorado Historical Society F6592)*

The first settler in the James Creek area was George Zweck, who had a herd of cattle which he brought there in 1860. Galena ore, containing lead and silver, was discovered along James Creek in 1864 by Johnny Knoop and Joe Hutchinson. The two men returned to Black Hawk and purchased supplies, then traveled back to James Creek using pack mules to get into the area. There were no roads and it took them three days. The two men sunk a

The George Walker family arrived in 1872 and built this beautiful log home. *(Kenneth Jessen 101C11)*

shaft ten feet deep in the bank of the creek and recorded their claim, naming it the Buckhorn. A twenty pound ore sample was brought back, and it assayed at $233.50 per ton.

In 1865, the men returned again to the mine accompanied by three others. One of them built a steam-powered saw mill and began harvesting trees along James Creek while the others concentrated on mining. Soon, a badly needed stamp mill was constructed by a couple of experienced miners from Gold Hill.

Once the news of the discovery got out, hundreds of prospectors poured into the area. Some simply turned around and went home; either the ore was not rich enough, or the weather was too severe. But for those that stayed, milled lumber made the construction of cabins and shanties much easier.

A storm in May, 1866 dropped three feet of snow and temporarily isolated the camp, which had now grown to 600 residents. That summer, the residents petitioned the U.S. Postal Department for a post office under the name of Camp Jimtown. The post office elected not to use the name, but for some reason used Jamestown instead. The first post master was appointed in January, 1867.

To solve its transportation problems, the Left Hand and Jamestown Wagon Road Company was incorporated in March, 1872. The company charged a 15 cents toll for a wagon pulled by one animal, 20 cents for one pulled by two animals, and 35 cents for one pulled by four animals. A trip up the toll road on a saddle horse cost 10 cents.

To prevent disputes over the size of mining claims and to provide some means of filing claims, the Central Mining District was formed. This was the first formal law and order in the area.

Several stores opened in Jamestown along with a meat market. The town grew to include six mills, a blacksmith shop, church, a school with fifty to sixty students, and many homes. A stage coach line provided triweekly service from Boulder.

The first boom ended in 1870 when the easily processed, oxidized gold ore was depleted. The town's population declined to sixty men and six families. The depression in Jamestown lasted until 1871, when tellurium ore, containing gold and silver, was discovered in the area.

The population was listed as only 100 in 1879, but the town was growing. In July, 1883, Judge Sylvester Downer filed a plat for the town. That same year, the *Jamestown Whim*, weekly newspaper, was first published. It cost $2 per year or a nickel a copy; Mary F. Lee was its editor and publisher. By then, the town had grown to include ten general mercantile stores and two drug stores. It also had a couple of jewelry stores, a hardware store, four dance halls and many boarding houses where a miner could stay for a quarter a night and a quarter a meal. A second weekly newspaper also appeared later that same year, the *Jamestown Miner*.

The Budweiser Palace was one business worthy of note. It had a corner sign which read "1883 Von Richthofen." Yes, Baron Von Richthofen came to Jamestown from Prussia in the early 1870s. His nephew was the great World War I flying ace, Manfred Von Richthofen, known as the Red Baron.

Another Jamestown celebrity of sorts was Griffith Evans and his family. In 1874, they sold their land in Estes Park to Lord Dunraven. The Evans family established the St. Vrain Hotel in Longmont, then returned to Estes Park to open the Estes Park Hotel. Griffith quarried stone in Lyons and even built a stone house which still stands. Griffith and his wife had six children by the time they arrived in Jamestown. They opened a hotel called the Evans House, which was completed in 1892. Evans is credited with establishing a traditional Christmas celebration in Jamestown and used his talent to play Christmas music.

But Griffith Evans was most noted for killing "Rocky Mountain" Jim Nugent during a dispute in 1874, when Evans operated a small guest ranch in Estes Park. During the altercation, pieces of shot from Evans shotgun penetrated Nugent's brain. Jim Nugent was moved to Fort Collins were he eventually died of his wounds. Evans was charged with the crime, but was released with no bond set. Because the one and only witness suddenly disappeared just before the trial, Evans was acquitted for lack of evidence.

In 1899, there was an interesting incident during a square dance. The town bully insisted on edging in on the dancing couples, leaving one man without a partner. The bully was thrown out several times only to return. Finally, he went to his cabin to get a gun. Somehow on his way back, he was seriously wounded by a gunshot. Then, an open grave mysteriously appeared in the town cemetery, possibly as a warning. It is not known why the bully decided to leave town, but perhaps it was for his health.

Jamestown also had a violinist with the bad habit of putting his feet on the piano. This annoyed the pianist, who told him if he did it again he would put a hole in the violinist's foot. The violinist was game and stuck his foot in defiance back on the piano. The pianist pulled a gun and shot off one of the violinist's toes. According to the story, the dance went on!

To process the low grade ore, the Wano Mill was constructed in 1907. A decade later, it was rebuilt to produce fluorspar used as a flux in the steel-making process for the World War I effort.

In 1894, a flood destroyed the lower portion of town built along James Creek. A second flood in 1913 destroyed the lower portion of the town again, and in 1969, a flood took out several more buildings. As a result of repeated flooding, Jamestown is only a shadow of its former glory days. The town has always been occupied, even as the mining industry faded. People discovered that it was a nice place to live throughout the year or as a location for a summer home.

There are many newer homes in town, but one historic residence worth seeing is east of the Jamestown Cafe and General Store. It is the George Walker home, occupied by the Walker family for five generations. George moved from Ward in 1872 and built this beautiful log home. He was in the freighting business and also hauled wood to be used for fuel by the mills. He also opened a meat market, which was eventually taken over by his son.

The reader is discouraged from getting too close to some of the mines in the Jamestown area, especially the Burlington Mine. This mine is west of Jamestown where the graded dirt road begins its climb up Balarat Hill. A large underground cavity has reached the surface forming a sink hole.

A contemporary view of the Jamestown Cafe and General Store, a popular place for locals and for those visiting this old mining town. *(Kenneth Jessen 106D1)*

Frank Fossett, *Colorado, its Gold and Silver Mines*, C. G. Crawford, New York, 1879, p. 97.

Frank Hall, *History of Colorado*, Vol. III. The Blakely Printing Company, Chicago, 1895, pp. 307-308.

Jann Gurnsey, Barbara Heaton, and Jean King, *Mountain Memories: A History of Jimtown*, Colorado, pp. 1-27.

KEYSPORT
Utopian Colony

- *Boulder County, North Beaver Creek drainage*
- *Accessible via graded dirt road*
- *Town did not have a post office; no standings structures remain*

What the mining camp of Keysport was in terms of its size and population is difficult to say. Donald Kemp, in his book *Silver, Gold and Black Iron,* says that Keysport was only a gleam in the eye of a dreamer.

The town company was organized in 1870 by Alfred Tucker, one of the gold-seekers who came to Gregory's Diggins (later named Mountain City) in 1859 with the first wave of prospectors to enter Colorado. Tucker would give any person a free lot just for putting up a building. His idea was to found a cooperative community where all worked toward the common good, sharing

equally in the assets. Tucker formed the Grand Island Lumber Company as the central industry in Keysport. A tract of uncut timber was purchased to feed the mill, and part of site was located on a 160-acre ranch. There were several gold claims near Keysport to add to its economic base, and a primitive arrastra was used to crush samples of gold ore for evaluation.

The cooperative began with ten men and a cook. With the exception of the cook, who drew regular wages, all shared in the profits equally. The lumber company expanded to include a sash and door factory and household furniture factory.

However, just like other Colorado cooperative attempts, the enterprise failed. How many structures once stood in Keysport and how many people called the place their home is unknown. One can speculated that the place did not amount to much more than the saw mill.

The Keysport site is about half way between Nederland and Cardinal on the Coon Trail where Hicks Gulch enters North Beaver Creek. *For a map showing Keysport, see "Cardinal."*

Donald Kemp, *Silver, Gold and Black Iron,* Sage Books, Denver, 1960, pp. 85-86.

LAKEWOOD

- *Boulder County, Middle Boulder Creek drainage*
- *Access limited by private property*

Rather than a town or a camp, Lakewood was a mill site where a few mill workers lived. C. F. Lake began using the Boulder County Mill at Cardinal to reduce tungsten ore during the 1909 tungsten boom. As the demand picked up during World War I, Lake decided to build a large mill dedicated to tungsten ore. It was called the Primos, and was located above and north of Nederland. To handle the large volume of tungsten concentrate, the Colorado & Northwestern put in a 639 foot spur track at a stop it called Lakewood. The Primos Mill was one and one half miles away; for passengers, it was a flag stop.

Current access to the site is limited by private property. **For a map showing Lakewood, see "Cardinal."**

Forest Crossen, *The Switzerland Trail of America*, Pruett Press, Boulder, 1962, p. 202, p. 334.

MAGNOLIA

On Big Hill

- *Boulder County, Boulder Creek drainage*
- *Accessible by paved road; occupied site with access limited by private property*
- *Town did have a post office*

Magnolia was a small mining camp located high on a ridge, which divides Keystone Gulch from Boulder Canyon. Many modern homes now dot the area. *(Colorado Historical Society F7475)*

The original mining camp of Magnolia was founded in 1875 in what was called the Big Hill district. Hiram Fullen discovered the first lode. Area mines included the Keystone, Mountain Lion, Washington, Little Nand and Lady Franklin.

Magnolia was split into several locations with one place referred to as Jackson's Camp below the main portion of Magnolia. The camp itself was located on the ridge, which divides Keystone Gulch from Boulder Canyon. Muriel Sibell Wolle reported that she

183

sketched Magnolia during the 1930s, and by the late 1940s, most of the structures were gone.

The life of the camp was extended with the construction of the mill built by the Redemption Mines Company. The biggest operation in the area, the Keystone mine, was located about a mile below Magnolia. It had a boarding house for the miners as well as several homes.

The road to Magnolia, located on the opposite side of Boulder Canyon from the turnoff to Sugarloaf on Colorado 119, is one of the steepest paved roads in the state. It climbs the south wall of Boulder Canyon in a succession of hairpin turns and over-looks Keystone Gulch. Magnolia is located about two miles from the turnoff. A few mine dumps and some mining equipment are visible along the side of the road. There are also several rundown shacks on both sides, but much of the original town of Magnolia is hidden in the trees, and access is restricted by private property. The remains of Magnolia do not suggest an organized, neatly laid out town, but it did have a post office from 1876 to 1920.

Beyond the town site, the Magnolia Road turns into a graded dirt road and heads west to the Peak-to-Peak Highway just south of Nederland.

Muriel Sibell Wolle, *Stampede to Timberline*, Sage Books, Chicago, 1949, 1974, p. 492.
Robert L. Brown, *Jeep Trails to Colorado Ghost Towns*, Caxton Printers, Caldwell, Idaho, 1973, p. 128.

NEDERLAND
Built On Mining Three Metals

- *Boulder County, Boulder Creek drainage*
- *Accessible by paved road*
- *Town has a post office and school; fully occupied town; several original structures remain*

In 1861, the headwaters of Middle Boulder Creek were sparsely settled. The town of Dayton was not much more than an accumulation of cabins on the north bank of Middle Boulder Creek at the base of a glacial ridge. One of the earliest settlers was Nathan Brown, known locally as "Bolly" because he was partially bald. Powerfully built, Bolly was quite genial and easygoing, but only when sober. Bolly was in the 1859 gold rush to Pikes Peak and tried his hand at prospecting in Gregory's Gulch outside of Central City. He eventually turned to agriculture as a means of supporting his family. Bolly's homestead consisted of forty acres of meadow

Nederland in 1916 during the tungsten boom. *(Denver Public Library, Western History Department K-199)*

below the eastern limit of Dayton. He constructed a comfortable two-story log home fifty-six feet by thirty-three feet, large in comparison to the typical miner's cabin. Using an extra room, he found he could supplement his income by taking in guests. This led to the construction of Brown's Mountain Home.

A wagon road was built from Ward to Black Hawk. Today's Peak-to-Peak Highway follows the approximate route of this old road. Midway between these two important mining camps and just where the new road crossed Middle Boulder Creek was Bolly Brown's Mountain Home. The crossing became known as Brown's Crossing, and nearby Dayton was sometimes referred to as Brownsville. The two names were used interchangeably until 1871 when the U.S. Postal Service established a post office with the name Middle Boulder. The post office retained this name until 1874. One possible explanation the name Dayton was not used by the post office is that the Lake County seat was also called Dayton. The name Brownsville had already been used by a town in Clear Creek County.

At first, Bolly Brown was good to his guests, and his wife Caroline prepared excellent meals. Excessive drinking, however, resulted in occasional fights, and his neighbors took him into court several times for disturbing the peace. Poor at business matters, mounting debt eventually cost Bolly his ranch and his hotel. In 1872, three of his four children died in a diphtheria epidemic. Soon after, his wife divorced him, and Bolly left the area never to be heard from again.

Thomas Hill settled north of Middle Boulder on North Boulder Creek. Here he cut hay on his ranch and, due to his good business sense, exploited the demand for hay. The mining towns in the area used many draft animals and were in constant need for feed. The high demand eventually drove the price of hay to ninety dollars a ton, and Hill was able to earn $65,000 during his first decade of ranching. This was at a time when $900 a year was considered good wages. Hill also cut cord wood to fuel the many boilers used at the mines.

In 1873, Tom Hill married Bolly Brown's former wife Caroline, and the family settled in on the Hill ranch. However, in less than two months Caroline found herself a widow when Tom died of unspecified causes.

The rich silver mine at Caribou needed a mill to process its ore. Since the mine was located near the Continental Divide where the weather was

The old Caribou Mill in Nederland was used first to process silver ore, then converted to handle tungsten ore. It was renamed the Wolf Tongue Mill. A fire destroyed the original mill in 1926, but it was quickly rebuilt. *(Kenneth Jessen 101C1)*

simply too severe for mill work, the mine owners elected in 1871 to construct their mill at the western end of Middle Boulder. This location was more than eleven-hundred feet lower than the mine and was connected to the mine by a good road known as the Coon Trail. A large mill was built, and it was successful from the very start. Mill workers earned $3.00 a day, double that of a common laborer.

The nearly pure silver provided by the mill was cast into seventy pound bars. The bars were hauled by wagon from Middle Boulder to the First National Bank in Central City where they eventually transferred to the Denver Mint. In April, 1873, President U. S. Grant, during his visit to Central City, stepped out of his carriage in front of the Teller House onto a street that had been paved temporarily with bars of solid silver from the Caribou mill in honor of the occasion.

The mill brought prosperity and continual growth to the town. A road was constructed from Boulder up Boulder Canyon, and stage coaches began running to Middle Boulder three times a week. The coaches on the Ward-to-Central City route exchanged passengers, mail and freight, raising the importance of the town as a transportation center.

It was at this time that the Caribou Mill and Mine was purchased by a Dutch mining company who renamed the place Nederland. The post office followed suit in 1874, and Nederland was officially incorporated in 1875.

Up to this point, the town had been run rather informally. The new Nederland town board appointed a committee to examine the records of the former town clerk. A few weeks later, the committee reported that the only records, written in pencil, were on slips of dirty paper and essentially meaningless. The town did not seem to suffer from this problem, but tough times were ahead.

When the United States abandoned the silver standard and stopped minting pure silver coins, the price of silver fell. It was called the "Silver Panic of 1893," and the silver mines in Colorado never recovered from this blow. The Caribou Mine was forced to close along with its mill, and Nederland's population quickly fell to seven families. The business district was abandoned, mail service stopped, and stage coaches came up Boulder Canyon only occasionally.

This photograph was labeled "Middle Boulder," one of the earlier names for Nederland. *(Colorado Historical Society F3254)*

Gold was discovered just before the turn of the century in the area around Eldora to the west of Nederland. This resulted in a second boom, but based on gold and not silver. Summer tourism was also becoming a factor in the economy, and to satisfy the demand the Antlers Hotel was built in 1897.

For years, the milling processes for the area's gold and silver were hampered by "...that damned black iron." Believed to be magnetic iron oxide, it was said to be worthless. At the turn of the century, however, the black iron was correctly identified as tungsten, which was used in producing hardened steel. Sam Conger was among the first to realize its value and leased an old mine rich in "black iron" that was just north of Nederland. The Conger, as the mine was called, became one of the largest tungsten producers in the world and brought Nederland into yet a third boom era.

The old Caribou Mill, originally constructed to handle silver ore, was rebuilt with new machinery to handle the tungsten ore. The mill operated throughout World War I and did not shut down until after World War II. At some point in time, the mill's name was changed to the Wolf Tongue. It operated twenty-four hours a day, seven days a week, shutting down only for Christmas, the Fourth of July and Thanksgiving. When it burned to the ground in 1926, it was quickly rebuilt as a fire-proof structure. The old mill still stands on the western edge of Nederland as a reminder of its bygone mining days. From its low point of seven families, Nederland grew to a population of three thousand by 1915. Unfortunately, fire and time have eliminated many of the original structures.

Nederland's economy is now tied to summer residents and tourism.

Donald Kemp, *Silver, Gold and Black Iron*, Sage Books, Denver, 1960, p. 87-88.
William H. Bauer, James L. Ozment, John H. Willard, *Colorado Post Offices*, Colorado Railroad Museum, Golden, Colorado, 1990, p. 98.

ORODELL

A Camp With Many Names

- *Boulder County, Boulder Creek drainage*
- *Accessible by paved road*
- *Camp had a post office; unknown if any original structure survives*

Orodell was a small mining camp located near the mouth of Four Mile Creek where it joins Boulder Creek. On some maps, it was also called Orodelfan or Orodelphan. Ghost town historian Muriel Sibell Wolle stated that at various times the place was called Maxwell's Mill, Hortonville and Hunt's Concentration Works. The Greeley, Salt Lake & Pacific Railroad called it Oredel. The camp did have a post office from 1876 to 1881 under the name Orodelfan.

In 1865, Captain C. M. Tyler and James P. Maxwell ventured into Boulder Canyon from Central City. Maxwell was in charge of building the first toll road up Boulder Canyon at the time. The two men constructed a steam-powered sawmill at the confluence of the two creeks and put in a log dam across Boulder Creek. The dam was used to capture logs cut higher in the canyon. It was common practice along the Front Range to cut timber during the winter and drag the logs to the closest creek. During the spring run off and with some help from the loggers, the logs were floated down the creek to a sawmill. The Tyler-Maxwell sawmill stopped operating in 1870, and on the same site, Hunt and Barber built a smelter.

During 1907 through 1910, a hydroelectric plant was constructed farther up Boulder Creek. Orodell was used as the staging point for the materials, and the railroad built two spur tracks to accommodate all the rail traffic.

It is impossible to determine how many people lived in Orodell, but one home shows up in a historic photograph. Although several old photographs show that the slopes surrounding Orodell had been denuded by logging, the location today is so overgrown as to render the place unrecognizable. It is not believed that any of Orodell's original structures survive today, however, there are several old buildings on private property on the south side of the creek.

Forest Crossen, *The Switzerland Trail of America*, Pruett Press, Boulder, 1962, pp. 31, 199, 304.

Muriel Sibell Wolle, *Stampede to Timberline*, Sage Books, Chicago, 1949, 1974, p. 488.

William H. Bauer, James L. Ozment, John H. Willard, *Colorado Post Offices*, Colorado Railroad Museum, Golden, Colorado, 1990, p. 108.

PUZZLER
Yields Good Ore

- *Boulder County, Left Hand Creek drainage*
- *Accessible by foot*
- *Town had post office; no standing structures remain*

Ths photograph, taken by professional Denver photographer Louis McClure for the Colorado & Northwestern, illustrates that Puzzler was more than just a place on a map. *(Denver Public Library, Western History Department MCC-1060)*

Puzzler was located on the hillside south of Left Hand Creek. From 1898 to 1903, this small mining camp had its own post office, and eventually the town built its own schoolhouse.

Around 1890, Robert Duncan discovered and developed a mine he named The Puzzler in California Gulch located above Left Hand Canyon. He took out $39,000 in high grade gold ore in just one month. Later he constructed a mill on the property to handle the lower grade ore.

The Colorado & Northwestern arrived in 1898 and constructed a small frame station with a loading platform at the south end of the trestle across the gulch. The railroad also had a siding 430 feet long.

Not only did Puzzler supply business for the railroad, silver ore from the White Raven Mine was also shipped from the station. The low grade ore was placed in open gondolas while the high grade ore was locked in box cars.

After a dam above the town burst in 1918 and took out the trestle across California Gulch, trains operated only as far as Puzzler. The Colorado & Northwestern, unable to make a profit, was at the end of its life. Passengers would stop for lunch at the boarding house run by Mrs. M. F. Thompson before continuing on to Ward or Estes Park by Stanley Steamer.

A historic photograph of Puzzler shows the mine immediately below the track along with the mill and another mine structure. There were several homes on both sides of California Gulch. The ruins of the mill are all that remain today.

For a map which shows where Puzzler was located, see "Big Five Mine."

Forest Crossen, *The Switzerland Trail of America*, Pruett Press, Boulder, 1962, p. 322, p. 324.
William H. Bauer, James L. Ozment, John H. Willard, *Colorado Post Offices*, Colorado Railroad Museum, Golden, Colorado, 1990, p. 117.

QUIGLEYVILLE

- *Boulder County, Left Hand Creek drainage*
- *Accessible over a graded dirt road*
- *Camp did not have a post office; no standing structures remain*

It is tragic that history books do not tell us how Quigleyville got its name. It was a small camp located in Spring Gulch east of Ward. It was laid out by Colonel Wesley Brainard who also founded Camp Talcott. Not much else is known about Quigleyville.

Nothing remains today except for some stone foundations set back from the road.

Muriel Sibell Wolle, *Stampede to Timberline*, Sage Books, Chicago, 1949, 1974, p. 513.

ROWENA

- *Boulder Canyon, Left Hand Creek drainage*
- *Accessible by paved road*
- *Town had a post office; several original structures remain*

Rowena still appears on topographic maps and is occupied today. Its location is not too far below the steep Lickskillet Road to Gold Hill, but past Glendale. This road, incidentally, drops one thousand vertical feet in a little over a

A frame homes in the mining camp of Rowena located in Left Hand Canyon. *(Kenneth Jessen 106A8)*

mile. During the mining days, the wheels on loaded ore wagons had to be chained. Opposite Lickskillet Road is the stone foundation for the Prussian Mill, which processed much of the gold ore mined in the Gold Hill region. The mill provided employment for those living in Rowena. There are a number of small frame homes in Rowena, which could easily date back to the mining era. A post office was established in Rowena in 1894 and closed in 1918.

For a map showing Rowena, see "Springdale."

Muriel Sibell Wolle, *Stampede to Timberline*, Sage Books, Chicago, 1949, 1974, p. 513.

William H. Bauer, James L. Ozment, John H. Willard, *Colorado Post Offices*, Colorado Railroad Museum, Golden, Colorado, 1990, p. 124.

SALINA
Named For A Kansas Town

- *Boulder County, Four Mile Creek drainage*
- *Accessible over a paved road*
- *Town had a post office; occupied site; several original structures remain*

Salina during its boom years. This photograph was taken in the 1882-1884 period of time. *(Colorado Historical Society F49965)*

Founded by O. P. Hamilton and six other men, Salina was named for their home town in Kansas. By 1873, thirty families called Salina, Colorado their home. As the placer deposits in Gold Run were worked out, prospectors drifted down to Salina to join the Kansas party, and by 1875, Salina had over one hundred residents. A school was also constructed this same year for the town's eighteen children. The town gained a store, a saloon and an assay office. By 1881, Salina had a hotel called the Salina House, several stores and three mills.

Henry Von Myrinck, a carpenter by trade, came to Salina

when he heard there
was work building a
mill. Unfortunately, he
was laid off immediate-
ly while the owners
waited for material to
arrive. He took a job at
the Fourth of July mine
at the head of the North
Fork of Boulder Creek.
On the long walk back
from the mine, he
prospected. One ver-
sion of the Von Myrinck
story has him sitting

Church of the Pines is located up Four Mile Creek in the mining town of Salina. *(Kenneth Jessen 106D8)*

down under a tree to eat lunch. After he finished he went back to
the boarding house, but forgot his Navy jacket. During supper, he
overhead a conversation about a man digging around the place
where he left his jacket. Apparently the man had discovered some
rich gold ore. Without any further thought, Von Myrinck traveled
to the nearest claim office and filed on the place where he left his
jacket. He named the mine the Melvina after his mother and
became a rich man.

Another version of the discovery of the Melvina has a couple of Von Myrinck's friends poking fun at him by having him
climb to the top of a nearby mountain and dig for gold in the cool
shade. They recommended the experience because of its excellent view never thinking any gold ore would be discovered. An
experienced miner happened by as Von Myrinck shoveled out
some dirt. The miner recognized the dirt as gold ore, and a partnership was formed between Von Myrinck and three other men to
develop the property. The first shipment of ore to a Black Hawk
smelter yielded over eight thousand dollars.

Von Myrinck sent for his wife and children and the family
settled in Salina in 1879. The Melvina shipped ore valued as high

as $10,000 to $12,000 per ton. Von Myrinck sold the mine and invested in a horsehair mattress business. He was swindled out of his money, however, and his income was reduced to his $21 per month Navy pension.

Other big mines in the area were the Black Swan, Emancipation, Richmond and Ingram.

Salina was on the Greeley, Salt Lake & Pacific, a narrow gauge railroad originating in Boulder. After this railroad was destroyed by a flood, the Colorado & Northwestern rebuilt the line on higher ground. Salina got a 20 x 30 foot frame station with a waiting room and a freight room. Salina was also the site of the steepest grade on the railroad at about 5%. A siding 1250 feet long accommodated the freight business.

Not much is left of the original town. Modern homes now occupy most of the site, although the old schoolhouse still stands.

For a map showing Salina, see "Crisman."

The primary sources of employment in Salina were the mines and these mills. The town also had rail service provided by the Colorado & Northwestern. *(Colorado Historical Society F6442)*

Delores S. Bailey, *God's Country U.S.A.*, p. 17.
Forest Crossen, *The Switzerland Trail of America*, Pruett Press, Boulder, 1962, p. 309.
Muriel Sibell Wolle, *Stampede to Timberline*, Sage Books, Chicago, 1949, 1974, p. 487.
Silvia Pettem, *Red Rocks to Riches*, Stonehenge Books, Boulder, Colorado, 1980, p. 35.

SPRINGDALE

- *Boulder County, James Creek drainage*
- *Accessible by paved road; access to site restricted by private property*
- *Town did not have a post office; several original structures remain*

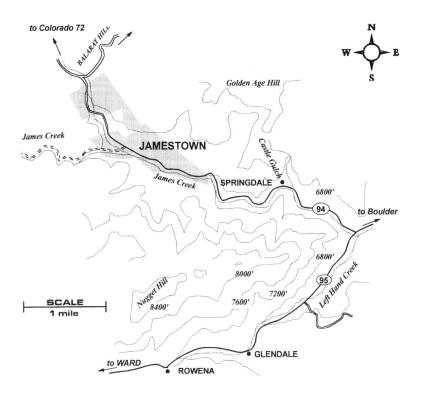

to Colorado 72

BALARAT HILL

Golden Age Hill

James Creek

JAMESTOWN

Castle Gulch

James Creek

SPRINGDALE

6800'

94

to Boulder

6800'

8000'

Nugget Hill

7200'

95

Left Hand Creek

SCALE
1 mile

8400'

7600'

GLENDALE

to WARD

ROWENA

Halfway between the mouth of James Creek and Jamestown is Springdale. It is still indicated on topographic maps because much of the property is filled with summer homes. There is one old structure sitting below the road plus a cabin sitting above the road on the north side, which might have belonged to the original settlement.

Springdale was founded in 1874 as a mining town, with a row of houses up Castle Gulch. It was also known for the Peabody Mineral Springs whose spring water, at least for a time, was bottled and sold commercially.. Estimates place the peak population at around 300, but based on what little exists at the site today, this seems somewhat high. A summer resort, called the Seltzer House, was established with cabins for rent. The flood that badly damaged nearby Jamestown in 1894 also destroyed much of Springdale.

Springdale is located along James Creek at Castle Gulch.

Muriel Sibell Wolle, *Stampede to Timberline*, Sage Books, Chicago, 1949, 1974, p. 510.

SUGARLOAF

- *Boulder County; on the divide between Boulder Creek & Four Mile Creek*
- *Accessible by paved road*
- *Town had a post office; occupied site; several original structures remain*

This appears to be one of the original log homes in Sugarloaf. There are several other log homes located along Old Post Office Road. *(Kenneth Jessen 105C2)*

The town of Sugarloaf sits at the base of a treeless mountain by the same name. The town is located high above and north of Boulder Creek. A paved road runs past the old town site. Access to the site is via a side road marked Old Post Office Road. The remains of the United States Gold Corporation mill can also be seen just outside the town site. The rest of the area is now an expensive mountain housing development with commuters hurrying to and from work.

The first gold prospectors came into the area in 1860 and used an arrastra to crush their ore. This was a primitive device where a center pivot allowed a horizontal arm to be powered by a horse walking in a circle. To the arm was tied a large stone. In a groove worn in the base rock of the arrastra, the large stone, by its circular motion, was used to crush the ore. When a steady supply of water was run over the arrastra, the lighter, worthless rock was washed away leaving the heavier, gold bearing rock.

Once the free milling surface ore was depleted, Sugarloaf was abandoned. A second boom occurred in 1873 when tellurium, containing gold and silver, was found, and new mines were opened. Thus the history of Sugarloaf parallels that of other towns such as Gold Hill and Salina.

The Livingston Mine at Sugarloaf produced $300,000 in gold, and after it closed, a prospector named Miles found some rich gold ore in 1902 in a potato patch a few hundred feet from the mine. In a week, the prospector pulled $20,000 in gold from the potato patch using a simple scraper. This became the Potato Patch Mine and resulted in a new boom in Sugarloaf.

In 1915, the United States Gold Corporation constructed a large cyanide mill to process the lower grade ore. The mill was idle by 1940, and during the scrap drives of World War II, was gutted of its machinery.

Except for a brief period of time between 1868 and 1869, Sugarloaf had its own post office until 1944.

Muriel Sibell Wolle, *Stampede to Timberline*, Sage Books, Chicago, 1949, 1974, p. 442, p. 490.
William H. Bauer, James L. Ozment, John H. Willard, *Colorado Post Offices*, Colorado Railroad Museum, Golden, Colorado, 1990, p. 137.

SULPHIDE
Flag At Half Mast

- *Boulder County, Middle Fork of Boulder Creek drainage*
- *Accessible by paved road*
- *Had no post office; no standing structures remain*

At the Sulphide site (also known as Sulphide Flats), an elaborate plat was laid out for a town of substantial size and promoted by a Colorado Springs realtor. Sulphide was located 1.3 miles downstream from Eldora, close to the point where the road to Lake Eldora leaves the main road. A two-story hotel, the St. Julian, was constructed overlooking a small pond on the flats; it had forty guest rooms, but apparently the hotel was never fully completed. There were also a couple of false-front stores along what was to have been Sulphide's main street.

The real estate promoters from Colorado Springs set up a grand opening for Sulphide complete with a band, free lunch, coffee, speeches, fireworks and a flag raising. The free lunch had a lot of local appeal and attracted several hundred people from the surrounding towns. At noon, a stick of dynamite was set off followed by the free lunch, then the sales pitch by the promoters amid carefully marked-off lots. The ceremony was concluded by the flag raising on a forty-foot pole near the partially complete hotel. A pretty girl was selected for this duty and began to haul the flag up the pole by its halyard. This was done as *The Star Spangled Banner* was sung. The wind whipped the halyard against the pole causing the rope stick in the pulley with the flag not quite at the top. One of the men jerked the halyard and broke the line at the pulley causing the flag to fall toward the ground. A second gust of wind picked up the falling flag causing it to stick at half mast. This ended the ceremony.

Some of the prospective buyers picked out choice lots and stood on them admiring the view. When it came time to close the sale, not a single individual put up the down payment.

The Colorado & Northwestern built its narrow gauge railroad through Sulphide in 1904, and during the construction of the Barker Dam east of Nederland during 1907 through 1910, a switch was installed at Sulphide for a spur track. A wye for turning locomotives and a water tank were also built. The spur ran east through Nederland, down Barker meadow to the dam. Tons of cement and other building material were switched off the main line at Sulphide to be hauled down this spur.

Today there is nothing to see at Sulphide except for a gravel pit and pond. The hotel was razed many years ago, but the water tank, still standing in the 1970s, has since disappeared. The railroad grade, however, is visible to the north where it enters the flat.

For a map showing Sulphide, see "Cardinal."

Donald Kemp, *Silver, Gold and Black Iron*, Sage Books, Denver, 1960, pp. 204-206.

SUMMERVILLE

- *Boulder County, Four Mile Creek drainage*
- *Accessible over graded dirt road*
- *No post office; several original structures remain*

The small mining camp of Summerville is located at the base of the first switchback on the graded dirt road known as Gold Run, between Salina and Gold Hill. There are several original structures, which have been fixed up for summer use, plus one abandoned shack along side the road. The camp was settled in 1872 with several good mines close by. The large combination log and wood frame home in Summerville served as a hotel/boarding house. After the high grade ore was exhausted, new methods of treating low grade ore extended the life of Summerville. The town did not have a post office.

The old hotel in Summerville, built in 1877, is located on the road from Salina to Gold Hill. Several additions have expanded the original structure. *(Kenneth Jessen 106D10)*

John K. Aldrich, *Ghosts of Boulder County*, Centennial Graphics, Lakewood, 1990, p. 32
Perry Eberhart, *Guide to the Colorado Ghost Towns and Mining Camps*, Sage Books, Chicago, 1959, pp. 85, 90.
Muriel Sibell Wolle, *Stampede to Timberline*, Sage Books, Chicago, 1949, 1974, p. 486.

SUNSET

A Railroad And Mining Town

- *Boulder County, Four Mile Creek drainage*
- *Accessible by graded dirt road*
- *Town had a post office; occupied site; several original structures remain*

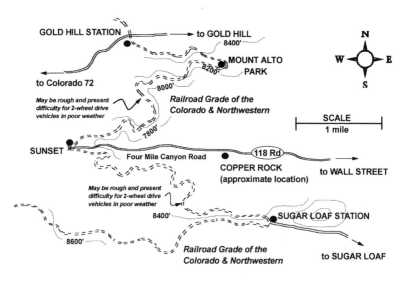

Sunset is at the end of a graded dirt road lead-ing from Salina and is at the beginning of rough, but graded dirt roads both to the north and to the south following the old grade of the Colorado & Northwestern.

Sunset, located at the end of a graded dirt road up Four Mile Creek, was unique in that it served as the terminus for the Greeley, Salt Lake & Pacific narrow gauge railroad, which originated 13.2 miles away in Boulder. At the time the railroad was completed in 1883, the town was called Penn Gulch or Pennsylvania

Gulch. A severe flood in 1894 so badly damaged the railroad that the tracks were removed.

In 1897, a second railroad, the Colorado & Northwestern, constructed a new narrow gauge railroad over basically the same route, but in places on higher ground. That same year, the narrow gauge line was extended across the north wall of the canyon and around several mountains to Ward, a distance of 12.8 miles. In 1904, a second major portion of the Colorado & Northwestern was completed to Eldora, a distance of 20.1 miles. It climbed up of the canyon directly opposite the other grade.

Enough people had settled in Sunset by 1883 that a post office was established, and it remained active until 1921.

Sunset has always remained a small town. Its one hotel, the Columbine, was complimented by three general merchandise stores. Sunset also had a meat market. In 1890, the town had forty residents, and by 1894, it had grown to 175. Between 1901

This log home is located at the old Boulder County mining town of Sunset at the head of Four Mile Creek. *(Kenneth Jessen 106D4)*

and 1903, the population had dwindled to just 75 people, and in 1921, only 30 people lived in the town. The first governor of Colorado, John L. Routt, was one of the owners of the Free Coinage Mine at Sunset.

The Colorado & Northwestern could not make ends meet as a mining railroad so it made itself into a tourist railroad. Excursions stopping at Sunset were common. The railroad constructed a 20 x 30 foot frame depot, a siding and a wye. The railroad hauled up two old wooden box cars and set them on the ground to use for storage. Italian section hands, who maintained the track, lived in Sunset in the section house.

The Columbine Hotel in Sunset charged $5 per week for room and board, and it was common for a visitors to stay for a week at a time. Its dining room had four long tables and excellent home cooking. Mountain raised beef, vegetables and fruit were served.

As shown on the map in this section, Sunset is quite easy to get to from Boulder. A right-hand turn from Colorado 119 in Boulder Canyon leads to Salina. A left hand turn at Salina up Four Mile Creek passes through Wall Street then Sunset. From Sunset, the opposing railroad grades can usually be driven by car, however, the old grades are quite rough and rocky in places. They afford excellent views of the surrounding country and end up on the Peak-to-Peak Highway.

Forest Crossen, *The Switzerland Trail of America*, Pruett Press, Boulder, 1962, p. 319.

Robert L. Brown, *Colorado Ghost Towns - Past and Present*, Caxton Printers, Caldwell, Idaho, 1977, p. 259-260.

Tivis Wilkins, *Colorado Railroads*, Pruett Publishing Company, Boulder, Colorado, 1974, pp. 51, 147.

SUNSHINE

- *Boulder County, Boulder Creek drainage*
- *Accessible by graded dirt road*
- *Town had post office and school; seasonally occupied; several original structures remain*

Just the name alone is enough to paint a picture of this wonderful small community located west of Boulder. Sunshine was founded in 1873 when rich gold ore was discovered. This was a late find since gold was first discovered in the Gold Hill area in 1859. The American, Interocean, Osceala, Tille Butzel, Sheridan, Grand View and White Crow mines quickly developed and dominated the landscape. The stores and homes, which made up the town of Sunshine, were mixed in with the mines and mine buildings wherever there was room. There weren't any neat right angle intersections, and Sunshine was anything but symmetrical.

The beautiful stone Sunshine School was constructed in 1900, entered in the National Register of Historic Places in 1981 and restored in 1991. *(Kenneth Jessen 096B4)*

By 1874, the population of Sunshine had grown to a couple of hundred, and a post office was established inside the general store. The post office was really just a postal cabinet mounted to the counter. A small window with vertical iron bars served to separate the patron from the "postal employee," who was in reality the store clerk. A wire basket could be pushed through the bars to give patrons their mail, stamps and so on. In a town as small as Sunshine, this was as much formality as required.

By the centennial year of 1876 when Colorado became a state, Sunshine had grown to over a thousand residents, although the town was not incorporated until 1885. After the other mines had begun to play out, it was the American Mine which kept the place going. Fullen Jackson discovered the American lode, took out $17,500 in high grade gold ore, and sold it for another $17,500. The new owner, Hiram Hitchcock, hired Professor Alden Smith of Central City to continue to develop the mine. Hiram cleared $196,000 during the following twenty months! At the Centennial Exposition in Philadelphia in 1876, a spectacular piece of gold ore from the American Mine was displayed. Chunks of ore were held together by rare native wire gold similar to that found at the

Wire Patch near Breckenridge. When the vein of ore finally "pinched out," the American had shipped a million and a half dollars in gold.

The local newspaper was *The Sunshine Courier,* and it advertised that its editorial policy was "...strickly a miner's journal and the only paper in Colorado that keeps its columns from politics." Early Sunshine hotels

One of the older buildings in Sunshine is the home of Forest Jones, one of the town's pioneers. *(Kenneth Jessen 096B5)*

included the Minneapolis House, Howard House, the Grand View
Hotel, the American House, the Mountain House, the Forest
House and the Miner's Hotel. Sunshine also had two general
merchandise stores, three blacksmith shops, but only two
saloons. Saloons, by the way, were required to close on Sunday
by virtue of a local ordinance. The livery stable, barbershop and
boot repair store rounded out Sunshine's businesses. A telegraph
line connecting Sunshine to Boulder was an unusually progres-
sive feature for a mining town.

The original wood-frame Sunshine school was replaced in
1900 by a finely crafted stone schoolhouse. It was entered on the
National Register of Historic Places in 1981 for its sophisticated
neoclassical design. Restoration work was completed on the
building, and it is one of the finest historic stone structures in
Colorado.

A year after Sunshine's population hit over a thousand, the
town declined to only 800. This was typical of the ups and downs
of a Colorado mining town. All the mines eventually played out
and in 1908, Sunshine's population had dwindled to about 200
and the town was partially abandoned. A few hardy souls hung
on through World War I, and in 1920, the post office and telegraph office were closed along with the last surviving store. What
mail there was for Sunshine's scattered residents was brought up
from Boulder on horseback. During the depression of the 1930s,
it almost became a ghost town.

Sunshine is easy to reach over a paved road up Sunshine
Canyon or over a graded dirt road from Gold Hill. There are relatively few original structures, but Sunshine is worth the visit.
Many newer summer homes have been constructed in recent
years, and the original cabins have been converted into summer
homes. *Sunshine is shown on a map in "Crisman."*

Frank Fossett, *Colorado, its Gold and Silver Mines*, C. G. Crawford, New York, 1879, p. 275.
June Peterson Howard, *Stories of Sunshine*, The Book Lode, Longmont, Colorado, 1994, pp. 1-64.

TUNGSTEN
Hardens Steel

- Boulder County, Boulder Creek drainage
- Access limited by private property
- Town had post office and school; no standing structures remain

Although Tungsten still appears on topographic maps, there is little to suggest that a town ever existed at the base of the Barker Dam below Nederland. Today's highway is high above the town site, and it appears that only newer buildings occupy the site. When Muriel Sibell Wolle first visited Tungsten in 1926, the Boulder Tungsten Mill was still standing along with many of the town's buildings. Bob Brown visited Tungsten during the 1960s to take a photograph using the same view as a historic photograph. At that time, approximately ten structures including the school remained. Access to the town site today is limited by private property, but it appears looking down from Colorado 119 that time and changes in property ownership have caused the old town of Tungsten to vanish.

Originally called Steven's Camp, the name was changed to Ferberite, then, during the World War I tungsten boom, to Tungsten. Samuel Conger is credited with finding tungsten ore at his mine above Nederland. It was called black iron and fouled the milling process for gold and silver. Even though it was identified as tungsten around the turn of the century, it still had little value until metallurgists found it could be used as an alloy to harden steel. The demand for tungsten dramatically increased in World War I for use in tool steel and in the steel for gun barrels. An estimated 5,000 people came into the vicinity of Tungsten to live and to work the mines. In 1916, Tungsten got its post office, which remained opened until 1949.

At the peak of the tungsten boom, the town had seventeen mills running. A constant stream of new arrivals came up Boulder Canyon in the Stanley Steamers used by the stage companies. The boom subsided after the war was over. Although the demand for tungsten rose again when the U.S. entered World War II, cheaper sources of tungsten were discovered overseas. The mines closed for good during the late 1940s, and the town was abandoned.

Muriel Sibell Wolle, *Stampede to Timberline*, Sage Books, Chicago, 1949, 1974, p. 496.

Robert L. Brown, *Ghost Towns of the Colorado Rockies*, Caxton Printers, Caldwell, Idaho, 1977, pp. 371-374.

William H. Bauer, James L. Ozment, John H. Willard, *Colorado Post Offices*, Colorado Railroad Museum, Golden, Colorado, 1990, p. 143.

WALL STREET
Caryl's Utopia

- *Boulder County; Four Mile Creek drainage*
- *Accessible by paved road*
- *Several original structures remain; large stone foundation*

To the left of the stone foundation for the Gold Extraction Mining and Supply Company Mill at Wall Street is the tramway used to bring ore to the top of the mill. *(Kenneth Jessen collection)*

Exploration for gold ore in Four Mile Canyon dates back to the 1860s. A small town sprang up named Delphi. Charles W. Caryl, using five million dollars he raised on New York City's Wall Street, founded the Gold Extraction Mining and Supply Company in 1896. He consolidated sixty gold claims in the Delphi area, then renamed the location Wall Street.

Caryl had an unusual spin on social structure. He wanted to not only own and operate a successful gold mining business, but he wanted to turn Wall Street into a utopian colony. Each man, he said, should be able to produce up to his personal potential and to receive pay according his contributions. Caryl created seven distinct classes of workers with the lowest class doing menial work, such as shoveling dirt, handling freight, and so on. For this, he would pay $2 per day. His "privates" would get $3 per day for work requiring some experience, and the "sergeants", who had skills as mechanics, accountants, teachers, musicians, and so on, would receive $4 per day. The "lieutenants" would jump to $6 as professional people, and "captains" were next at $10 per day. General managers, at $15 per day, were Caryl's "majors." As for Caryl, he classified himself as a "general" and would pull in $25 per day. This notion of class was extended to the living quarters to be built at Wall Street. The workers would live in simple houses in contrast to the top rung of Caryl's social ladder, the "generals" who would have palaces with lakes, boating and boulevards.

The company constructed an enormous mill in 1902 to process the gold ore from the Nancy group of mines. The most prominent feature in Wall Street today is the tall stone foundation, which acted as the cooling pit for the chlorination process. The entire mill cost upwards of $175,000, a large sum of money for its day. The mill processed not only ore from the Nancy, but from other area mines. The Colorado & Northwestern brought in much of the ore, and a tramway was used to elevate the ore to the mill's highest level. After crushing, the ore was treated in a complex process, which ended with cyanide leaching and precipitation over zinc filings to recover the gold. In July, 1903, a pair of refined

425 ounce gold bars were put on display at Boulder's First National Bank.

The Gold Extraction Company's mill did not last long. In 1904, the mill shut down due to mounting debts. The Nancy Gold Mine was sold at a sheriff's auction. The mill never reopened, and at a bankruptcy sale a few years later, was liquidated for just $20,000. It was dismantled and some of the machinery was moved to a mill at Sugarloaf.

In 1898, one photograph shows only a handful of structures at Wall Street. There were four homes plus a small hotel and various buildings associated with the mining and milling industry. After the Gold Extraction Mining and Supply Company constructed its large mill, the number of structures in the town increased. The assay and mine office, which still stands today, was built from stone hauled all the way from Gunnison. The base of the mill was

This well-preserved schoolhouse is located west of Wall Street. It has been converted into a private residence. *(Kenneth Jessen 106D5)*

also constructed from this same material. A two-story hotel was also built along with a general store. The population of Wall Street, however, probably never exceeded much more than one hundred.

The town of Wall Street was officially laid out in 1898 with a plat, which shows it to be six city blocks long and a

The imposing foundation for the large Gold Extraction Mining and Supply Company Mill sits as a silent reminder of Wall Street's glory days. *(Kenneth Jessen 012C12)*

half a block wide with numerous town lots. The lots varied in size from 50 x 25 feet to 115 x 25 feet.

So what happened to Charles W. Caryl? After trying to promote the mill at the Wall Street disaster, he established a colony to educate Denver's homeless children. This venture also failed, and Caryl founded a cult in California, the Brotherhood of Light, with ten thousand followers. Eventually, Caryl ended up in the Denver County Jail for sending obscene material through the U. S. Mail.

It is very worthwhile to visit Wall Street. The assay and mine office is a beautiful structure and forms the centerpiece for the present town. The stone buttress, which once supported the mill, is very imposing, and an interpretive sign explains the mill's history.

See "Crisman" for a map showing Wall Street's location.

Delores S. Bailey, *God's Country U.S.A.*, Robinson Press, Fort Collins, 1982, pp. 51-54, p. 63.
Silvia Pettem, *Red Rocks to Riches*, Stonehenge Books, Boulder, Colorado, 1980, pp. 74-84.

WARD
Calvin's Town

- *Boulder County, Left Hand Creek drainage*
- *Accessible by paved road*
- *Occupied town; many original structures remain*

An 1890 street scene in Ward shows how the town looked during its boom years. *(Colorado Historical Society F2619)*

Ward is not a ghost town, nor has it ever been completely abandoned. Nevertheless, it has lost much of its glitter, and due to a devastating fire in 1900, many of its buildings are gone. Although both of its churches are still standing, the Catholic Church is unfortunately a disgraceful ruin at the edge of town and used as a garage to house highway maintenance trucks. Ward is laid out like many Colorado mining towns, kind of haphazardly in a small valley, but it does have a well defined main street. Part of the town sits up on the old railroad grade of the Colorado & Northwestern above the rest of the town.

Calvin M. Ward located the first claim in the area and named it the Miser's Dream. This happened in the spring of 1860. A more important discovery, however, was made the following year when Cy Deardorff discovered the Columbia lode. The Columbia group of claims yielded five million dollars in easily milled gold.

C. H. Merill paid fifty dollars for one of the Columbia claims only to sell it in two years for less than what he paid. It was then sold to Davidson and Breath for $50,000. They constructed a simple, six-stamp mill to recover the gold. To continue to develop the property, which was called the Ni-Wot, they needed capital. A half million dollars from eastern bankers allowed them to develop the mine. The machinery for a larger mill was hauled across the plains and up Left Hand Canyon by wagon to the mine. No sooner had the mill began operating than it burned to the ground.

Davidson and Breath sold the mine for $300,000 to a company that turned around and sold the property again, but this time for a half million dollars. The Big Five Syndicate, owners of other mines in the area, eventually ended up with the Ni-Wot. From their operations, the mine yielded a million and a quarter dollars in gold. Just about everyone seemed to win.

Looking down Rundell Ave., the Ward business district looks substantial. All but the stone building on the right was destroyed by fire in 1900. *(Colorado Historical Society F2618)*

The Ward schoolhouse now serves as the town's post office. *(Kenneth Jessen 101B5)*

Ward was called Columbia City at first, and only after Calvin Ward's discovery did the name change. Located above 9,000 feet, winters were hard and spring was slow to come. The population reached 400 during Ward's early years and climbed to 600 by 1865. Ward was incorporated in 1896, and *The Ward Miner,* the town's one and only newspaper, was published for a brief period of time.

The trip to Ward from Boulder by stage coach took twelve hours over dusty, rough wagon roads. When the Colorado & Northwestern narrow gauge railroad arrived in 1898, it greatly improved the economy of Ward and made travel more comfortable. Ward was located at milepost 26.1 as measured from Boulder. Now low grade ore, uneconomical to process in Ward's

A fire in 1900 destroyed fifty-three structures in Ward. The town was not rebuilt, and insurance covered only 10% of the loss. *(Colorado Historical Society F32107)*

mills, could be transported to smelters in Black Hawk or Denver. Much of this ore had been simply discarded in the tailings piles. After the railroad was abandoned in 1919, the former railroad agent, R. D. Ward, purchased the depot, moved it to the west side of the right of way, and converted it into a store. The structure remains standing today just off of Colorado 7 overlooking the rest of the town of Ward.

A devastating fire struck Ward in 1900 and destroyed fifty-three build- ings. By using a water brigade, residents were able to save both churches and the school. Fanned by strong winds, the fire burned unchecked for six hours . Freezing tempera- tures hampered efforts to put the fire out. Insurance covered less than 10% of the losses. The Boulder County Commissioners sent provisions by rail to Ward the next day.

The only surviving hotel in Ward, Columbia Hotel, is wedge-shaped to conform to the layout of the streets. *(Kenneth Jessen 101C9)*

It is difficult to determine what Ward's peak population was during its boom years, but based on the size of the town relative to other mining towns, it must have been well over one thousand. However, when Muriel Sibell Wolle visited the town during the 1940s, her estimate at that time placed Ward's population at less than twenty hardy souls. Today, many of the town's homes have been restored and a grocery store remains open year-round.

Forest Crossen, *The Switzerland Trail of America*, Pruett Press, Boulder, 1962, p. 329.

Muriel Sibell Wolle, *Stampede to Timberline*, Sage Books, Chicago, 1949, 1974, pp. 516-517, 520.

Robert L. Brown, *Colorado Ghost Towns - Past and Present*, Caxton Printers, Caldwell, Idaho, 1977, pp. 285-289.

WILLIAMSBURG

- *Pennsylvania Creek drainage*
- *Accessible just off paved road*
- *Town did not have a post office; no standing structures remain*

Of the original ghost town books, only Perry Eberhart's *Guide to the Colorado Ghost Towns and Mining Camps* mentions this obscure camp. The site is located just below the Peak-to-Peak highway near the head of Pennsylvania Gulch not far from Glacier Lake. At the time Eberhart wrote his book in 1959, several milled lumber shanties were still standing. The area is now so overgrown with new aspen trees that finding the site is difficult. Nothing but some debris from the buildings remains.

Williamsburg got its start in 1871, and at the time, it appeared that the rich silver ore would rival that found at Caribou. The town was platted the following summer.

Beginning just ten feet below the surface, silver ore valued at $328 per ton was mined. The property was named the Washington Avenue. The Mayflower Mine, located a mile and a half from Williamsburg, produced silver for several years. However, the ore deposit at Williamsburg wasn't as extensive as originally believed, and as with other Boulder County mining camps, poor roads and isolation hampered development.

The Colorado & Northwestern constructed its narrow gauge line from Sunset to Eldora past Williamsburg in 1904. Eberhart writes that the name of Williamsburg was changed by the railroad to Switchville, but this cannot be confirmed by other sources.

Perry Eberhart, *Guide to the Colorado Ghost Towns and Mining Camps*, Sage Books, Chicago, 1959, p. 89, pp. 101-102.

AREA FOUR 4

Gilpin County

AREA 4: Gilpin County
Selected Towns

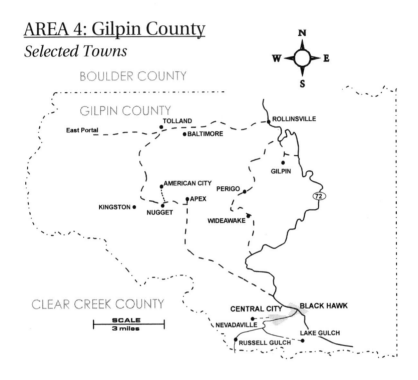

Introduction to Gilpin County

During the first two decades of Gilpin County history, nearly three quarters of a billion dollars in gold and other precious metals, as evaluated in today's dollars, was taken out of its mines. The story begins in 1859 with John H. Gregory's discovery of gold in Gregory Gulch near Mountain City, located between Central City and Black Hawk. Thousands of prospectors poured into the area to stake their claim; few ended up wealthy.

It did not take long before the narrow Gregory Gulch became choked with mines, mills, smelters, businesses and homes. Growth was not planned. At the west end, Central City emerged as the business center while at the east end, where Gregory Gulch joins the North Fork of Clear Creek, Black Hawk became the mill town. Nevadaville, located above Central City, at one time had a population greater that either of the other two towns, but lack of a good water supply spelled its doom.

The development of mining in Gilpin County got off to a good start, but during the mid to late 1860s, it looked like the entire mining economy would collapse. The placer gold in the sands of Clear Creek was exhausted and surface ore, which was decomposed by natural forces, was also depleted. This ore was known as "free milling" since simple crushing followed by amalgamation was all that was required for the recovery of gold. As the mines got progressively deeper, refractory ore containing sulfides was encountered. This ore required roasting followed by smelting, a far more costly and complex process than any mine owner had to deal with up to this time. Many residents packed up and left. Mills sat idle, filled with rusting machinery, and many of the mines of Gilpin County began to close.

Then in 1867, Professor Nathaniel Hill from Brown University in Rhode Island opened a smelter in Black Hawk capable of treating refractory ores. As a result, the mines began to reopen. The mining boom resumed with renewed hope in the area as the earth began to yield its treasures of gold, silver and other metals; it soon became known as the richest square mile on earth.

Through the 1870s, 1880s and into the 1890s, Gilpin County experienced a steady growth. Eventually, the mines reached a depth where pumping water became a major expense. The Newhouse Tunnel, drilled from Idaho Springs, solved this problem for approximately one hundred claims by undercutting them to allow drainage. Finished in 1910, the Newhouse Tunnel also served as a ore haulage tunnel. In 1913, the giant Argo Gold Mill was constructed at its portal. The Newhouse Tunnel will be covered later in this introduction in more detail.

Even with sufficient drainage, the richest gold ore was eventually exhausted and only low grade ore remained. By the 1950s, only a handful of mines were in limited operation, and Gilpin County went into steady economic decline. Central City tried its best to attract tourists with a variety of saloons and its famous opera house. This was only seasonal, however. Black Hawk had less to offer in entertainment, but managed to hang on. Other Gilpin County mining towns were abandoned.

The "silver bullet," at least in the eyes of those that lived in Gilpin County, was limited stakes gambling. Beginning October 1, 1991, gambling started in the two towns with a rush of new construction. Entire city blocks, which stood empty for decades, were purchased by the casinos. Modern buildings, made to look old, were erected. Gambling made a big difference, and today, the streets are crowed with pedestrians. The narrow road up Gregory Gulch between Black Hawk and Central City is now choked with traffic, especially on weekends. The complexion of the two towns has changed forever, and many of the long time residents have sold out and moved. Some of the once abandoned mining towns in the area have been re-occupied.

Although gambling has drastically altered Gilpin County's mining towns, much of its historic character remains. In Black Hawk, however, some of the new casinos overpower its original buildings. In this chapter, the majority of its towns, both occupied and abandoned, will be covered.

Gregory's Discovery

The story of Gilpin County's mining era, and many of its towns, is largely the story of Gregory Gulch. In 1859, John H. Gregory had just completed a wagon trip to Fort Laramie when he heard of the discovery of gold along the banks of Cherry Creek by W. Green Russell. Gregory had originally planned to travel to the Canadian Northwest, but instead, he turned south drawn by gold fever. Gregory traveled along the eastern edge of the Front Range and tested the sands in each stream he crossed looking in his pan for "color" in the form of gold flakes. He found nothing until he reached Vasquez Creek, later called Clear Creek. He panned his way up Clear Creek to the point where the north and south forks join, and here he made a decision. The flecks of gold were more plentiful in the North Fork, so off he went until he came to a gulch coming in from the west. Beyond this gulch and farther up the North Fork, Gregory found no color in his pan. He turned west into the gulch and began to explore it until he was driven out by a heavy April snow storm.

Remembering the exact spot where his exploration stopped, Gregory retreated to the small settlement of Arapahoe. It was there that he met another prospector named Wilkes DeFreese, who was

John H. Gregory was the first to discover gold in what would become Gilpin County.

traveling with about a dozen other men in hopes of finding gold. Gregory, normally a loner, trusted DeFreese with his discovery, and the two men made the three-day trip back to the same spot where Gregory had stopped his exploration just a few weeks before. It was May 6, 1859, and the men immediately hit pay dirt in the form of sand rich with gold flakes. Gregory's first pan netted him $4, which converted to today's prices would be close to ninety dollars. Gregory and DeFreese washed forty dollars from the gravel before returning for the rest of the party. The men named the lode and the gulch after Gregory. After just a week, John Gregory had panned over fifty ounces of gold dust valued at nearly $20,000 at today's gold prices.

The Gregory Mining District was set up by this original party of prospectors and recognized 100-foot claims. The district established laws governing such matters as claim jumping, sale of claims and so on. For his efforts, Gregory got two choice claims.

William Newton Byers, founder and publisher of the *Rocky Mountain News*, visited what was then known as "Gregory

William Newton Byers, founder and publisher of the *Rocky Mountain News*, was among the first journalists to report on gold discoveries in the Colorado mountains. *(Colorado Historical Society)*

Diggings" in June, 1859, to see if the rumors were true. He saw that the strikes were not only legitimate, but very rich. Back in Denver, he printed a special issue telling of the discovery of gold, thus opening the flood gates for thousands of gold-seekers. In one month, an estimated 2,000 to 3,000 men were prospecting and panning in Gregory Gulch. Claims on the richest surface ore had already been taken by the original group of prospectors, and the new arrivals tried to force the mining district to amend its laws by reducing the size of its claims to 25 feet. But the founders of the Gregory Mining District held fast.

Horace Greeley, editor of the *New York Tribune*, visited Gregory Diggings that year and estimated that 5,000 people were crammed into the area. He observed 500 arriving each day while 100 discouraged prospectors left each day. Greeley reported the growth of the area by predicting, "A provision store will soon follow; then groceries; then dry goods; then a hotel, etc., until within ten years, the tourist of the continent will be whirled up to these diggings over a longer but far easier road..."

After a couple of hectic months, John Gregory decided mining took too much physical effort and sold both of his original claims for $21,000. As a common laborer at the going wage of $1.50 per day, Gregory would have had to work 14,000 days to earn this much money.

Gregory's new occupation was that of consultant with an irrefutable reputation for finding gold. He charged $200 a day and later located the Gregory Extension, the Gregory No. 2, and the

Bates. He also built a small mill which he sold immediately for six times its cost. Although he spent his winters in his native Georgia, he returned to Gregory Gulch for the following three summers. After 1862, he was never heard from again and probably lived out a quiet life.

Bedposts Served as Gilpin County's First Jail

In 1861, when Gilpin County was separated from Arapahoe County, a fellow named William Cozens became sheriff. Though supplied by the county with a Sharps rifle, a couple of Colt revolvers, a set of handcuffs and a set of leg irons, the new sheriff had no office or jail. As stated later by Sheriff Cozens, "We had no jail of any kind, so when we arrested someone, we had to see to it that he got a pretty speedy trial."

Late one afternoon in 1861, Cozen arrested a couple of horse thieves. The judge was not available until the following morning. Cozens remembered swift justice and later recalled, "You know before we got our court working, it was the custom of the camp to hang a man who stole a horse or robbed gold out a of sluice box, and there never was a lengthy ceremony over such an affair either."

The problem facing Sheriff Cozens was that the local judge was trying hard to bring law and order to Gilpin County mining camps by replacing the miner's form of quick justice with a rope to one with due process for the defendant. Cozens had to set a good example, and simply letting a couple of thieves get hung without a trial was not good for public relations. Therefore, he had to somehow figure out what to contain the two thieves with until the following morning.

Only a few days had passed since Mrs. Cozens gave birth to their first child, Willie. She was still in bed nursing the infant. The only idea Sheriff Cozens could think of was to take the two criminals home with him and put them in his wife's bedroom! This he did, handcuffing them to the bedpost at the foot of her bed, and telling the men to lay down on the floor. Cozens then drew his Colt revolver, shoved it into the faces of the two men, and threatened to blow their brains out if they made even the slightest noise. The thieves knew he meant every word. During the night, the horse thieves never stirred or made a sound.

William Cozens became the first sheriff of Gilpin County and lived in Central City for many years. Still standing are two of the homes Cozens built for his family. *(Denver Public Library, Western History Department F27016)*

The next morning, however, Mrs. Cozens opened fire verbally on her husband. She said it was an outrage to turn her bedroom into a jail and that she would not allow such an event to take place ever again. Cozens said later, "When I tell you that she didn't like it, I mean she didn't like it with all the emphasis you can put on the words. She wasn't mealy-mouthed about what she had to say to me either. I told her I was in a hell of a fix, that I had to keep those men in our house because I had no other place to put them."

After this episode, Sheriff Bill Cozens knew he had to take immediate action for fear he would have to arrest more criminals after the court had closed for the day and face a similar dilemma. So he rounded up the County Commissioners and demanded that they build a jail. The Chairman replied, "Billy, we know damn well you ought to have a jail, but we are just getting this County government started and we have no money...If we had some money, we'd build you a jail, but just now, we can't do anything for you."

The Sheriff, however, would not let up and continued his demands that construction on a jail begin immediately. He suggested that the county go into debt to purchase some lime for mortar, a few iron bars, some planks, and a few nails. Cozens said he would take care of the rest, and the County Commissioners eventually agreed to his request.

Once the material arrived, Cozens began rounding up his work crew. "There was a lot of bad ones loafing around the camp that I had come to know pretty well, and to know that they weren't at all anxious to have the new law officers dig into their past records. You know, you can do a lot with that kind of a man if you go at him right; he's afraid of you." First the Sheriff would tell a prospective worker that the County Commissioners were not going to stand for a lot of dirty bums loafing around Black Hawk and Central City. He then threatened to search the wanted posters and to check the records in the surrounding states until he discovered what law they had broken. If an individual proved unwilling, he told them that a few days of hard work were better than a long jail sentence. Using this technique, he literally forced each individual to work on a chain gang building Gilpin County's first permanent jail along Eureka Street opposite the Central City Opera House. The structure was completed in 1862.

Republicans Crash Through Floor

What may be the oldest standing structure in Central City is Washington Hall opposite the Teller House on Eureka Street. Although it appears to be of frame construction with clapboard siding, it is actually built of massive hand-hewn square logs.

William Gilpin, the first governor of Colorado Territory, approved the creation of Gilpin County in 1861 and established Central City as its county seat. Up to this time, the mining district enforced the law, but now William Cozens, the new sheriff, took over this responsibility.

The new County Commissioners leased part of the Central City post office for their offices, but there wasn't any jail and very little room for county business. Sheriff Cozens convinced the commissioners to accept a plan for a new jail constructed on a city lot he owned. The County Commissioners had but little choice and leased the jail from Cozens for $35 per month. They also made Cozens the jailer at a salary of $600 per year.

The idea of having the sheriff act as the jailer and own his jail apparently worked. Cozens then added a second story to the structure to serve as the courtroom and county offices. The lower floor was expanded, and the County Recorder moved into that area. A vault was constructed at one end of the lower office for the county records. Now the county found itself leasing all of its space from its own sheriff.

Sheriff Cozens did have to pay some of the expenses, however. He was required to buy chamber pots, blankets, silverware and dishes for the prisoners. He also had to invest in beds. Cozens was compensated at the rate of $1.25 per day for each prisoner.

The building became known as Washington Hall and served not only the needs of the county, but in off hours, was a citizen's meeting place. A singing school was held in the courtroom, and the Methodists rented the place for Sunday services. Without question, the most exciting meeting held on the second floor of Washington Hall was the Republican's Saturday night meeting on March 18, 1871. They gathered to nominate party members to run for various local offices. Between 300 and 400 crowded their way into the small second-story courtroom to either be nominated or to vote for their favorite candidate.

Sheriff Cozens never anticipated such high floor loading when he added the second floor. During the meeting, 250 men stood in a small 24 by 30 foot area near the bench. This was simply too much weight, and both floor joists snapped at once without warning sending the Republican Party from the second floor to the first floor. Fortunately for their reputation, none of the Republicans ended up dropping into the jail since this part of the floor held up.

The furniture fell in on top of the men, and one of the oil lamps started a fire which could have proved fatal. Using coats and hats, the Republicans quickly smothered the fire. They then scurried to get out. Some climbed up the remains of the floor to escape through second story windows. Others used a more direct route through ground story windows with no serious injuries. The floor joists were later replaced by massive 8 by 8 timbers supported by equally massive posts. Eventually, Cozens sold the facilities at Washington Hall to Gilpin County.

Washington Hall, which may be the oldest structure in Central City, was built in the early 1860s and owned by Sheriff William Cozens. It contained the county jail, recorder's office, county offices, and courtroom. Gilpin County leased the structure from Cozens and also paid him as sheriff. *(Kenneth Jessen 010D1)*

Professor Hill Introduces Modern Smelting

The progression of mining in Colorado began with placer mining, where gold pans and sluice boxes were used, and later progressed to hydraulic mining, where vast amounts of gold-bearing gravel were washed down at once. In certain areas, large gold dredges appeared and operated for decades.

Oxidized gold ore, found in decomposed quartz near the surface, required only simple mechanical milling techniques. Such mills were often referred to as quartz mills. The placer deposits in the gravel along Clear Creek were eventually exhausted, and as lode mines got deeper, the naturally oxidized ore ran out. The ore was just as rich, but became complex to treat. Primitive milling techniques were no longer adequate.

For the Central City and Black Hawk area, when the sulfides containing gold were encountered, the mines began to close. For this type of ore, the area's stamp mills, using amalgamation, could only recover 5% of the gold. The ore deep in the earth was "refractory," meaning that heat was required to first drive off the sulphur after which the ore was melted in the smelting process. Nathaniel P. Hill, chemistry professor at Brown University in Providence, Rhode Island, was only thirty-two when he visited the mines of Colorado in 1864. His original purpose was as a consultant on mineral deposits in the southern part of the state. By 1865, he was involved in a couple of mining investments and was hired by James Lyon to help evaluate the use of smelting in the Black Hawk area.

James Lyon fired up his Black Hawk smelter in 1866 with some ore to test the process, but it seemed like little gold was recovered and Lyon gave up. What Lyon didn't know was that the furnace was poorly built, and the molten metal leaked out into the soil.

Hill, in the mean time, returned to Rhode Island to do some research into smelting techniques. He invested in a trip across the Atlantic to Swansea, Wales to observe the smelting of ore similar to that found in Gilpin County. Hill's next step was to purchase seventy tons of high-grade ore from the Bobtail Lode between Black Hawk and Central City and have it shipped at great expense to Wales.

Sustained heat, in a process called roasting, was used to drive off the sulphur. This was followed by melting the ore in a furnace along with a flux and reducing agent. The reducing agent converted the metallic oxides into pure metal. The waste rock, lighter than the metals, floated to the surface as slag and could be skimmed off. Piles of black slag can still be seen along Colorado 119 leading into Black Hawk. The molten metal, called matte, could be drawn from the bottom of the furnace and cast into ingots. The matte was composed of copper, gold and silver, which were separated later during the refining process.

Since the experiment was a complete success, Professor Hill obtained the financial backing to build a Swansea-style smelter in

Black Hawk. Avoiding past mistakes, Hill hired experienced brick masons from Wales to construct the furnaces. His company, the Boston & Colorado Smelting Company, began operating in June, 1867, and was an immediate success in precious metal recovery. Richard Pearce was hired by Hill to act as the metallurgist.

News spread quickly of Hill's new smelter and the mines began to reopen. For his family, Hill constructed a beautiful home near the mouth of Chase Gulch which remains standing today.

After the smelter's first full year of operation in 1868, the area's gold production was over thirty million dollars at today's gold prices. Gold production continued to climb, and in 1871, Gilpin County produced a record 156,000 ounces of gold valued at nearly sixty million dollars.

The biggest problem Hill and other smelter operators faced was the short supply of fuel. As clearly illustrated in historic photographs, the hills around Black Hawk and Central City had been stripped of all timber and cord wood had to be hauled in from other locations.

Hill's smelter was followed by many others creating an environmental disaster in the narrow Clear Creek Canyon. Hill discovered that the local ore needed to be roasted for six weeks in open air to drive off the sulfur. The byproduct was sulfur dioxide which was released into the air. This toxic gas was released into the atmosphere, where when mixed with rain, it formed a mild solution of sulfuric acid. At times, the sulphur dioxide would probably reach dangerous levels in Black Hawk.

The narrow gauge

An engraving of Nathaniel P. Hill *(from "The City of Denver" by Edward Roberts)*

Colorado Central Railroad completed its line from Golden to Black Hawk in 1872, and coal could now be transported from coal fields near Boulder. It was still expensive, however, and in 1878, Hill decided to build a new smelter just outside of Denver. The place was called Argo, and there was plenty of room for expansion. It was cheaper to transport ore down from the mountains than to haul coal up to the mines. The Argo opened in 1879, and at the same time, Hill closed his Black Hawk smelter. Ore was now hauled from many other mining locations down to Argo.

There is little doubt that without the contributions of Professor Hill, mining might have died during the late 1860s in Gilpin County. Other experts would have eventually come along to treat the sulfide ore, but it was Hill that kept the economy rolling.

Though not known for his political ambitions, Professor Hill ran for a position in the United States Senate in 1879 and was elected to office. He also became the owner of the *Denver Republican.*

Gilpin County's Gold Tram

The only commercial two-foot gauge railroad to operate in Colorado was the Gilpin Gold Tram. It served over fifty mines in and around Central City. In all, this diminutive railroad reached a total length of 26 miles with over a dozen switch-backs used to gain altitude. The zig-zag tram wound its way around the hills from Black Hawk, up Chase Gulch, around Winnebago Hill, over to Quartz Hill, past Russell Gulch and up to the Banta Mill which is located above today's Miner's Mesa parking lot.

The grade of the old tram is easy to spot on the north side of Central City high above the town. It crosses Eureka Street above town and is distinguished by the fine rock wall running across Winnebago Hill just above Central City's residential area. The railroad used small locomotives called Shays to climb steep 6% grades and negotiate tight curves, some with a radius of only sixty feet.

On its uphill runs, the Gilpin Gold Tram hauled coal and

supplies to the mines, as well as an occasional miner or two. Coming back down grade, it brought untreated ore to the nearly two-dozen mills in Black Hawk. Each ore car was capable of handling only three-quarters of a ton. For comparison, modern standard gauge hopper cars have a 100 ton capacity.

Construction on the Gilpin Gold Tram began in 1887. After operating successfully for thirty years, the line was scrapped during the decline in mining activity in the Central City area.

This photograph was taken around 1890 at the Gilpin Gold Tram's engine house north of Black Hawk on the North Fork of Clear Creek. *(Denver Public Library, Western History Department F8008B)*

Arthur Chapman, *The Story of Colorado*, Rand McNally & Company, New York, 1924, pp. 95-102.

George B. Thomas, *The Old Sheriff*, Margent Press, New York, 1937, pp. 8-12.

Keith Pashivia, "The Gilpin Line - Snapshots in Time," *Narrow Gauge and Short Line Gazette*, (Part 1) March/April pp. 44-49 and (Part 2) May/June, pp. 38-42.

Liston E. Lyendecker, "Washington Hall," *CSU History Bulletin No. 1.*

Mallory Hope Ferrell, *The Gilpin Gold Tram*, Pruett Publishing Company, Boulder, Colorado, 1970.

Sandra F. Pritchard, *Men, Mining & Machines*, Summit Historical Society, Breckenridge, Colorado, 1996, pp. 40-42.

Terry Cox, *Inside the Mountains*, Pruett Publishing Company, Boulder, Colorado, 1989, pp. 7-11, 22-29.

AMERICAN CITY

- *Gilpin County, Elk Creek drainage*
- *Access to within site of structures four-wheel drive vehicle, site on private property*
- *Town did not have a post office; several original structures remain*

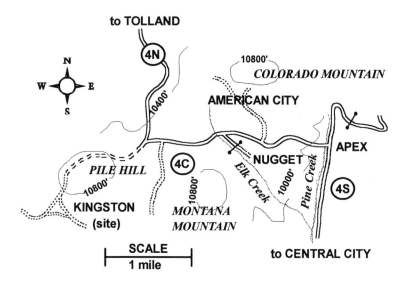

American City is located on a steep side road running north from the Elk Park road.

A merican City was founded during the 1890s in the Pine Creek Mining District, in which the towns of Nugget, Kingston and Apex are also located. This was three decades after the boom years when towns such as Central City, Nevadaville and Black Hawk were founded. The Boston-Occidental Mine and Mill Company dominated American City and may have owned the site. The structures in American City included the Hotel Del Monte, a school and a number of cabins. Muriel Sibell Wolle also mentioned a place called the St. Elmo Hotel. A large mill, called the Mascot, was constructed near the town.

High above Central City and about eight miles to the northwest is the old mining town of American City. At one time, a mill stood and hotel stood at the site. Today, the area is fenced off and posted. American City was the site for a 1911 Tom Mix silent film. *(Kenneth Jessen 015B8)*

In 1911, American City was selected for a Tom Mix silent film, one of many westerns Mix made during his life. His leading lady was Myrtle Stedman whose brother worked as a saloon keeper in Nevadaville. Mix was a legend in his own time and was a champion horseman, bronco buster and fancy trick rider. He was best remembered for his pioneering efforts in the early days of silent film westerns. American City was selected by the film company for its scenic location in a high saddle over looking the Indian Peaks.

The site is located north of the Kingston Road which runs east and west between Apex and Elk Park. The road to American City takes off half way between these points and is steep, rough and requires high ground clearance. The buildings at American City can be viewed from outside the posted fence line, but access to the site is restricted.

Gilpin County Observer, October 10, 1911, "American City, talking Motion Pictures"

Muriel Sibell Wolle, *Stampede to Timberline*, Sage Books, Chicago, 1949, 1974, p. 37.

Perry Eberhart, *Guide to the Colorado Ghost Towns and Mining Camps*, Sage Books, Chicago, 1959, p. 64.

Robert L. Brown, *Jeep Trails to Colorado Ghost Towns*, Caxton Printers, Caldwell, Idaho, 1973, pp. 39-41.

APEX
Bloomed Late

- *Gilpin County, Pine Creek drainage*
- *Accessible via graded dirt road*
- *Town had a post office; a number of original structures restored for seasonal use*

Apex today only has a fraction of the number of structures it once had as evidenced by this historic photograph. Note the stores lining the main street and a second, parallel side street. *(Colorado Historical Society F4205)*

The first town in Colorado to be named Apex lies below an earthen fill at Heritage Square shopping area in the foothills near Golden. The second town to have this same name is located northwest of Central City. This second Apex was founded in 1891,

240

three decades after Central City, Black Hawk and Nevadaville, and grew out of the need for a satellite town close to the mines.

Apex was never very large, but it did have two hotels, a Miners Hall and the Palace Dance Hall. At one time, the town also had several churches and a school. Its peak population was estimated at 1,000, a number which was reached in about 1896. Its newspaper was called *The Apex Pine Cone.* Newspapers written at the time boasted that Apex had one hundred businesses along its main street. The number of foundations which can be found today suggest closer to two dozen businesses.

The Mackey was the best mine, and was named for its original owner, Dick Mackey. The property was later leased by a man named Mountz, who formed a partnership. After the removal of $30,000 in gold ore, his partner stole the money leaving Mountz with just $400 to keep the mine operating. This might not seem like much money, but Mountz worked the mine alone. He just knew the mother lode was somewhere inside the mountain. Optimistically, he drove a cross-cut to try to reach that elusive vein of rich gold ore. He took his tunnel ninety feet farther and gave up. He was out of money and in his anger and frustration, he placed all of the remaining dynamite at the end of the tunnel, lit the fuse and went home.

When he returned, the explosion uncovered what he had been seeking all long...rich gold ore. He telephoned Denver and on credit, ordered a thousand sacks for the ore and also ordered a wagon from a Central City livery stable. The assay results showed that the mine could produce ore valued at $1,800 a ton. Mountz paid his bills and had nothing to worry about after that. Eventually, a mill was constructed at the site.

To get to Apex from Black Hawk, follow Colorado 119 north past Chase Gulch. There is a graded dirt road, called Apex Road, which follows the North Fork of Clear Creek then swings to the right and heads due north up Pine Creek to Apex. There are a number of modern homes along this road. Midway through the town of Apex, which has a few seasonal residents, the Kingston

Road heads west and leads past the turn off to American City, past
Nugget, through Elk Park and eventually to Tolland.

 *For a map showing the location of Apex, see "American City."*

The town of Apex is not quite a ghost. It was established during the 1890s, three
decades after other Gilpin County mining towns such as Central City and Black Hawk.
Relative to the town's original size, there is not much left of Apex except for this old store
and several cabins which are occupied seasonally. *(Kenneth Jessen 015B5)*

Muriel Sibell Wolle, *Stampede to Timberline*, Sage Books, Chicago, 1949, 1974, pp. 34-36.

BALTIMORE

Had An Opera House

- *Gilpin County, Coal Creek drainage*
- *Private property; access to site restricted*
- *Town had a post office; several standing structures remain*

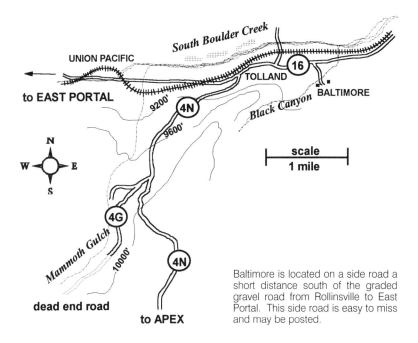

Baltimore is located on a side road a short distance south of the graded gravel road from Rollinsville to East Portal. This side road is easy to miss and may be posted.

By road, Baltimore is located about a mile east of Tolland, just off the graded dirt road between Rollinsville and the East Portal of the Moffat tunnel. The town site is in a densely wooded area and has several cabins and the remains of the town hall. It is private property, and a couple of the cabins have been restored for seasonal use.

There is very little history on Baltimore. Despite its remote location, it had an opera house that was still standing when Muriel Sibell Wolle visited the site in 1935. There was also the Baltimore Club, a saloon. Its bar was moved to Central City after the saloon closed. Wolle found that when she returned in 1943, many of the cabins were no longer abandoned and had been converted into summer homes. The town also had a two-story hotel which had collapsed by the late 1960s when Robert Brown visited the site.

The Baltimore post office was opened for a few months in 1896 then opened again in 1898. It closed in 1904, and mail delivery was moved to Tolland.

This is the Baltimore "City Hall" which sits in a beautiful meadow surrounded by a dense forest. Baltimore is located off the main road to Tolland, and at one time, had its own opera house. *(Kenneth Jessen 010D3)*

Muriel Sibell Wolle, *Stampede to Timberline*, Sage Books, Chicago, 1949, 1974, pp. 37-38.

Robert L. Brown, *Jeep Trails to Colorado Ghost Towns*, Caxton Printers, Caldwell, Idaho, 1973, pp. 57-59.

William H. Bauer, James L. Ozment, John H. Willard, *Colorado Post Offices*, Colorado Railroad Museum, Golden, Colorado, 1990, p. 16.

BLACK HAWK

County's Smelter Town

- *Gilpin County, North Fork of Clear Creek drainage*
- *Access via paved roads*
- *Town has a post office; many original structures remain*

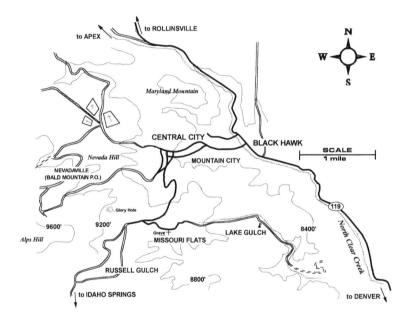

Black Hawk is situated east of Central City, but is located along North Clear Creek. The stream provided a steady supply of water critical for milling the gold ore recovered from the mines in the surrounding area.

An early photograph of Black Hawk looking west up Gregory Street with the Colorado Central's trestle crossing over the business district. *(Colorado Historical Society F40753)*

Black Hawk, Central City, Mountain City, Nevadaville and other mining towns in the general area owe their existence to John H. Gregory's gold discovery on May 6, 1859. The discovery was made at the western boundary of Black Hawk. Central City evolved into a town with a business district, hotels, saloons and a residential area. Black Hawk, with its abundant supply of water from the North Fork of Clear Creek, evolved into a mill town for processing the ore from the numerous area mines.

Black Hawk got its name from an early mining company. The owners named their quartz mill "Black Hawk" for a famous Indian Chief. The mill was constructed in 1860 and was located in the town's center. Black Hawk got its post office under the name of "Black Hawk Point" in December, 1862, and in 1871, the name was simplified to "Black Hawk." In 1895, the name was changed again to "Blackhawk," and in 1950, it was changed back to "Black Hawk."

In 1887, a two-foot gauge railroad, called the Gilpin Gold Tram, was constructed starting on the north end of Black Hawk. Its grade ran around the hillside to the mouth of Chase Gulch then up the north side of the gulch, and around Winnebago Hill. It crossed Eureka Street well above Central City's business district and continued on to Russell Gulch. At its peak, the railroad reached a length of 26 miles. For more details, see "Gilpin County's Gold Tram" located in the introduction.

When Bayard Taylor visited Black Hawk in 1866, he observed that it was busy and noisy with the constant thump of the stamp mills. Gregory Street, the main thoroughfare, was rough, winding and dusty. It was lined with wooden buildings including hotels, saloons, bakeries, a few homes and even a brewery. The stream from Gregory Gulch was muddy and polluted with a mixture of waste water from the mines and human waste. Historian Frank Hall made a specific reference to this situation, "I have a lively remembrance of its original charm. Clear Creek had not then been polluted by the sewage from a score of mills and sluices, streams of offal that flow from numberless habitations. Its waters were almost transparent, and every pebble in its depths could be seen...When the deluge of immigration came in 1865-66, on its mission to redeem the wilderness, the greater part of its splendor disappeared..." Historic photographs also reveal extreme air pollution from the numerous smelters and mills which used either coal or cord wood as fuel.

After the placer gold and decomposed quartz ore was exhausted, Black Hawk and the surrounding towns fell into a slump during the late 1860s. As the mines got deeper, complex

The famous Lace House in Black Hawk, a National Historic Landmark, was constructed in 1863 by Lucien K. Smith, tollgate keeper for the toll road to Empire. In 1997, prompted by the need for more casino parking, the Lace House was almost moved. A court decision prevented its relocation. *(Kenneth Jessen 013B6)*

sulfide ores were encountered which could not be milled by the primitive stamps. The town was on the verge of being abandoned. The independent miner could no longer make a living, and the mining industry was about to enter into the world of big business.

What was needed was a smelting process where the ore was first heated to drive off the sulfur followed by smelting. It was Professor Nathaniel P. Hill who brought this technology to Black Hawk in the form of a successful smelter, opened in January, 1868. Hill's Boston & Colorado Smelting Company was responsible for allowing many of the area's mines to reopen. See "Professor Hill Introduces Modern Smelting" in the introduction to this area.

The town of Black Hawk was incorporated in March, 1864 and by the early 1870s, reached a population of 2,000. It had the state's first cemetery and the district's first jail. The school, which remains standing today, was built in 1870 for $15,000, a generous sum in those days. It eventually became a grade school and students would graduate to the high school in Central City. The enrollment was nearly 400 students.

In 1877, Black Hawk's smelters were processing half of all the ore mined in Gilpin County. The old stamp mills, now rendered useless, were converted into concentrators. Their purpose was to separate the worthless rock from valuable ore-producing concentrates which were sent to the smelters to produce a copper, gold, and silver matte.

The Colorado Central, under the leadership of W. A. H. Loveland, built its narrow gauge line from Golden through Clear Creek Canyon to Black Hawk. It reached the town in 1872 and used the abandoned Fitz-John Porter's mill as a depot. The mill was a large structure located along the North Fork of Clear Creek, and the railroad converted it into the West's most unusual depot by adding large doors at either end. Tracks were laid all the way through so that entire trains could be brought indoors for the comfort of the passengers and for those who handled the freight. The structure was abandoned when the Colorado Central extended its line to Central City in 1878. A new but conventional depot

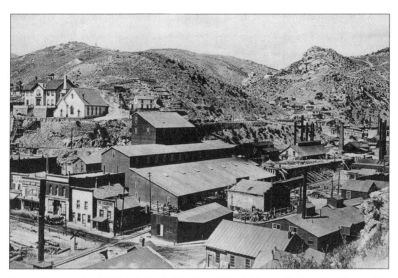

Local photographer H. H. Lake took this view of Black Hawk with its mills. The road to Central City begins off to the left in front of the business district. A casino now occupies the site where the large mill (center of the photo) was located. The school and church up on the hill to the left remain standing today. *(Colorado Historical Society F13793)*

was built to the south across from the Gilpin Hotel. By 1937, the roof of the original depot had collapsed along with two of its walls. Nothing remains today of either depot.

The distance to Central City was only a little over a mile, but the increase in elevation was 500 feet. This forced the Colorado Central to resort to the use of switchbacks. The line was extended past Black Hawk up Clear Creek a short distance to the first switchback. The leg of the switchback came back through Black Hawk, but at a slightly higher elevation. To get to the opposite side of the gulch, the railroad constructed a trestle right over Black Hawk's business district along Gregory Street. At the end of this leg, trains reversed directions once again at a switch located near the Miner's Mesa access road. This arrangement produced three levels of track, one coming up Clear Creek Canyon into Black Hawk, one across the trestle and along the hillside, and a third on the upper leg to Central City.

After 1878, when Professor Hill constructed a new smelter at

Argo just outside of Denver, concentrates were loaded into rail cars in Black Hawk for the trip down the canyon. The Boston & Colorado Smelter in Black Hawk was closed.

During the early 1870s, Black Hawk's population peaked then went into a steady decline as the ore was depleted. Mills closed and homes were abandoned. By 1916, only one mill remained in operation. By 1925, only 200 people lived in what was fast becoming a ghost town. During the Great Depression, there was a momentary revival of placer mining in the area. As World War II approached, many of the homes were razed for firewood. Almost all of the area's mills were dismantled and the machinery removed for scrap metal.

Located at the intersection of two narrow canyons, Black Hawk was prone to flooding. During the 1860s, the hillsides were stripped of their timber, and no vegetation was left to hold back the runoff from severe summer storms. It was used for a multitude of purposes including homes, mine structures, timbers, railroad ties and cord wood to fuel the many boilers at area mines and smelters. The need for space in Black Hawk became so severe that Clear Creek was confined to a narrow covered flume. The creek in Gregory Gulch was also confined to a flume. At various times, floodwaters proved too great for the capacity of these flumes, and raging torrents swept

This is a portion of the original Polar Star Mill, constructed in 1867. Practically every square inch of the bottom land on Colorado 119 through Black Hawk was covered with mills or railroad tracks. The Polar Star had rail service from both the three-foot gauge Colorado Central and the two-foot gauge Gilpin Gold Tram. *(Kenneth Jessen 090A10)*

through Black Hawk's business district.

In August, 1881, Joe Gerrich was caught in a flash flood at the Buell mine-mill complex between Central City and Black Hawk. The force of the water pinned poor Joe against debris which had piled up at the mouth of the flume, and he drowned within sight of horrified spectators. His body was swept down to Black Hawk where it was found later under a pile of debris.

In Black Hawk, the water reached above the lower window level and washed through many structures, sweeping away furniture. All of the cellars along Gregory Street were flooded and filled with sand. Merchants lost a substantial amount of their inventory. The tracks of the Colorado Central were buried under ten feet of silt.

Another flood in 1910 came straight down Gregory Street and literally buried the street itself for a depth of several feet. A path was cleared, and the railroad laid tracks up the street. A string of flat cars was brought in, and the debris was shoveled directly onto the cars for disposal.

In 1914, disaster struck Black Hawk again. A violent thunder storm struck towards the end of July and the entrance to the flume along Gregory Street quickly became clogged. Water swept over the top of the flume and washed away the kitchen of one home and the bedroom of another. Again the street through Black Hawk was buried in mud and debris.

Once the vegetation grew back on the hillsides and the covered flume was removed, little flooding has occurred.

On October 1, 1991, small stakes gambling began in Black Hawk and Central City. The once partially abandoned town became a lively place, but this time it was the sound of slot machines and not stamp mills which filled the air. New buildings constructed on vacant lots intermingled with the town's historic structures. An attempt was made to blend them in architecturally, but their new brick betrays them as modern structures. Gregory Street is once again choked with traffic and pedestrians, but the original character of this old mining town has changed.

Gregory Lode.   Bobtail Mill.

This accurate engraving of Black Hawk shows the mill portion of town in the foreground, the business district as well as its residential housing. *(Colorado, its Gold and Silver Mines by Frank Fossett, 1879)*

Black Hawk is well worth visiting, however, since many of the original Victorian homes still stand above the town and up Chase Gulch. The old school dominates the area above Gregory Street and the Polar Star Mill still stands at Colorado 119 and Chase Street. The grade of the Gilpin Gold Tram is now an informal hiking trail up Chase Gulch.

Cornelius W. Hauck, *Narrow Gauge to Central and Silver Plume*, Colorado Railroad Museum, Golden, Colorado, 1972, pp. 34, 144.

Frank Hall, *History of Colorado*, Vol. III. The Blakely Printing Company, Chicago, 1895, p. 320.

"Miner Dies," *Rocky Mountain News*, August 9, 1881.

Minnie B. Morgan, *Historical Souvenir of Central City*, Colorado, 1941 , pp. 36-37.

Robert L. Brown, *Central City and Gilpin County*, Caxton Printers, Ltd., Caldwell, Idaho, 1994, pp. 74-85.

Sarah J. Pearce and Christine Pfuff, *Guide to Historic Central City and Black Hawk*, Cordillera Press, Evergreen, Colorado, 1987, pp. 7-22.

"Senator Nathaniel P. Hill," *Harpers Weekly*, November 1, 1879.

"Streets Running Rivers," *Central City Register-Call*, July 31, 1914.

Tivis Wilkins, *Colorado Railroads*, Pruett Publishing Company, Boulder, Colorado, 1974, p. 23.

William H. Bauer, James L. Ozment, John H. Willard, *Colorado Post Offices*, Colorado Railroad Museum, Golden, Colorado, 1990, p. 21.

BORTONSBURG

- *Gilpin County, Illinois Gulch drainage*
- *Exact location unknown*

Among the most obscure mining camps in the Central City area was Bortonsburg. It was located near the Glory Hole at the head of Illinois Gulch. It was founded in 1861 by Colonel Bortons. By the 1940s, only foundations remained. It does not show up on topographic maps even as far back as the 1940s and must have been short-lived.

Perry Eberhart, *Guide to the Colorado Ghost Towns and Mining Camps*, Sage Books, Chicago, 1959, p. 25.
Robert L. Brown, *Central City and Gilpin County*, Caxton Printers, Ltd., Caldwell, Idaho, 1994, p. 68.

CENTRAL CITY

- *Gilpin County, Gregory Gulch drainage*
- *Accessible via paved road*
- *Town has a post office; many original standing structures; fully occupied*

In this 1864 view of Central City, the outhouses, which lined Gregory Gulch, are evident behind each building. The human waste was mixed with animal waste and contamination from mining. These pollutants flowed downstream to Black Hawk. All of these structures in Central City's business district were destroyed in 1874 by fire. *(Colorado Historical Society F2075)*

Prospectors started arriving by the thousands as word got out about the fabulous gold ore in Gregory Gulch. In June, 1859, Horace Greeley paid "Gregory Diggings" a visit and told of a hundred or so log cabins, while most miners lived in tents. Gregory Diggings was soon called Mountain City.

The Gregory Mining District was organized to bring law to the claims and to lay some ground rules for the types of claims that could be held. Punishment for various crimes was also defined and varied from a simple fine, to whipping, and even hanging. A circuit judge came by periodically to try cases.

Some historians say that the name Central City was first suggested by William Newton Byers, founder and publisher of the

The first Central City classes were held on the first floor of the gambling hall/saloon. The town needed something better for its children, and voted in favor of a bond issue to finance this school building. Completed in 1870, it is the second oldest permanent school in Colorado. *(Kenneth Jessen 012D12)*

Rocky Mountain News. The name reflected its central location near John H. Gregory's original gold discovery made on May 6, 1859. Other historians, such as Frank Hall in his *History of Colorado*, relate that in 1859, Jesse Trotter opened a miner's supply store he named the Central City Store. It located where Central City's Main and Lawrence streets join. Trotter persuaded his customers to change their mailing address from Mountain City to Central City.

Although the population began to rise during 1859 and 1860, Central City came into its own in 1861 when the Territory of Colorado was formed. With it, Gilpin County was defined and Central City became the county seat. In 1866, Central City was platted by a local engineer, George Hill, and consisted of 629 acres. When the Civil War began, the growth of Central City stagnated as many men left to join either the Union Army or the Confederate Army.

In 1865, Samuel Bowles visited the Central City area and commented that six or seven thousand were crowded into the narrow canyon between Black Hawk and Nevadaville including

Central City. As for the towns, he commented, "These (towns) are most uncomfortably squeezed into little narrow ravines, and stuck into the hill-side, on streets the narrowest and most tortuous that I ever saw in America..." He then went on to paint a more optimistic picture, "But there these towns are thriving, orderly, peaceable, busy, supporting two of them each its daily papers, with churches and schools..." Frank Hall described Central City as rows of cheap and ugly frame buildings held up on stilts along densely populated ravines. He went on to note that these structures extended up and down Gregory Gulch from Black Hawk to Nevadaville.

Violence was not as common in Colorado mining towns as one might suspect given the rough character of the miners who populated these outposts. But every now and then, an incident would occur such as the one involving George Harrison. He was a resident of Central City, and in 1862, constructed a theater which he named the National Theater. Soon after its completion, Harrison got into a quarrel with a young prize fighter named Charley Switz. Switz operated an entertainment business of a little different sort. It was a saloon which included variety shows, often a front for prostitution.

After a vicious quarrel between Switz and Harrison, both men swore that their next encounter would be settled with firearms. George Harrison went on a long trip back East to bring in a troupe of actors for his theater. After quite a while, Harrison returned with his troupe. They came up Gregory Street from Black Hawk by stage coach. Charley Switz, upon hearing of their impending arrival, put a brace of revolvers in the belt of his pants. He positioned himself in a saloon next to Harrison's National Theater. A crowd gathered to witness the shootout.

After the stage coach pulled up in front of the theater, Switz watched as the passengers got off. Harrison was not among them. Harrison apparently was aware that he was going into an ambush and slipped off the stage below Central City. He made his way on foot to a back door of his theater and got his shotgun. He also took a loaded revolver with him just in case. Harrison made his way quietly onto a balcony, which ran across the second story of the theater. He was able to see the crowd in the street below, but more important, he spotted Charley Switz with his guns in his belt. When Harrison had a clear view, he fired both barrels at Switz followed by multiple shots from his revolver. Harrison watched Switz fall dead in the street as blood quickly flowed onto the pavement from the multiple gunshot wounds. Harrison then turned and went back into the theater to go about his business of getting ready for opening night.

The victim was taken into his own saloon, stripped, washed and laid out. Only a sheet covered the corpse. Those that wanted to pay their last respects could. A pair of concentric holes were visible in the body from the blasts from Harrison's shotgun.

Harrison was arrested, but not placed in jail. He was tried for the murder of Charley Switz, but not convicted of the crime. Harrison opened his theater with a series of plays, and at the end of the season left for the mountains, never to be seen again in

This photograph was taken during Central City's rebuilding period following the 1874 fire, which leveled most of the business district. Many of these structures still stand today, including the church in the left center and the school to its right. *(Colorado Historical Society L565)*

Eureka Street in Central City looks very much the same today as it did in 1879 when this engraving was published. *(Colorado, its Gold and Silver Mines by Frank Fossett)*

Central City.

The ups and downs of gold mining were clearly illustrated just two years later, when another journalist commented on the numerous idle mills and rusting machinery at Central City. As with other towns in the Gilpin County area, the mining and smelting processes evolved. By the mid-1870s, the population of Central City stabilized at about 3,000.

Much of the original Central City was burned down in a terrible fire, which began one May morning in 1874. It started in a Chinese "washee house" near the corner of Spring and Gregory streets, in what was called the Chinese Quarter. This fire would redefine Central City, and many of the unsightly shanties randomly distributed on either side of Gregory Gulch near various claims would be incinerated. No wind was blowing that day, and the fire burned for twenty minutes unchecked before it broke through to adjoining buildings.

A rather bigoted account of the fire in the *Central City Register* reported that, "From the best information obtainable, it appears tolerably certain that the Asiatic were engaged with their women in some sort of heathen worship, or celebration of rites known only to themselves..."

The fire company did its best to stop the spread of the fire, but fighting the blaze directly was out of the question. The best that could be done was to destroy the buildings in the fire's path. As the intensity built, the fire leaped from roof to roof. So intense was the heat, that row after row of frame structures were consumed in minutes. As put by a reporter, "The hell of the flames tore madly down the street consuming with the velocity of a whirlwind all that had been left to consume..." Then the fire reached the storm stage where it created its own superheated wind. Thousands fought the blaze to no avail.

Lin Sou, the leader of the Central City Chinese settlement, marched directly to the offices of the *Central City Register* and denied that the Asiatic occupants of the house, where the fire originated, were engaged in any so-called religious ceremony. He told the newspaper when the occupants were in the process of making breakfast, a flue fire broke out in the attic above them. Lin Sou complained that the Chinese were frequently blamed for anything that went wrong in a town.

The fire destroyed 150 structures with an estimated value of $500,000 as measured in the currency of the day. Today, this would amount to a loss of well over five million dollars.

It took eight days before the safe at a mercantile business was cool enough to open. Inside the store records were charred beyond recognition. The fire was so hot that glass light fixtures on the exterior of the Teller House melted.

The fire was turned into a golden opportunity for Central City. The town was to be rebuilt, but first, its roads were widened, straightened and graded. The frame buildings were replaced with substantial structures built of brick or stone. A distinct business district emerged along its main streets, and the homes were located up above the town in an orderly residential area. Many of these buildings remain standing today. Central City learned a lesson and installed a fire protection system including a water supply for hydrants. Domestic water, however, had to be purchased privately.

Central City was well connected to the outside world with two daily stage coach services, one from Denver and the other from Georgetown. The town also had three banks and its own public school attended by over 300 students. An additional 100 students attended a parochial school.

The *Central City Register* began publication as a weekly in 1862, and in 1876, the newspaper became a daily. The town also had six churches and three banks. An opera house opened in 1878.

Central City was a fairly well-rounded town with a wide variety of items carried by local merchants. The Central City Brewery and Boarding House might have been fun to stay at, but not especially restful! It is instructional to look at a list of the Central City businesses in 1876:

5 boots & shoe stores	*4 attorneys*
2 stage companies	*2 watchmakers & jewelry stores*
2 house & sign painters	*4 contractors, builders*
2 drug and mill chemical stores	*3 grocery stores*
2 civil and mining engineers	*1 fire insurance company*
3 physicians	*3 hotels*
1 dentist	*2 bakeries*
1 book and stationery store	*1 clothing store*
1 furniture store	*1 assay office*
1 bank	*1 livery stable*
3 hardware and lumber stores	

and then there was

Joseph Tishler's California Fruit Store
J. Collier - Photographer
N.A. Sears - ice
Wilson Brothers - dairymen
W. C. Hendricks - sewing machines, pianos, organs
Central City Brewery and Boarding House
J. R. Morgan - Carriage and Wagon Manufacturing

Each building has a history, but one of the most impressive structures is the St. James Methodist Church located on Eureka Street opposite the Central City Opera House. Construction on this handsome stone structure started in 1864, but was not completed until 1872. The *Rocky Mountain News* reported that it cost $30,000.

One of the most impressive structures in Central City is the St. James Methodist Church. Construction started in 1864 and was completed in 1872. *(Kenneth Jessen 010D2)*

The Methodists organized in July, 1859 under the guidance of Rev. W. H. Goode, making them among the first religious groups in Gregory Gulch. The church got off to a good start with 35 members. In 1860, a hand-hewed log church was constructed, but was destroyed by a fire the following year. The congregation began meeting in various places including Washington Hall, Aunt Clara Brown's home, and the old City Hall. Some meetings were even out doors.

Although the Methodists began raising money in 1864 for a new church, construction delays did not allow the St. James Methodist Church to open until 1872.

Of great historic importance is the massive Central City Opera House, still active in presenting a variety of fine programs. The success of *The Bohemian Girl* in the old Belvidere Theater in 1877 led to the formation of the Gilpin County Opera House Association, with its primary objective to build a suitable opera house for major stage productions. It took just a year to raise the money and the building was completed in 1878. Success did not last long and the structure was sold to the county for use as a courthouse. As put by H. William Axford, biographer for the life of Peter McFarlane, "This move to turn Gregory Gulch's cultural monument into a habitat for local politicians produced a strong wave of protests." Soon the Central City Opera House was the property of a fifty-nine member opera house association. Peter McFarlane eventually took its management and made extensive repairs using his own money. He eventually purchased the structure and continued to operate it for the cultural benefit of the public for twenty-eight years.

Following World War II, there was a long period of stagnation for Central City. The town tried to provide entertainment in

The massive stone Central City Opera House, completed in 1878, is still active in presenting a variety of fine programs. *(Kenneth Jessen 012D10)*

its saloons and the opera house. Only on summer weekends, however, were places like the Gilded Garter and the Silver Slipper lively. But it wasn't until casino-style gaming came to Central City on October 1, 1991 that the town boomed once more. A great deal of new construction, using an architectural style in keeping with existing buildings, filled many of the vacant city blocks. Many of the

The Peter McFarlane home, on Eureka Street, was constructed in 1873. The McFarlanes owned the Central City Opera house for nearly thirty years, presenting a fine variety of programs. McFarlane served as the town's mayor for 1878 to 1879. *(Kenneth Jessen 097C9)*

old Victorian homes were restored. Escalating real estate prices and higher property taxes drove out the majority of old residents, changing the character of the town. New construction has leveled off and so has the gaming industry, but the face of Central City has been changed forever.

For a map showing the location of Central City, see "Black Hawk."

Bayard Taylor, *Colorado*, G. P. Putnam's Sons, New York, 1867.

"Dedication of St. James" *The Daily Central City Register*, June 23, 1868.

Don and Jean Griswold, *Colorado's Century of "Cities"*, Self Published, 1958, pp. 54-60.

Frank Fossett, *Colorado, its Gold and Silver Mines*, C. G. Crawford, New York, 1879, pp. 284-354.

Frank Hall, *History of Colorado*, Vol. III. The Blakely Printing Company, Chicago, 1895, pp. 405-411.

Robert L. Brown, *Central City and Gilpin County*, Caxton Printers, Ltd., Caldwell, Idaho, 1994, pp. 45-57.

Samuel Bowles, *Across the Continent.*

Samuel Cushman and J. P. Waterman, *The Gold Mines of Gilpin County*, Colorado, 1876.

"Terrible Conflagration," *The Central City Register*, May 22, 1874.

"Stone Contract Let" *The Daily Central City Register*, June 28, 1868.

GILPIN

Named For First Governor

- *Gilpin County, Ellsworth Creek drainage*
- *Accessible via graded dirt road; access limited by private property*
- *Town had a post office; at least one original structure standing*

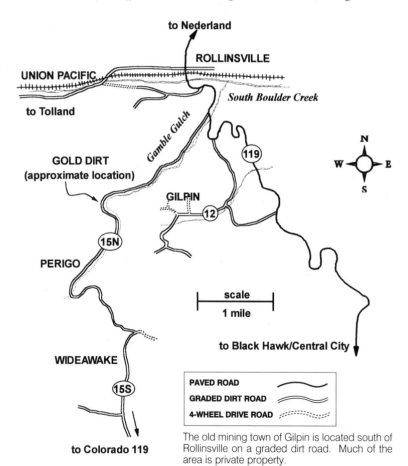

The old mining town of Gilpin is located south of Rollinsville on a graded dirt road. Much of the area is private property.

264

Gilpin has been recently subdivided and is dominated by modern homes. The character of the original town is completely lost in the new construction. Founded during the late 1890s, the town was named for William Gilpin, the first governor of Colorado Territory. A post office, established in 1897, lasted until 1970.

An early photograph speaks volumes about this town. There are approximately twenty structures (excluding outhouses) and a main street with stores. Little written history exists, however.

Ester Rings, resident of Gilpin since 1953, reports that there are a number of original structures in Gilpin. Only her cabin, however, has not had major changes to its exterior.

To reach Gilpin from the north, drive past Rollinsville on

Ester Rings cabin, restored for summer use, is the only cabin in Gilpin which has not had a major renovation to its exterior. *(Kenneth Jessen 106A1)*

Colorado 119 and across the bridge over the tracks of the Union Pacific. When climbing the switchbacks above Rollinsville, the third graded dirt road is marked as RD 12 and leads to Gilpin. Farther south on Colorado 119, RD 13 heads west to Gilpin. At least one original home is still standing along what was the town's main street while other vintage buildings may be hidden in the trees. Private property limits the exploration of Gilpin.

Robert L. Brown, *Central City and Gilpin County*, Caxton Printers, Ltd., Caldwell, Idaho, 1994, p. 96.

GOLD DIRT
Switched Counties

- *Gilpin County, Gamble Gulch drainage*
- *Accessible via graded dirt road*
- *Town did have a post office; no standing structures remain*

Gold Dirt was located a mile below Perigo in Gamble Gulch. Mining began in Gamble Gulch in 1860, and the gulch was soon lined with primitive "arrastras" powered by a draft animal dragging a heavy stone around in a circular motion, quartz mills, sluice boxes, cabins, stores and saloons. Gold Dirt and Perigo were two communities that sprang up at the same time, and the two towns combined had 500 voters. Perigo survived, but little remains of Gold Dirt.

One of the most unusual factors in Gold Dirt's history is that it was originally located in Boulder County, but after a new survey of the area, it fell just inside Gilpin County.

Gold Dirt qualified for its own post office in 1861, but it was closed in 1867. According to Frank Fossett, early historian and author, Gold Dirt's mining history was a story of abandoned and lost mines. The camp fell into decay after the post office closed, and soon the ruined mine and mill buildings were all that were left of what was a once flourishing village. Gradually, Gold Dirt was almost forgotten.

John Q. A. Rollins owned some isolated claims near the town and preferred to let them remain idle until he could get title to adjoining properties. Other mine owners paid little attention to the annual assessment work required by an act of Congress in 1875 to maintain a claim. Rollins seized the opportunity and took over many of these claims which had not been kept current. Over a period of a few years, Rollins gained title to a variety of placer deposits, lodes and timber land until he owned virtually the entire area.

Rollins began mining on a large scale, sinking a shaft 1,000 feet deep on a mine called The Savage. The town of Gold Dirt was revived and its buildings were once again occupied. Other mines were developed, including the Ophir and Virginia, all under Rollins' ownership. Rollins own wealth increased by an estimated quarter of a million dollars in gold from just one of his claims, which measured 33fi feet long. Ore was hauled to a mill Rollins owned located at Rollinsville.

By 1879, Gold Dirt was abandoned again. As the mines got deeper, the only ore found was in the form of sulfides, which were more difficult to mill. Local processing facilities could not handle this type of ore, and the lack of cheap transportation limited the ability to ship the ore to distant smelters.

For a map showing the location of Gold Dirt, see "Gilpin."

Frank Fossett, *Colorado, its Gold and Silver Mines*, C. G. Crawford, New York, 1879, pp. 344-345.
John K. Aldrich, *Ghosts of Gilpin County*, Centennial Graphics, Lakewood, Colorado, 1989, p. 24.

HUGHESVILLE

- *Gilpin County, Missouri Creek drainage*
- *Camp did not have a post office; one standing structure remains*

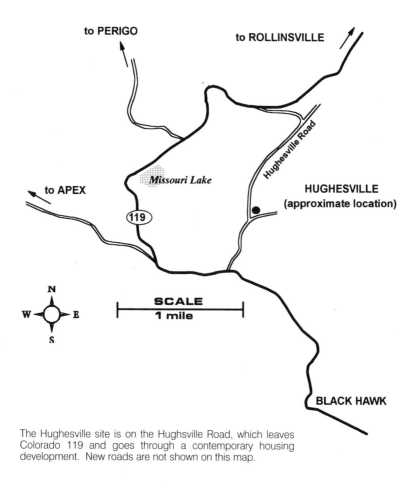

The Hughesville site is on the Hughsville Road, which leaves Colorado 119 and goes through a contemporary housing development. New roads are not shown on this map.

North of Black Hawk between Missouri Creek and the Golden Gate Canyon road was an obscure mining camp called Hughesville. Silver ore was discovered around 1870, and as many as 100 men worked the mines in this area. Hughesville did not have any organized town structure with stores or a post office, but it did have a school.

When Muriel Sibell Wolle visited the site in the 1970s, she found the ruins of a cabin and some prospect holes. Apparently the ore body was not large, and Hughesville lasted but a short time.

The Missouri Lake mountain property development, with its network of new graded dirt roads, makes reaching Hughesville easy by car. Juniper Road leaves Colorado 119 (the Peak-to-Peak Highway) north of Black Hawk and intersects Hughesville Road. By turning right on the Hughesville Road and heading downhill, a collapsed home and a small frame home, which has been restored, will be seen on the right. Farther down the road, the canyon narrows and a mine building sits on the right. The Hughesville Road continues south until it intersects Colorado 119 about two and a half miles from Black Hawk.

This mine building sits along the Hughesville Road near the Hughesville site north of Black Hawk. *(Sonje Jessen SJ110)*

Muriel Sibell Wolle, *Timberline Tailings,* Sage Books, Chicago, 1977, pp. 16-17.

KINGSTON
On Pile Hill

- *Gilpin County, Clear Creek drainage*
- *Accessible on a graded dirt road*
- *Town did not have a post office; no standing structures*

If Kingston was an actual town, it's site is certainly allusive. Muriel Sibell Wolle placed Kingston on the road between Apex and Tolland where it makes a right angle turn. Although there are no signs of cabins at that point, there are two collapsed cabins to the west on the Kingston Peak road (four wheel drive) about a half mile apart, and there area the remains of another cabin on the Elk Park side. John Aldrich places Kingston in and around Pile Hill,

These are the remains of a cabin near Kingston mining camp near Pile Hill. This cabin sits on the Elk Park side with American City off in the distance hidden in the trees. The remains of other structures can be found to the west. *(Kenneth Jessen 107A6)*

which agrees with early maps that define Kingston's location as the cabins spread out in this general area.

There were a number of mines in the area near the head of Mammoth Creek. Of note is the London mine below the Kingston site at the head of Mammoth Basin.

To reach the Kingston site from

the graded dirt road from Rollinsville to Tolland, take the turnoff to the left (south) just west of the homes in Tolland. The road is rough in places as it begins a steady climb across the mountainside. It narrows as it goes across a slide area, but it is graded. In good

Christopher Jessen stands besides the remains of a building at the London Mine at the head of Mammoth Gulch. The mining camp of Kingston sits directly above this mine. *(Kenneth Jessen 106C10)*

weather, it is usually suitable for a car provided caution is used. At the first fork, the road to the right enters Mammoth Gulch. Stay to the left on the road that climbs up above the gulch and heads south. At the top of the hill at timberline, this road turns sharply to the left toward Apex. By heading to the right, this road gets rough and may be more suitable for a four-wheel drive vehicle and is marked as such by a Forest Service sign. It leads to the Kingston site as it hugs the side of the mountain above Mammoth Basin. The site, according to early maps, is where this road intersects with another road coming up from the south. An old cabin sits in a willow thicket near this intersection, but do not expect to see the remains of a town.

The London Mine is up Mammoth Gulch about two miles where a gate across the road denotes private property. This is a rough dirt road and may not be suitable for an automobile. Next to the mine are the remains of a large log structure, and a large boiler sits near the mine entrance.

See "American City" for a map showing the location of the Kingston site.

John K. Aldrich, *Ghosts of Gilpin County*, Centennial Graphics, Lakewood, Colorado, 1989, p. 24.
Muriel Sibell Wolle, *Timberline Tailings*, Sage Books, Chicago, 1977, p. 16.

LAKE GULCH
Site Of First School

- *Gilpin County, Lake Gulch drainage*
- *Accessible via graded dirt road; limited access, private property*
- *Town did not have a post office; remains of school still standing*

The people of Lake Gulch distinguished themselves with Gilpin County's first school near the Clay County mine. The school was built near the head of the gulch and was completed in 1864. Lumber donated from a saw mill located to the south was hauled to the site. Volunteer carpenters constructed the school. Money to pay the teacher was by subscription, and the school year was restricted to the summer months. The original frame school building was replaced in 1905 by a brick structure, the remains of which sit along side of the road in Lake Gulch.

Lake Gulch appears to have been more of a camp distributed along the gulch rather than an actual town with a business district. It was known for the Hermit of Lake Gulch who lived in a crude cabin and never seemed to be home when visitors stopped by. The only way people knew of his existence was when he picked up his supplies.

One day, the hermit made a trip to Idaho Springs during World War II. He slapped down the cash needed to purchase the food items he had selected and was told that he needed ration stamps. The stamps were part of the war effort to conserve certain food. Naturally, the hermit had never head of ration stamps nor did he have any idea of what was going on. The grocer firmly refused to sell him the food items until the hermit produced ration stamps. At that, the hermit pulled out a gun and left with his groceries, probably happy with his persuasive ability.

Jerome Chaffee, a Colorado senator and one of the state's wealthiest men, had mining interests in Lake Gulch. Chaffee owned the Lake House overlooking a small lake at the head of the gulch.

The mines in Lake Gulch were simply not as rich as mines in other parts of Gilpin County. In addition, the camp was in a relatively remote location.

The Clay County Mine, with its modern mine structures, is located alongside of the old school. The site is located directly south of the Miner's Mesa parking lot, which was built for the gaming industry. In addition to the school and the mine, there are the other ruins along the road down the gulch.

It is easy to reach Lake Gulch from the Miner's Mesa parking lot above Black Hawk by turning left just prior to the parking lot entrance structure and following a dirt road south to the intersection with the road in Lake Gulch. Another access is from the parking lot off the Virginia Canyon road above Central City. Continue east past the Missouri Flats site (and the child's grave), past the casino bus service area to the head of Lake Gulch.

See "Black Hawk" for a map showing Lake Gulch.

This is the old brick school in Lake Gulch. Lake Gulch was the site of Gilpin County's first school, built in 1864, and was replaced in 1905 by this structure. *(Kenneth Jessen 107C11)*

John K. Aldrich, *Ghosts of Gilpin County*, Centennial Graphics, Lakewood, Colorado, 1989, p. 25.

Minnie B. Morgan, *Historical Souvenir of Central City*, Colorado, 1941, p. 40.

Perry Eberhart, *Guide to the Colorado Ghost Towns and Mining Camps*, Sage Books, Chicago, 1959, p. 29.

MISSOURI FLATS

Marked By A Child's Grave

- *Gilpin County; Clear Creek drainage*
- *Accessible by graded dirt road*
- *Town had a post office; no standing structures remain*

L ocated on the plateau a few miles southwest of Central City was Missouri Flats (sometimes called Missouri City). Today, the road past the Missouri Flats site is access to large parking lots associated with the gambling industry. This road leaves the Virginia Canyon road at the top of the steep switchbacks above Central City on the way to Russell Gulch.

The Missouri Flats founders tried to encourage the Leavenworth & Pikes Peak Stage Company to establish its terminus in the town. The town grew to the point where it qualified for a post office, which was established in 1860, but was closed three years later. Missouri Flats was listed as having a population of 597. It served as the headquarters for the Consolidated Ditch Company, important to the supply of water to Central City, but ironically, the town's own water supply was inadequate.

Central City was at a lower elevation and as a result, had a somewhat milder climate. By the time ghost town historian Muriel Sibell Wolle visited Missouri Flats in the 1940s, there was nothing left but the grave of a child, surrounded by an iron fence. The child died in 1865 at the age of one year, twelve days. At the time, the grave had a marble headstone, but today that is gone. Missouri Flats has been a ghost site for many years and is about to be paved over as the parking lots for the gambling industry are expanded.

See "Black Hawk" for a map showing Missouri Flats.

This child's grave is the only physical reminder that Missouri Flats ever existed. The child died in 1865, and this grave may have been the start of the town's cemetery. *(Kenneth Jessen 107A8)*

Don and Jean Griswold, *Colorado's Century of "Cities"*, Self Published, 1958, pp. 60-61.

Muriel Sibell Wolle, *Stampede to Timberline*, Sage Books, Chicago, 1949, 1974, p. 31-3

MOUNTAIN CITY

County's Early Settlement

- *Gilpin County, Clear Creek drainage*
- *Lower portion of town on paved road, upper portion on private property*
- *Town had a post office; several original structures remain*

Mountain City was a community where one portion of the town was spread up and down the Gregory Lode, while the rest of the town was located along the main road between Black Hawk and Central City. *(Denver Public Library, Western History Department L-304)*

Mountain City was founded about the time of the first gold strike by John H. Gregory in May, 1859, and was originally known as "Gregory Diggings." Mountain City grew haphazardly with some of its business district situated along the main road

276

between Black Hawk and Central City, with other businesses located up Packard Gulch on a steep road called Bent Street. The Mountain City post office was one of the earliest in Colorado Territory, established in January, 1860. It lasted nine years before being moved to Central City.

Why the town was named Mountain City is obvious; the town was built on the side of a mountain so steep that terraces had to be graded for most of its buildings. Based on what is left to see today, its hard to believe such an important town ever existed at this site. Mountain City had its own log theater, the first saloon in a Colorado mountain town, and on June 12, 1859, it was the site of the first religious services held in a Colorado mountain mining town. Mountain City was also the site of Colorado's first Masonic Temple.

By August, 1859, the town had two weekly newspapers, *The Rocky Mountain Gold Reporter* and *The Mountain City Herald.* They lasted only until October!

Businesses include the Mountain City Brewery, located up Packard Gulch, and next to it was a jewelry shop and a butcher shop. Along the main road to Central City was a restaurant, the Masonic Temple, a general store, the office of L. W. Borton Attorney at Law, and a claims recorder's office. A saloon, sawmill, boarding house, carpenter shop, blacksmith shop and a second butcher shop rounded out Mountain City's businesses.

By January, 1860, the population of Mountain City was estimated at 800. The demand for housing was tremendous as the number of miners and prospectors grew daily, but there was little space available for the construction of homes in Mountain City. As a result, other towns, such as Black Hawk, Nevadaville and Central City, sprang up and eclipsed Mountain City. In 1880, Mountain City was annexed into Central City, and its last listing for businesses in the *Colorado State Business Directory* was for 1878.

The Colorado Central completed its railroad to Black Hawk from Golden in 1872 and using a long switchback, extended its line through Mountain City to Central City in 1878. The grade is

This is one of the few remaining structures in the upper portion of Mountain City. Based on what little is left today, it is hard to believe that this town was once the home for 800 people. The town itself was absorbed into Central City in 1880. *(Kenneth Jessen 094A3)*

still visible and until recently, was used by a tourist line originating in Central City.

Up Packard Gulch the remains of a frame home plus several mine buildings can be found. The largest structure in Mountain City was the Gregory-Buell Consolidated Gold Mining and Milling Company. The mill was razed many years ago but the remains of the stone walls for the power plant sit between the one way branches of the Black Hawk to Central City road. Next to the power plant is the granite marker commemorating the first gold discovery by John H. Gregory.

The deep scar running diagonally across the hillside through the Mountain City site is the Gregory Lode. Here, mining began as a tunnel and as the ore was removed, great hollow caverns were created. Eventually, the cavities collapsed to the surface leaving the deep and dangerous scar across the hillside.

Don and Jean Griswold, *Colorado's Century of "Cities"*, Self Published, 1958, pp. 53-54.

Muriel Sibell Wolle, *Stampede to Timberline*, Sage Books, Chicago, 1949, 1974, p. 24.

Muriel Sibell Wolle, *Timberline Tailings*, Sage Books, Chicago, 1977, pp. 12-13.

Robert L. Brown, *Central City and Gilpin County*, Caxton Printers, Ltd., Caldwell, Idaho, 1994, p. 15.

William H. Bauer, James L. Ozment, John H. Willard, *Colorado Post Offices*, Colorado Railroad Museum, Golden, Colorado, 1990, p. 101.

NEVADAVILLE

Larger Than Denver

- *Gilpin County; Clear Creek drainage*
- *Accessible by graded dirt road*
- *Town had a post office (Bald Mountain); several original structures remain; site occupied by several families*

Nevadaville was a mixture of mine buildings, mine cars tracks, homes, mills, businesses and churches. Typical of so many Colorado mining towns, city planning was unheard of. *(Colorado Historical Society F4993)*

Nevadaville was founded just three weeks after John H. Gregory made his initially gold discovery on May 6, 1859. The town site was formed by A. D. Gambell and Sam Link. The Burrows Lode was what put Nevadaville on the map, and this

This contemporary photograph of the Masonic Lodge in Nevadaville shows that it is still in good condition. A sign in the window says, "Nevada Lodge No. 4, 2nd and 4th Saturday, Nevadaville, Colorado." *(Kenneth Jessen 098B2)*

became the site of the largest concentration of mining activity in Gilpin County.

Joseph Stadley, who discovered gold ore nearby, named the town. It was also known as Nevada or Nevada City. When Colorado Territory was created in 1861, the post office elected to use the name Nevada. This, however, created confusion with a placed called Nevada, California, and some of the mail destined for Nevada, CO. may have ended up in Nevada, CA. In 1869, the post office changed the name to Bald Mountain, but residents resisted and continued calling their home Nevadaville. Postal officials would not yield, and neither would its residents. The post office continued as Bald Mountain until its closure in 1921. This created an unusual situation where the name of the town was different than the name of the post office.

Nevadaville was a very large Colorado town by 1860 standards with a population of 2,705, making it slightly larger than Denver. In 1864, the town opened up a school with initial enrollment of one hundred students. The structure was a long, low, one-story building located on the side of a hill and divided into four rooms.

Nevadaville wanted no part of the wild night life common to other mining towns, and in a meeting held in 1860, resolved that, "...there be no Bawdy Houses, Grog shops or Gambling Saloons within the Limits of this District." The fine was $50 in a time when wages ranged from $1.50 to $2 for a day's work. If the violations continued, banishment from the district was the next step.

The district also appointed its own sheriff to enforce the law, and as an added incentive, the sheriff got to keep half of the fines.

Samuel Mallory wrote about his stay in Nevadaville in 1860. He camped in his wagon with the top of a barrel serving as his desk and his trunk as his chair. He realized that he could not survive at this elevation during the winter and paid $500 for a house to be built of milled lumber.

At the time, forty quartz mills were in operation in Nevadaville. They were used to grind the gold ore and recover the gold using amalgamation with mercury. A year later, a fire leveled fifty homes in Nevadaville, but life went on and the town was rebuilt. In 1863, a missionary visited the area and reported that there was a continuous town from Black Hawk, up the road past Central City, and on to Nevadaville. He also said that the best stores, hotels and theaters were in Central City and that, "...Nevada is the least aristocratic in character."

Aristocratic or not, a few famous people came to Nevadaville including Henry Stanley, who later became a famous African explorer seeking the source of the Nile river. Schuyler Colfax, the Republican candidate for United States Vice President, also visited Nevadaville.

Prosperity and growth continued until the Leadville boom of 1879. Many left Nevadaville and other Gilpin County towns and moved over the mountains to mine silver. Miners had little loyalty to a town. George Crofutt, in his 1885 grip-sack guide, placed the population of the area at 2,000 and listed Nevadaville as

City Hall is one of the few frame structures, in what was downtown Nevadaville, to escape destruction by fire. *(Kenneth Jessen 098B1)*

little more than a suburb of Central City. Even at the turn of the century, there were still one thousand people living in Nevadaville, which was quite remarkable for a Colorado mining town. By 1919, only two hundred remained, and in 1930, Nevadaville's population was listed at two. The Great Depression and an increase in the price of gold caused a minor boom, and Nevadaville came back to life. After World War II, only four residents remained.

Along its now deserted, dusty, empty street, Nevadaville had a substantial business district including a number of saloons, two barber shops, a shoe store, and a grocery store. A dry goods store, where lamps, tinware, china and the like could be purchased, opened up as the Colorado Trading and Investment Company. The largest structure in town was the Red Men's Building, which housed the town's butcher shop where patrons could purchase not only beef, but wild game. Nevadaville did not have a bank, and merchants accepted normal currency as well as gold dust for payment.

A much needed medical practice was opened up by Dr. Bourke in 1890. He also operated a drug store, which was a common side-line for physicians.

Nevadaville had its own baseball team, and the Cornish introduced the game of cricket. A club was formed, called the Mountain Daisy Cricket Club, and commissioned a silversmith to make a loving cup. The club then boasted that it would yield its valuable silver cup to any cricket club in Colorado who could beat them. This was a safe bet because Colorado cricket clubs were few and far between.

Nevadaville's biggest problem was a good water supply, and this was what ultimately limited the town's success. A ditch was dug in 1860 from Peck Gulch to bring water to the town. In 1876, a bigger ditch was completed from the Fall River. Despite improvements in the water supply, it was still inadequate and could not prevent the town from burning to the ground no less than five times during its history. The last fire was in 1914, and the town was never fully rebuilt.

Today, only a few structures remain along Nevadaville's unpaved main street, where at one time, there were dozens of businesses and hundreds of homes. Once a vibrant mining town, it is now almost a ghost town. Nevadaville can be reached easily by driving up a steep dirt road, which heads southwest from Central City's Main Street. The distance is a little over a mile. *For a map showing Nevadaville, see "Black Hawk."*

After the end of the mining boom, Nevadaville was slowly abandoned and its business district left to deteriorate. *(Colorado Historical Society F5070)*

George Crofutt, *Crofutt's Grip Sack Guide of Colorado 1885*, Johnson Books, Boulder, Colorado, 1966, 1981, p. 70.

Nolie Mumey, *History and Laws of Nevadaville*, Johnson Publishing Company, Boulder, Colorado, 1962, pp. 1-27.

Robert L. Brown, *Central City and Gilpin County*, Caxton Printers, Ltd., Caldwell, Idaho, 1994, pp. 99-118.

Samuel Mallory, "Overland to Pikes Peak with a Quartz Mill," *The Colorado Magazine*, Vol. VIII (May, 1931), p. 112.

William H. Bauer, James L. Ozment, John H. Willard, Colorado Post Offices, *Colorado Railroad Museum*, Golden, Colorado, 1990, pp. 16, 104.

NUGGET

- *Gilpin County, Clear Creek drainage*
- *Part of site accessible on a graded dirt road; private property*
- *Town had a post office; one standing structure remains*

Nugget was large enough at one time to have its own post office, which lasted from 1895 to 1901. After 1901, residents collected their mail at Apex. The Nugget town site is located near the Elk Creek crossing on the Kingston Road between Apex and Tolland. This

Chris and Ben Jessen stand near a remaining structure at the town of Nugget in Elk Park between Apex and Kingston. *(Kenneth Jessen 103D3)*

road is usually negotiable by car, but can be quite rough. There is a short side road to Nugget, which angles to the south below the main road. The side road has a posted gate, but outside the gate is the one remaining structure in Nugget. Muriel Sibell Wolle found three foundations on the site when she visited Nugget during the 1970s.

Opposite the town site in a willow thicket along Elk Creek is a snow bank that lingers most of the summer.

For a map showing Nugget, see "American City."

Muriel Sibell Wolle, *Timberline Tailings*, Sage Books, Chicago, 1977, p. 38.
Robert L. Brown, *Central City and Gilpin County*, Caxton Printers, Ltd., Caldwell, Idaho, 1994, p. 97.

PERIGO
Blown To Bits

- *Gilpin County, Coal Creek drainage*
- *Accessible by car over graded dirt road; private property*
- *Town had post office; two standing structures remain*

Perigo, in Gamble Gulch, was a boom town during the 1880s when this photograph was taken. Only two structures survive today, and the forest is so dense that this view is impossible to recreate. *(Denver Public Library, Western History Department L-580)*

Access to Perigo is up Gamble Gulch, named for A. P. Gambell (note the difference in spelling). Gambell located some placer claims during the winter of 1859, making him one of the very first successful prospectors in Colorado.

After his discovery, Gambell returned to Denver to get supplies. He was followed back into the mountains by a group of men who forced him to reveal the location of his claim. These

285

men, along with Gambell, formed the Independent District and within this district, the towns of Perigo and Gold Dirt emerged.

Another prospector, B. F. Longly, staked out a claim in Gamble Gulch and named it the Deadwood Diggings. The biggest producing mine was the Tip Top located along the main road through the gulch. The camp that grew up around the Tip Top was named Perigo, and a second camp, Gold Dirt, came into being just a mile below.

Perigo had a social club, which sponsored dances. Apparently the club tried to attract big name shows from Central City, but was not successful. Perigo's "matrons" had to be content with attending events in other area towns. A stamp mill, with thirty stamps, was constructed to process the gold ore from the Tip Top and the mines above town. The mill was purchased by Peter McFarlane from Central City.

A post office opened in Perigo in 1895 only to close a year later, then to reopen in 1897. The Perigo post office remained active until 1905.

As for Perigo's neighbor Gold Dirt, it apparently was a John

Recently restored, this was the home of the assayor at Perigo and is privately owned. *(Kenneth Jessen 106C2)*

Q. Rollins project. He built a small stamp mill in 1860-1861 and at some later point in time, enlarged the mill. The mill was fed with gold ore from the mines above Gold Dirt using a long flume.

The demise of Perigo happened during modern times when the owner of the town got tired of paying property taxes. She lived in California and argued with Boulder County officials that the old buildings in Perigo could not be occupied and that taxing them was unreasonable. Boulder County officials were unsympathetic, so she took a box of dynamite and blew up the structures on her property. She then invited officials to visit Perigo and see the condition of the flattened structures. This may account for the fact that the only two structures in Perigo are located downstream from the actual town center.

To reach Perigo, take the second turn right off of Colorado 119 south of Rollinsville where the Peak-to-Peak Highway begins a series of switchbacks. This is RD 15, and Perigo is about six miles up this road. It is a rough road and narrow in places, but in good weather should be passable by car. Nothing remains at the Gold Dirt site, and Perigo is easy to miss since the two remaining structures are off on the right side (west) of the road in the trees. The first (lower) home was where the assayer lived and had his office.

For a map showing the location of Perigo, see "Gilpin."

Muriel Sibell Wolle, *Stampede to Timberline*, Sage Books, Chicago, 1949, 1974, p. 38.

Perry Eberhart, *Guide to the Colorado Ghost Towns and Mining Camps*, Sage Books, Chicago, 1959, pp. 76-77.

William H. Bauer, James L. Ozment, John H. Willard, *Colorado Post Offices*, Colorado Railroad Museum, Golden, Colorado, 1990, p. 112.

ROLLINSVILLE

Named For John Q. Rollins

- *Gilpin County, Coal Creek drainage*
- *Accessible by paved road*
- *Town did have a post office; at least two original structures remain*

This town is easy to reach and is located along the Peak-to-Peak Highway, between Nederland and Black Hawk where the highway crosses the Union Pacific tracks. The old stage station has been converted into a restaurant and sits on the north side of the bridge over the tracks. There is also an old store near the stage station, which may date back to the early years of the town. Rollinsville has become quite a little community of newer homes.

The town was founded by John Q. Rollins, who prohibited such things as gambling halls, dance halls, and saloons. A stamp

Rollinsville, about 1930. The stage station down the street on the left remains standing today. *(Denver Public Library, Western History Department L-408)*

(Top Photo: Colorado Historical Society F7260)

mill was constructed in 1861 to handle the gold ore from nearby mines. It was located was on a terrace with a flume running along its upper end to supply water to the mill. Initially, the mill had a dozen stamps powered by an eighty horsepower stationary steam engine. Rollinsville got a post office in 1871.

This old store possibly dates back to Rollinsville's early years and is located near the town's historic stage station. *(Kenneth Jessen 107C6)*

Rollins also built a wagon road forty miles long heading west up South Boulder Creek over Rollins Pass to Middle Park. He operated it as a toll road, and part of this pioneer road can still be seen in the Rollins Pass area at timberline. For a while, his toll road enjoyed a monopoly on the supplies shipped into Middle Park, but the pass proved more difficult to negotiate than Berthoud Pass. When the toll road over Berthoud Pass opened, the Rollins Pass road saw little service.

Not only did Rollinsville have a stage station but it also had a train station below the town along the tracks of the Denver, Northwestern & Pacific. The railroad constructed its line up over the Continental Divide at Corona, passing very close to the toll road.

A large ice house stood until a few years ago along the tracks west of the highway bridge. In the days before mechanical refrigeration, this is where refrigerator railroad cars received new blocks of ice on their journey across the country. The ice was cut during the winter at area lakes and packed in sawdust until used.

John Q. A. Rollins, Jr. "John Q. A. Rollins, Colorado Builder." *Colorado Magazine XVI.*, No. 3 (May, 1939)

Muriel Sibell Wolle, *Stampede to Timberline*, Sage Books, Chicago, 1949, 1974, p. 38.

William H. Bauer, James L. Ozment, John H. Willard, *Colorado Post Offices*, Colorado Railroad Museum, Golden, Colorado, 1990, p. 124.

RUSSELL GULCH
A Town With Equal Opportunity

- *Gilpin County, Clear Creek drainage*
- *Accessible over graded dirt road*
- *Town had a post office; partially occupied site; several original buildings remain*

William Green Russell was among the very early prospectors to enter the Colorado mountains in 1858. He discovered small amounts of gold while panning Dry Creek near the future site of Denver and reasoned that the mother lode was located somewhere to the west in the mountains. In 1859, he panned his way up Clear Creek taking the north fork and eventually discovered gold in a gulch south of Central City. The gulch was subsequentially named Russell Gulch, and a town by the same name grew near William Green Russell's cabin.

William Green Russell, a pioneer prospectors in Gilpin County, was the founder of the town of Russell Gulch, which grew up around his cabin.

When news of the discovery reached the outside world, there was a stampede up Clear Creek Canyon to Gregory Diggings and also to Russell Gulch. By the end of September, 1859, an estimated 800 men were working the gravel in the area using pans and sluice boxes. When winter came and the stream froze over, a meeting was held to set up a mining district to protect claim holders. Within the laws set forth and under the heading "Discovery Claims," it says that females have the same right as males, but that

Once the home for 2,000 people, Russell Gulch was one of Gilpin County's early gold mining towns. This overview shows its homes and the school house. *(Colorado Historical Society F1869)*

youths under the age of ten shall not be allowed to hold claims. This reflected an unusually liberal attitude for the time.

Early Denver was filled with scalpers willing to take advantage of the numerous prospectors in the hills needing supplies. Denver merchants not only lowered the exchange rate for gold dust from $18 an ounce to $17 per ounce, but charged outrageous prices as well. Russell Gulch miners banned together in an "indignation" meeting supporting their own local merchants and threatened to haul their own supplies across the prairie if necessary. Their ultimatum was published in the *Rocky Mountain News*. It is not clear if the protest had any effect on prices.

Russell Gulch miners decided to take a day off from digging and celebrate the Fourth of July. They began by firing their revolvers into the air, and one volley of shots was given to honor the Pikes Peak gold rush, another for William Green Russell and a final volley for John H. Gregory. The closest American flag at this time flew over Fort Laramie hundreds of miles to the north in Wyoming. The miners decided that an American flag was important and fabricated one out of blue overall material, white shirts and red flannel drawers. How accurate this replica was probably didn't matter. A banquet concluded the celebration complete with a printed menu, and among the items were "brook trout, a la catch them first," and coffee served in tin cups, "...to be washed clean for the occasion."

In 1860, the population of Russell Gulch topped 2,000 and a school was built. The business district had many stores, saloons and a meat market.

William Green Russell left his town in 1862 to enlist in the Confederate Army in his native state of Georgia. After the war, he returned to Colorado for a number of years and finally settled in Oklahoma.

The placer gold was quickly exhausted, and in four years, the population of Russell Gulch dwindled. Hard rock mining replaced placer mining, and by the 1880s, only about 400 people lived in Russell Gulch. The population continued to shrink, and today there are just a few people living among the many ruins.

This stone and brick store survives along Russell Gulch's main street, a street once lined with other stores. (Kenneth Jessen 012C4)

Russell Gulch is located along the road which connects Central City with Idaho Springs. This road descends Virginia Canyon into Idaho Springs and is often referred to as the "Oh My God Road" due, in part, to its exposure. Recent improvements, including a guard rail, widening and partial paving, have tamed it and in the process, have diminished its thrilling quality.

The large, two-story, red brick school

house sits immediately below the road and dominates the Russell Gulch site. Other buildings include a store and several homes. The population is scattered about in a shallow valley. It is worth stopping and looking at the picturesque, partially collapsed stone structures. All of Russell Gulch is on private property.

See "Black Hawk" for a map showing the location of Russell Gulch.

Drawing by Julia McMillan

Muriel Sibell Wolle, *Stampede to Timberline*, Sage Books, Chicago, 1949, 1974, 33-34.

Robert L. Brown, *Ghost Towns of the Colorado Rockies*, Caxton Printers, Caldwell, Idaho, 1977, pp. 301-306.

Robert L. Brown, *Central City and Gilpin County*, Caxton Printers, Ltd., Caldwell, Idaho, 1994, pp. 85-96.

TOLLAND

- *Gilpin County, Coal Creek drainage*
- *Accessible by graded dirt road*
- *Town had a post office; many original structures remain*

Tolland is now a place for summer homes, and many of the original buildings, both log and frame construction, still stand along the hillside above the town site. Originally, Tolland was called Mammoth, named for Mammoth Gulch immediately above the town. The small town was renamed Tolland for the Charles B. Toll family who settled in this area. Mrs. Toll, in fact, was the postmistress and operated a large hotel. Originally a mining town, Tolland became a stage stop for the route over Rollins Pass to

This is an early overview of Tolland taken by renowned Colorado photographer Louis C. McClure. *(Colorado Historical Society F14944)*

294

Middle Park. It later became a stop along the Denver, Northwestern & Pacific (The Moffat Road).

The post office, originally located in Baltimore, was moved in 1904

The Tolland schoolhouse sits near the original town site close to the tracks, while the rest of the town is to the south of the main road. *(Kenneth Jessen 106C12)*

to Tolland and was active until 1944.

After the arrival of the Denver, Northwestern & Pacific in 1904, many new facilities were constructed in Tolland, including a beautiful railroad depot with a long covered platform. There were lunch rooms and souvenir shops set up along the town's main street. The railroad brought thousands of people from Denver for day excursions during the summer months. Activities included fishing, hiking and just relaxing while eating a picnic lunch.

The original town site, according to historic photographs, was located down near the railroad tracks. No doubt, some of the original structures have been moved. The schoolhouse, however, still sits down near the tacks.

See "Baltimore" for a map locating Tolland.

Edward T. Bollinger and Frederick Bauer, *The Moffat Road*, Sage Books, Denver, 1962, pp. 65, 93, 97-98, 116, 126.

Perry Eberhart, *Guide to the Colorado Ghost Towns and Mining Camps*, Sage Books, Chicago, 1959, pp 74.

Tivis Wilkins, *Colorado Railroads*, Pruett Publishing Company, Boulder, Colorado, 1974, p. 149.

William H. Bauer, James L. Ozment, John H. Willard, *Colorado Post Offices*, Colorado Railroad Museum, Golden, Colorado, 1990, p. 142.

WIDEAWAKE
Named By Alert Miners

- *Gilpin County, Missouri Creek drainage*
- *Graded dirt road runs near site; no access to site, private property*
- *Town did not have a post office*

This small camp was located right at a mine. There are a few buildings left standing, but private property limits access to the site. The camp is located on upper Missouri Creek, which flows south toward Colorado 119, just below the divide with Gamble Gulch.

One source states that the town had a mill and a post office. An official listing of all Colorado post offices fails to confirm this.

After several meetings to decide on the name for the new camp, the miners were told that there would be one more meeting and that they would have to be wide-awake. The miners were weary of these meetings and wanted to get back to work digging their fortune out of the hills. Instead of holding that meeting, one of the miners suggested that the town simply be named "Wideawake," and the matter was settled.

For a map locating Wideawake, see "Gilpin."

Muriel Sibell Wolle, *Timberline Tailings*, Sage Books, Chicago, 1977, p. 17.

Perry Eberhart, *Guide to the Colorado Ghost Towns and Mining Camps*, Sage Books, Chicago, 1959, p. 77.

AREA FIVE 5

Clear Creek County

continued

AREA 5: Clear Creek County
Selected Towns

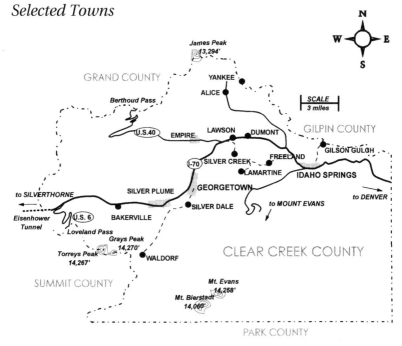

Introduction to Clear Creek County

Clear Creek County is one of the original seventeen counties approved in 1861 by the Colorado Territorial Legislature. It is now part of the modern-day I-70 corridor and encompasses the Clear Creek drainage and its tributaries.

Prospectors first entered the area in 1859 making them among the earliest settlers in Colorado. Placer gold was discovered first, and it wasn't until after the placer gold was exhausted that any serious attention was given to other metals such as silver. It would be silver that would come to dominate the area's economy.

There are relatively few true ghost towns in this county since most of the towns abandoned after the end of the mining era have been repopulated. The economy made a shift from mining to tourism, which was amplified by the construction of I-70. The true ghost towns are in the high country away from Clear Creek Canyon.

Frank Dibben built this primitive smelter in 1868, and it was one of the first such plants in the Argentine District near Georgetown. Dibben was noted for being the first mill operator to attempt to extract silver bullion from ore in Georgetown. *(Denver Public Library, Western History Department F141)*

Smelting the First Silver Ore

Silver was discovered in the Georgetown area as early as 1860, but for the most part, this precious metal was ignored. Prospectors were intent on duplicating the success of rich gold deposits discovered by Jackson and Gregory. At the time, the U. S. Government placed silver coins on the open market at less than their metallic value. This meant that a great deal of silver currency was melted and sold. Even though the U.S. was on a bimetallic standard, gold dominated the currency.

High assay values, in dollars per ton, placed on early silver lodes got the attention of many of the area's prospectors. In 1864, the Civil War caused high inflation in paper currency, and prices for precious metals reflected this fact.

Economics drove prospectors and mine owners to focus on silver, but it would take several years before the ore could actually be converted into bullion. To reduce the cost of transportation, Georgetown mine owners began to build their own mills. During 1866, three mills were under construction, but none had actually converted ore to bullion.

In 1867, Caleb Stowell completed a furnace specifically designed for silver ore from a mine located high on McClellan Mountain to the south of Georgetown. The furnace failed to yield

A train of jacks was a common sight on the streets of Georgetown. In this case, the animals each have a pair of rails destined for some area mine. *(Denver Public Library, Western History Department F7323)*

any silver so, Stowell turned to experienced mill operator Frank Dibben. Dibben, to make it more interesting, bet Stowell $500 that he could produce silver bullion within 24 hours.

The wager was accepted and Dibben worked frantically behind closed doors using Stowell's mill. An hour before midnight, Dibben admitted defeat. He was replaced by black mill operator Lorenzo Bowman who knew how to treat this type of ore. Bowman, a member of a group of blacks who

The chimney is all that remains today of the historic Frank Dibben smelter in the Argentine Mining district. It stands along a four-wheel drive road which parallels the Argentine Central roadbed and is located between Sydneyville and Waldorf. *(Kenneth Jessen 106B5)*

arrived in Clear Creek County in 1865, had fifteen years of experience with galena-lead ore and a smelter operation in Missouri.

He had been secretly watching Dibben and his assistants through a knot-hole in the wall of the mill and knew just what mistakes were made. Bowman told Stowell that Dibben would certainly fail and asked for the opportunity to try his hand. Stowell granted Bowman permission, and by noon of the following day, Bowman was casting silver bullion simply by using more heat during the roasting process. This was the first silver bullion cast in Clear Creek County and marked a turning point in the history of the region.

The Pelican-Dives Feud

The Mining Law of 1872 indirectly cost the lives of two Georgetown men. It permitted the owner of a mining claim the exclusive right to work all veins and ore bodies throughout the entire length of a claim if the apex or highest point of the vein were within the claim's rectangular limits. If the vein strayed out of the claim somewhere deep in the earth, the owner could legally follow the vein literally to China. It became known as the Apex Law, and such a law was made for the legal profession.

The Pelican-Dives Feud was based on this law. The Dives claim dated back to 1869, while the Pelican claim was not filed and worked until 1871. The Pelican overlapped part of the Dives claim, a fact which went unnoticed until legal action was taken. The owners of the Pelican started work during the summer of 1877, located some 800 feet above Cherokee Gulch on the steep side of Republican Mountain. They dug a series of adits into the side of Republican Mountain which permitted exploration of the ore body. The proposition paid for itself in that the ore mined during exploration yielded the necessary funding to continue mining.

In June, 1872, the Pelican owners struck a rich ore body 1,400 feet long. By now, some sixty men had been hired for the work in two shifts. By the summer of 1874, four tunnels had been opened, and employment grew to one hundred miners. The mine yielded hundreds of thousands of dollars. The *Colorado Miner* claimed that the Pelican was the richest mine in the state with ore running between 800 and 1,000 ounces of pure silver per ton.

The original Dives claim was staked out in 1869, and its owner sold an interest to entrepreneur William A. Hamill. Hamill made part of his living through the blackmail allowed by Apex Law litigation. The Dives had the potential of becoming a very rich property with assay results running as high as 680 ounces of silver per ton. The ore body became richer as the mine increased in depth.

In 1873, the owners of the Dives were being rewarded with high grade ore running as much as 700 ounces of silver per ton. The vein was two feet thick, but by 1874, the rich seam had dwindled to just a few inches.

Based on the Apex Law, the Pelican owners filed a law suit against the Dives. Their claim was that this rich vein of silver ore was higher on their property than on the property belonging to the Dives. No less than twenty-three law suits followed during the feud between these mines.

The battle lines then shifted underground. The owners of the Dives were not going to be denied what was rightfully theirs and cut into a lode owned by the Pelican by digging twenty-three feet lower than the active portion of the Pelican. The Dives owners had their miners remove a great deal of rich ore. They claimed they were simply following the same vein on which their original claim was based. In the three dimensional world of tunnels, the two mining companies were soon mining above and below each other until an injunction stopped progress.

The outcome of the approaching trial was very important to Georgetown residents since their lives and occupations depended on silver mining. The *Georgetown Courier* noted that the courtroom was a walking arsenal and that the judge had as his "advisors," two large revolvers. The judge finally agreed to a change of venue to El Paso County to prevent an all out war in the court room.

The owners of the Pelican had to prove in court that they occupied the disputed ground first and that the disputed vein was actually separate from the rest of the Dives. The Pelican's lawyers won this round, and an injunction was issued against the Dives.

Naturally, a counter suit was filed in the form of a statement which attempted to establish the Dive's prior claim on its lodes. The Dives also pointed out that they sank the discovery shaft near the Pelican claim and that its owners had never objected.

The Dives added a grievance covering the illegal entry by a number of Pelican miners into the Dives 160 feet below the surface and the removal of a large quantity of silver ore. The Dives tried to get an injunction against the Pelican to prevent them from processing ore stored at various locations. There was no practical means of accurately determining what ore had been removed from which lode. The ambiguity of the situation allowed the legal wizards to make their money at the expense of the mine owners. One thing was certain, both the Pelican and Dives companies were trying to extract rich silver ore from the very same location under the earth's surface.

Matters became so complex that the only recourse for the court was to enter the mining business. The judge hired miners to sink a winz and define the vein and which way it ran. As a result, the court ordered the Dives to erect a gate at the end of its drift where it entered the workings of the Pelican. The gate was to be kept locked except for inspection purposes. In the world of mining, gates are of little consequence, and both the Dives and Pelican kept on mining rich silver ore in the disputed area.

The legal battle continued throughout 1873. To continue to extract ore, the Dives resorted to operating from midnight on Saturday until midnight Sunday. The ore was transported down the mountain side in the dark. The Dives paid its miners extremely high wages to maintain their secrecy. They also hired armed guards to protect the mine and the ore. This operation lasted several weeks. Ore worth $65,000 was taken to Georgetown, then transported to Black Hawk for processing. When questioned, the Dives management simply said that the ore had been stolen.

The feud between the Pelican and Dives was not without its humor, however. Deputy Sheriff P. C. Baily was instructed to commandeer ore coming from the Dives. When he saw one of their covered wagons, typically used for transporting high-grade ore, he intercepted it and ordered the driver to take it down to a Georgetown stable. At the stable, a crowd gathered to see what would happen. Baily ordered the cover unlocked, and the driver refused. When it became clear that Baily was going to break the lock, the driver acted out his role perfectly and relented. When the lid was opened, the surprised sheriff found two miners inside and no ore! The miners stood up in the wagon much to the delight of the crowd. In the meantime, an open ore wagon, full of rich ore from the Dives, passed the stable and went to a local mill where the ore was deposited.

After the court ruled in favor of the Pelican, the injunction was lifted and mining resumed. The legal settlement allowed the Dives miners to work one particular drift

This was the office of the Dives and Pelican Mining Company. The two properties were consolidated in 1890 after seven years of feuding. Although its windows have been modified, this historic buildings still stands in Georgetown. *(Denver Public Library, Western History Department F5136)*

which the Pelican sought for itself. On the night of April 24, 1875, a force of armed men from the Pelican broke into the lower portion of the Dives. The miners from the Pelican had been waiting in a connecting tunnel and took possession of the Dives by force. This allowed the Pelican to work a rich section of the Dives touching off another round of legal battles.

Along with a force of around two hundred men working both mines, another twenty or so well-armed men stood guard duty on the surface. The two mines were within easy rifle shot of each other, and the area was unsafe for visitors. A Central City judge issued an injunction against the Pelican to stop robbing ore from the Dives. Deputy Sheriff P. C. Baily had the unfortunate task of delivering the writ and was almost shot for his efforts. The men at the Pelican said they would resist any attempt by Baily and his posse to enter the mine. Out gunned, Baily backed off and posted men at what he believed were all the mine openings in hopes of starving out the Pelican invaders. Knowledge of a hidden tunnel allowed food and water to be smuggled into the Pelican miners.

During the standoff, a watchman at the Pelican left his post to get a drink of water. He slipped and fell several feet down a steep incline. He was carrying a loaded pistol in his hand, and it accidentally discharged, killing him.

Jacob Snider was experienced at mining and milling. Snider became involved with the Pelican when he began crushing its ore in a Silver Plume mill he supervised. In 1874, he purchased an interest in the Pelican. During the feud, Snider was shot to death on a Georgetown street by Jackson Bishop. Snider thus became the second casualty of the Pelican-Dives Feud.

Deputy Sheriff Baily continued to have his problems. Not only was he denied access to the Pelican, he was also sent threatening notes from Central City lawyer Henry Teller, who represented the Pelican. The first such note ended with "...the Pelican people will be justified in defending their property, if they are compelled to kill you and your posse." A second note said "...and if Streeter and McCunniff (the Pelican owners) serve you right, they will shoot you and your men like dogs." Teller refused to give up the ground mentioned in the writ and simply defied the law. The frustrated Baily then kidnapped one of the Pelican's officers right out of his chair in his Georgetown office. He placed the surprised man in a buggy with three armed posse members and hauled him up to the mine. The posse tried to use this man as a human shield, but the men guarding the mine apparently were willing to kill one of their own if necessary.

Pressure was placed on the lawyers to settle the feud once and for all. The reputation of Georgetown as a sophisticated, law-abiding town had been shattered. Its population had been polarized between the two factions. After the legal community had been paid an estimated half a million dollars over a period of years, the Dives and Pelican owners finally agreed to stop their legal proceedings against each other. Eventually, in 1880, William Hamill consolidated the claims forming the Dives and Pelican Mining Company. Some owners lost, others gained, but the biggest winners in the feud were the lawyers.

Miner's Companion Is His Violin

High above the mining town of Silver Plume, a rich vein of ore was discovered in the late 1860s by Clifford Griffin. This young Englishman was one of the first miners to come to the Silver Plume area. Little was known about him except that his fiancee had been found dead the eve of their wedding. Griffin came to the rocky Mountain to enter the mining business and possibly to forget his sad past.

Griffin discovered a rich vein of ore and named his mine the Seven-Thirty. It contained mainly silver with some gold ore. The

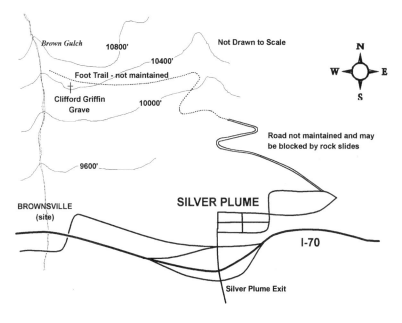

The trail to the Clifford Griffin grave starts out as a wagon road, but becomes a narrow, exposed foot trail. The trail is not maintained and has deteriorated over the years.

High above Silver Plume and the sound of I-70 is the Clifford Griffin monument which was erected to honor a lonely miner who took his life one spring evening in 1887 after playing his violin. *(Kenneth Jessen 074C7A)*

deeper the mine was developed, the richer the ore. The young Englishman soon became the wealthiest mine owner in the area. Nothing, however, caused him to forget his fiancee's untimely death, and he withdrew socially from the other miners and their families.

On the side of the steep mountain near his mine, Griffin constructed a simple cabin. His sole companion was his violin, and after the end of a day's work, he would stand at the front of his cabin and play. The sad music would drift down into Silver Plume, and miners and their families would come outside and look up to see the lonely musician by his cabin. Sometimes one of the miners would request a special tune. After he completed his mountainside recital, the miners would applaud, with the sound echoing off the canyon wall.

Directly in front of his cabin on a point of rock clearly visible from today's I-70, Griffin dug a grave in the solid rock. One spring evening in 1887, he played especially well. The miners and their families applauded, then watched him walk toward the grave. Suddenly, the sharp report of a gun reverberated through the hills. Clifford Griffin was found face down in his own grave with a bullet though the heart.

In his cabin was a note requesting that he be left in the stone grave. The miners not only followed his last instructions, but erected a granite marker over the grave with the following inscription:

Clifford Griffin, Son of Alfred Griffin Esq. of Brand Hull, Shropshire, England, Born July 2, 1847, Died June 19, 1887 and in Consideration of His Own Request Buried Here

Although a strenuous hike, this marker can be visited using an old mining road leaving Silver Plume's north side and passing the Pelican-Dives mine. The road becomes a narrow foot trail traversing the steep mountainside. For the arm chair traveler, the granite shaft over the grave of Clifford Griffin can be seen from Silver Plume at the edge of a rock outcrop over Browns Gulch.

Samuel Newhouse and the Newhouse Tunnel

Born in New York City, Samuel Newhouse graduated from public school and later from a Philadelphia law school. Although he was admitted to the bar, he never practiced law. Just a year after his graduation, he went to Leadville, arriving in 1879.

He started a transfer business with one team. He met a beautiful sixteen year old girl at her mother's boarding house in Leadville. After the two were married, they ended up managing the Swell Claredon Hotel in Ouray.

This is the interior of the Newhouse Tunnel, which provided drainage and transportation of ore for many Gilpin County mines. To allow passage of ore cars, the first two and a half miles of the tunnel was double track, and the tunnel width was twelve feet. *(Colorado Historical Society F35542)*

   Eventually, the Newhouse family settled in Denver, and this was when Samuel got the idea of a great drainage tunnel to "unwater" the mines around Central City. He got financing from an Englishman his wife had nursed back to health while the couple lived in Ouray. Through a variety of investments, Newhouse became a wealthy man.

   Newhouse started the Newhouse Tunnel in 1893, and by this time, over $70 million dollars in gold had been removed from Gilpin County mines. The tunnel's economics were based on the fundamental needs of all mines: transportation and drainage. By this time, mining in the Central City area was on the decline because of pumping costs. Sometimes chain reactions took place where the water in one abandoned mine would fill a working mine through hydrostatic pressure.

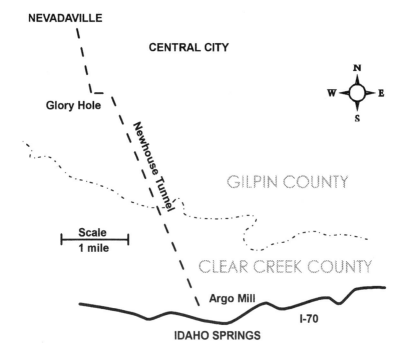

This map shows the approximate location of the Newhouse Tunnel drilled to drain mines in the Central City area.

Drilling continued for sixteen years on the Newhouse Tunnel until by 1910, it was a little over four miles long. It intersected directly or by side passages an estimated one hundred mines. *(Colorado Historical Society F37900)*

The geography of the area is such that the bottom of Clear Creek Canyon is well over a thousand feet lower than the deepest mines in the Quartz Hill area above Central City. The tunnel was the most ambitious and costly venture ever undertaken in either Clear Creek or Gilpin County. Drilling continued for sixteen years until by 1910, the tunnel was a little over four miles long. It intersected directly or by side passages an estimated one hundred mines. At the end of the tunnel near Nevadaville, the tunnel was 1,300 feet below the surface. Mines which had been closed for many years reopened using the Newhouse Tunnel for drainage. The largest mines serviced by the Newhouse Tunnel were the Ophir-Burroughs, California, Gold Coin-Kansas, Prize, Concrete, Gunnell and Grand Army.

To allow passage of ore cars, the first two and a half miles of the tunnel was double track and the tunnel width was twelve feet. Beyond the end of the double track, the width of the tunnel decreased to ten feet. Electric locomotives were used for haulage.

In 1913, the Argo Gold Mill was constructed using the latest milling processes. Some of the mine owners paid the tunnel company to haul ore out to Idaho Springs to the mill. The combination of an ore haulage tunnel and a mill right at its portal was a success, and operations continued for forty years.

On January 19, 1943, four miners were drilling and blasting in the tunnel to open up the Kansas mine. This mine had been drained by the Newhouse Tunnel for over thirty years. An unexpected underground lake was penetrated by the miners and the tunnel immediately filled with water. All were killed, and the Newhouse Tunnel was shut down for good.

This is the Argo Gold Mill as it looks today. It dominates the view of Idaho Springs from I-70. It was constructed in 1913 and operated up until 1943 when the Newhouse Tunnel, to the left of the mill, flooded. *(Kenneth Jessen 047C5)*

Liston Leyendecker, *The Pelican-Dives Feud*, The State Historical Society, Denver, 1985, pp. 39-59.
Muriel Sibell Wolle, *Timberline Tailings*, Sage Books, Chicago, 1977, p. 128.
Terry Cox, *Inside the Mountains*, Pruett Publishing Company, Boulder, Colorado, 1989, pp. 36-41.
"Mining Pioneer Samuel Newhouse Dies in Paris, France," *Denver Post*, September 24, 1930.
"Argo Tunnel Progresses," *The Denver Times*, January 1, 1896. *The Denver Times*, June 24, 1896.

ALICE, SILVER CITY and NINETY-FOUR

- *Clear Creek County, Fall River drainage*
- *Site accessible via paved road or a short hike; private property*
- *Town of Alice had a post office; several original structures remain*

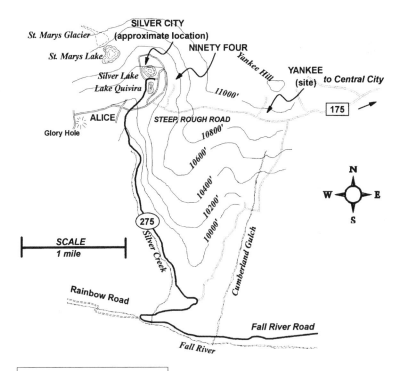

PAVED ROAD	
GRADED DIRT ROAD	
4-WHEEL DRIVE ROAD	

Alice, Silver City and Ninety-Four were close together, but offset in time. All of these sites were located at the head of Silver Creek. Yankee is also shown on this map.

313

The mines around the town of Alice had the typical progression in mining methods starting with gold panning, then hydraulic mining in 1881, and finally lode mining. A stamp mill was constructed when lode mining began, and the operation expanded into an open pit creating a glory hole. Ore was transported by mine cars to the mill over a long trestle from the glory hole. As the mine got deeper pyretic ores were encountered, and the stamp mill was no longer effective. The ore had to be treated in a smelter. Transportation from Alice, located at the head of the Fall River, was not economical, and the entire operation closed in 1898.

The town of Alice had a school plus several log and milled lumber homes. The post office didn't open until the end of the mining era in 1898 and remained open less than a year. It

The ghost camp of Ninety-Four still has several standing structures including this frame home located near the base of Yankee Hill, above Mine Road. *(Kenneth Jessen 107B8)*

reopened in 1900 and closed in 1925. It was also opened between 1936 and 1938.

Today, new housing overshadows the original town, and access to the site is limited by private property. There are a few original structures which have been converted to seasonal homes, and the Alice school has been restored.

Alice can be reached by driving up the Fall River Road (State Highway 275) from Clear Creek Canyon. This road has its own exit off of I-70. Near the head of the canyon, just prior to the switchbacks below Silver Lake, Alice Road takes off to the left. It is only about a quarter of a mile to the town site at the intersection of Silver Creek Road and Alice road.

The earliest town at the head of the Fall River drainage was short-lived Silver City. It was founded in the summer of 1860 and was said to have had a thousand prospectors in the general area. Claims were made which gave hope to these men that they might strike it rich. The silver ore they found, however, required smelting. At the time, no smelters had been built in Clear Creek County to handle refractory ore, and transportation to smelters outside the region was not economical. Silver City soon died, and its log structures have long since vanished. The log buildings at Silver Lake today are not part of the original town. The largest is the St. Marys Glacier Lodge.

Another camp in the general area was Ninety-Four and as the name suggests, it was founded in 1894. The mines which supported Ninety-Four were the Ninety-Four, the Lalla and the Princess Alice. The camp was a cluster of buildings in the general vicinity of the mines, but it was never a town as such. It did not have such things as a store, post office or school. The steep mountainside precluded Ninety-Four from expanding. Besides, the town of Alice was just across the valley. The view, however, from Ninety-Four was spectacular and included two peaks in excess of 14,000 feet and across the valley, the St. Marys Glacier.

Still standing is the restored general manager's office for the Ninety Four Mining Company. There is also an abandoned frame home, an abandoned cabin and a mine building, possibly the compressor house. Up until the 1960's, another large mine structure stood near the manager's office, but time and heavy snow caused its collapse. The Ninety-Four site is a few hundred feet north of the base of Yankee Hill Road near where it meets Mine Road. From Mine Road, it takes only about ten minutes to hike to Ninety-Four.

The Alice school, built in 1906, is fully restored and sits near the intersection of Alice Road and Silver Creek Road, only a few hundred feet west of the Fall River Road. *(Kenneth Jessen 107B6)*

John K. Aldrich, *Ghosts of Clear Creek County*, Centennial Graphics, Lakewood, Colorado, 1984, p. 40.

Robert L. Brown, *Jeep Trails to Colorado Ghost Towns*, Caxton Printers, Caldwell, Idaho, 1973, pp. 27-28, 149-150.

William H. Bauer, James L. Ozment, John H. Willard, *Colorado Post Offices*, Colorado Railroad Museum, Golden, Colorado, 1990, p. 11.

Muriel Sibell Wolle, *Timberline Tailings*, Sage Books, Chicago, 1977, p. 108.

Don and Jean Griswold, *Colorado's Century of "Cities"*, Self Published, 1958, pp. 74-75.

BAKERVILLE and GRAYMONT

- *Clear Creek County, Clear Creek drainage*
- *Accessible via paved road; access limited by private property*
- *Towns had post offices; no original structures remain*

In 1865, John Baker discovered the gold ore on Kelso Mountain, and four years later work began on the mine. The camp which evolved below the mine in Clear Creek Canyon was named Bakerville. Early photographs show a boardinghouse, a store and a mine building. A mill was constructed several years later and was owned by the Baker Silver Mining Company. The mill was destroyed by fire in 1871 and not rebuilt. Several homes were also constructed at Bakerville.

In 1870, the boarding house began taking in guests who were not there to work in the mines, but to climb Grays Peak. The Methodists also began to hold church services in the camp. During the construction of the railroad in 1882, workers camped at Bakerville. A post office opened that same year. The population of Bakerville grew to 200.

The post office went under the name "Yates," named for Charles Yates, Bakerville's first postmaster. He was a successful Georgetown businessman and operated a dining room and a bakery. He opened Georgetown's Yates House in 1872. A decade later, he and his wife moved to Bakerville. When he made out the application to the Postmaster General, he gave his own name to the post office and ignored the legitimate name of Bakerville. The Yates post office lasted only a year from 1882 to 1883.

Confusion exists over the location of Graymont relative to

Bakerville. When the Georgetown, Breckenridge & Leadville narrow gauge railroad was extended past Silver Plume, its directors decided to terminate the line at the eastern edge of the established town of Bakerville. This avoided contending with existing land owners. Named after Grays Peak, the railroad called its station Graymont, and a box car was taken off the track and used as the station. One leg of the wye used to turn locomotives extended a short distance into the Bakerville site.

The railroad was completed to its Graymont station in July, 1884 with the running of a special train for Union Pacific officials. Excursions soon followed carrying hundreds of people.

The Jennings Hotel, built in 1884, was a two-story log structure built on the Graymont site. It had an addition which extended a right angles to the rear coming within a few feet of the railroad track and its box car depot.

The hotel's owner, John Jennings, also applied for a post office which was to be located in the hotel. Permission was granted, and the post office opened in May, 1884, under the name Graymont. It served seventy-five residents and closed five months later.

As the ore body was depleted from the mines along Kelso Creek, tourism became the primary business. The railroad advertised round trip tickets from Denver to the top of Grays Peak at over 14,000 feet. From Graymont, passengers were transferred to horses. The railroad continued to haul milled lumber out of Graymont.

The canyon below Graymont-Bakerville was very narrow and the railroad wisely purchased the toll road running along the creek for its right of way. A flume paralleled the railroad forcing the wagon road to Graymont-Bakerville on the north side of the canyon. From I-70, portions of the old wagon road and the railroad grade are still visible.

The Jennings Hotel dominated the Graymont site, but the town did have some cabins, ore storage bins and a saloon called the Fox and Hounds. Activity continued at the two adjacent towns

The Jennings Hotel at Graymont. *(Colorado Historical Society)*

until 1898 when dwindling business forced the railroad to close.

The Highlands Lodge was constructed many years later and burned to the ground during the 1980s. Today, only its chimney is left. About four to five seasonal homes have been constructed on the Graymont-Bakerville site, but no original structures remain.

Erl H. Ellis and Carrie Scott Ellis, *The Saga of Upper Clear Creek*, Jende-Hagan Book Corporation, Frederick, Colorado, 1983, pp. 151, 167, 194, 203-205, 218-222.

Tivis Wilkins, *Colorado Railroads*, Pruett Publishing Company, Boulder, Colorado, 1974, p. 55.

Perry Eberhart, *Guide to the Colorado Ghost Towns and Mining Camps*, Sage Books, Chicago, 1959, p. 54.

William H. Bauer, James L. Ozment, John H. Willard, *Colorado Post Offices*, Colorado Railroad Museum, Golden, Colorado, 1990, p. 65.

BROWNSVILLE
Buried

- *Clear Creek County, Clear Creek drainage*
- *Accessible via paved road*
- *Town did have a post office; site buried*

This etching is an accurate representation of Brownsville. It was a small mining town west of Silver Plume complete with an Odd Fellows Hall, restaurant, saloon, boarding house and about a dozen homes. *(Colorado, its Gold and Silver Mines by Frank Fossett)*

Silver ore was discovered during the 1860s by a prospector named Brown near the base of Browns Gulch above and west of Silver Plume. The town of Brownsville grew during the 1870s when the area mines were in full production due to its central location. Not only did area miners live in Brownsville, construction workers involved with the ambitious Atlantic and Pacific Tunnel along Kelso Creek also called it home. This tunnel,

320

incidentally, was to go under the Continental Divide and allow the passage of narrow gauge trains from Clear Creek County to Summit County.

As the town grew, the Lampshire Boarding House was completed. Brownsville also had an Odd Fellows Hall, a restaurant, a saloon, another boarding house and about a dozen homes. There was also a large smelter in the center of the town operated by the Colorado Silver Mining Company. A post office opened in 1871, and in 1875, it was combined with the Silver Plume post office not too far away. Brownsville even had its own band.

The reason nothing is left today of Brownsville is that it was located in a geologically hazardous area. The tailings high above the town in Browns Gulch at the Seven-Thirty Mine and several other smaller mines became saturated with spring runoff. The mine owners had not provided adequate drainage around or underneath the tailings. In the 1880s, heavy rain caused part of the Seven-Thirty tailings to slide down into the town. The next slide occurred in June, 1892. Although it buried several homes, part of the mill and the town's saloon, people continued to live in Brownsville. On June 15, 1895, a large mass of saturated tailings made it way down the gulch and demolished the boarding house. Several of the Seven-Thirty's buildings were taken down with the slide, but once again the people continued to live in Brownsville.

One day in June, 1912, there was a thunderous sound from the mountains and an immense mud, rock and tailings slide made its way down the gulch. Residents and workers evacuated town. This time every thing in Brownsville was buried or demolished, including a couple of loaded railroad cars. The flow continued many hours and people came from the surrounding towns to witness the slide. This time there wasn't any town to return to.

Today, on the north side of I-70 just west of Silver Plume, the headframe for the Terrible Mine sits high above the highway on top of the Brownsville site.

The headframe for the Terrible Mine sits on top of the Brownsville site west of Silver Plume on the north side of I-70. *(Kenneth Jessen 099B11)*

David Digerness, *The Mineral Belt*, Vol. III, Sundance Publications, Silverton, Colorado, 1982, p. 189.

William H. Bauer, James L. Ozment, John H. Willard, *Colorado Post Offices*, Colorado Railroad Museum, Golden, Colorado, 1990, p. 24.

Robert L. Brown, *Ghost Towns of the Colorado Rockies*, Caxton Printers, Caldwell, Idaho, 1977, pp. 61-67.

DOWNIEVILLE

Was Free America

- *Clear Creek County, Clear Creek drainage*
- *Accessible via paved road*
- *Town did not have a post office; no original structures remain*

John Coburn, his wife and sixteen-year-old daughter Kate came into the Clear Creek area in 1871 with plans to build a town called Free America. John had seen others succeed by opening a new town, selling lots and becoming wealthy. What better place than the booming Clear Creek Canyon at a time when the silver mines were just starting to produce. Coburn built a hotel and laid out his town around the hotel.

John's first and biggest problem, however, was young Alex Lawson. Lawson was the wagon master who took John, his wife and daughter into the mountains from Denver. Lawson took an immediate liking to Coburn's daughter, Kate, and John did not approve of the young wagon master. Lawson had worked many different jobs and possibly to seek Coburn's approval, Lawson settled down on property just outside Free America. He built a hotel and bar and followed Coburn's lead by founding the town of Lawson.

This just infuriated Coburn even more because the new town of Lawson was a threat to his own town of Free America. Lawson sold hard liquor at his bar, something Coburn did not approve of in the least. Soon miners began building shanties at Lawson, near the bar, and not in Free America. So intense was their conflict that young Alex was obligated to elope with Kate.

Coburn gave up on the idea of a town and settled into the hotel and ranching business. He called his place the Downieville

Ranch, named for his birth place in Ireland. The hotel had thirty-two rooms and after a number of years, was converted into a boarding house. Fire destroyed the old hotel and other ranch buildings in 1947. Only modern structures are on the Downieville site today.

For a map showing the location of Downieville, see "Silver Creek."

History of Clear Creek County, Specialty Publishing Inc, Denver, Colorado, 1986, pp. 42, 233-234.

DUMONT

The Mill Town

- *Clear Creek County, Clear Creek drainage*
- *Accessible via paved road*
- *Town did have a post office; several original structures remain*

The old Mill City House in Dumont, constructed in 1860, has served as a hotel, saloon and stage stop over the years. Ulysses S. Grant once stayed here. *(Kenneth Jessen 101B10)*

The town of Dumont got its present name in 1880 for Colonel John M. Dumont, a Clear Creek pioneer and mine owner. Prior to 1880, the place was called Mill City. It was founded in 1859, making it one of the very earliest towns in Colorado. Under the Mill City name, a post office opened in 1861 and closed in 1863 only to reopen three years later. The post office reflected the boom to bust to boom mining in the region as a transition was made from mining surface ore and placer claims to hard rock or lode mining. In 1880, the post office changed its name to Dumont.

Arrastras were the first mills constructed at Mill City and were powered by a burro or a mule. The construction of several stamp mills followed. As refractory ores were encountered, the place was abandoned and the mines closed. John M. Dumont purchased many of the claims and using modern mining methods, put them back in operation. He also used better milling techniques and introduced smelting to reduce refractory ores.

In 1880, Dumont's population reached 100, and businesses included two hotels, a general store, school and fire house. The log hotel was called the Mill City House and was built in 1860. It served as a stage stop and housed the first saloon west of Denver. There was a billiard table in the Mill City House shipped from New York. The upper floor was used for meetings and as an opera house for live stage performances. Ulysses S. Grant once stayed in this historic hotel, and it still stands along the frontage road near

the bridge over I-70.

The original school was replaced in 1909 with a fine brick structure, which also stands today on the north side of the frontage road west of the Mill City House. The construction of I-70, however, covered much of the southern part of the original town.

For a map showing the location of Dumont, see "Silver Creek."

The Dumont school, built in 1909, serves as a community meeting place for special events. *(Kenneth Jessen 094A10)*

History of Clear Creek County, Specialty Publishing Inc, Denver, Colorado, 1986, p. 41.

William H. Bauer, James L. Ozment, John H. Willard, *Colorado Post Offices*, Colorado Railroad Museum, Golden, Colorado, 1990, p. 47, p. 98.

Frank Hall, *History of Colorado*, Vol. III. The Blakely Printing Company, Chicago, 1895, p. 315.

EMPIRE
Named For The Empire State

- *Clear Creek County, West Fork of Clear Creek drainage*
- *Accessible via paved road*
- *Town has a post office; town site occupied; a number of original structures still standing*

The original settlers in the Empire area were four prospectors from Spanish Bar, a placer camp one mile west of Idaho Springs. They organized the Union Mining District in 1860 based on flakes of gold they found in their pans in the broad valley where Empire is located today. A couple of these prospectors, George Merrill and Joseph Musser, constructed a cabin were Bard

The majority of early Empire was located along the Bard Creek road running over Union Pass to Georgetown. *(Colorado Historical Society F23965)*

327

Creek, Lion Creek and the West Fork of Clear Creek join. Originally named Valley City sometime in 1861, the Valley City Town Company was dissolved, and the camp remained unnamed for several weeks. The name Empire City was suggested by a settler from the Empire State of New York, Henry DeWitt Clinton Cowles. The "City" was dropped in 1886 in favor of just Empire.

The second cabin built at Empire was a modest log courthouse and recorder's office for the Union Mining District. The sheriff, James Ross, also had his office in this cabin and it served as the town hall. The recording fee for a mining claim was fifty cents and other records cost fifty cents per one hundred words.

An example of the type of laws passed by this mining district included prohibiting timber cutting in the immediate vicinity except for the construction of cabins. If someone was caught stealing, the thief had to give back the stolen property, and if the guilty party did not comply, a specified number of lashes were administered periodically until the person left the area! For offenses where the value of the property exceeded $100, the thief was hanged until dead. Hanging also applied to horse stealing.

Henry DeWitt Clinton Cowles became the judge in the miner's court, and he believed that this small, primitive mining camp could eventually blossom into something of great importance. No sooner had the town been named than it got its post office.

In 1860, wire gold was discovered on Eureka Mountain to the north and another camp called North Empire was formed. The camp was about two miles north of Empire in the Lion Creek drainage. As a town, it amounted to nothing more than a disorganized accumulation of cabins and buildings near the mines.

The first woman to settle in Empire was the wife of the sheriff, Mrs. James Ross. The town gave her a choice building lot. At the home they constructed, Mrs. Ross churned the first butter in Clear Creek County.

Another early settler was Dr. Richard Bard who successfully panned gold in an unnamed creek which was eventually called

Bard Creek. He and his brother tried to start a dairy farm in the valley, but the severe winter weather and short growing season quickly ended this venture.

By the spring of 1861, Empire had its own blacksmith shop, general store, post office, and a dozen or so homes. It was a prosperous place for two decades. Ernest Ingersoll in his book,

The D. W. King house in Empire dates back to 1861 and has been nicely restored. *(Kenneth Jessen 107C3)*

Knocking Around the Rockies, reported that Empire was virtually abandoned by 1883. He pointed to its wide streets and estimated that the population reached 1,500 just ten years before. Only six families remained.

The history of Empire was like that of so many other Colorado mining towns with many ups and downs. Empire survived into modern times and was never totally abandoned because of its strategic location along the shortest route between Denver and Middle Park. It is the last town before Berthoud Pass. The Peck House, built in 1862, still stands today and represents a combination stage stop and hotel.

The most unusual story associated with Empire happened in 1860 before the town got its name. A band of around 300 Ute Indians came through the valley and with them was a white girl. She was about nineteen and quite attractive which got the immediate attention of the miners. She spoke only the Ute language and few could communicate with her. She was not a prisoner of the Indians, but might have been abducted from a white family as a child. She showed no desire to leave her band, but she had a faint recollection of a covered wagon and a man digging for gold.

She told one miner who knew the Ute language that the Utes dug gold in an area about two days away. She produced several nuggets as evidence of this claim and presented one to the miner as a gift.

The young girl returned in the fall as the Utes traveled toward Middle Park. The miner asked her permission to go with her to where the gold was found. She said that her people would kill him. She did volunteer directions to the gold, however. She told him to travel north for a full day then west stopping at a pair of isolated mountains. At the base of the mountains would be the gold.

The miner teamed up with another man and set out to find the gold. They got lost in a storm, were separated, and the miner wandered for days before coming to a cabin at the head of the Fall River. Never again did the miner attempt to find the source of the Ute gold.

Also associated with Empire was Empire Station along the Colorado Central. It is east of Empire where the West Fork of

Clear Creek joins Clear Creek. The interchange between I-70 and U.S. 40 occupies this location today. In an isolated area within this intersection, the old Colorado Central depot still stands, although extensively remodeled.

The Peck House in Empire was constructed in 1862 and remains open to this day. *(Kenneth Jessen 094D5)*

Don and Jean Griswold, *Colorado's Century of "Cities"*, Self Published, 1958, pp. 78-80.
History of Clear Creek County, Specialty Publishing Inc, Denver, Colorado, 1986, p. 35.
Louise C. Harrison, *Empire and the Berthoud Pass*, Big Mountain Press, Denver, 1964, pp. 33-36.
Rocky Mountain News, May 13, 1861.

FALL RIVER and GLENARD CITY

- *Clear Creek County, Fall River drainage*
- *Accessible by paved road*
- *Towns did not have a post office; several standing structures remain*

The old site where the mining camp of Fall River was once located is passed every day by thousands of motorists on I-70 west of Idaho Springs at the mouth of the Fall River Canyon. Highway construction has obliterated most of the site. Early photographs indicate that Fall River was not very large and consisted of about eight or nine structures.

This is the only remaining structure in the small mining town of Fall River along Clear Creek, west of Idaho Springs. *(Kenneth Jessen 107B4)*

Silver ore discoveries at Fall River date back to July, 1860 and predate silver strikes in the Georgetown area. The ore at Fall River, however, was hardly worth mining. Claims were staked up the Fall River all the way to the St. Marys Glacier.

Fall River was kept alive after hopes of rich ore faded. It was along the primary stage coach route from Georgetown to Central City over Yankee Hill. Passengers would stop at the Fall River

House, a clapboard sided frame structure, two-stories high. The small town also had several homes and several stores. Fall River was also where the road up to Alice left Clear Creek Canyon.

In 1942, ghost town historian Muriel Sibell Wolle reported that two mills were still standing at Fall River. Today, there is only one frame house, half hidden in the trees.

Another small camp was Glenard City, 3.2 miles from the mouth of Fall River Canyon. Little is know about it, but there are the collapsed remains of a cabin plus a frame house which has been restored.

See "Gilson Gulch" for a map locating Fall River.

Muriel Sibell Wolle, *Stampede to Timberline*, Sage Books, Chicago, 1949, 1974, p. 108.

David Digerness, *The Mineral Belt*, Vol. III, Sundance Publications, Silverton, Colorado, 1982, p. 227.

Robert L. Brown, *Ghost Towns of the Colorado Rockies*, Caxton Printers, Caldwell, Idaho, 1977, pp. 158-162.

Frank Hall, *History of Colorado*, Vol. III. The Blakely Printing Company, Chicago, 1895, p. 315.

FORKS CREEK

On The Colorado Central

- *Jefferson County, Clear Creek drainage*
- *Accessible via paved road*
- *Town did have a post office; no standing structures remain*

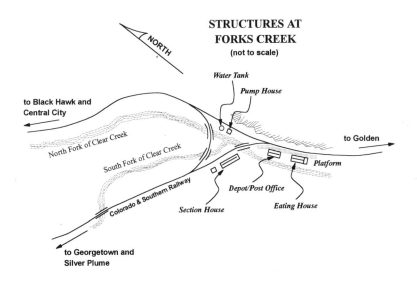

STRUCTURES AT
FORKS CREEK
(not to scale)

F orks Creek could hardly be classified as a town or even a mining camp for that matter. It was one of those places supported
by the railroad and consisted of a small cluster of buildings at the
point where the North Fork of Clear Creek joins its South Fork.

The Colorado Central, using Union Pacific money, built a
narrow gauge railroad up Clear Creek Canyon from Golden and
reached Forks Creek in 1872. At this location, a little over a dozen
miles from Golden, one branch turned right for Black Hawk and

the other branch turned left for Idaho Springs and Georgetown.

Forks Creek became a fueling station for the railroad, complete with a coal bunker and water tank. It had a two-story depot with living quarters, and a wooden platform was built which covered 2,000 square feet running a considerable distance along the track allowing long trains to be unloaded. Passengers headed to Georgetown or Silver Plume were allowed to get off, eat or simply stretch from riding in the confined narrow gauge cars.

A post office opened in 1878 and changed its name from "Forks Creek" to "Forkscreek" in 1895. The post office, located inside the railroad depot, continued to operate until 1927.

So that trains coming from Black Hawk could head up the canyon to Georgetown or visa versa, a wye was constructed to allow the smooth movement of trains. Up until 1997, one of the stone abutments for the bridge across Clear Creek could be seen just below Colorado 119. Recent changes to the highway related to high traffic volume to Back Hawk's casinos has obliterated the Forks Creek site.

The mining boom was in the distant past when the last train passed through Forks Creek in 1941. This brought to an end nearly seven decades of use of its facilities. After the tracks were removed, highway construction in Clear Creek Canyon forced the removal of the buildings at Forks Creek.

Robert L. Brown, *Ghost Towns of the Colorado Rockies*, Caxton Printers, Caldwell, Idaho, 1977, pp. 161-166.

William H. Bauer, James L. Ozment, John H. Willard, *Colorado Post Offices*, Colorado Railroad Museum, Golden, Colorado, 1990, p. 56.

FREELAND

On Trail Creek

- *Clear Creek County, Trail Creek drainage*
- *Accessible via graded dirt road*
- *Town did have a post office; at least two original structures remain*

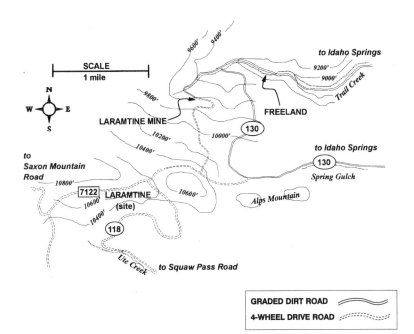

Freeland can be reached via a graded dirt road up Trail Creek or from Spring Gulch south of Idaho Springs. The Trail Creek road is steep, but can usually be negotiated by an automobile.

The Freeland town site is on Trail Creek south of I-70. Now so overgrown, it is hard to recognize the place based on historic photographs. During the mining boom practically all of the trees near Freeland were cut. Lumber was used for buildings, homes, cord wood and supports within the mines.

The Freeland Lode, discovered in 1877, consisted of rich silver ore. The following year, a Georgetown newspaper reported that seventeen homes had been built in Freeland. A week later, the same newspaper reported that thirty-four homes were complete and occupied. J. D. Armstong opened a grocery store which was soon followed by a meat market owned by John T. Jones. The Freeland post office opened in 1879 and was located in Armstrong's general store. There was a small store in the corner of the large mill at the Freeland site. The assay office, essential to any mining town, and a blacksmith shop were also part of Freeland. The town had its own public school, opened in 1879, starting with twenty-one students.

More than a dozen structures show up in early photographs taken around the turn of the century with the New Era Mine most prominent. The road up Trail Creek served as Freeland's main street.

By 1881, the population of Freeland reached about 400, and the town had eighty homes. As the ore was exhausted, the town began its decline, and by 1901, only 100 people lived in Freeland. The post office closed in 1908. When ghost town historian Muriel Sibell Wolle visited Freeland during the 1940s, she reported that most of the cabins and homes were deserted, but there were still a few families living in the old mining town. Robert Brown, in his *Ghost Towns of the Colorado Rockies* (published in 1977), took a contemporary photograph of Freeland using the same angle as a historic photograph. Out of the many structures which once stood, only one original building was still standing. A resident of Freeland told the author in 1996 that his log home and one other building were all that remained.

One of the two remaining original structures in Freeland, located up Trail Creek near Idaho Springs. *(Kenneth Jessen 101B11)*

To get to Freeland, exit I-70 at Idaho Springs and head west up the frontage road which parallels I-70. The frontage road crosses to the south side of Clear Creek immediately west of Idaho Springs while I-70 continues along the north side of Clear Creek. A little over a mile beyond Idaho Springs a sign marks the graded dirt road up Trail Creek. The Trail Creek road heads south and is very steep. In wet weather, it may require a 4-wheel drive vehicle, but otherwise, a car can handle the grade. Freeland is about two and a half miles from the frontage road and can be recognized by a log home on the right hand side of the road. Beyond this home are numerous mine dumps.

History of Clear Creek County, Specialty Publishing Inc, Denver, Colorado, 1986, p. 48.

Robert L. Brown, *Ghost Towns of the Colorado Rockies*, Caxton Printers, Caldwell, Idaho, 1977, p. 168.

Muriel Sibell Wolle, *Stampede to Timberline*, Sage Books, Chicago, 1949, 1974, p. 108.

William H. Bauer, James L. Ozment, John H. Willard, *Colorado Post Offices*, Colorado Railroad Museum, Golden, Colorado, 1990, p. 59.

GENEVA

- *Clear Creek County, Geneva Creek drainage*
- *Access restricted by private property*
- *Town did not have a post office; standing structures unknown*

The Geneva site is located in the extreme southwestern corner of Clear Creek County at the head of Geneva Creek near the Britannic and Sill mines. Its elevation is approximately 11,600 feet. Until recent years, it was possible to reach the site with a four-wheel drive vehicle, however, a property owner has blocked the road with a metal gate.

The road up Geneva Creek leaves the Geneva Park Campground, and the gate is located 3.7 miles up the road. The site is approximately three to four miles father with a considerable elevation gain.

According to ghost town historian John Aldrich, several cabins and mine buildings remained at the site in the 1980s. Original structures included a two-story boarding house, a general store and several cabins.

John K. Aldrich, *Ghosts of Clear Creek County*, Centennial Graphics, Lakewood, Colorado, 1984, p. 18.

Perry Eberhart, *Guide to the Colorado Ghost Towns and Mining Camps*, Sage Books, Chicago, 1959, p. 158.

GEORGETOWN

The Silver Queen

- *Clear Creek County, Clear Creek drainage*
- *Accessible via paved road*
- *Town has a post office; numerous original structures remain*

This historic view of Georgetown, looking southeast, shows how densely packed the town was in the narrow Clear Creek Valley with stores lining 6th Street cutting across the photograph. The large, white, two-story structure on the right is the Clear Creek County Courthouse. Few of the structures in the foreground survive today. *(Denver Public Library, Western History Department F659)*

Rumors of gold in the Rocky Mountains swept across the prairie through Kansas Territory like a wildfire in 1858. William Green Russell and a small party of prospectors were able to pan a few hundred dollars in gold from a South Platte tributary. This modest discovery precipitated a gold rush where hundreds, then thousands of prospectors entered what was to become Colorado Territory.

Among the early arrivals were brothers George and David Griffith from Kentucky. They came to the new settlement of Auraria where Cherry Creek and the South Platte River joined. It was the fall of 1858, and the brothers constructed one of the first cabins in this fledgling town and settled down for the winter.

Believing that the early bird gets the worm, George A. Jackson and John H. Gregory made secret strikes during the early part of 1859. These were placer deposits located in the forks of Clear Creek, and when the news got down to Auraria and Denver, anxious prospectors headed into the hills.

By the time the Griffith brothers arrived at what was to

It all began with the discovery by George and David Griffith of rich gold ore, but it would be silver which made Georgetown famous. This is the covered portal to the Capital Prize Mine located near the original Griffith Mine at the east end of 11th Street at the top of a mine dump. *(Kenneth Jessen 099B9)*

become Central City, the place was overrun, and in their estimation, all the good claims had been taken. The brothers moved on, and in June, 1859, they worked their way up the South Fork of Clear Creek past George Jackson's discovery at Chicago Creek, and traveled west to the end of a broad, unoccupied valley. They camped along the South Fork of Clear Creek, and here they discovered that panning yielded fifty cents to a dollar in gold flakes in every pan. Encouraged by their discovery, the brothers constructed a cabin at a location which would later become Georgetown. A couple of days later, George discovered the Griffith Lode on the side of what was later named Griffith Mountain. The ore consisted of decomposed gold-bearing quartz which the brothers crushed and panned.

During the summer of 1859, the Griffith brothers recovered an estimated $500 in gold. Other prospectors arrived, and more claims were staked out. A camp began to form around the Griffith cabin and was christened George's Town.

David wrote the family back in Kentucky of the discovery. His two other brothers, John and William, their father along with John's wife, Elvira, made the long trip to Colorado and up Clear Creek to George's Town. It must have been a difficult trip since only a primitive trail provided access to the area. Elvira was the first white woman to enter the valley.

To provide order and prevent claim jumping, the brothers formed the Griffith Mining District. Officers were appointed, and George became the recorder to register all mining claims. Gulch or placer claims were limited to one hundred feet in length in the gulch where a discovery was made, while lode claims were confined to one hundred feet by fifty feet in size. A 640-acre plat was laid out for George's Town, and it wasn't long before the name Georgetown was used.

Getting mining equipment to Georgetown was next to impossible, so in 1860, the Griffiths took time away from mining and built a wagon road. It started near Central City at the head of Eureka Gulch and went over the mountains to Georgetown. It cost $1,500. It wasn't long before the Griffiths used their new twenty mile long road to haul machinery for a stamp mill to crush their gold ore.

The brothers charged a toll of $1 per round trip in an effort to recover their investment. They took in a little over $150 that first summer. The following spring, 1861, they added a toll gate.

The *Rocky Mountain News* suggested that an assessment be made on all the mines in the Central City - Georgetown area to buy the road from the Griffiths. The road was purchased and opened to the public.

The mill built by the brothers was powered by water brought by a flume from Clear Creek. The diverted water fell over the top of a water wheel to power six stamps used to crush the gold-bearing rock. The mill began pounding rock into powder in 1861 and was the second mill to begin operations in Georgetown.

The Griffith mine was located high on the mountainside; an ore chute a thousand feet long was used to get the ore to the valley floor. The Griffith Lode was mined through a twenty-five foot deep shaft.

Downstream from Georgetown, the Griffith brothers claimed part of the Clear Creek valley on behalf of their father, Jefferson Griffith. In 1861, they built a cabin for him, but unfortunately, he passed away the same year. The place became known as Mill City, and its name was later changed to Dumont.

By March 1861, Georgetown had forty residents, and the future looked bright. As summer approached, mining activity began to decline. The ore was becoming more difficult to mill as the depth of the mines increased. No longer was it possible to use primitive mechanical crushing methods followed by amalgamation with mercury. Near the surface, ore was naturally decomposed, but at depth, more sophisticated milling techniques were required. Much of the ore contained silver, but the milling process at the time focused only on gold.

These mining difficulties were compounded by Elvira's fear of invasion by Indians. The Griffiths moved from the area in September, 1862, and in January of the following year, sold their property to Stephen Nuckolls. Nuckolls paid $10,000 for the Griffith property. In the fall of 1863, he rebuilt the mill, and it operated under the ownership of a company in New York.

The most important discovery in the Georgetown area did not take place until two years later. In September, 1864, the

On the left and in front of a mining company office is Jesse Summers Randall, founder and editor of *The Georgetown Courier*. On the right is pioneer founder and editor of *The Rocky Mountain News*, William N. Byers. Ben Catren, Sr., local mine owner, is in the middle. This structure stands today and is a small store. *(Denver Public Library, Western History Department F33031)*

ex-Provisional Governor and resident of Georgetown, R. W. Steele, along with James Huff and Robert Layton found silver ore south of Georgetown at the head of Leavenworth Creek. The place became known as the East Argentine District. The vein of ore was exposed at the surface and was named the Belmont. Later it became the Johnson Lode.

The discovery was made by reasoning that the ore found near Snake Creek on the other side of the divide extended under the mountains. After prospecting for two or three days, James Huff found an outcropping on McClellan Mountain. Immediately, the men broke open the vein and extracted several pounds of ore. A Central City assay office confirmed its rich silver content. Later, an estimate was made on the value of the lode using six samples. The average value of the ore was $827 per ton in silver and gold as valued in the dollars at the time.

When news got out, prospectors rushed up Leavenworth

Creek to find their own lode. It was at a time when placer mining had pretty well exhausted the supply of gold and lode mining was just beginning.

After this discovery, Georgetown began to grow once again. Men with experience in processing the complex silver ore arrived which insured success. The Argentine Mining District was established to handle the numerous claims. As for Georgetown, the crude cabins began to be replaced with more substantial structures made of milled lumber. Local saw mills were kept busy. By 1868, the town's population reached 1,500.

Prior to this time, the U.S. Government placed silver coins at less than their metallic value on the open market which meant that a great deal of silver currency was melted and sold. Even though the U.S. was on a bimetallic standard, gold dominated the currency. Initially, the high silver content in the ore was ignored. The Civil War caused rapid inflation in paper currency. As a result, the price of silver soared making silver mines an attractive investment.

The Hamill House is owned and operated by Historic Georgetown Inc. as a museum. It represents the height of wealth and prosperity achieved by its owner, William Hamill. Originally built by his brother-in-law in 1867, Hamill purchased the house in 1874. As Hamill's wealth began to grow, he added to the structure. Of particular note is the solarium on the left, made up of curved pieces of glass custom manufactured and shipped all the way across the country. *(Kenneth Jessen 057C)*

To reduce the cost of transportation, Georgetown mine owners began to build their own mills. During 1866, three mills were under construction within the town. Mine owner John Herrick supervised the construction of the Georgetown Smelting Works, powered by Clear Creek water. A fourth mill, called the Washington, was started in November, 1867.

In 1864, the Mount Alpine Mining Company located its office in a small open piece of land south of Georgetown. A separate settlement grew up around their operation, and was named Elizabethtown in honor of Elizabeth Griffith. Several buildings were erected, and a swampy area filled with willows defined the boundary between Elizabethtown and Georgetown. As the two towns grew, this boundary became indistinguishable. Georgetown got its post office in 1866, and the following year, the two towns agreed to merge under the Georgetown name. Elizabethtown had its own survey, and as for Georgetown, the original survey done by pioneer David Griffith had been lost. A new survey was done to neatly combine the two towns. A town charter was granted by the Territorial Legislature in 1868, and Georgetown became the Clear Creek County Seat. From this point on, Georgetown was known as the "Silver Queen," and for decades to come, silver mining was its primary industry.

The life of William A. Hamill is often synonymous with that of Georgetown history. He moved from Philadelphia to Central City in 1865 to run a cigar and tobacco store for his brother-in-law, Joseph Watson. The lure of quick riches through silver mining brought Watson to Georgetown in 1866 and Hamill followed. A year later, Hamill moved his wife and two sons to Georgetown. In 1867, Watson constructed a modest home on the corner of Argentine and 3rd Street.

Watson ran into some bad luck with his own mining ventures and moved to Salt Lake City in 1871. Watson sold his home, and in the process, William Hamill became the owner.

William Hamill became one of the richest men in Colorado using a strategy of buying and selling mining property. He began by purchasing undervalued claims on Brown Mountain about two and a half miles west of Georgetown and above Silver Plume. His tactic was to become owner of a claim adjacent to a productive mine and then force the productive mine into extensive litigation.

By 1872, Hamill owned almost all or part of many silver

claims on Brown Mountain to the west of Silver Plume. The one mine he did not have, however, was the British-owned Terrible Mine at the base of Brown Gulch. When Hamill became the manager of the Dives in 1875, he begin working on the Silver Ore Mine next to the Terrible. He intentionally broke into the Terrible, and forced it into litigation and closure. The legal battle lasted from 1875 to 1877, preventing either mine from being worked profitably. The lower levels of the Terrible were at the center of the dispute, and the mine owners allowed these tunnels to flood. Hamill and his partner, Jerome Chaffee, eventually forced the British company to buy them out for roughly a million dollars and consolidate the Terrible with the Silver Ore.

Part of the payment to Hamill was a third interest in the consolidated property. This allowed Hamill to vote himself in as the manager. Hamill did such a good job as manager that by 1883, the company was able to pay its stockholders a dividend. The British, however, became fed up with Hamill's high-handed management style. Hamill reported to the board of directors only as he saw fit and ruled over the mining operations with an iron hand. The directors, however, found it difficult to unseat a major stock holder and a member of their own board. One large shareholder finally agreed to buy out William Hamill's stock.

The British formed a new mining company and began production. The tailings from the mine, however, became so extensive that they began to bury a property called the Rainbow. Of all the bad luck, it was owned by Hamill who had the court slap an injunction on the British company forcing them to stop mining. This left the British paying Hamill an additional $75,000 to buy the Rainbow.

From 1874 to 1881, William Hamill used his wealth to transform the simple, two-story Watson home into the largest, most elegant mansion in Georgetown. He hired Denver architect Robert Roeschlaub to design the addition. It became a show place for Hamill's parties and a source of pride for Georgetown residents. In addition to expanding the house, two substantial buildings were added to the rear of the property. One was a large two-story carriage house, and the other was a two-and-a-half story office building.

Expensive furnishings, such as the mirrors over the fireplaces, were purchased. Camel's hair wallpaper was hung on the walls. In the library, an embossed leather-like wallpaper was used. Alternating strips of maple and walnut made up the parquet flooring. Possibly the most spectacular room in the mansion was the solarium,

Jacob Snetzer constructed this classic false-front shop at Taos and 5th Street in Georgetown. Snetzer was known for the excellent quality of his work, and he charged $18 for a pair of pants and another $35 for a coat and vest. This building still stands today, but has been highly modified. *(Colorado Historical Society F38142)*

built in 1879. It was covered with curved panes of glass. Imported marble was used for the fireplace in the master bedroom. The exterior of the home was complimented by a beautiful lawn, garden, and shade trees surrounded by a low, decorative granite wall.

During this time in Colorado history, mining and politics went hand in hand. Eventually, Hamill became a leader in the Republican Party and was elected to the state senate in 1876. He served as chairman of the State Republican Party and was seriously considered as a gubernatorial candidate.

Hamill gave a great deal to the town of Georgetown. He was not only a civic leader, but an investor in the town's future. He was not universally liked, however, since some of Georgetown's residents had been victims of his litigation over mining claims. Hamill paid to have the first flagstone sidewalk laid in front of his house and a hotel called The American House. This was a departure from the wooden sidewalks which dominated Georgetown. The Alpine House No. 2 wanted a fire bell, and Hamill paid all of the expenses, including transportation, for a 1200 pound bell which still hangs today in that firehouse. He also donated money to the local Catholic Church for a bell. The Grace Episcopal Church also got its bell courtesy of William Hamill.

In 1881, Hamill constructed a two-story brick building in downtown Georgetown. Known as the Hamill Block, it remains in use today on Rose Street between 5th and 6th streets. Other

The Maxwell House, shown in this sketch, is rated as one of the finest examples of Victorian architecture in the United States. It was originally constructed by a Georgetown storekeeper named Potter and began as a modest two-story home. Potter struck it rich and expanded the original building. Frank Maxwell, a mining engineer, purchased the house from Potter and lived in it for fifty years. *(drawing by Kenneth Jessen)*

investments included a ranch in Middle Park, a farm near Denver, and a wagon road over Berthoud Pass.

Sometimes called "General" Hamill, he was named Brigadier-General in the state militia by Colorado Governor Pitkin after the Ute Indian uprising in 1879 on the White River Agency. During this time, he made field trips to insure that the Indians remained confined to their reservation. No conflict occurred.

At one time, Hamill was part owner of the *Denver Tribune* and also loaned Jesse Summers Randall money needed to start *The Georgetown Courier* in 1877. The loan was later repaid by Randall. Both men wanted a local paper with a Republican slant.

William Hamill raised four sons and a daughter in his Georgetown house. His fortunes were closely tied to the price of silver. When the Sherman Silver Purchase Act was repealed in 1893, the market for silver sharply declined along with William Hamill's wealth. He moved to Denver and passed away in 1904.

Historic Georgetown Inc. purchased the Hamill House in 1971 and began an extensive restoration project. They have spent an estimated half million dollars and keep the house open to the public for tours.

Christine Bradley, *William A. Hamill*, Colorado State University, Fort Collins, Colorado, 1977.

Frank Hall, *History of Colorado*, Vol. III. The Blakely Printing Company, Chicago, 1895, pp. 317-320.

"Our Town is Nicknamed Silver Queen," *The Colorado Miner*, June 6, 1872.

"Georgetown - The Christening," *The Georgetown Courier*, December 25, 1920.

Muriel Sibell Wolle, *Stampede to Timberline*, Sage Books, Chicago, 1949, 1974, pp. 114-122.

Liston E. Leyendecker, *Georgetown, Colorado's Silver Queen*, 1859-1976, Centennial Publications, Fort Collins, Colorado, 1977.

Georgetown - Silver Plume Guide to the Historic District, Cordillera Press Inc., 1990, pp. 7-19.

The Story of a Valley, Colorado Historical Society, 1984, selected pages (Note: This book does not have numbered pages)

David S. Digerness, *The Mineral Belt*, Vol. I, Sundance Publications, Silverton, Colorado, 1977, pp 23-33.

Frank Fossett, *Colorado, its Gold and Silver Mines*, C. G. Crawford, New York, 1879, pp. 355-403.

History of Clear Creek County, Specialty Publishing Inc, Denver, Colorado, 1986, pp. 23-27, 189, 196-197, 202.

GILSON GULCH

- *Clear Creek County, Clear Creek drainage*
- *Access limited by private property, site can be seen from public road*
- *No standing structures remain from original town*

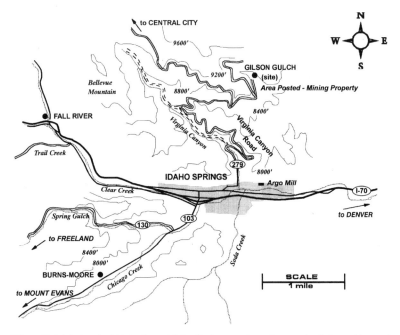

Gilson Gulch is located high above Idaho Springs and can be reached via a side road off the Virginia Canyon Road between Idaho Springs and Central City.

The town of Gilson Gulch once sat in the gulch by the same name high above Idaho Springs on the Clear Creek side of the mountain separating Gilpin and Clear Creek counties. The access road to the Gilson Gulch site exits the road up Virginia Canyon

about halfway up the hill from Idaho Springs. At the end of this
road is the Franklin Mine which covers most of the site.

What is disappointing is how little is left of this small mining town. Approximately fifteen structures show up in early photographs and none of them remain. Modern mine buildings
dominate the site today.

Gilson Gulch was founded during the late 1870s, well after
Central City and Idaho Springs got their start. The Gilson family
were the first residents, and they began mining a rich gold-bearing lode. After a while, a small community formed around the
mine to house the miners. The camp was somewhat disorganized
with homes intermingled with mine structures. Most residents
were Italian with some Frenchmen and Germans as well. Based
on the number of structures, the camp probably had less than
one hundred residents.

The Gem Consolidated Mines took over and sunk a shaft
down to the Newhouse Tunnel. This tunnel was drilled from
Idaho Springs to drain the mines in and around Central City.
The Newhouse Tunnel was also used for ore haulage directly to
the large Argo Gold Mill in Idaho Springs.

In 1893, a boarding house was opened by the Dumont family. The camp also had a saloon and a grocery store. To eliminate
taking children for a long daily trip to Idaho Springs, the town
constructed a school and hired a teacher. With no place to stay in
Gilson Gulch, it was the teacher that had to commute back and
forth from Idaho Springs.

It is not known when the town was finally abandoned. It
may have occurred slowly as the new mine owners expanded
their operations.

Robert L. Brown, *Ghost Towns of the Colorado Rockies*, Caxton Printers, Caldwell, Idaho, 1977,
pp. 179-183.

IDAHO SPRINGS
Was Jackson's Diggings

- *Clear Creek County, Clear Creek drainage*
- *Accessible via paved road*
- *Town has a post office; fully occupied town with many original structures*

Idaho Springs in the 1860s when its economy was linked to placer mining. *(Colorado Historical Society F31136)*

George Andrew Jackson set out in January, 1859 to explore what was then called Vasquez Creek, now known as Clear Creek. As he traveled up the creek to a point where it widened, he saw a mist rising in the distance. He thought it was an Indian camp. He exercised a great deal of caution as he crept through the snow until he could get a clear view. It wasn't an Indian camp, but a large herd of mountain sheep grazing on green grass in the middle of the winter. The vapors from a hot spring produced the mist and its warmth kept the grass green.

The following night, Jackson camped at the confluence of Chicago Creek and Clear Creek. His campfire melted a small area of the sand bar, and the next morning, he used his hunting knife to dig into the sand. He panned what he could dig up with his drinking cup. Much to his amazement, he got about nine dollars in gold flakes, nearly a week's wages. He marked the spot and returned to Golden.

Jackson waited until April to return to his find. He brought with him twenty-two men and wagons. The trip was very slow and required road building up the canyon. In places, the wagons had to be unloaded, dismantled and put back together on the other side of some of the narrow places. After a week or more, the men finally reached the spot where Jackson made his discovery. The first week alone yielded nearly two thousand dollars in gold dust.

At first, the camp which evolved around the gold-bearing sand bar was called Jackson's Diggings, then it became Sacramento City. Finally, the name Idahoe or Idahoe Bar was used, and in 1886, the word "Springs" was added. Historians have presumed that Idahoe was actually the Arapahoe word "edau hoe" meaning "gem of the mountains." Later the "e" was dropped, and the town became known as Idaho Springs.

By June, 1859, approximately 400 prospectors were at the sand bar. A mining district was organized to maintain law and order in filing claims.

Idaho Springs was selected as the county seat in 1861 and held on to the position until 1867 when it was moved to Georgetown. After a number of surveys, the Idaho Springs town site was officially registered at the land office in Central City in 1973. Land prices at the time were $1.25 per acre. By 1877, the town had over eighty structures.

The first post office was established in 1862 in a candle box partitioned into pigeon holes. Mrs. R. B. Griswold was post-mistress, and she place the box on her parlor table where it was convenient for her to sort the mail.

In 1860, F. W. Beebee and his wife constructed a primitive log cabin at Illinois Bar below Idaho Springs. They soon gave up on placer mining and moved to Idaho Springs near Virginia Canyon. The couple opened a log hotel which they called the Beebee House and charged $30 a week for room and board. They served what was available at the time, mainly bacon, beans, hominy, bread, dried apples, tea and coffee.

The first newspaper was published in Idaho Springs in 1873, but it didn't last. A second paper, the *Iris*, came along in 1879 and was followed by the *Idaho Springs News*.

The Colorado Central reached Idaho Springs in 1877 and solidified the town's economic future. It became a mill town, but also a place for miners to live. A good wagon road was built up Virginia Canyon to Central City to serve the many mines in this area. Another road was built south along Chicago Creek to serve these mines.

The hot springs, consisting of a mild carbonate and sulphate of soda solution, were commercialized in 1863 when Dr. Cummings purchased the land. He built a small, cheaply constructed bath-house and charged for bathing. Harrison Montague purchased the springs in 1871 and constructed the Ocean Bath House to replace the original structure and swimming pool. After the rail-road arrived in 1877, the springs became popular with Denverites. He also added a small hotel, and the name was changed to Saratoga of the Rockies. A number of notable people stayed at the hot springs including poet Walt Whitman, not so notable Frank and Jesse James and mining millionaire Horace Tabor. The springs changed hands again under the ownership of the Big Five Company at the turn of the century. A new hotel was opened and over the years, other improvements were made. It changed names again to Hot Springs Hotel and was partially destroyed by fire in 1951. Rebuilt, it is now called Indian Springs Resort.

The Castle Eyrie, possibly Idaho Springs' most unusual home, was constructed in the 1880s by Governor Bryon of British Columbia. He was one of the investors in gold mines in the area. He modeled the castle after his family home in England. The Chinese who worked the placer deposits in the Idaho Springs area were hired to build the castle out of locally quarried granite. Dr. Robert Metzler purchased it in 1965 and added a drawbridge and moat.

Other mining areas in the immediate vicinity of Idaho Springs included the small camp of Spanish Bar. It was a mile west of the town center. After the gravel beds were thoroughly mined during 1860 and 1861, the gold diggers turned to hard rock mining. They had little luck and most moved on. Spanish Bar was named for a party of Mexicans who joined in the gold rush.

A twenty stamp mill, owned by the Silver Springs Mining Company, was constructed at Spanish Bar by an aristocrat named Colonel Hart. Water was used to power the mill. Hart built a small stone house for his personal use and as an office. Decomposed gold-bearing quartz was milled, but the results were not profitable.

The small company town of Burns-Moore was located 1.4 miles southwest of Idaho Springs on Chicago Creek. The town consisted of a row of at least five cottages, and based on historic photographs, miners and their families lived in the town. One of the original structures is still standing on the site. *See "Gilson Gulch" for a map showing Burns-Moore.*

Hose No. 2 in Idaho Springs is a classic small fire station. It is located at the west end of town on Colorado Boulevard. *(Kenneth Jessen 107B11)*

Immediately west of Idaho Springs are the Whale and Hukill lodes, first developed in 1861. They were not profitable until John M. Dumont purchased them a decade later. He began to realize immediate profits and sold the mine after five years for what would be two million dollars in today's currency. The mine still had in its reserves thousands of tons of ore. John M. Dumont and E. S. Platt owned the adjoining Whale Mine and turned this property over to the Hukill Mining Company in 1878. This allowed the co-development of both properties. The property was sold again in 1879 to the owners of the Freeland Mine on Trail Creek. At one time, a brick building 300 feet long housed an ore concentrator at the Hukill-Whale property. The Hukill Mine, its headframe and buildings, still stand today on an isolated narrow piece of land bounded by I-70 on the north and Clear Creek on the south.

Probably no history of Idaho Springs would be complete without mentioning the water wheel immediately south of the I-70 bridge over Clear Creek at Bridal Veil Falls. It has been a landmark since 1945. This large wheel was once used to power a five stamp mill and other machinery at Charley Tayler's mine on Ute Creek to the south of Idaho Springs. Opinions vary as to when Tayler built the wheel, but it was sometime between 1893 and 1907. After Charley's death in 1939, the wheel was given to the town of Idaho Springs and was subsequently moved to its present location. It was an immediate sensation among tourists who stopped to see the wheel turning slowly powered only by water.

Over the years, the wheel suffered from neglect. The wood had decayed and money was donated to rebuild the old wheel. It was placed back in operation in 1974, but a little over a decade later, it had fallen into ruin again. Pieces of the rim were missing as a result of chunks of ice falling from above. This led to the wheel's complete reconstruction using new materials in 1988 with a new concrete foundation and supporting timbers.

This water wheel once powered machinery at Charley Tayler's mine on Ute Creek. It is now a popular Idaho Springs tourist attraction. After having been rebuilt several times, little remains of the original wheel. *(Kenneth Jessen 103D2)*

History of Clear Creek County, Specialty Publishing Inc, Denver, Colorado, 1986, pp. 7-8, 21, 349.

Frank Hall, *History of Colorado*, Vol. III. The Blakely Printing Company, Chicago, 1895, pp. 311-312.

William H. Bauer, James L. Ozment, John H. Willard, *Colorado Post Offices*, Colorado Railroad Museum, Golden, Colorado, 1990, p. 76.

LAMARTINE

- *Clear Creek County, Chicago Creek drainage*
- *Accessible via graded dirt road*
- *Town had a post office; partially standing structures remain*

Lamartine is more than a mile from the mine of the same name leading to confusion over its exact location. The Lamartine site is located at the junction of four roads, one which comes up from the Lamartine Mine on Trail Creek, one up Ute Creek, one from the east along the high voltage power lines and another road over Saxon Mountain from Georgetown. The town site is located in a high saddle above 10,000 feet between Alps Mountain to the east and Saxon Mountain to the west. The site sits in a meadow which slopes down toward Ute Creek.

When ghost town historian Muriel Sibell Wolle first visited Lamartine in 1946, two dozen cabins were still standing. When she returned in the 1970s, little remained, but several cabins still had their roofs intact. Today, there are the collapsed remains of two buildings, and in another decade or so, nothing but this high meadow will mark the site. There are many foundation platforms upon which cabins once sat located like stairs stretching from the bottom of the meadow to its top.

A historic photograph taken at the turn of the century shows eighteen homes and cabins. The town had its own post office, established in 1889, two years after mining began in the area. The ore was dominated by silver, but also contained gold and lead. Estimates place Lamartine's population at under five hundred.

The easiest way to reach the Lamartine site is up Trail Creek, beyond Freeland, by first driving to the large Lamartine Mine on a

Dusty Arnold and Ben Jessen at one of the few remaining cabins at the ghost town of Lamartine. There are numerous foundations from the lower portion of the meadow, where this cabin is located, up to the head of the meadow. *(Kenneth Jessen 101A7)*

good graded dirt road. At the mine, a narrow graded dirt road takes off up the steep hillside to the town site. The distance to the site is about a mile. This road could be impassable in bad weather for 2-wheel drive vehicles. The other roads to the town site require high ground clearance and four-wheel drive.

See "Freeland" for a map showing the location of Lamartine.

History of Clear Creek County, Specialty Publishing Inc, Denver, Colorado, 1986, p. 50.

Muriel Sibell Wolle, *Timberline Tailings*, Sage Books, Chicago, 1977, p. 35.

Robert L. Brown, *Jeep Trails to Colorado Ghost Towns*, Caxton Printers, Caldwell, Idaho, 1973, p. 122.

William H. Bauer, James L. Ozment, John H. Willard, *Colorado Post Offices*, Colorado Railroad Museum, Golden, Colorado, 1990, p. 85.

LAWSON

Named For Alex Lawson

- *Clear Creek County, Clear Creek drainage*
- *Accessible via paved road*
- *Town had a post office; several original buildings remain*

Originally a saloon constructed by Adolf Coors, founder of Coors Brewing Company of Golden, it was purchased by Walter E. Anderson and converted into a combination grocery store and gasoline station. When I-70 was constructed, traffic no longer flowed by Anderson's store and Walter retired. *(Kenneth Jessen 101B9)*

Alex Lawson, after his discharge from the Union Army in 1866, became one of the many prospectors seeking gold in Clear Creek County. By this time, most of the placer deposits had been exhausted, and the era of hard rock mining had started. It was difficult to make a living with a shovel and a pan.

After several days of panning, young Lawson was discouraged and moved into the freight transfer business. The nearest railhead was in Kansas, and he did some long hauls up to the gold fields of Colorado. The Denver Pacific reached Denver in 1870, and Alex began regular freight service up Clear Creek Canyon. He also opened his own stage line.

He settled down and married an attractive young woman named Kate. His courtship wasn't easy since Kate's father disapproved of Alex, and the couple ended up eloping. In the town he founded called Lawson, he constructed the Six Mile House and continued to operate the stage coach line. Soon other miners began buying lots and building in Lawson. The Six Mile House sold hard liquor which may have influenced the miners' decision to select Lawson as their home. Young Lawson's stage coach made its daily meal time stop at the Six Mile House adding to the business. The arrival of the Colorado Central in 1872, however, made stage coach travel unnecessary.

Kate and Alex had five girls, five boys and raised the orphaned children of Kate's sister. After their retirement, Alex and Kate settled in Middle Park.

The Lawson post office opened in 1877 and was absorbed into the rural delivery route in 1966.

In 1885, George Crofutt reported Lawson's population at 500 with four stores, the Six Mile House, a school and several places of public worship. At this time, the mines above Lawson were producing enough ore to fill three to five narrow gauge railroad cars each day. The ore was hauled to Denver for processing.

Lawson remains a viable town to this day. It may have lost some of its luster, and a trailer park may dominate its structures, but it is alive and never became a true ghost town.

The Lawson School, built in 1876, is privately owned and is kept well maintained. *(Kenneth Jessen 094A11)*

William H. Bauer, James L. Ozment, John H. Willard, *Colorado Post Offices*, Colorado Railroad Museum, Golden, Colorado, 1990, p. 88.

History of Clear Creek County, Specialty Publishing Inc, Denver, Colorado, 1986, (Within this work, the Lawson family history written by James C. Dedman.) p. 43, 185, 327-328.

Frank Hall, *History of Colorado*, Vol. III. The Blakely Printing Company, Chicago, 1895, pp. 315-316.

RED ELEPHANT

- *Clear Creek County, Clear Creek drainage*
- *Accessible by graded dirt road*
- *Camp had a post office; no standing structures remain*

Above Lawson on the north side of Clear Creek Canyon was the Red Elephant Mine and a small mining camp by the same name. Red Elephant was also the name of the mining district. D. C. Dulaney discovered the first silver ore in the area in 1876. After the mine was in production, it supported a crew of 120 men.

Red Elephant's post office opened in 1878 and closed three years later as mining activity tapered off. Structures in the community included a boarding house, company store and several cabins.

Muriel Sibell Wolle commented that, by the late 1940s, few buildings stood at Red Elephant. The mill, located below in Lawson, remained intact for many years with a trestle over the highway. From the trestle hung a sign with the outline of a red elephant. John K. Adrich, ghost town historian, reported that today Red Elephant is difficult to locate and that there are ruins scattered throughout the gulch.

For a map showing the location of Red Elephant, see "Silver Creek."

Muriel Sibell Wolle, *Stampede to Timberline*, Sage Books, Chicago, 1949, 1974, p. 38.

William H. Bauer, James L. Ozment, John H. Willard, *Colorado Post Offices*, Colorado Railroad Museum, Golden, Colorado, 1990, p. 120.

David S. Digerness, *The Mineral Belt*, Vol. III, Sundance Publications, Silverton, Colorado, 1982, pp. 222, 224.

Perry Eberhart, *Guide to the Colorado Ghost Towns and Mining Camps*, Sage Books, Chicago, 1959, p. 57.

Frank Fossett, *Colorado, its Gold and Silver Mines*, C. G. Crawford, New York, 1879, pp. 382-383.

Frank Hall, *History of Colorado*, Vol. III. The Blakely Printing Company, Chicago, 1895, p. 316.

SANTIAGO

- *Clear Creek County, Clear Creek drainage*
- *Accessible over rough dirt road; travel by car may be limited*
- *Town did not have a post office; no standing structures remain*

This was one of many mines in Clear Creek County that had a seasonal population. Santiago was located at over 12,000 feet and about 500 vertical feet above Waldorf. The mine was served by a railroad spur built in 1909-1910 from the Argentine Central's extension to the top of Mt. McClellan.

Santiago was still active when Muriel Sibell Wolle visited it during the 1940s. By the 1960s, there was only one structure left, and today nothing remains except mine tailings and scattered pieces of lumber.

The ore body was located in 1898 by William Rogers, but the mine was most productive after the turn of the century. At this time in history, the U.S. had just taken Santiago, Cuba during the Spanish-American War and the assumption can be made that this is how the mine got its name. A tramway was constructed in 1913 down to Waldorf. Little is know about how many miners lived at Santiago, or how long the camp lasted.

For a map showing the location of Santiago, see "Waldorf."

Muriel Sibell Wolle, *Timberline Tailings*, Sage Books, Chicago, 1977, p. 124.

John K. Aldrich, *Ghosts of Clear Creek County*, Centennial Graphics, Lakewood, Colorado, 1984, pp. 41.

SILVER CREEK

- *Clear Creek County, Clear Creek drainage*
- *Accessible by four-wheel drive road*
- *Town did not have a post office; no standing structures remain*

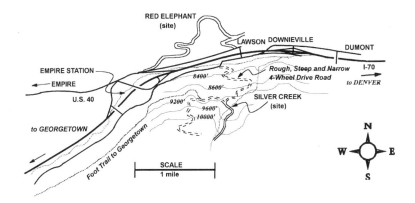

Silver Creek is located south of Lawson up a rough, steep and in places, narrow four-wheel drive road.

A rough, steep, four-wheel drive road leads up to the site of the old mining town of Silver Creek high above Lawson. To reach the road, head west from Lawson on the frontage road and just after it crosses Clear Creek, take a left. A few hundred feet up this dirt road is a branch to the left which leads to a private residence. The right hand branch heads to Silver Creek and becomes very steep beyond this point. At the top of the steep portion the road is built on a rock shelf. Farther ahead, the road switches back and becomes very rocky. It is easy to drive, but the large river gravel requires some navigation. Eventually, the road levels off and comes into the meadow at the site of Silver Creek with the creek dividing the town site.

Large mine dumps at the upper end of the valley testify to the extent of the mining in Silver Creek. Although no structures remain, there is the foundation of a small stone building which could have been a wine cellar or a powder magazine. (Some early saloons did incorporate wine cellars into their construction.)

The incredible Silver Creek to Georgetown wagon road, built in 1887 by the Georgetown Mining & Business Association, begins above the Silver Creek site and runs for seven miles south across the side of Saxon Mountain as a narrow shelf road to Georgetown. The idea was to provide a relatively flat route to the smelters in Georgetown for ore mined at Silver Creek. On the Georgetown end, it has been converted into a spectacular hiking trail.

Silver Creek started in 1884 as Chinn City or Daileyville. Where the name Chinn City came from is uncertain. James Dailey was the manager of one of the larger mines in the area and it seemed appropriate to name the town for him. Since the small stream coming out of this valley was already called Silver Creek, the residents decided to change the name to Silver Creek.

The school in this unincorporated town had 25 pupils. Since the town lacked its own post office, mail was picked up in Lawson daily. There was one saloon, one store, and one hotel.

In a historic photograph of Silver Creek, an attractive home or office was built at the Joe Reynolds Mine on its dump high above the rest of Silver Creek. In a 1904 photograph of the town itself, there were at least fourteen structures on either side of the creek which could have been homes while the rest of the buildings belonged to the mining industry.

Although there were two good producing mines, what ended large scale mining at Silver Creek, and all of the other silver mines, was the 1893 repeal the Sherman Silver Purchase Act. After 1905, newspapers made little mention of Silver Creek.

When ghost town historian Muriel Sibell Wolle visited Silver Creek in the 1940s, she reported that almost all of the buildings

This home or mine office building, overlooking the town of Silver Creek, seems out of place. All other buildings in Silver Creek were simple milled lumber structures. *(Colorado Historical Society F17835)*

were gone. Decades later, others reported seeing only sportsmen's cabins. Today, one can only ponder what life was like in the beautiful setting and whether or not those that toiled in the mines could enjoy their surroundings.

David S. Digerness, *The Mineral Belt*, Vol. III, Sundance Publications, Silverton, Colorado, 1982, pp. 217-220.

Muriel Sibell Wolle, *Stampede to Timberline*, Sage Books, Chicago, 1949, 1974, p. 112.

Muriel Sibell Wolle, *Timberline Tailings*, Sage Books, Chicago, 1977, pp. 37-38.

Robert L. Brown, *Colorado Ghost Towns - Past and Present*, Caxton Printers, Caldwell, Idaho, 1977, p. 51.

SILVER DALE

Underground Party

- *Clear Creek County, Clear Creek drainage*
- *Accessible via graded dirt road*
- *No post office; no standing structures remain*

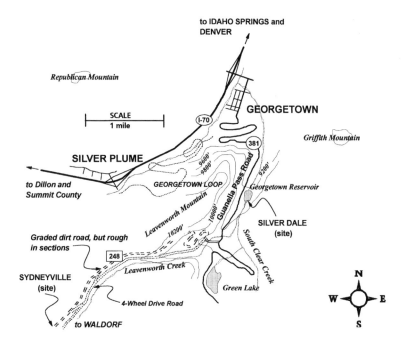

The Silver Dale site, where several stores were located, is located at the south end of the Georgetown Reservoir just below the Guanella Pass Road. A number of other structures, also part of Silver Dale, were distributed south of the reservoir.

Silver Dale's existence depended solely on the mineral wealth in the immediate vicinity, including the Colorado Central Mine at the confluence of Leavenworth and South Clear Creek. Silver Dale never had the population required for a post office, but it did have a one room school house which saw service for many years.

Mining along the Guanella Pass Road began to develop in 1864 with the discovery of silver ore. By 1873, Silver Dale had seventy-five residents, and on a map dated 1878, fifty-two structures are shown. The town also had two boarding houses. A dozen buildings sat at the town center on the shore of the Georgetown Reservoir.

A diphtheria epidemic in 1879 cost the lives of many of the town's children. Although almost obliterated by time, a few graves can be found along the south edge of the Georgetown Reservoir.

Silver Dale may best be remembered by an unusual party. It was given in the underground workings of the Marshall Silver Mining Company's tunnel above the town. The normal dark confines of the mine were illuminated for the occasion, and an estimated 800 to 1,000 people attended. A popular Georgetown group, Gordon's String Band, provided the music. Dignitaries included General Frank Marshall, president of the company. Most notable among the guests was Stephen Decatur Bross, editor of *The Colorado Miner*. In his earlier life, Bross had abandoned both his first and second wives and their children. His second wife knew nothing of the existence of his first wife until told by one of Decatur's relatives.

Another interesting resident of Silver Dale was Ada LaMonte, a well known prostitute who went "straight." Ada's real name was Ellen A. Mohier, born in New York City. She started a career as a bareback rider in a circus before heading across the vast prairie with her first husband. He disappeared, and she thought she lost him to another woman. She arrived in Denver in about 1860 and started a brothel. A fashionable two-story house on Arapahoe Street became her home. She specialized in high class clientele and ran what was termed a "clean" house.

Years later, a friend of hers used the same route across the prairie to reach Denver. Members of her party discovered a skeleton of a man with a bullet hole in his skull, clutching a Bible. It turned out that this was the very Bible Ada gave her husband, and was identified by its inscription. She now realized that she had falsely accused him of running off with another woman. Depressed, Ada began to drink. She moved to Georgetown where she opened another brothel.

After she married a mine owner named Sheridan, she moved to the portal of her husband's mine near Silver Dale and settled into a life of sewing and cooking. Presumably she lived to a ripe old age.

The Colorado Central Mine near Silver Dale alone produced between eight and eleven million dollars, and the combined output of the area was over twenty million dollars primarily in silver. After the Sherman Silver Purchase Act was repealed in 1893, most of the area mines closed. Only a few individuals stayed on in Silver Dale, and by 1905, just four or five cabins remained

Silver Dale consisted of mine buildings and cabins scattered along South Clear Creek above the Georgetown Reservoir. The mine dump for the Marshall Mine dominates the center of this photograph. Today, the Silver Dale site is void of buildings. *(Colorado Historical Society F25284)*

standing. A large mill to reprocess tailings was built in 1917, but failed financially. A mud slide in 1925 took out some of the town's structures, killing two boys. The body of one of the boys wasn't discovered until 1961.

To reach the Silver Dale site, drive up the Guanella Pass Road from Georgetown. After the climb up a series of switchbacks, look for the Georgetown Reservoir on the left. At the upper end of the reservoir was the lower portion of the town of Silver Dale. To reach the site, drive a short distance farther, and turn left down to a parking lot. From the parking lot, which is maintained by the Forest Service, cross a foot bridge and go left down to the reservoir. The town site sat on the gravel bed at the reservoir, and hardly a stick of wood remains.

History of Clear Creek County, Specialty Publishing Inc, Denver, Colorado, 1986, pp. 45-47.
Clark Secrest, *Hell's Belles; Denver's Brides of the Multitudes*, Hindsight Historical Publications, Aurara, Colorado, 1996, pp. 78-79.

SILVER PLUME
Mining And Tourism

- *Clear Creek County, Clear Creek drainage*
- *Accessible via paved road*
- *Town has post office; many original structures remain*

Silver Plume, looking west, in 1900. *(Colorado Historical Society F35842)*

Silver Plume became known as a miner's town while George-town, a short distance away, was the home of many wealthy mine owners.

Most of the silver lodes around Silver Plume were discovered during the mid to late 1860s with the largest concentration on Republican Mountain and Brown Mountain north of town. Big producers were the Pelican-Dives, Pay Rock, Seven-Thirty and the Terrible.

The town of Silver Plume was founded in 1870, after many of the initial discoveries were made, and the town was incorporated a decade later. A distinct commercial district grew up along Main Street and included a wide variety of stores. Fraternal organizations were active and some constructed lodges. Soon after its founding, the population exceeded 1,000. Ethnic groups included the Cornish, Irish, English, Italian, German and Scandinavians. Many of these immigrants had previous experience in the mining industry.

Silver Plume had nine saloons and two churches. It also had grocery stores, a drug store, clothing stores, shoe stores and a jeweler. During the town's peak years during the 1880s, about 2,000 people called Silver Plume their home.

On the 4th of July, Silver Plume hosted a large celebration geared around the skills of the miners. This included a variety of drilling contests. A hose cart contest was also held for volunteer fire departments, and from 1902 to 1910, the town had one of the best bands in the state. In 1913, a ski club was organized and included twenty-four charter members.

Just when Silver Plume's future looked good, a fire broke out on a November day in 1884. The fire started in a saloon and was soon out of control. The Silver Plume Hook and Ladder did its best to contain the fire as it steadily consumed the business district. Without fire hydrants or even a fire engine, it was a hopeless battle. The Star Hook and Ladder Company from Georgetown came up the wagon road, which connected the two towns, to help. They got the fire under control, but not until it leveled everything on both sides of Main Street. Silver Plume was rebuilt, and added fire fighting equipment, but never fully recovered.

The town of Silver Plume was almost abandoned in 1893 when the price of silver plunged. Although there were periods of time when mining would resume, activity was nothing like the boom years of the 1880s.

More by accident than by design, Silver Plume moved into the tourism era. The Georgetown Loop, located in the valley

Constructed by William Banton immediately after the 1884 fire, this Silver Plume building became a dry goods store. *(Kenneth Jessen 014D7)*

between Georgetown and Silver Plume, became a major tourist attraction. Many excursions ran from Denver ending at Silver Plume. At the wye, where locomotives could be turned, a depot was built. Later under the ownership of the Colorado & Southern, a large pavilion was constructed for the comfort of visitors. A covered platform provided shelter from frequent afternoon thunderstorms, and a tall, rustic, wooden clock tower allowed tourists to see the time.

The platform and clock vanished many years ago, but the pavilion was used as an after ski bar until it was destroyed by fire in the 1960s. The old Silver Plume depot was restored and is now used by the Georgetown Loop Railway.

Another Silver Plume attraction was the Sunrise Peak Aerial Tramway, completed in 1907. It was a short walk from the pavilion. Primitive buckets, more suitable to carrying ore, were used to transport the passengers. The buckets were suspended below a set of trolley wheels which ran on a heavy wire rope. The supporting rope was held high off the ground by a succession of wooden towers up the mountainside, and a second wire rope was used to pull the buckets along. The tramway climbed nearly to the top of Leavenworth Mountain and reached an elevation of 12,491 feet. A covered pavilion at the top provided minimal shelter from the sometimes violent afternoon storms and high winds. The trip up the Sunrise Aerial Tramway took about three-quarters of an hour and gained three thousand vertical feet in elevation.

With its head quarters in Silver plume, the narrow gauge Argentine Central used a series of spectacular switch backs to climb up Mount McClellan, reaching an elevation of 13,040 feet. The railroad's literature as well as a sign used for photographs at the end of track boasted that it reached an elevation of 14,007 feet. Never the less, the Argentine Central was the highest adhesion railroad in the world, and its lower terminal was near the Colorado & Southern pavilion. The line was so steep that it required geared locomotives.

The Argentine Central was constructed in 1905 and 1906 to serve the mines around Waldorf, but lack of rich ore combined with high operating costs produced insufficient pay-back. The railroad continued to operate, but as a tourist line. It was abandoned and the rails removed in 1918.

Today, the Georgetown Loop Railway is Silver Plume's primary tourist attraction. Trains run several times a day during the summer over the Devil's Gate viaduct to a the Silver Plume depot.

A 1926 photograph shows a Colorado & Southern train at the pavilion in Silver Plume. The pavilion was constructed specifically for tourists. *(Colorado Historical Society F44150)*

Using a geared locomotive, a train on the Georgetown Loop is shown crossing the Devil's Gate Viaduct located between Georgetown and Silver Plume. This bridge forms part of a spiral where the tracks cross over themselves. *(Kenneth Jessen 040A3)*

History of Clear Creek County, Specialty Publishing Inc, Denver, Colorado, 1986, p. 25.

Muriel Sibell Wolle, *Stampede to Timberline,* Sage Books, Chicago, 1949, 1974, pp. 127-130.

Georgetown - Silver Plume Guide to the Historic District, Cordillera Press Inc., 1990, p. 35.

SYDNEYVILLE

- *Clear Creek County, Leavenworth Gulch*
- *Accessible via rough dirt road*
- *Camp did not have a post office; no standing structures remain*

This was a station and water stop for the Argentine Central and not a town. Some miners lived near the Sydney Tunnel at Sydneyville, named for Matt Sidney. The mine, located below the Argentine Central grade, was quite extensive, but only a couple of structures remain standing, including the collapsed hoist house.

The site can be reached by leaving Georgetown on the paved Guanella Pass road. At the first intersection past the Georgetown Reservoir, the road to Waldorf leaves to the right and eventually joins the grade of the old Argentine Central railroad. Sydneyville is located a short distance beyond where this road levels off on the old railroad grade.

The remains of a hoist house at Sydneyville, located below the Argentine Central grade in Leavenworth Gulch. *(Kenneth Jessen 106B4)*

Perry Eberhart, *Guide to the Colorado Ghost Towns and Mining Camps*, Sage Books, Chicago, 1959, p. 54.
Dan Abbott, *Stairway to the Stars*, Centennial Publications, Fort Collins, Colorado, 1977, p. 77.

WALDORF

- *Clear Creek County, Clear Creek drainage*
- *Accessible over rough dirt road; travel by car may be limited*
- *Town had a post office; no standing structures remain*

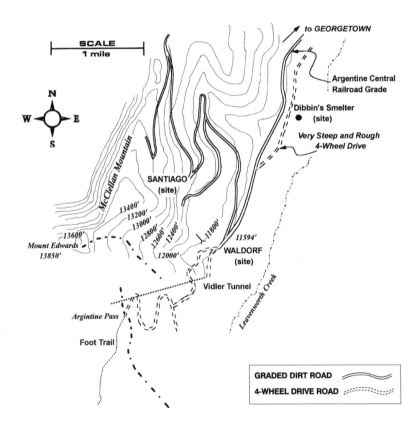

The Waldorf site is located in a relatively flat area near the headwaters of Leavenworth Creek at an altitude of 11,594 feet. The road to the site is graded, but is rough in places.

When this photograph was taken, the town of Waldorf was still occupied. Note the tracks of the Argentine Central and the post office. *(Colorado Historical Society F2781)*

The road to Waldorf leaves the Guanella Pass Road a short distance beyond the Silver Dale site at the Marshall Tunnel. At first, this road is narrow and steep, then it intersects the abandoned railroad grade of the Argentine Central. From that point, the grade continues at a steady 6% to Waldorf through some rugged country.

Waldorf just barely qualifies as a town. It sat on a hillside with structures on either side of the narrow gauge tracks of the Argentine Central. A large mill dominated the town. Its population was estimated to have reached 300, but this must have been a very optimistic figure.

Waldorf was part of the East Argentine Mining District, and mining in the area began early in Colorado's mining history during the 1860s. A large deposit of silver sulfide was discovered in 1864. Edward John Wilcox saw potential in the district and founded the Waldorf Milling and Mining Company. A large boarding house was constructed for the men who operated the mill. Waldorf also had a small store, a stable for the livestock, a machine shop and a power house. A tiny post office was opened in 1906, and it closed in 1912, after the railroad was abandoned. At an elevation of 11,666 feet, this was the highest post office in the United States. About four million dollars in precious metals were extracted during the life of the mines.

Wilcox also funded the Argentine Central. Construction of a railroad to such a high elevation was a bold move, but he needed low cost transportation for his mine. Track laying began in Silver Plume in 1905, and the line was finished the following year. A depot and water tank were constructed at Waldorf. A spur was built from Waldorf to the Vider Tunnel. The tunnel was drilled partially for mining and partially as a railroad transportation tunnel. Had it been completed, it would have allowed Argentine Central trains to run to Summit County under the Continental Divide.

The ore from the area mines was milled at Waldorf into a concentrate which was loaded into railroad cars and hauled to smelters in Silver Plume. Income from this operation couldn't pay the bills. As a result, the railroad was extended as a tourist attrac-

At an elevation of 13,040 feet, the Argentine Central was the highest adhesion railroad in North America. The tracks ended near the summit of Mt. McClellan. *(Denver Public Library, Western History Department MCC-686)*

tion almost to the top of Mt. McClellan using a series of switch backs. The end of this spectacular railroad was at approximately 13,040 feet. Many historic photographs show tourists holding a sign which read "14,007 feet." Near the end of track was a mine called the Crystal Palace filled with ice crystals all year round. This became part of the standard attractions of the route.

The railroad went bankrupt in 1912 and the rails were removed. The roadbed was turned into an automobile road. Waldorf was publicized as one of Colorado's most accessible ghost towns. Vandalism took its toll and the old hotel, which had stood through many severe winters, was set on fire in about 1960. The boarding house as destroyed in 1962, and the small post office stood until the early 1970s. All that is left to see at Waldorf is a small shack which probably does not date back to the town's boom years. There is a granite marker telling a little of the town's history.

Beyond Waldorf, there are a number of roads. A four-wheel drive road goes up to Argentine Pass. The railroad grade to Mt. McClellan can be driven with a vehicle having sufficient ground clearance.

William H. Bauer, James L. Ozment, John H. Willard, *Colorado Post Offices*, Colorado Railroad Museum, Golden, Colorado, 1990, p. 149.

Dan Abbott, *Stairway to the Stars*, Centennial Publications, Fort Collins, Colorado, 1977, p. 36.

Robert L. Brown, *Jeep Trails to Colorado Ghost Towns*, Caxton Printers, Caldwell, Idaho, 1973, p. 216.

YANKEE

- *Clear Creek County, Clear Creek drainage*
- *Accessible by four wheel drive vehicle*
- *Town had a post office; no standing structures remain*

Yankee was spread out across Yankee Hill at timberline. This area has reforested itself during the last century, and virtually nothing is left of this remote town. *(Denver Public Library, Western History Department L-288)*

Yankee (also called Yankee Hill) is noted on some contemporary topographic maps, yet nothing remains at the site. It was the terminus for the Yankee Hill Stage and Mail Route, run by John West, providing service six days a week from Idaho Springs via the Fall River Canyon. A second stage line provided service from Central City.

Yankee had a post office from 1893 to 1910. The town was spread out over a hillside with no apparent town center or main street. It started as a tent city when rich surface gold ore was discovered. Since the nearby mountain was named Yankee Hill by Northern sympathizers during the Civil War, it was logical that the town be called Yankee.

Bachelor miners stayed in a privately run boarding house while the married miners lived in cabins. The town had a small saloon. The North Star Mine was the largest employer at Yankee. The Gold Anchor Mine constructed its own concentration mill in 1905 near the town site. Another mining company constructed a small five stamp mill near the town. All in all, however, the ore was not as rich as investors originally thought nor was the deposit extensive. What must have been impressive, however, were the winters at 10,900 feet.

Electric power reached Yankee in 1902 via the Fall River, and a year later, a telephone line was brought across the mountains to Yankee. Ore was shipped by wagon from Yankee down the Fall River Canyon to Idaho Springs. This road, incidentally, is quite steep, and this must have made for some hazardous trips for the teamsters.

During the 1940s, Muriel Sibell Wolle was unable to drive all the way to Yankee and was obligated to hike. She found the old Gold Anchor Mill complete with a trestle and ore cars. She also found the remains of several cabins near the various mines in the area, but she did not find a town as such.

Robert L. Brown visited the Yankee site for his book, *Colorado Ghost Towns - Past and Present*, during the late 1960s. He found a historical photograph (shown to the left) with fourteen structures scattered at timberline across the hillside, and his contemporary view shows no trace of any of the buildings.

One way to reach Yankee is up the Fall River Road from its exit off of I-70 towards the St. Mary's Glacier Lodge. Below the lodge, a graded dirt road takes off to the right (east) and is marked Mine Road. At the apex of Mine Road, a very rough, steep four-wheel drive road goes to the right straight up the mountain. This is the Yankee Hill Road.

The other route is extremely difficult to follow even when armed with the latest maps, but it is far more interesting. This route uses a four-wheel drive road which leaves the graded dirt road to the Columbine Campground west of Central City. At the first major intersection, the way to Yankee heads north or to the right. Farther on, the road passes a small pond named Pisgah Lake. This is FS 175.3, and it continues north past many side roads, through a creek, past a small open meadow to another intersection. The left fork goes up the very steep, rocky Yankee Hill Road and is marked FS 175.3. At the junction with the Kingston Mountain Road near the top of a steep grade and a mile beyond the last intersection, the route to Yankee continues to the left. The next intersection is with a road which descends to the left into the Fall River drainage. At the top of a second steep grade are mine dumps, and where the road levels off and comes out of the trees is the Yankee site. Only a careful search will reveal the faint traces of this ghost town. The road continues over another saddle and down to Mine Road.

For a map showing the location of Yankee, see "Alice, Silver City and Ninety-Four."

Robert L. Brown, *Central City and Gilpin County*, The Caston Printers, Caldwell, Idaho, 1994, p. 156.

William H. Bauer, James L. Ozment, John H. Willard, *Colorado Post Offices*, Colorado Railroad Museum, Golden, Colorado, 1990, p. 154.

Robert L. Brown, *Colorado Ghost Towns - Past and Present*, Caxton Printers, Caldwell, Idaho, 1977, p. 312-317.

AREA SIX 6

Summit County

continued

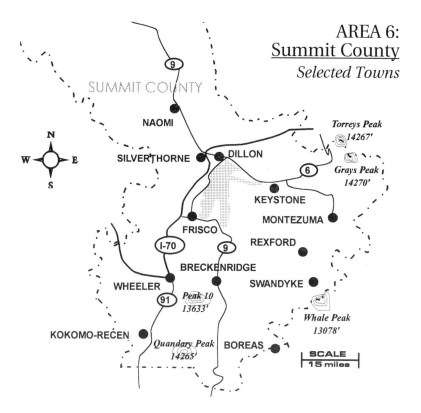

AREA 6:
Summit County
Selected Towns

Introduction to Summit County

Summit County is rich in mining history. Its towns and mining camps were scattered over a wide area in the Blue River Valley and its tributaries. Placer gold, found along the Blue River and up several of its tributaries, was the first precious metal discovered. Silver ore was discovered next along Tenmile Creek and in the Snake River drainage.

Beginning in 1882, well after placer mining was starting to yield to hard rock mining, two railroads entered the county, adding to its development.

Gold mining methods advanced from simple panning to hydraulic mining and then to dredges. Using outside capital, lode mining was used to recover silver ore and for mines like the Wire

Patch, where pure wire gold was recovered. Gold mining in Summit County spanned eighty years, while the boom years for silver mining were relatively short-lived.

The recovery of precious metals fueled the creation of numerous towns, varied in location, size and elevation. Many of these towns were abandoned a century ago as the sources of the mineral wealth were exhausted. Other old mining towns lasted into this century. Although partially abandoned, a few towns managed to remain intact through World War II.

Summit County was rediscovered, not by prospectors, but by outdoor enthusiasts wishing to get away from city life. The Dillon Reservoir, built during the early 1960s, began to change Summit County into a recreation-based economy. Cross country and downhill skiing developed at this time, and golf courses added balance to the activities. Bicycle trails, constructed in recent years, added another dimension to Summit County recreation. In the process, the old mining towns of Breckenridge, Keystone and Frisco were reborn, and their once empty stores are now fully occupied. Vacant lots are being filled by new construction.

There are many ghost towns in Summit County worth a visit. Preston is one of the easiest to reach, and if the road is dry, an automobile can negotiate the route. Surrounded by high peaks, Sts. John can usually be reached by car, although the road is rough. Farther up the valley at timberline is Wild Irishman, a mining camp with several standing cabins. Another ghost town which can be reached by car is Parkville, former Summit County seat. Swandyke, with its ghostly two-story log structure, requires a four-wheel drive vehicle. Rexford is equally picturesque, but also requires a four-wheel drive vehicle. The road over Boreas Pass goes through several ghost town sites now void of buildings. The remains of old gold dredges sit in ponds on both the Swan River and French Creek. Breckenridge and Frisco were never completely abandoned and have many well preserved Victorian homes.

Thanks to the Summit Historical Society and the Frisco Historical Society, much of the history of Summit County has

Wapiti is one of many ghost sites in Summit County. It included cabins and this large combination mine office, living quarters and post office. *(Kenneth Jessen 103C2)*

been published in the form of books and booklets. Many structures have been preserved and some are open to the public. There are also museums in Frisco, Breckenridge, Montezuma and Dillon. Of all of the mountain counties in Colorado, it is fair to say that the people of Summit County have been the most effective in their preservation efforts.

Colorado's No-Man's-Land

Conflicting territorial claims, changes in sovereignty, and inaccurate maps produced a no-man's-land unclaimed by the United States in the middle of Colorado.

It all began with Christopher Columbus in 1492, followed by claims by Spain and Portugal covering the New World. Exploration by Dominguez, Escalante, and others strengthened Spain's claim

on lands west of the Rio Grande River. The French claim of its
Louisiana Territory overlapped that of the Spanish. The French
explorer LaSalle claimed the entire Mississippi River drainage.

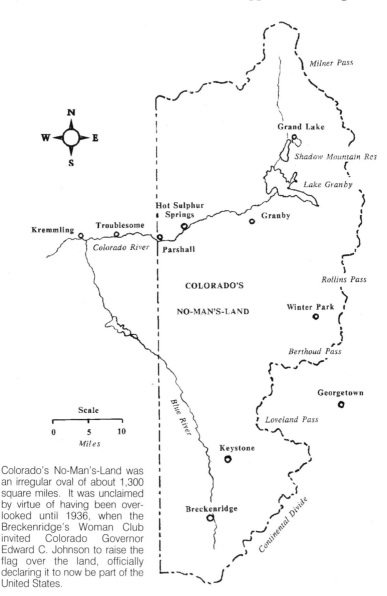

Colorado's No-Man's-Land was
an irregular oval of about 1,300
square miles. It was unclaimed
by virtue of having been overlooked until 1936, when the
Breckenridge's Woman Club
invited Colorado Governor
Edward C. Johnson to raise the
flag over the land, officially
declaring it to now be part of the
United States.

The primary area of uncertainty was the border between the western edge of the Louisiana Territory and the eastern edge of the lands included by the Spanish. Since this area was inhabited only by Native Americans, no real effort was made to resolve its borders.

In 1762, France ceded its Louisiana Territory to Spain. After nearly four decades, Spain gave the land back to France. England, meanwhile, claimed all land east of the Mississippi River, with the exception of Spanish-held Florida. The American Revolution in 1776 changed the sovereignty of England's claim. In 1803, the French sold the vast Louisiana Territory, with its poorly defined boundaries, to the United States. The only certainty was that the territory included the Mississippi River watershed, west to the Continental Divide, and as far south as the future site of Salida, Colorado.

In 1819, the United States signed a Treaty with Spain to set its western boundary contingent on the location of the headwaters of the Arkansas River near Leadville. A boundary line was drawn north to meet the latitude of 42 degrees, which was Spain's northern territorial limit. Before it reached this latitude, the line intersected the Continental Divide. This formed a pocket between the Louisiana Territory, ending at the Continental Divide on its western extreme, and Spain's eastern border, ending along a meridian between 106 degrees, 9 minutes to 106 degrees, 25 minutes. The border depended on where the headwaters of the Arkansas River were defined.

Spain's territory, in what is now Colorado, traded hands to Mexico. In 1836, this territory was traded once again to Texas. In 1850, it became part of the United States, then subsequently became part of the State of Deseret, Utah Territory, only to become part of Colorado Territory in 1861. The pocket of land not included under treaty comprised an area roughly 70 miles by 30 miles, forming an irregular oval of about 1,300 square miles from Breckenridge north to Middle Park.

On August 8, 1936, the Breckenridge Women's Club sponsored a unique celebration to officially lay claim to this last piece of land. Colorado Governor Edward C. Johnson unfurled and hoisted the United States flag followed by the Colorado flag. The Governor said, "For that vast territory, he (Napoleon) received 15 million dollars, but this little oval of 'no-man's-land,' considered so unimportant that it was overlooked entirely, has produced more than four times the total cost of the fourteen states with which Napoleon so readily parted."

It was sarcastically put by Robert Black, III, in his book *Island in the Rockies*, that "Assuming a permanent division (between the U.S. and Spain), Fraser, Granby, and Hot Sulphur Springs would have found themselves in the United States. Troublesome and Kremmling would have appertained to the Crown of Spain; the formalities of customs and immigration would have been conducted close to the site of Parshall."

Barney Ford

Barney Ford was disappointed that three or four thousand greedy prospectors had already beat him to the gold fields around Breckenridge. He had already been forced off of one claim by claim jumpers (men who force claim holders off their land). When Barney arrived in 1860, a year had passed since gold was first discovered within the Breckenridge area. He found Breckenridge to be a lively place with plenty of saloons and a mint, which turned out $5 gold pieces.

Regardless of the fact that all of the placer deposits of rich gold along the Blue River had been claimed, thousands of men toiled at shoveling gravel into sluice boxes in hopes of recovering gold dust or even a nugget or two. Barney Ford and his four companions headed east up French Gulch, panning the stream as they went. When they saw the yellow gold in their pans, they stopped, and Barney staked out a claim.

He wrote his wife that he had finally struck it rich in Colorado, but not to come out until the spring. Making the journey with their small child would be too risky.

The yield in gold dust by Barney and his companions grew by the day. He kept the gold dust in a jar buried beneath the dirt floor in a cabin he and his companions occupied. By the first of September all of his cash was gone, so he brought some of his gold in a sack to Breckenridge to exchange it for $5

Barney Ford was forced off of his gold claim near Breckenridge along French Creek, in part, because he was black, and under the law at the time, blacks could not hold mining claims. He settled in Denver and became a successful business man. He returned to Breckenridge and operated a well-patronized restaurant. *(Colorado Historical Society)*

gold pieces. Once in town, he ran into an old enemy, Dode. Dode had harassed Barney out on the trail to Colorado. Afraid that Dode might rob him of his bright shiny gold pieces, Barney waited in town until dark before returning to his cabin.

Under the law at that time, blacks were not allowed to own homesteads or mining property. This law applied to Barney Ford, forcing him to file his claim in the name of a Denver lawyer who told him he would take 20% of the value of gold recovered as a commission. After some time had passed since the claim was presumably filed by the lawyer, Barney became worried. He had not received confirmation as promised by the lawyer that the claim had been properly filed.

One afternoon, the sheriff appeared at his cabin door and served Barney with an eviction notice. It was sworn out by none other than his Denver lawyer! The attorney had kept the claim and had no intention of letting Barney recover any of its riches. The agreement Barney had with the lawyer was based only on a handshake.

That night, Barney and his companions heard a group of

horsemen approaching the cabin. Barney hid the bottle of gold dust in his shirt, and he and his companions fled into the dense forest. They headed up the hillside south of French Creek leaving all of their belongings behind. It was now the middle of September, and the nights were getting colder.

The group was led by Dode. Dode and his men tore apart the cabin floor in search of the gold dust they knew must be hidden somewhere. Meanwhile, Barney and his companions continued up the hill and spent a cold night without shelter or even a blanket knowing that if they returned to the cabin, they might be killed. They traveled by foot to Swan City where they were able to purchase supplies from a miner. This cost Barney most of his hard earned gold dust.

Not finding any gold in the cabin, Dode spread the rumor that the gold was buried somewhere in the vicinity of French Creek above Breckenridge. As the story passed from mouth to mouth, the amount of gold grew until is was in the hundreds of thousands of dollars. The hill Barney and his companions escaped over was given the derogatory name of "Nigger Hill."

Barney Ford returned to Denver, where he eventually built the fabulous Inter-Ocean Hotel. He became a wealthy man and expanded his hotel business by opening a second hotel under the same name in Cheyenne. Barney accepted a lot of financial risk and eventually he went broke. In 1880, he returned to Breckenridge. It had been twenty years since he had been run out of the area. He rented a modest frame house and was joined by his wife and daughter. Together they opened a restaurant called Ford's Chop House.

The rumor about the buried gold dust persisted. As Barney became prosperous, others believed that the source of his wealth was the hidden treasure up on the hill above French Creek. Barney could not go for a walk at night without being followed. Just for his own amusement, he would occasionally walk up French Creek with the intent to lose his follower in the woods before returning to Breckenridge.

His chop house became a popular gathering place. The income allowed Barney to purchase the building. He also purchased the Oyster Ocean restaurant in Denver, forcing him to split his time between the two locations.

In 1882, he constructed one of the finest homes in Breckenridge at the corner of Main and Washington on a city block he owned. This house still stands today and is a historical landmark. Barney managed to make a quick trade on some mining property, which yielded quite a nice sum of money.

As he and his wife grew old, they longed to return to the milder climate in Denver. With his money, he was able to go back to Denver and enter the real estate business. Through his transactions, the construction of apartment houses, and other good business decisions, the Fords became millionaires, which seemed impossible for African Americans at the time.

Originally, Colorado was composed of a patchwork of pieces of Kansas Territory, Nebraska Territory, Utah and New Mexico. In 1861, Colorado was recognized as a territory and in 1876, was admitted to the Union. Barney Ford insured that the laws of the new state of Colorado did not contain elements directed against minorities. He was among the very few inducted into the Colorado Association of Pioneers, and his wife, Julia, was listed in the Denver Social Register.

After a century, someone with taste and intelligence recommended that the hill above Ford's original claim on French Creek be renamed "Barney Ford Hill." The name was changed in 1964.

Nott's Stagecoach Line

Silas W. Nott was a Georgetown livery stable owner who recognized the need for regular stagecoach service from Georgetown through Summit County to Leadville. With the advent of new mining activity along Tenmile Creek in 1878, Nott figured that the time was right to initiate service.

The specific plan was to establish a route out of Georgetown up over Argentine Pass and down the Snake River past the towns of Decatur, Chihuahua, Montezuma and Keystone. The route would then go across the Blue River Valley to Frisco and up past Kokomo-Recen, Robinson and Carbonateville. It would enter Lake County over Fremont Pass where the mining town of Climax was located. Nott used this route with one major modification; he entered Summit County over Loveland Pass, which was 1,500 feet lower than Argentine Pass.

In 1879, Nott began grading work over Loveland Pass on what became known as the High Line. It certainly was high since Loveland Pass comes within a few feet of reaching 12,000 feet in elevation. Work progressed through the winter, and the route was completed in June of the following year. Service from Georgetown to Kokomo ran on Monday, Wednesday and Friday with the return trip to Georgetown on Tuesday, Thursday and Saturday. The leg between Kokomo and Leadville was handled by two other men who eventually were bought out by Nott and became his drivers.

The mail contract which Nott received from the U.S. Government from Georgetown to Kokomo put Nott's High Line on firm financial ground. Nott began running his Concord coaches all the way to Leadville with a Georgetown departure time of 5:00 a.m., arriving in Leadville at 7:00 p.m. A one-way ticket was $7 to Kokomo and $10 to Leadville.

Most interesting is Nott's advertisement of no walking, no dust and no danger. Most of the time this was true, but on some trips, none of these claims were true. Nott's business, however, prospered due to the high demand for reliable transportation in a growing mining economy with no previous service.

The road over Loveland Pass was extremely primitive and portions of this original road can still be seen today on the west side of the pass. It was more like a rough four-wheel drive road, and along the route were abandoned wagons and dead draft animals. During the spring thaw, the bottom land was swampy and passage was impossible at times.

Winter operations posed special problems for Nott. He

boldly advertised he would run his stagecoaches all winter, but the reality of high country travel had a negative effect on his plans. High winds combined with drifting snow and avalanches closed the Loveland Pass route much of the time. Nott turned to light wagons and sleighs, and his drivers were decked out in long winter coats with burlap covering their feet.

Argentine Pass, despite its elevation, was blown free of snow much of the winter and was used by Nott. On the Peru Creek side, a long exposed traverse was built across a rock cliff making travel very hazardous. Sometimes the baggage had to be abandoned to be picked up later. Men were stationed along the route to clear the snow with shovels. At times, the animals would literally fall off the edge of the road and have to be lifted back on the road using the wagon or stagecoach tongue as a lever arm. The drivers would sometimes ask the passengers to help push a loaded stagecoach or to clear the road.

Despite these problems, Nott's stagecoach line was extended to Breckenridge and enjoyed immediate success. He changed the schedule so that passengers arriving by train from Denver could make connections with the Leadville stage. Nott's stagecoach line was to some degree responsible for the rapid development of the Ten Mile District. It was new technology that made the stagecoach obsolete. The arrival of narrow gauge railroads into Summit County eventually put an end to Nott's business. The Denver & Rio Grande extended its line into Summit County in 1882, followed two years later by the Denver, South Park & Pacific.

Mary Ellen Gilliland, *Summit*, Alpenrose Press, Silverthorne, Colorado, 1980, pp. 62-63.

Forbes Parkhill, *Mister Barney Ford*, Sage Books, Denver, Colorado, 1963, pp. 102-104, 182-184.

Stanley Dempsey and James E. Fell, Jr. *Mining the Summit*, University of Oklahoma Press, Norman, Oklahoma, 1986, pp. 80-82.

Robert C. Black III, *Island in the Rockies*, Grand County Pioneer Society, Grand Lake, Colorado, 1969, pp. 16-19.

ADRIAN

- *Summit County, Snake River drainage*
- *Accessible via paved road*
- *Site did not have a post office; no standing structures remain*

Adrian is still shown on topographic maps, yet it amounted to very little in the way of a town or a camp. It was located about four miles east of where the Montezuma Road leaves U.S. 6 and just before the turn off to Peru Creek.

Adrian was founded by Dr. McKenney from Illinois and was to have become more of a resort town than a mining camp. For the benefit of its guests, excursion boats were to operate on the Snake River. Several cabins were constructed, then Dr. McKenney passed away. The project was abandoned and the cabins moved or razed. Nothing remains today at the site.

For a map showing the location of Adrian, see "Chihuahua."

Verna Sharp, *A History of Montezuma*, Sts. John and Argentine, Summit Historical Society, Breckenridge, Colorado, 1971, p. 29.

Verna Sharp, "Montezuma and Her Neighbors," *Colorado Magazine*, Vol. XXXIII, No. 1 (January, 1956), p. 31.

BOREAS

Where The Cold Winds Blow

* *Summit County, Continental Divide*
* *Accessible via graded dirt road*
* *Camp had a post office; one standing structure remains*

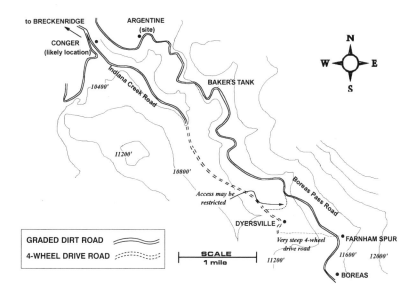

Boreas was at the top of Boreas Pass, elevation 11,491 feet. It can be reached via a graded automobile road, which at times, can be quite rough.

Boreas, god of the north wind, was the name of a station on the Denver, South Park & Pacific. Section hands and the station agent lived at Boreas, elevation 11,481 feet. Aptly named, the north wind blows constantly, and on a typical summer day, Boreas can be a cold place to visit.

The railroad reached Boreas Pass from Como in 1881, on its way to Breckenridge, and 600 feet of snowshed was erected to

The section house on Boreas Pass in 1974, prior to restoration. Its roof had partially collapsed along with other damage as a result of the relentless wind and driving snow. *(Kenneth Jessen 003B)*

protect the narrow gauge tracks from the constant blowing snow. The railroad also built a one and one-half story log section house with five rooms. This structure remains standing today and was recently restored.

Also at Boreas was a two-room log telegraph office, a log storage shed, a small depot built into the snow shed, a cabin and a home. The most spectacular structure was a 57 foot by 155 foot stone engine house with an enclosed turn table. Other railroad facilities included a coal bin and water tank.

Boreas had its own post office, which opened in 1896 and remained in operation until 1905. Trains were discontinued over Boreas Pass in 1910 and Boreas was abandoned.

Today, the ruins of the stone engine house are along the road over the pass. The section house, at one time partially collapsed, has been restored. The remains of a cabin can be found on the south side of the section house, and that is all that is left of this remote outpost.

Mary Ellen Gilliland, *Summit*, Alpenrose Press, Silverthorne, Colorado, 1980, pp. 208-209.

William H. Bauer, James L. Ozment, John H. Willard, *Colorado Post Offices*, Colorado Railroad Museum, Golden, Colorado, 1990, p. 22.

Mac Poor, *Denver, South Park & Pacific*, Rocky Mountain Railroad Club, Denver, 1976, pp. 444-445.

BOSTON
Colorado Style

- *Summit County, Ten Mile Creek drainage*
- *Accessible via four-wheel drive road*
- *Camp did not have a post office; several standing structures remain*

High above the spectacular Ten Mile Canyon in a natural amphitheater at the head of Mayflower Gulch was a camp called Boston. The Boston Mining Company owned a gold placer operation.

Mary Ellen Gilliland in her book, *Summit,* tells of a visitor who was born in Boston, Colorado many years ago and returned in 1979. He discovered what was left of his mother's brass bed and some of his old toys half-buried in the yard outside of the cabin where his family lived. A number of log cabins still stand at Boston. The Colorado Mountain Club maintains one of the cabins as an emergency shelter.

For a map showing the location of Boston, see "Kokomo-Recen."

Mary Ellen Gilliland, *Summit*, Alpenrose Press, Silverthorne, Colorado, 1980, p. 168.

BRADDOCKVILLE

And Bronco Dave

- *Summit County, Blue River drainage*
- *Accessible by paved road;*
- *No standing structures remain; also called Braddocks or Bronco*

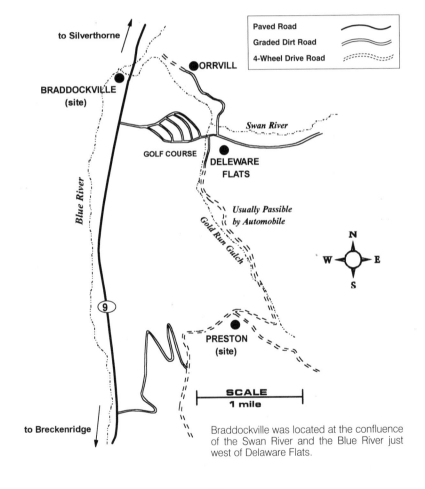

Braddockville was located at the confluence of the Swan River and the Blue River just west of Delaware Flats.

Bronco Dave Braddock was one of those rare enterprising individuals, the type of individual who gives an area its color and vitality. Dave was in his forties when he first arrived in Breckenridge in 1880. His first business venture was a stage line to the various mining camps in the Swan Valley to the north. He used the Domestic Bakery on Main Street as his ticket office. Business was great until someone shot one of his horses and put him out of work.

Dave Braddock was not deterred by this or any other setback. He decided to found a town and called it Braddockville. It was located at the confluence of the Blue River and the Swan River near Delaware Flats. When the Denver, South Park & Pacific built their narrow gauge line through the Blue River Valley in 1882, they constructed a ticket station at Braddockville giving the location some legitimacy. Mrs. Braddock was appointed station agent. The railroad also constructed a 1,072 foot siding to handle freight destined for the mining camps in the area. The railroad referred to the place as Braddockville or Bronco.

A few houses were constructed on the site, but Braddockville remained a very small community. It consisted mainly of Dave's home and a hotel he built called the Braddock House. The hotel opened in 1882 along with a dance hall. The editor of the Breckenridge newspaper recommended that families take their Sunday buggy ride down the Blue River to Dave Braddock's little town. Braddockville eventually gained a saloon and livery stable.

The following year, Bronco Dave saw a major business opportunity. He began to manufacture a "temperance drink." It was an alcohol-free beer and was distributed to area bars as an alternative to regular beer. The product received good reviews, and some forty-two dozen cases were sent up to Montezuma. As a sideline, Dave used the bottling plant for mineral water, which was also distributed throughout the Blue River Valley. During a severe wind storm, however, the bottling plant was destroyed. The front of the structure was first blown out, disconnecting the stove pipe from the roof and allowing sparks to ignite the structure. Bronco Dave rebuilt and expanded his business to include manufacturing operations in Breckenridge and Leadville.

A post office was established at Braddockville in 1884, with Dave as postmaster. Mail was carried on horseback during the summer to the surrounding mountain towns including Swan City, Parkville and Preston. In the winter, snowshoes were used.

In September, 1887, Bronco Dave went up and down the streets of Breckenridge yelling about fresh radishes and turnips. The produce was grown in his backyard garden and was an immediate success to the many households where fresh vegetables were rare. This was the first business of its type in the area, and soon Dave was tilling over one hundred acres next to his home. At an elevation of 9,640 feet, it was remarkable that he could grow anything and his crops received national attention in *Field and Farm* magazine. He was constantly experimenting with various crops to see which ones could grow during the short summer season. Crops had to survive occasional freezing weather at any time, even during July and August. Dave jokingly commented that he believed his farm was too wet for bananas!

Braddockville and Bronco Dave faded into history. The post office was closed in 1890. As late as 1891, Dave ran a stage line from Breckenridge to Lincoln up French Creek. From this point on, little is known about Dave Braddock and his family. Today, only the cinders from the narrow gauge steam locomotives mark the site were Braddockville once sat.

Mark Fiester, *Blasted, Beloved, Breckenridge*, Pruett Publishing Company, Boulder, Colorado, 1973, pp. 143-148.

Summit County Journal, January 30, 1882, March 8, 1882, June 25, 1888.

BRECKENRIDGE

Snubs V.P. And Changes Its Name

- *Summit County, Blue River drainage*
- *Accessible by paved road*
- *Occupied town; many original structures*

Breckenridge in the 1860s. Note how little water is in the Blue River. The miners diverted the water to allow them to dig down to bedrock where the gravel yielded the greatest concentration of gold. *(Colorado Historical Society F7836)*

Ruben J. Spaulding entered the Blue River Valley with fourteen other prospectors from South Park in August, 1859. The first mining claims were made about one-fourth of a mile north of the present town of Breckenridge. Spaulding and his party dug a hole into the rocky soil three feet deep on a sand bar. The very first pan yielded only 13 cents in gold, but the second pan contained 27 cents in gold and things got progressively better as the prospectors dug deeper. As much as two dollars a pan could be recovered, and initially, it was easy money in a time when wages were only $1.50 to $2.00 per day. Each member of the party staked off claims along the Blue River.

The Ute Indians caused a great deal of fear among the party. For protection, a primitive fort was erected of logs. It was dubbed Fort Mabery to honor the first white woman to cross over into the valley. The fort took the form of a square block-house, but its cramped quarters and lack of ventilation made for poor living conditions. Green logs were used in the construction, render-

The Edwin Carter Museum in Breckenridge was built in 1875 by naturalist Edwin Carter. He was among the first gold seekers in California Gulch near Leadville in 1860, but went on in life to carefully collect samples of the animals and birds in Colorado's high country. In 1892, he proposed moving his museum to Denver. This was the start of the Denver Museum of Natural History. *(Kenneth Jessen 104C4)*

ing the fort fire-proof. The roof was covered with sod. The small fort was occupied during that first winter of 1859-1860 as well as the following winter. The anticipated attack by the Ute Indians never came and the fort was eventually abandoned in favor of more comfortable cabins.

The name of the fort has been contested over the years. William Newton Byers, founder and editor of the *Rocky Mountain News*, called it Fort Mary B. while other sources, such as *Stampede to Timberline*, use Fort Meribeh. Others noted that its name was Fort Independence.

The miners teamed up to divert the Blue River using a flume four miles long, which was completed in the fall of 1860. With the water flowing around their claims, they could dig down to bedrock where the richest gold-bearing gravel was located. Trees were felled and whip-sawed into crude planks so that sluice boxes could be constructed. If the box was relatively long, it was referred to as a long Tom. Spaulding constructed three such boxes and began working in near freezing, ankle deep water with rope wrapped around his feet. After shoveling tons of gravel for a day, Spaulding recovered ten dollars in gold and also caught a bad cold.

Along with nine others, Spaulding spent the winter of 1859-1860 at Fort Mabery. They soon discovered that snow accumulated up to six feet deep in the valley. Among the prospectors were two Norwegians who constructed "snowshoes" consisting of 13-foot long boards, turned up in the front and four inches wide. Spaulding and a few others abandoned the fort, strapped on the Norwegian skis, and moved downstream. New claims were staked and a small cabin was constructed. This was, by the way, the first recorded incidence of skiing in the Blue River Valley.

Close to the Spaulding claim, William Iliff and his partner found a pocket of gravel that produced two dollars worth of gold per pan and in a space just forty feet square, $7,000 in gold was recovered in a few days. When the Iliff party returned to Denver and the gold-hungry prospectors actually saw the dust, a major stampede to the Blue River Valley took place. In March of 1860,

Eli Fletcher lived in this home at 100 N. High. He came to Breckenridge when he was just five years old and was among its earliest residents. This is actually a log building with clapboard siding. Fletcher was known for his handmade skis, which he fabricated in his garage. *(Kenneth Jessen 104B12)*

twenty men, one woman and four children stayed at Fort Mabery, but by the fall of that same year, an estimated 2000 people were camped along the Blue River.

Accounts vary as to exactly how Breckenridge got started. The miners were in search of easy gold and were not intent on the formation of towns. One of the stories relates that in August, 1859, General George Spencer, along with other prospectors, entered the Blue River Valley and built some cabins. Spencer laid out a 320 acre town, but some of the land had already been claimed. Spencer then moved up the Blue River and founded a second town next to a site that Felix Poznansky staked out. Spencer and his rival, Poznansky, met in South Park to resolve their differences over the town site. Spencer boasted that he would make the first "improvement," a necessary move to solidify his claim to the land, and meet the conditions of the Homestead Act. Poznansky managed to get a message to his son who happened to be in the Blue River Valley. He told his son to lay down some logs and loosely meet the requirements for the improvement. Spencer counterattacked by offering anyone at the Poznansky town site a free lot in his new town of Independence. As the story goes, Spencer's town won out.

But any self-respecting town needs a post office. How can a small mining town in the remote Territory of Colorado get Washington's attention?...name the town for the vice president of the United States, of course. This is exactly what Spencer did. The town became Breckinridge, named for John Cabell Breckinridge who served as vice-president under President Buchannan. This simple act got General Spencer what he wanted, a post office. As a bonus, he was named the postmaster.

In 1860, Vice President Breckinridge ran on the pro-slavery ticket, which lost to Abraham Lincoln and the Republican Party. Breckinridge resigned from the U.S. Senate and joined the Confederate Army, an act pro-Union residents of Breckinridge could not tolerate. The town did not abandon its name, but instead to show their contempt, the town modified the spelling of their town to Breckenridge.

The *Rocky Mountain Herald* reported that in June, 1860, ten houses were under construction. By October, the town of Breckenridge was reported to include sixty log homes with up to 4,000 miners engaged in gold mining, according to the *Golden City Western Mountaineer.* Supplies began to run short by the end of 1861, and the miners pleaded with Denver merchants to send wagon loads of food and clothing with the promise of handsome profits. None of the miners wanted to abandon their claims to travel the long distance to Denver. Any miner knows that placer gold found in the gravel is quickly exhausted. In addition, some of the miners were pulling in as much as twenty dollars per day. Nevertheless, the prospect of starvation forced many to leave, and the rest of the Blue River Valley miners stuck out the winter on flour and bacon.

When the spring of 1862 came, as many as two hundred miners per day were coming in over Georgia Pass along with pack trains of supplies. The canal, which diverted the Blue River around the claims, was enlarged. Ute Indians came into the area not to cause trouble, but to beg for food. As many as 1,200 were camped along the Blue River Valley near the present-day town of Frisco.

Breckenridge had one woman resident and hundreds of men. George Spencer opened up a law office and became the first professional in town. Several well-stocked stores opened. Along the various tributaries of the Blue River, prospectors fanned out and labored over their pans and sluice boxes. The banks along the streams became vast tent camps.

Things changed as the town grew. In 1880, the year Breckenridge was incorporated, it was ranked fifteenth in population among Colorado towns with nearly two thousand residents. It had double the population of any other Summit County town. By this time, there were 147 businesses including three banks and two telegraph offices.

Forest fires raged along French Creek set by careless miners. What timber didn't burn was harvested for cabins and sluice boxes. The pristine wilderness, which had remained untouched for thousands of years, was quickly destroyed. As all the good placer claims were taken, miners expanded into the more remote regions of the Blue River Valley. The Swan River Valley yielded fabulous amounts of wire gold, but at a heavy cost to the environment.

At a lower elevation with a milder climate, Dillon began to rival Breckenridge. The *Montezuma Mill Run* reported that in the November 1882 election, where the location of the county seat was put to a vote, Dillon cast over 1000 votes vs. 832 votes from Breckenrige. Dillon almost won the two-thirds of votes throughout the county necessary to move the county seat.

Breckenridge continued to grow and become one of the top mining camps in Colorado. However, when the last gold dredge operating in the Blue River Valley cut its power in 1942, Breckenridge almost became a ghost town. For two decades, the town had

The town surveyor, Charles Walker, constructed this log home in 1875. It is now a bed and breakfast. *(Kenneth Jessen 104B9)*

just a few residents. The ski industry revitalized the town, and it has been growing every since.

Breckenridge is a Colorado treasure worth visiting. Most of the older homes lie to the east of the main street, and many of these homes have an interesting history. Several original commercial buildings also survive. The Summit Historical Society has placed plaques on the most significant historic structures.

Father John Dyer took charge of the Blue River Mission in 1862 for the Methodist Church and carried the Word of God through the primitive mining camps in Summit, Lake and Park counties. This chapel was constructed by Father Dyer using volunteer labor in 1880. A number of additions, however, have been made next to the original building. The belfry was added in 1889. *(Kenneth Jessen 104C3)*

Golden City Western Mountaineer, October 25, 1860.

Jane Morton, *Dyer, Dynamite & Dredges*, Father Dyer United Methodist Church, Breckenridge, Colorado, 1990, pp. 1-11, p. 51-54.

Mark Fiester, *Blasted, Beloved, Breckenridge*, Pruett Publishing Company, Boulder, Colorado, 1973, pp. 15-24.

Muriel Sibell Wolle, *Stampede to Timberline*, Sage Books, Chicago, 1949, 1974, pp. 72-78.

The Summit County Journal, January 1, 1881.

The Rocky Mountain Herald, June 16, 1860.

The Montezuma Millrun, November 18, 1882, December 12, 1882.

CARBONATEVILLE
Short Lived

- *Summit County, Tenmile Creek drainage*
- *Town did not have a post office*
- *Site buried under tailings*

Although placer gold had been successfully mined in the area, it would be the discovery of silver ore that brought to life the town of Carbonateville in 1878. Most of the original prospectors came from Leadville. Carbonateville was located at the base of Fremont Pass about a mile south of Robinson and at the mouth of McNulty Gulch.

By 1879, a long list of businesses could be found in Carbonateville including a couple of clothing stores, four grocery stores, a shoe store, two barber shops, meat market, and paint store. The town also had a couple of doctors and several attorneys. There was a liquor store and seven saloons. The largest hotel in Carbonateville was the Delmanico of the Pacific, able to accommodate 100 guests. This two-story structure measured 36 feet by 60 feet. In addition to the Delmanico, the town had five other hotels and two boarding houses.

The first bank in the Ten Mile District was the Merchant's and Miner's Bank in Carbonateville. This bank could exchange gold dust by weight to currency. Another service was the exchange of foreign currency. A Yale time lock protected the safe. The owners were Anthony Blum and A. H. Reynolds, and in the fall of 1879, Blum wrote some questionable bank drafts and suddenly left Carbonateville. He had with him several thousand dollars belonging to local merchants, the type of theft the Yale lock could not protect against. A warrant was issued for his arrest, but lack of an organized law enforcement network allowed Blum to escape. Confidence in the bank dropped, and it eventually failed. But mining was not the only thing that supported the economy of Carbonateville. Judge John S. Wheeler, with his partners, built a sawmill under the name Ten Mile Saw Mill Company in Carbonateville. All types of lumber was harvested in the area to meet the high demand for shingles, siding, farming material and mine timbers. There were also building contractors and carpenters for hire in Carbonateville.

A post office opened in Carbonateville in 1879 only to close two years later as the population began to dwindle. During this same year, Frank Fossett provided an interesting description of Kokomo, Ten Mile (Robinson) and Carbonateville by saying, "The embryo cities of...presented a strange medley of log cabins, tents, and primitive habitations, and the prices of town lots compared in altitude with the places in which they were located."

By 1885, Carbonateville was all but dead and does not appear on the U. S. Geological Survey maps after that date. George A. Crofutt in his *Crofutt's Grip-Sack Guide of Colorado* reported, "It was once a booming camp...just east from the town site, which now contains only a store and a half a dozen buildings, is the once famous McNulty Gulch." The population had moved to Robinson, only a mile away, or to Kokomo-Recen, a little farther down Tenmile Creek.

See "Kokomo-Recen" for a map showing the approximate location of Carbonateville.

Frank Fossett, *Colorado, its Gold and Silver Mines*, C. G. Crawford, New York, 1879, p. 85.

George Crofutt, *Crofutt's Grip Sack Guide of Colorado 1885*, Johnson Books, Boulder, Colorado, 1966, 1981, p. 77.

Mary Ellen Gilliland, *Summit*, Alpenrose Press, Silverthorne, Colorado, 1980, pp. 169-170.

Stanley Dempsey and James E. Fell, Jr. *Mining the Summit*, University of Oklahoma Press, Norman, Oklahoma, 1986, pp. 82-84.

William H. Bauer, James L. Ozment, John H. Willard, *Colorado Post Offices*, Colorado Railroad Museum, Golden, Colorado, 1990, p. 28.

CHIHUAHUA

Required No Physicians

- *Summit County, Peru Creek drainage*
- *Accessible via graded dirt road*
- *Town had a post office; standing structures in the vicinity*

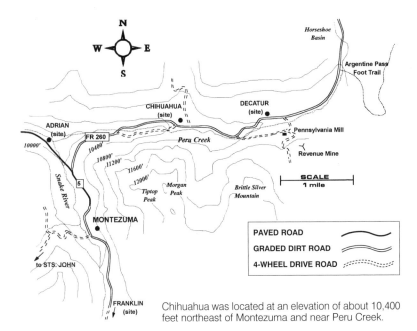

Chihuahua was located at an elevation of about 10,400 feet northeast of Montezuma and near Peru Creek.

Located along the Peru Creek Road about three miles northeast of Montezuma, Chihuahua was founded in 1879. Named for the State in Mexico, it was incorporated in 1880 and grew to a population of 200 by the following year. It was described in 1882 as having fifty-four "substantial" buildings, one hotel, three restaurants, three saloons, two grocery stores, a butcher shop, a

414

dry goods store and many homes. *The Montezuma Millrun* extolled the virtues of Chihuahua by saying, "There are no physicians as their services are never required. There are two lawyers, but they might as well take in their shingles as there is nothing for them to do..." And as for religion, the *Millrun* continued, "The clergy seldom visit this 'Arcadia of the Mountains', as their mission is to call the sinners not the righteous to repentance." Another report said that when politicians came to Chihuahua, parents used their names only to frighten their children.

Chihuahua also had a sawmill and reduction works. The nearest mine was the Peruvian, and the town was not far from the Pennsylvania Mine. In 1889, the business district was destroyed by a forest fire. The post office, which opened in 1880, closed in 1892. Apparently the fire did not consume the entire town.

The Summit School District No. 7, located between Chihuahua and Decatur, had 24 students in the 1881-1882 school year. The school served both towns. It was located inside the boundary of the local cemetery, for some reason. The children would play between the grave stones during recess and were told some of the legends about the people buried there.

The cemetery itself had an unusual beginning. A couple of prospectors, riding from Chihuahua to Decatur, passed a pretty place. It must have had that quiet feel of tranquility that small

A 1955 photograph shows a cabin in Chihuahua. *(Colorado Historical Society F1578)*

wooded areas often
have, and one prospec-
tor remarked that it
would make a fine spot
for a cemetery. Later,
while on his way home
after a night on the
town, the prospector
was thrown from his
horse. He died of his
injuries and was the first
one buried in the new
Chihuahua cemetery.

An old mine building sits near Peru Creek with the tailings of a large mine in the background. Near here, the wagon road over Argentine Pass left the Peru Creek road. *(Kenneth Jessen 097D4)*

The dander of the peace-loving Chihuahua residents was raised when a couple of prospectors were robbed and killed by a trio of road agents. The murderers were pursued and when apprehended, they were strung up from the nearest tree without the benefit of a trial.

Chihuahua was located approximately two miles north and east of where the Peru Creek Road divides from the road to Montezuma. Chihuahua is accessible by automobile under dry conditions during the summer months. It is where the four-wheel drive trail up Chihuahua Gulch departs from the Peru Creek Road, and the site is still indicated on topographic maps. One cabin still stands on the site.

Denver Daily Tribune, October 8, 1880.

Elizabeth Rice Roller, *Memoirs from Montezuma, Chihuahua and Sts. John*, Summit Historical Society, Breckenridge, Colorado, p. 4.

Mary Ellen Gilliland, *Summit*, Alpenrose Press, Silverthorne, Colorado, 1980, pp. 170-171.

Montezuma Millrun, June 24, 1882, June 24, 1882.

Muriel Sibell Wolle, *Stampede to Timberline*, Sage Books, Chicago, 1949, 1974, pp. 134-136.

Sandra F. Prichard, *Roadside Summit Part II*, Summit Historical Society, Breckenridge, Colorado, 1992, p. 71.

Verna Sharp, "Montezuma and her Neighbors", *Colorado Magazine*, Vol. XXXIII, No. 1 (January, 1956), p. 25, pp. 34-35.

William H. Bauer, James L. Ozment, John H. Willard, *Colorado Post Offices*, Colorado Railroad Museum, Golden, Colorado, 1990, p. 33.

CONGER'S CAMP
and ARGENTINE

- *Summit County, Indiana Gulch drainage*
- *Accessible by graded dirt road*
- *Town had a post office; no standing structures remain; also called Camp Conger*

Conger's Camp was a small mining town located in Indiana Gulch on the old stage coach route between Breckenridge and Boreas Pass. The town was founded based on a nearby silver lode called the Diantha; its discoverer was Colonel Samuel Conger. His life was more closely associated with Boulder County where he made his fortune. He was one of the prospectors who discovered the rich silver lode at Caribou and identified tungsten as the black metallic ore near Nederland.

Conger's Camp had a mill, several stores and at least twenty cabins. Its post office opened in 1880, just as the town began to grow. In 1881, postal records show the name was changed to Argentine, and it remained open until 1883 when the Diantha lode was exhausted. Mrs. Diantha Conger, Samuel Conger's wife, was postmistress of Argentine.

Eastern capitalists, believing Conger's Camp to be another Leadville, bought up the claims and poured money into developing the Diantha. Presumably, the ore ran as high as 250 ounces of silver per ton, but such assays were wildly optimistic when it came to the practical matter of mining. It wasn't long until the timber industry replaced mining as the primary source of income for Conger's Camp.

This should be the end of this ghost town story, however,

the location of Conger's Camp is elusive. As published in 1883 in the *Daily Journal* (Breckenridge), "Known when first established as Conger's Camp from S. P. Conger, the founder in 1879. It is located on the old stage road from Breckenridge to Como, three-quarters of a mile west of the Denver and South Park railroad." That would place Conger's Camp down in Indiana Gulch near the intersection of Indiana Creek Road and Argentine Drive, exactly where Summit County historian Mary Ellen Gilliland says it was in her book *The New Summit Hiker.*

From a 1921 article in the *Summit County Journal* comes this description of Argentine, "In crossing the range from Como to Breckenridge, the incoming passenger's attention is directed to the little village of Argentine, formerly and widely known as Conger's Camp." The bottom of Indiana Gulch is a good 600 feet below the railroad grade and three-quarters of a mile away.

Argentine had twenty or more buildings including cabins, businesses and well-built houses of the more prosperous mine owners. It was on the rail line as confirmed by Mac Poor in *Denver, South Park & Pacific*, and it had a two-story section house with a siding a little over eight hundred feet long. Adding to the confusion, Argentine was also called Bacon.

A detailed analysis of the Boreas Pass Road was done during 1974-1975 by John Daugherty. His conclusion was, "The location of Conger remains a mystery. I am not convinced that Argentine and Conger were the same towns, even though they probably were not far from each other. The site of Argentine is known, while descriptions place Conger in Indiana Gulch."

Conger's Camp faded away in 1881-1882 while Argentine's post office closed in 1883. The town gave its last gasp a few years later. Recent mountain property development in Indiana Gulch has obliterated the site of Conger's Camp and nothing but the out-line of a few foundations remain at the Argentine site. *For a map showing the probable location of Conger's Camp and the location of Argentine, see "Boreas."*

As a side note, another town named Argentine was established along Peru Creek in 1901. See "Decatur: The Ghost Town with Three Names."

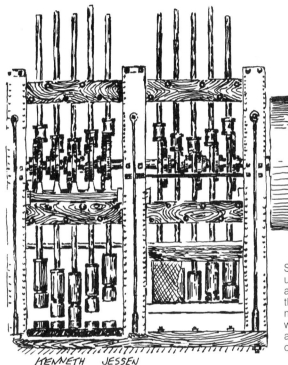

KENNETH JESSEN

Stamp mills were used to crush ore into a fine powder through the use of heavy metal rods. The rods were raised by a cam and allowed to drop on the ore.

"Argentine," *Breckenridge Daily Journal*, February 21, 1883.

Mary Ellen Gilliland, *Summit*, Alpenrose Press, Silverthorne, Colorado, 1980, pp. 171-172.

John Daugherty, *Historic Site Survey of Boreas Pass Road* (unpublished), pp. 27-31.

Mark Fiester, *Blasted, Beloved, Breckenridge*, Pruett Publishing Company, Boulder, Colorado, 1973, pp. 151-152.

Mary Ellen Gilliland, *The New Summit Hiker*, Alpenrose Press, Silverthorne, Colorado, 1983, p. 28.

"This is Argentine - Argentine A Swiss Chalet," *Summit County Journal*, March 26, 1921.

William H. Bauer, James L. Ozment, John H. Willard, *Colorado Post Offices*, Colorado Railroad Museum, Golden, Colorado, 1990, p. 13, p. 37.

CURTIN

- *Summit County, Ten Mile Creek drainage*
- *Accessible by bike path*
- *Camp did not have a post office; no standing structures remain*

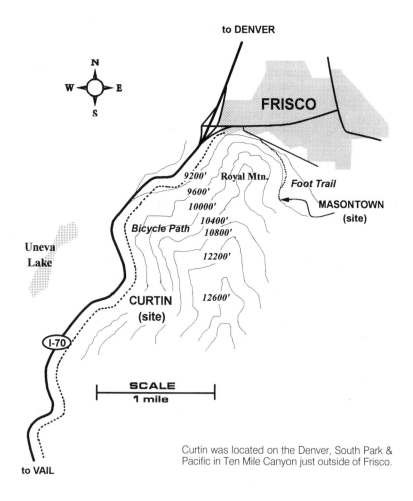

Curtin was located on the Denver, South Park & Pacific in Ten Mile Canyon just outside of Frisco.

A bout two miles south of Frisco in the Ten Mile Creek Canyon was the mining camp of Curtin. It was named for a railroad section hand, Bill Curtin and was served by the Denver, South Park & Pacific. The railroad ran right through the camp, which had a one and one-half story section house for the railroad workers and a long side track. A large mill dominated the camp on the west side of the tracks and on the east side was a boarding house sitting on a rise. A tramway brought the ore down to the mill from a mine high above. There were several homes at Curtin, some in the flat among the willows near the creek and others on the hillside. Curtin was also known as Uneva Lake for the nearby privately owned lake.

Hundreds of bicyclists, people on roller blades, and walkers pass the Curtin site every week during the summer. Only the overgrown crumbling remains of a brick foundation mark the spot.

Curtin was more of a mill site than a town, as shown in this 1908 photograph. The site is located along the bicycle trail between Copper Mountain and Frisco. *(Colorado Historical Society F8082)*

Mac Poor, *Denver, South Park & Pacific*, Rocky Mountain Railroad Club, Denver, 1976, p. 446.
Mary Ellen Gilliland, *Summit*, Alpenrose Press, Silverthorne, Colorado, 1980, pp. 172, 181, 222.

DECATUR
The Ghost Town With Three Names

- *Summit County, Peru Creek drainage*
- *Accessible by graded dirt road*
- *Town had a post office; no standing structures within town site*

A 1942 photograph taken at the Decatur-Rathbone-Argentine mine site. It appears to be an old boarding house with mine buildings off to the left. None of these structures are standing today. *(Denver Public Library, Western History Department X-5490)*

A bove the modern ski resort of Keystone, high up Peru Creek grew the mining town of Decatur. It was established in 1879 on the north side of the valley to support the Pennsylvania Mine just a half mile away. By 1881, Decatur had grown to 300, and steps were taken toward incorporation. The following year, an election was held. The town's success was short lived, however, as the ore in the Pennsylvania seemed to pinch out. Decatur's post office closed in 1885, and in 1893, the "Silver Panic" closed almost all of the area's silver mines.

Credit for founding Decatur is given to "Commodore" Stephen Decatur. He was the second son of Joseph Bross and was born in Sussex, New Jersey. Stephen learned the shoe making trade from his father. He attended several terms at Williams College in Massachusetts, went on to become a teacher and worked his way up to principal of an academy in New York. After his marriage a daughter was born, and it seemed like a wonderful, normal life was in store for Stephen.

Just before the war with Mexico broke out, Stephen Decatur Bross went to New York

Stephen Decatur Bross was editor of *The Georgetown Miner* for four years, and during that time, refused to divulge any of his past life. He had good reason since he abandoned his first wife and children to fight in the Mexican War and abandoned his second wife and children to come to Colorado. *(Kenneth Jessen collection)*

City on business and vanished. His wife and relatives made great efforts to find him and eventually assumed that Stephen had been murdered. His wife was pregnant at the time and gave birth to a son three months after Stephen's disappearance.

By dropping "Bross," he changed his name to simply Stephen Decatur and joined the U.S. Army. He marched under General Kearney to Santa Fe then south into Chihuahua, Mexico. He was well remembered by Colonel Clay Taylor as a brave soldier. After the Mexican War ended, Decatur operated a ferry boat near Council Bluffs, Iowa and also ran a shoe repair shop in the ferry house.

In Omaha, Nebraska, in 1857 or 1858, Stephen Decatur was recognized by a former pupil, none other than financier David H. Moffat. Moffat notified his brother who, in the meantime, had become Lieutenant Governor of the State of Illinois and worked for the *Chicago Tribune.* Lt. Governor William Bross immediately traveled to Omaha and recognized Stephen at once. In a strange turn of events, Stephen denied any relationship and even threatened the life of the Lt. Governor.

While living in Nebraska, Decatur married again and became the father of three children. He also founded the town of Decatur, Nebraska. Gold fever seized Decatur in 1859, and he abandoned his second family in Nebraska to disappear once again.

Lt. Governor Bross, upon hearing this, traveled to Nebraska to console Stephen's second wife. He told her of Stephen's previous marriage and the pattern of abandoning his family. She knew nothing about this and was crushed by the news.

Despite his sordid past, Stephen Decatur was counted among Colorado's pioneers and was a member of the Third Colorado Regiment. He participated in the infamous Sand Creek Massacre under Col. Chivington. For a while, he prospected in the Peru Creek area of Summit County. He represented Summit County in the Territorial Legislature in 1867 and 1868. In addition, he was one of the founders of the Georgetown and Snake River Wagon Road Company, organized in 1869. This company

When this photograph was taken in 1911 of Argentine, the town was a lively place. None of these buildings remain standing today, in fact, hardly a trace of the town can be found. *(Colorado Historical Society F5144)*

constructed the road over Argentine Pass, providing a link between the Peru Creek district and Georgetown.

In 1869, Stephen Decatur moved to Georgetown and began a career as associate editor of *The Georgetown Miner,* a job he held for four years. He remained a man of mystery who flatly refused to divulge any of his past life. His nickname was "Old Sulphurets", but he was also known as "Commodore" Decatur.

Decatur was responsible for entering Colorado in the Industrial Exposition in Philadelphia with a display of ores from various Colorado mines. Eventually, the state awarded Decatur $1,000 for his help in advertising Colorado's mineral resources.

While in Georgetown, he developed an insatiable appetite for liquor and drank from early in the day until evening. This impoverished him and eventually Stephen Decatur drifted south to Custer County to work as Justice of the Peace. For a decade, he lived in what was termed "reduced circumstances." Eventually, the U.S. Government recognized his contribution during the Mexican War and granted him a pension. For the most part, he relied on the kindness of the residents of Rosita who provided him with a place to live and food. Decatur died alone in May, 1881 and is buried in an unmarked grave in the Rosita Cemetery.

Opinions about Stephen Decatur Bross made during his life vary considerably. In an 1870 letter to *The Georgetown Colorado Miner,* the author said, "Under the guidance of Commodore Decatur, I passed over the range to Montezuma and Breckenridge... Everybody in Colorado knows the Commodore, and a few, at least, of the incidents of his strange, eventful life. To ride and camp with him is to acquire a 'liberal education' of life in the mountains. The Commodore is literally saturated with their beauty and grandeur, and in their presence sees 'sermons in stones and books in the running brooks.' To the ripe experience of manhood, he adds the ingenuous simplicity of youth and the tenderness of a woman."

The Pennsylvania Mine hung on and demand for housing once again grew. Decatur was reborn as Rathbone, complete with

An old, picturesque barn located below the site of Decatur-Rathbone-Argentine, along Peru Creek. Nothing is left of the town itself except for traces of foundations. *(Kenneth Jessen 097D6)*

a new post office. The winter of 1898-1899 was especially hard with extremely heavy snowfall. Decatur-Rathbone sat in a meadow exposed to avalanches at the base of a high mountain. A spring avalanche reduced the town to splinters.

New silver strikes after the turn of the century caused a rapid growth in population. By 1902, 200 miners were employed by various mines along Peru Creek. The demand for housing was high, and the old town of Decatur-Rathbone was rebuilt as the new town of Argentine. This name is confusing because of another ghost town by the same name located on the Boreas Pass Road. For more details, see "Conger's Camp and Argentine."

A school was constructed, stores established and the town of Argentine developed sort of a main street lined with cabins and false-front businesses. Argentine was occupied for years, and the final end came when the mines closed for good.

Lula Myers remembered a sad trip during the dead of winter one moonlit night. Lula and her husband lived on a ranch at the old town of Dillon, the site now under the waters of Lake Dillon. Her husband was called by phone one night from the Pennsylvania Mine with news that a miner had been killed in an accident. He was summoned to get the body. Lula decided to go along. After passing through Decatur-Rathbone, the couple arrived at the mine. The miners loaded the now rigid corpse into the wagon bed. On the trip back, Lula began to sing to break the tension of this sad trip. The horse picked up the pace on the downhill grade. Where the road to Montezuma forks south from the main road, Lula looked back to see an empty wagon bed. Their cargo had fallen out in the snow. They turned around and headed back up Peru Creek. They soon found the dead miner, reloaded him and took a more leisurely pace back to Dillon.

Today, the only sign that a town once existed on the site of Decatur-Rathbone-Argentine are rows of shallow foundations on either side of the Peru Creek road. Below the town site, there is an old barn, which may have served as a livery stable.

For a map showing the location of Decatur, see "Chihuahua."

The old Pennsylvania Mill is located on Peru Creek near the Decatur town site. *(Kenneth Jessen 097D1)*

"A Double Life," *The Georgetown Courier*, June 6, 1888.

Muriel Sibell Wolle, *Stampede to Timberline*, Sage Books, Chicago, 1949, 1974, pp. 135-138.

Robert L. Brown, *Colorado Ghost Towns - Past and Present*, Caxton Printers, Caldwell, Idaho, 1977, pp. 10-16.

The Georgetown Colorado Miner, letters to the editor, July 7, 1870.

Verna Sharp, *A History of Montezuma, Sts. John and Argentine*, Summit Historical Society, Breckenridge, Colorado, 1971, pp. 21-25.

DICKEY
A Railroad Junction Town

- *Summit County, Blue River drainage*
- *Site below the Dillon Reservoir*
- *Town had a post office*

Just six miles north of Breckenridge was the railroad town of Dickey, originally called Placer junction. Dickey was named after Dickey Myers, a local rancher. The Denver, South Park & Pacific's branch line to Keystone left the main line at Dickey.

The Denver, South Park & Pacific built a three-stall roundhouse and coal bin at Dickey. A depot was constructed measuring twenty by sixty-three feet, which included living quarters for the agent. Dickey also had a side track three quarters of a mile long. A post office was established in 1892, but closed the following year.

On December 11, 1897, the depot was demolished by a half dozen ore cars, which broke loose in Breckenridge. It is not known if the structure was replaced.

The Dickey town site is under the water of the Dillon Reservoir. *For a map showing the location of the Dickey site, see "Dillon."*

Mac Poor, *Denver, South Park & Pacific*, Rocky Mountain Railroad Club, Denver, 1976, p. 446.

Mary Ellen Gilliland, *Summit*, Alpenrose Press, Silverthorne, Colorado, 1980, pp. 175, 212.

The Colorado Prospector, Vol. 4, No. 11, p. 5.

William H. Bauer, James L. Ozment, John H. Willard, *Colorado Post Offices*, Colorado Railroad Museum, Golden, Colorado, 1990, p. 45.

DILLON
A Town On The Move

- *Summit County, Blue River drainage*
- *Accessible by paved road*
- *Town has a post office; several original structures remain*

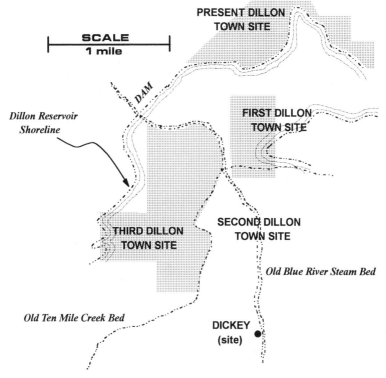

This map shows the location of all four Dillon town sites including the modern-day Dillon. *(based on research done by Sandra Pritchard in her book Roadside Summit Part II)*

Dillon was probably named for an early pioneer into the Blue River Valley, Tom Dillon. He certainly could be challenged for lack of good judgement when he set out into the Colorado mountains to hunt gold with several companions, but ended up traveling alone. A blizzard struck and somehow, he managed to survive and make it back to Golden. Tom Dillon told others about the wide valley where the three streams met (the Blue River, Ten Mile Creek and the Snake River).

Using Tom Dillon's description, settlers came to the area and established a stage stop and trading post at the confluence of the Snake River and the Blue River. The community was named Dillon. Elizabeth Roller, a Summit County historian, believes that Dillon got its start as early as 1873, and was well established by 1879. Wagon roads and stage routes over the various passes in the Blue River Valley all came through Dillon making it a transportation hub.

The Dillon Mining Company patented a 320 acre town site in 1881, which extended from the original town site to the north across the Snake River. This new town site was never developed.

When the Denver, South Park & Pacific arrived in the valley in 1882, Dillon moved across the Blue River to a point on the west side of the Blue River, but on the east bank of Ten Mile Creek. Dillon also became the terminus for the Denver & Rio Grande's

Wagons travel down Dillon's main street before the arrival of railroads. This photograph of Dillon was taken at its third site. *(Colorado Historical Society F8174)*

route over Fremont Pass. Apparently this location did not suit residents. A third move was made to the west side of Ten Mile Creek. It was after this last move that the town of Dillon was incorporated in 1883. It was here that the town of Dillon would remain until 1962 when its residents were forced to move for the construction of the Dillon Reservoir.

The original 1884 Dillon school is one of the structures to survive the town's relocation when the Dillon Reservoir was constructed and filled. It is now a museum operated by the Summit Historical Society. *(Kenneth Jessen 096D10)*

The Dillon post office opened in 1879, and except for a brief period of time in 1881, has remained in continuous operation despite the fact that the town has been in four locations.

A boost to the buildings in Dillon came in 1882 when some structures were moved from Frisco. Maybe Dillon held out the promise of a better economic future. Among these buildings were Graff's Hall, a large two-story structure, which became the I. O. O. F. Lodge Hall. Homes were also moved, as well as one saloon.

A school was constructed in Dillon in 1884 and started with seven girls and six boys in its first class. It remained in use until 1910 when it was replaced by a modern structure. The old school then served as the Union Church and later as the Dillon Community Church.

Dillon Number Three grew to become a nice community with general stores, a butcher shop, drug store, barber shop, two blacksmiths, two cafes, a telephone office, doctor's office, two livery stables, two hotels, the post office and the town newspaper, *The Blue Valley Times.* A second newspaper, *The Dillon Enterprise,*

Of great historical importance to Summit County is the original Myers ranch house, constructed in 1885, and now located in Dillon. It was the home of Colonel James Myers and his wife Lula. The house was originally located along the Snake River near the present-day Keystone Skyway Gondola. The Myers played a significant role in the formation of the county. *(Kenneth Jessen 096D11)*

also did business in the town until it moved to greener pastures in Breckenridge. The town also had four saloons and a pool hall.

As for public facilities, Dillon had a picnic ground on the edge of town. There was also a dance pavilion and a band stand. The big event of the year was the 4th of July picnic sponsored by the Denver & Rio Grande Railroad.

Around 1912, skiing became popular in Dillon and a ski slope was built above town on Lake Hill. Skiers had to hike up and ski down, but the hill remained the longest ski run in the country for many years. In 1919, Adres Hangen set the world's record in ski jumping at 213 feet.

Time ran out for Dillon Number Three when the Denver Water Board met with the town's people in 1955 to explain that a large reservoir would be built on the site. Property owners were given several options including swapping their land in the old town for land in a proposed new town as well as simply selling their property to the water board. Through purchases, the water board owned much of the old town through sales for back taxes. Eventually all of the land belonged to the Denver Water Board, and eviction notices were issued forcing everyone to leave by April 1, 1961. This was no April Fool's joke either!

Sad photographs show four structures on the north end of Main Street demolished then burned. The central business district, including Kremmling's Store, Dillon Drug and other false-front stores, was razed. The Lucky Horseshoe Inn and a home that sat next to it were bulldozed down to kindling. The new (1910) schoolhouse was felled by a wrecker's ball. But many structures were saved and moved up to new Dillon, including the 1884 schoolhouse.

The original Dillon cemetery, established in 1885, was the only cemetery in the county patented under federal law. The patent was signed by President McKinley in 1901. All three hundred plus graves were moved to a new cemetery to make way for the reservoir.

New Dillon is a planned community designed for the recreation industry.

Muriel Sibell Wolle photographed this two-story store in Dillon. It was razed to make way for the Dillon Reservoir. *(Denver Public Library, Western History Department X-5479)*

Anna Emore, Dillon, *The Blue River Wonderland*, Summit Historical Society, Breckenridge, Colorado, 1976, pp. 1-22.

Mary Ellen Gilliland, *Summit*, Alpenrose Press, Silverthorne, Colorado, 1980, pp. 80-81.

Mary Ellen Gilliland, *Lula*, Summit Historical Society, Breckenridge, Colorado, 1990, p. i, p. ii, p. 1.

Sandra F. Prichard, *Roadside Summit Part II*, Summit Historical Society, Breckenridge, Colorado, 1992, p. 64.

Sandra Pritchard, *Dillon-Denver and the Dam*, Summit Historical Society, Breckenridge, Colorado, 1994, pp. 26-29.

William H. Bauer, James L. Ozment, John H. Willard, *Colorado Post Offices*, Colorado Railroad Museum, Golden, Colorado, 1990, p. 45.

DYERSVILLE

Founded By Father Dyer•

- *Summit County, Blue River drainage*
- *Accessible by four-wheel drive vehicle or on foot*
- *Town did not have a post office; several partially collapsed structures remain*

John L. Dyer was a circuit-riding, Methodist minister who, in 1861, left his home in Minnesota for Colorado Territory. On July 4th of that year, he decided to walk from Denver to Buckskin Joe near Alma to preach to the miners rather than pay $10 to ride the stage coach. To earn enough money just to stay alive, Dyer took on odd jobs including carrying the mail over the Continental Divide. He became famous for his winter crossings of Mosquito Pass at an elevation above

Etching of Father John L. Dyer appeared in his book, *The Snow-Shoe Itinerant*, published in 1890.

13,000 feet. He used seven-foot skis and carried up to twenty-six pounds of mail. Since the mining camps of Colorado were filled primarily with young men, the old preacher was given the title of "Father" and was known throughout Park, Chaffee and Lake counties. For this reason, Father Dyer provides one of the few links between mining towns in Colorado. He also authored a detailed account of his own experiences in a book titled *The Snow-Shoe Itinerant* published in 1890.

During 1880, Father Dyer was living in Breckenridge and took in a couple of young prospectors as boarders. He decided to join the two men in a prospecting expedition in the spring. The young men found it difficult to keep up with the sixty-eight-year-old reverend who was used to the rigors of mountain life. The men found some promising ore, and all but Thompson returned to Breckenridge. Thompson kept on looking and eventually staked a claim. Father Dyer suspected that Thompson's claim was on or near one that he had previously staked out for himself. Upon investigation, Dyer found the new claim next to his own so he staked out the ground to either side. The two men agreed to merge their holdings and look for a buyer.

Thompson was offered $250, and Dyer told him to hold out for a thousand dollars. This is the amount they received and split between them.

The mine that developed was called the Warrior's Mark, and it opened in the summer of 1881 with fifty men at work. In just six months, between $75,000 and $80,000 in silver ore was removed, and the mine continued to operate profitably for many years.

A picturesque Dyersville on a warm summer day. Four structures are still standing among the tall trees near a crystal clear creek. *(Kenneth Jessen 096C11)*

Father Dyer founded a small town near the mine. It was tucked away in a dense grove of tall trees along a crystal clear stream below Boreas Pass. Father Dyer built a cabin in Dyersville hoping to get away from gambling, prostitution and lawlessness. The cabin measured 17-foot by 17-foot and stood story-and-a-half high. Possibly to his disgust, a saloon called the Angele's Rest opened in Dyersville, but on a positive note, a branch of a prominent Breckenridge clothing store, the Adamson's Blue Front Store, also opened its doors. The small town built its own school.

Although the Warrior's Mark lasted up to the turn of the century, longer than most mines, the ore eventually played out, and the miners left. The town was abandoned.

Ghost town historian Bob Brown provides more detail on Dyersville in his book *Ghost Towns of the Colorado Rockies* where the author says, "The ride to Dyersville is one of the prettiest and most rewarding trips in Colorado..." A visit to Dyersville does require a four wheel drive vehicle with low range, and can be reached via a steep trail from the Boreas Pass road at the Farnham Spur site. Dyersville can also be reached by driving up Indiana Gulch. There is a foot trail from the Boreas Pass road that intersects the Indiana Creek road and provides access to Dyersville. This trail, however, crosses private property. At the site, there are four structures in a state of partial decay.

A map showing the location of Dyersville can be found in the section titled "Boreas."

Jane Morton, *Dyer, Dynamite & Dredges*, Father Dyer United Methodist Church, Breckenridge, Colorado, 1990, pp. 1-7.

Mary Ellen Gilliland, *Summit*, Alpenrose Press, Silverthorne, Colorado, 1980, pp. 175-176.

Robert L. Brown, *Ghost Towns of the Colorado Rockies*, Caxton Printers, Caldwell, Idaho, 1977, pp. 124-131.

FARNHAM SPUR

- *Summit County, Indiana Creek drainage*
- *Accessible via graded dirt road*
- *Town had a post office; no standing structures remain*

The collapsed remains of the old Farnham mill, and one fallen-down cabin are all that is left at this site located along the old railroad grade of the Denver, South Park & Pacific. The grade has been converted into an automobile road, which runs from Breckenridge to Como. It is possible to find railroad ties embedded in the tundra marking the siding, which served the mill.

This is all that remains of Farnham Spur, a high camp along the tracks of the Denver, South Park & Pacific on the Boreas Pass road. *(Kenneth Jessen 103C10)*

Railroad cars were loaded with concentrate from several area mines including the Warrior's Mark mine below the grade. Farnham Spur gained its own post office in 1881 when the Denver, South Park & Pacific reached the site as it constructed its narrow gauge route into Summit County. The post office remained open until 1885 when the population at the mill dwindled. At its peak, the population of Farnham Spur was probably no greater than fifty. *See "Boreas" for a map showing Farnham's Spur location.*

Mary Ellen Gilliland, *Summit*, Alpenrose Press, Silverthorne, Colorado, 1980, p. 176.

William H. Bauer, James L. Ozment, John H. Willard, *Colorado Post Offices*, Colorado Railroad Museum, Golden, Colorado, 1990, p. 53.

FILGER CITY
And The Winning Card

- *Summit County, North Fork of the Snake River drainage*
- *Exact location of site unknown*
- *Camp did not have a post office; no standing structures remain*

On 13,204 foot Lenawee Mountain, which forms the cirque where A-Basin ski area is located, was the approximate site of Filger City. Rich ore was discovered by Isaac Filger, and he named his mine the Winning Card. Some of the miners who worked the Winning Card did so on a lease basis while others contracted their work. Hopes of a continual supply of rich ore ran high, and a few cabins were built at Filger City. In an 1885 issue of the *Montezuma Millrun*, the paper printed a list of the town's elected officials. Suddenly, the rich ore gave out, and no more ore could be located. Filger City was abandoned, and its exact location is unknown.

Verna Sharp, *A History of Montezuma*, Sts. John and Argentine, Summit Historical Society, Breckenridge, Colorado, 1971, p. 29.

Verna Sharp, "Montezuma and Her Neighbors," *Colorado Magazine*, Vol. XXXIII, No. 1 (January, 1956), p. 31.

FRANKLIN

- *Summit County, Snake River drainage*
- *Accessible via graded dirt road*
- *Site did not have a post office; no standing structures remain*

Franklin (also spelled Franklyn) was to have been the head-quarters for the Montezuma Silver Mining Company, and a Victorian style, two-story residence was constructed on the site. The mining company helped with the construction of the Webster Pass road and owned several mining properties in the area.

The house was beautifully furnished, and this is where the company superintendent, George Teal, lived and entertained. It was called the Franklin House and became a local show place. Prospective investors were invited to this residence to hear about the mines and their potential. The town was to have grown up around this residence, and eventually, a boarding house and sawmill were constructed. The location was one and one-half miles south of Montezuma along the Snake River near its junction with Deer Creek.

The Colorado Miner, October 19, 1878.

Verna Sharp, *A History of Montezuma*, Sts. John and Argentine, Summit Historical Society, Breckenridge, Colorado, 1971, p. 29.

Verna Sharp, "Montezuma and Her Neighbors," *Colorado Magazine*, Vol. XXXIII, No. 1 (January, 1956), p. 30.

A Victorian style residence constructed at Franklin, located south of Montezuma, for a mining company's superintendent. It was used to entertain prospective investors. *(Colorado Historical Society F1579)*

FRISCO CITY

- *Summit County, Ten Mile Creek drainage*
- *Accessible by paved road;*
- *Town has a post office; several original structures in a historic park*

Frisco was one of Colorado's mining towns that made the transition from mining to recreation and survived. By the time this photograph was taken in 1910, mining activity had declined, and Frisco would have its share of abandoned buildings. *(Colorado Historical Society F10590)*

Frisco came along well after Ruben Spalding's placer gold discovery along the Blue River in 1859. While 8,000 or more prospectors flooded the Blue River Valley in 1860 at what would soon become Breckenridge, the wide open area to the north at the mouth of Ten Mile Canyon remained untouched. Its potential mineral wealth was recognized by a Swedish immigrant named Henry Recen who constructed the first cabin at what would become Frisco.

Captain Henry Learned, a government scout, tacked up a sign over Recen's cabin door reading "Frisco City." The town burst into life in 1878 when rich silver ore was found in the rugged Ten Mile Canyon. Over on the other side of the valley, the easy placer gold was exhausted, and possibly prospectors populated the Frisco area from the Breckenridge area. The towns of Kokomo and Robinson were founded at the same time as Frisco.

Frisco City was also strategically located where the wagon road over Boreas Pass entered Ten Mile Canyon and joined the wagon road over Argentine Pass from Georgetown. A new wagon road was constructed over Loveland Pass in 1879, also passing through Frisco City.

The *Denver Daily Tribune* announced in April, 1879, that the new town of Frisco City had been born and credited Captain Learned with selecting the 1,500 acre town site.

Frisco City was actually composed of a federally granted town site of 150 acres with another 1,350 acres owned by the Frisco Town Association. Articles of incorporation were filed by the town company in 1879 and stock was issued.

A post office was opened in 1879 and remains in service to this day. At first, however, it served only fifty residents.

In a July issue of the Central City *Daily Register*, Frisco City was said to have had a stage station plus eight or nine cabins. The *Rocky Mountain News* touted in a September, 1880 article, that Frisco was free from lawyers, gamblers, fallen women and ministers. At the time, its population stood at 480. Businesses included two grocery stores, two hotels, three saloons, two stables and three blacksmith shops. The sawmill of C. G. Shedd produced ten thousand board-feet of lumber per day. In October, 1879, telephone service to Decatur, Breckenridge, Kokomo, Robinson and over Fremont Pass to Leadville began.

A town board was elected in 1880 as Frisco moved toward incorporation. The board was an eclectic collection of people from all over including an Englishman, a railroad mechanic from Golden, an Ohio-born lumber yard owner, an unmarried prospector as mayor and a Virginian as town recorder.

Of historic interest is the length of time it took for the patent application for the town site to be filed at the county seat in Breckenridge; the answer is almost a century! In 1882, a judge and an attorney agreed to accept town lots in exchange for their legal services. They drew up the necessary papers and filed them with the Federal Land Office. After revising the paperwork, the patent was granted to Frisco in 1885. The records were forwarded to the county seat in Breckenridge to be recorded, but the recording fee was not paid. The bill for the fee of just $5 did not arrive until 1899. The Frisco trustees simply overlooked the bill, and the patent certificate was lost until 1924 when it was mailed to the Frisco postmaster. He promptly put it with his personal papers. In 1979, his son discovered the document and turned it over to the town board who promptly paid the $5 fee thus making the patent official.

In 1880 and for the astounding price of $5, a person could purchase a town lot in Frisco. For $10, a corner lot could be acquired, and the Frisco Town Association quickly sold 150 lots. A lot was set aside, optimistically of course, for a courthouse, assuming that Frisco would grow to become the county seat.

The Denver & Rio Grande constructed its narrow gauge line over Fremont Pass to Wheeler Junction in 1881 and took the rails down Ten Mile Canyon the following year through Frisco. The railroad stopped construction at Dillon although it graded its line all the way north along the Blue River into Middle Park. In 1882, the Denver, South Park & Pacific laid its narrow gauge tracks over Boreas Pass to Dillon and the following year, constructed its line through Frisco to Kokomo. This gave Frisco two railroads. The arrival of the iron horse, however, put Silas W. Nott's "High Line" stage route from Georgetown to Kokomo out of business.

The history of Colorado mining towns is one of boom to bust to boom and eventual stagnation. Captain Henry Learned tried to hold the town government together, but the trustees quit showing up for meetings. An April, 1892 spring blizzard forced the cancellation of a town election followed by a twenty-three month interval without enough board members for a quorum. All of the meetings were cancelled until 1899, but by this time, Frisco was on its decline. The Sherman Silver Purchase Act had been repealed in 1893, and the price of silver dropped to almost half of its previous market price.

Frisco's population fell to 175, and only the sawmills kept the town alive. Back taxes put many rich silver mines on the auction block. The Excelsior, for example, sold for under $20 and the Victoria sold for two bucks. But mining came back with new capital to extend the tunnels thousands of feet into the mountains to gold ore.

Once the gold reserves had been depleted, the mines closed. The Denver & Rio Grande tore up its tracks over Fremont Pass in 1912, and the Colorado & Southern (successor to the Denver, South Park & Pacific) raised its prices. The real blow to Frisco came in 1937 when service on the Colorado & Southern

This is one of the structures in Frisco's Historic Park, located along Main Street. Many of the town's original structures are in this park for preservation and to make way for modern structures associated with the recreation industry. *(Kenneth Jessen 096B12)*

was terminated, cutting the town's only viable link to the outside world. At the time, the Loveland Pass road was not good enough to qualify as a four-wheel drive road. Those wanting to get to Denver had to use Hoosier Pass into South Park. Hoosier, however, was closed much of the winter. Another route was down the Blue River to Kremmling, then over Berthoud Pass. Frisco's isolation, closure of its mines and exhausted resources caused the town to almost be completely abandoned. The town had only a dozen permanent residents during the 1940s. It would be the post-World War II recreation boom that would bring life back to Frisco.

See "Curtin" for a map showing Frisco's location.

Tivis Wilkins, *Colorado Railroads*, Pruett Publishing Company, Boulder, Colorado, 1974, pp. 37-51.

William H. Bauer, James L. Ozment, John H. Willard, *Colorado Post Offices*, Colorado Railroad Museum, Golden, Colorado, 1990, p. 59.

Mary Ellen Gilliland, *Frisco!*, Alpenrose Press, Silverthorne, Colorado, 1984, pp. 5-42.

HAYWOOD
Stage Stop

- *Summit County, Snake River drainage*
- *Accessible via paved road*
- *Site had a post office; no standing structures remain*

Haywood was a stop for Silas Nott's High Line and other stage-coach services, which converged on this important intersection. Haywood was located where the road from Montezuma met the road coming down from Loveland Pass. Stages ran over Argentine Pass down the Snake River and over Webster Pass to this same intersection. A combination post office, hotel and restaurant was Haywood's primary structure. There was also a livery stable for fresh horses. Mrs. Kate Haywood was the post mistress. There also may have been a few cabins at Haywood, but the place certainly would not qualify as a town.

The post office opened coincident with the opening of the High Line in 1879, and the post office closed in 1882 when stage service was discontinued as a result of the completion of a narrow gauge railroad into the area. By 1890, Haywood had been abandoned.

The specific location was a few hundred feet northwest of the present-day U.S. 6 junction with the Montezuma Road.

Mary Ellen Gilliland, *Summit*, Alpenrose Press, Silverthorne, Colorado, 1980, pp. 176-177.

John K. Aldrich, *Ghosts of Summit County*, Centennial Graphics, Lakewood, 1986, pp. 34-35.

William H. Bauer, James L. Ozment, John H. Willard, *Colorado Post Offices*, Colorado Railroad Museum, Golden, Colorado, 1990, p. 70.

KEYSTONE

- *Summit County, Snake River drainage*
- *Accessible by paved road; town had a post office*
- *Many original structures remain, some on private property*

The old town of Keystone when it was still serviced by the Denver, South Park & Pacific. Many of these buildings remain standing today. *(Colorado Historical Society F31523)*

Keystone is not just a ski resort; it is also an old ghost town. The old town of Keystone is located west of the ski lifts and modern condominiums. Some of the original cabins sit abandoned while other more substantial structures are used by the Keystone Science School.

The story of old Keystone is closely linked to the Denver, South Park & Pacific Railroad, founded by Colorado Governor John Evans in 1872. It was absorbed by the powerful Union Pacific Railroad in 1880. The U.P. had big plans for this small narrow-

447

gauge, mountain railroad. It wanted direct access to the lucrative Leadville mining district, but surveyors quickly found that the Blue River Valley was also an active mining area. Breckenridge, therefore, became an immediate objective for the railroad.

The Denver, South Park & Pacific planned to enter the Blue River Valley from two directions: from the north over Loveland Pass using the Colorado Central from Georgetown and from the south over Boreas Pass. The intention was to have the two lines join at Dillon. The site of old Dillon, by the way, is under the Dillon Reservoir. To reach Leadville, plans called for a branch to be built over Fremont Pass.

The extension from Georgetown involved the creation of a spiral where the railroad looped over itself on a high bridge to gain elevation to reach Silver Plume. It became known as the Georgetown Loop, and tourist trains operate over this section today. Beyond Silver Plume, however, the railroad came to grips

This cabin in old Keystone, dating back to the 1880s, was constructed by Scandinavian loggers. The original Keystone railroad depot is just beyond this cabin. Many of the original buildings are used today by the Keystone Science School. *(Kenneth Jessen 096D12)*

with the choice between a difficult route above 11,000 feet over Loveland Pass or a long tunnel. The expense was simply too great.

In the meantime, the Denver, South Park & Pacific entered Breckenridge in 1882 over Boreas Pass from Como and built a spur to the north ending at Keystone. The residents above Keystone at the mining towns of Montezuma, Chihuahua, and Decatur campaigned to get the railroad extended. Grading was completed all the way to Montezuma, but no rail was laid. Keystone then became an active railhead with stagecoaches and ore wagons from Peru Creek and the Snake River meeting the trains. A substantial logging industry emerged, and a great deal of milled lumber was shipped out. Keystone remained an important town in the region for many years, and in 1937, the rails were finally removed. After all of the available timber was cut and the mines closed, Keystone became a ghost town. It would be the ski industry that caused its awakening.

Mac Poor, *Denver, South Park & Pacific*, Rocky Mountain Railroad Club, Denver, 1976, p. 446.
Mary Ellen Gilliland, *Summit*, Alpenrose Press, Silverthorne, Colorado, 1980, p. 178, pp. 213-214.
Sandra F. Prichard, *Roadside Summit, The Human Landscape Part II*, Summit Historical Society, Breckenridge, Colorado, 1992, p. 110, p. 143.

KOKOMO-RECEN

- *Summit County, Ten Mile Creek drainage*
- *Site not accessible, but can be viewed from public roads*
- *Site is on private property; town had a post office; no standing structures remain*

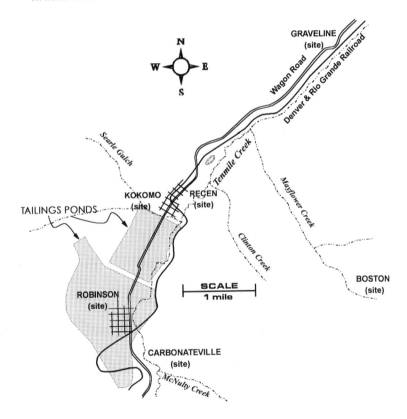

Kokomo-Recen, shown on this map derived from the United States Geological Survey work done in 1880-1882, was located along Tenmile Creek. The site was abandoned, and the buildings removed in 1965 by AMAX to meet the need for the expansion of the tailings ponds. Modern roads are not shown.

Miners from Indiana named the town Kokomo after Kokomo, Indiana. It is an Indian word for young grandmother. Kokomo had a twin just below it named Recen, platted by the Recen brothers. The two towns eventually grew together and became indistinguishable. Henry Recen, a member of the Swedish Recen family, constructed the first cabin at what would become the town of Frisco.

Kokomo-Recen was at first an isolated place. The Loveland Pass road opened in 1879, and this heralded the beginning of stage coach service from Georgetown. The road, however, was very primitive and reached an elevation of nearly 12,000 feet. It was closed much of the winter. A good road was constructed by those in Kokomo-Recen and other Ten Mile towns over Fremont Pass to Leadville.

Construction in Kokomo-Recen went on at a frantic pace during the early 1880s with four saw mills turning out milled lumber. Prices were extremely high due to transportation costs with flour at $12 a sack. This was at a time when a normal day's wages were just $1.50 to $2.00.

Kokomo-Recen's isolation was further reduced with the arrival of the Denver & Rio Grande narrow gauge railroad in 1881. Its depot, constructed in Recen, forced passengers to walk uphill to the Kokomo-Recen business district. The Denver & Rio Grande had constructed its narrow gauge line over Fremont Pass from Leadville and then down Ten Mile Canyon. Building in the opposite direction was the Denver, South Park and Pacific, and in 1883, this railroad came up the canyon from the Blue River Valley to Frisco. In Ten Mile Canyon, the two railroads paralleled each other with the Rio Grande on the north side and South Park on the south.

Railroads often avoided the purchase of land within an established town to avoid both the cost and the taxes. It was not unusual for railroads to enter into the land promotion business either. The Denver, South Park & Pacific surveyed Junction City adjacent to Kokomo-Recen hoping to eclipse both towns. If successful, they could sell lots at a handsome profit, but they soon

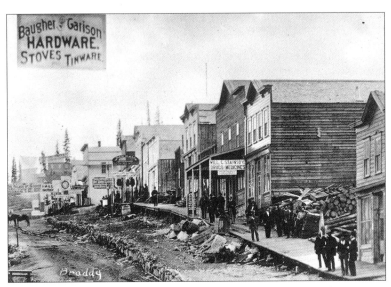

Kokomo-Recen in 1882, when the towns were booming. Note the awful condition of the uneven and unpaved street strewn with rocks. *(Colorado Historical Society F5479)*

discovered that the site was on the Recen brothersS placer claim.

The Denver, South Park & Pacific ended up in a right-of-way dispute in Kokomo. This forced the South Park to construct two trestles to cross over the Rio Grande and back over again.

The lots in Kokomo-Recen cost upwards to $650 where just a few miles down the canyon in Frisco, lots sold for $5 to $10. For one fellow, who paid full price for his Kokomo-Recen lot, was excavating the basement for what was to be a three-story home, a vein of silver ore four feet wide was struck. This more than made up for the amount paid for the lot.

Kokomo did have a weekly newspaper, the *Summit County Times,* founded in 1879. Its editor, Thomas Bowenlock, made the self-serving comment by predicting stagnation and death for any town that did not support its local newspaper. At an elevation of 10,632 feet, it was the highest newspaper in Summit County.

The Kokomo post office opened in 1879 and remained opened until the town was vacated in 1965 for expansion of the tailings pond from the AMAX molybdenum mine on Fremont Pass.

The remarkable growth of Kokomo-Recen is illustrated by the buildings that existed by the end of its first year in 1879. The hundreds of silver mines in the area supported two smelters. Dance halls were popular including the Jardin Mabille, the Variety Theater Comique, the Red Light Dance Hall (probably a very accurate name for some of its activities) and the Light Fantastic. The town had an assay office, five attorneys, five bakeries, a bank, a barbershop and seven boot and shoe stores. In an 1879 business directory, twenty-four carpenters and builders were listed indicating the construction activity in Kokomo-Recen. Another interesting statistic was its seventeen grocery stores, far more than other mining towns. As expected, the liquor establishments were quite numerous with twenty-three listed. To round out the businesses, there were four druggists, four dry goods store, four freighters, a furniture store, several stores selling "gentlemen's goods," four hardware stores, and eleven hotels. The first hotel, incidentally, began as a collection of tents. The town also had a couple of physicians and five surveyors. In the way of civic activities, Kokomo had its own brass band.

A look at Kokomo-Recen in the middle of the summer would be the kind of place only the most hardy could survive. Most of its business structures had false fronts, a style used during the 1800s. A single, narrow door was often in the center of the structure and was flanked by tall, narrow windows. Many of Kokomo-Recen's buildings were log with vertical planking nailed up to give it a more refined appearance. Other log buildings would receive clapboard siding. In front of the commercial buildings were wide wooden boardwalks with short flights of stairs at each end. The main street through Kokomo-Recen was unpaved, traversed by drainage ditches and very muddy. Wagon ruts made it exceedingly rough.

The populace of Kokomo-Recen wore a variety of outfits. Businessmen had on suits, usually dark, with a white shirt and tall hat. Miners and prospectors dressed in bulky clothing of virtually any description. What few women lived in Kokomo-Recen wore long, full dresses to the ground.

Following the tradition of several other Colorado mining towns, the first female to become a resident was given a town lot. This happened to be the daughter of a Mr. Stern.

Kokomo-Recen's main street, Ten Mile Avenue, was lined with the businesses described above. It was closely packed, and the buildings were all of wood frame construction. The town had no water supply or a fire department. In October, 1881, virtually all of the business district was reduced to ashes by an intense fire.

The town, however, was still in its economic prime and was rebuilt in Recen. The name became Kokomo-Recen and eventually, just Kokomo.

By 1885, Kokomo had a city hall, police department and most important, a fire department. At the time, Recen remained separate with its own city government. And as for the businesses, Mary Ellen Gilliland in her book, *Summit*, comments that, "the 1885 *Colorado Business Directory* lists enough saloons to slake an army's thirst..."

A. R. Wilfley lived with his family in Kokomo-Recen and became its most famous citizen. He invented the Wilfley Table, important in handling a high volume of gold ore. It used a clever scheme of a large, rectangular vibrating table with riffles.

The abandonment by the United States of the silver standard for coinage in 1893 caused the price of silver to drop nearly in half. This closed most of the silver mines in Colorado including those in Kokomo-Recen. A short-lived surge in the price of silver after the turn of the century produced a momentary return of activity to the town. Kokomo-Recen would never be the same; its population dropped to 350. The next blow to the town came when the rails of the Colorado & Southern (successor to the Denver, South Park & Pacific) were removed in 1937. The Denver & Rio Grande had removed its rails years before. Kokomo-Recen was now isolated with only poor roads in and out of the area.

During and after World War II, the American Smelting and Refining company mined base metals in some of the old Kokomo-

Recen mines.
When the AMAX
molybdenum mine
at Climax on
Fremont Pass
began to expand,
its tailings filled
upper Ten Mile
Creek. It needed
more room.
Mining was the
reason Kokomo-
Recen was born,
and it was also the
reason it died. The
site was purchased,
residents asked to
move, and the town was razed.

The community church in Kokomo-Recen was among the few structures left standing by 1958. Eventually, all of the structures were removed by AMAX for the expansion of the tailings ponds. *(Colorado Historical Society F26253)*

The Kokomo-Recen site can be seen from either Colorado 91 or from a graded dirt road on the north side of the canyon, but direct access to the site is restricted. The site is located at the foot of the lower tailings pile for the molybdenum mine, and a water treatment plant sits along the creek on part of the site.

A small town with several structures called Graveline was located about three miles to the northeast of Kokomo-Recen. It is not listed among the stations along the Denver & Rio Grande or along the Denver, South Park & Pacific. Nothing is known about this town's origins or when it was abandoned. The site is empty today.

Mary Ellen Gilliland, *Summit*, Alpenrose Press, Silverthorne, Colorado, 1980, pp. 243-250.

Stanley Dempsey and James E. Fell, Jr. *Mining the Summit,* University of Oklahoma Press, Norman, Oklahoma, 1986, p. 89.

William H. Bauer, James L. Ozment, John H. Willard, *Colorado Post Offices*, Colorado Railroad Museum, Golden, Colorado, 1990, p. 83.

LAKESIDE

- *Summit County, Blue River drainage*
- *Location had a post office*
- *Site under Green Mountain Reservoir*

Under the Green Mountain Reservoir between Otter Creek and Black Creek was the small town of Lakeside. The McDonald Flat campground is about a mile southeast of the site.

The 1892 census listed 88 males of voting age are at Lakeside, and according to historian Mary Ellen Gilliland, the Guyselman Ranch was where a stage stop was located for the line operating between Dillon and Kremmling. The ranch building became the Lakeside post office, which opened in 1882 and closed just four years later. It is not know how many other structures were located at Lakeside.

Under new ownership, the ranch was expanded, and a clubhouse was constructed to act as a social center for area ranchers. In 1943, the Green Mountain Dam inundated the Lakeside site.

Mary Ellen Gilliland, *Summit*, Alpenrose Press, Silverthorne, Colorado, 1980, pp. 178-179.

William H. Bauer, James L. Ozment, John H. Willard, *Colorado Post Offices*, Colorado Railroad Museum, Golden, Colorado, 1990, p. 84.

LAURIUM

- *Summit County, Illinois Creek drainage*
- *Access limited by private property; town had a post office*
- *Two standing structures remain; other spellings, Laurim or Larium*

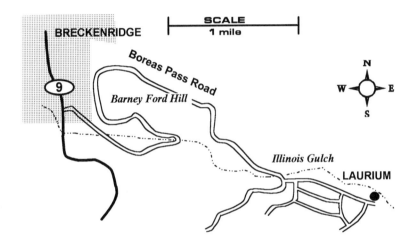

This very small mining camp was located near the Laurium mine in Illinois Gulch at 10,700 feet. The town site now sits amid a modern housing development in a maze of roads and can be difficult to locate. It is above the Boreas Pass road on the highest loop road in Illinois Gulch and is difficult to see from the public road.

The camp got its post office in 1895, only to close four years later. Judging from the size of the tailings, the Laurium mine must have operated for many more years.

The two remaining structures are up by the mine's portal and have been repaired for seasonal use. Access is restricted by private property. Little else is known about this obscure camp.

Such as it is, this is Laurium, an obscure mining camp located above the Boreas Pass road in Illinois Gulch. *(Kenneth Jessen 103C9)*

John K. Aldrich, *Ghosts of Summit County*, Centennial Graphics, Lakewood, 1986, p. 39.

Perry Eberhart, *Guide to the Colorado Ghost Towns and Mining Camps*, Sage Books, Chicago, 1959, p. 160.

William H. Bauer, James L. Ozment, John H. Willard, *Colorado Post Offices*, Colorado Railroad Museum, Golden, Colorado, 1990, p. 86.

LINCOLN CITY

And The Wire Patch

- *Summit County, French Gulch drainage*
- *Accessible via graded dirt road*
- *Town had a post office; several standing structures remain*

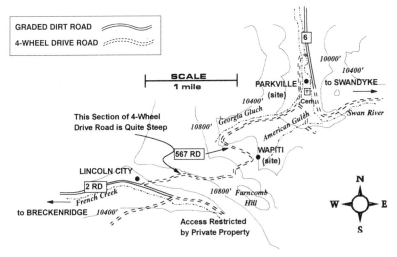

Lincoln City was located east of Breckenridge up French Creek.

arry Farcomb discovered remarkable twisted strands of pure crystallized gold in the gravel along French Creek east of Breckenridge. Before any other prospectors got word of this discovery, Farcomb wisely purchased as much of the land as possible in the area, especially above his placer claim. This was the source of the wire gold and was later named the "Wire Patch." News of the discovery leaked out, and prospectors quickly discovered that Farncomb owned practically every square inch in the area.

459

Resentful prospectors waged war on Harry Farcomb to get his rich property. The battle was fought in the courts at first, then escalated to gun play. A seven hour shoot-out by forty men along French Creek ended in death for three, while others lay wounded. The matter was settled when Farcomb was bought out. And as for Farcomb's fate, he ended up becoming a very rich man.

Lincoln City was founded during the "war" in 1861, not long after Breckenridge was settled. The town got its post office that year, and the post office remained open until 1894. Amazing amounts of gold were recovered at the initial discovery, and silver-galena was also successfully mined. The town of Lincoln City peaked in the 1880s, and in an 1885 visit by George Crofutt, he noted that its population was 250. The town had one store, a couple of hotels, several smelters plus a stamp mill. The population dropped to 25 by 1893, and just two years later, a Colorado business directory dropped Lincoln from its listing.

After the end of placer mining and lode mining, a dredge camp up French Gulch left huge piles of sterile rock. What effect

One of the remaining cabins at the town of Lincoln City in French Gulch, about four miles from Breckenridge. The photograph, taken on July 3, 1995 during a heavy snow storm, illustrates that summers in the high country are very short. *(Kenneth Jessen 097B8)*

this had on Lincoln City is unknown. Modern housing developments have necessitated leveling the old tailings. There are a
number of modern structures at the Lincoln City site along with
several original buildings. The steep four-wheel drive road up to
Wapiti down Georgia Gulch to Parkville leaves the graded road
near the town site.

The collapsed remains of a gold dredge sits west of the Lincoln City site. This dredge
made its way up French Creek, processing thousands of tons of gravel as it went and
leaving behind piles of sterile river rock. *(Kenneth Jessen 105D11)*

George Crofutt, *Crofutt's Grip Sack Guide of Colorado 1885*, Johnson Books, Boulder, Colorado,
1966, 1981, p. 115.

Mary Ellen Gilliland, *Summit*, Alpenrose Press, Silverthorne, Colorado, 1980, pp. 179-181.

Muriel Sibell Wolle, *Stampede to Timberline*, Sage Books, Chicago, 1949, 1974, pp. 78-80.

William H. Bauer, James L. Ozment, John H. Willard, *Colorado Post Offices*, Colorado Railroad
Museum, Golden, Colorado, 1990, p. 89.

MASONTOWN
Destroyed By An Avalanche

- *Summit County, Blue River drainage*
- *Site accessible by foot trail*
- *Town did not have a post office; no standing structures remain*

Some of Colorado's ghost towns succumbed to avalanches, and among them was Masontown located at the base of Royal Mountain above Frisco. General Buford opened up the Victoria mine containing gold and copper ore in 1866 and constructed a mill. Not much came of this venture. In 1872, the Masontown Gold Mining and Milling Company worked on improving the mine and also constructed a large mill to treat the complex ore. A great deal of money was invested in the project. The mill included twenty stamps with the ability to concentrate the ore. The investors were from Masontown, Pennsylvania, and the small camp formed at the mine and mill was named Masontown. Projected income was to have reached upwards of $1,000 per day. Development work included five tunnels. Some gold and silver was shipped to the Denver Mint, but profits were limited by high transportation costs. It wasn't until 1882 when the Denver, South Park & Pacific constructed its line over Boreas Pass, down the Blue River Valley, and through Frisco that transportation costs were low enough to make the mine pay.

An early photograph shows five structures at the site including the mill. The settlement was estimated to contain a dozen cabins.

Activity at Masontown began to slow down around 1910. Others came along and leased the property, but had little luck. The mine was worked up to about 1917, and after this,

This early view of Masontown shows that it was a small mining camp. The town was reduced to splinters by an avalanche many years after it was abandoned. *(Colorado Historical Society F7950)*

Masontown was deserted. When Prohibition came along in 1920, the then abandoned town was used by moonshiners to make their illegal whiskey.

A wet spring snow slide, which began high on the slopes of Mt. Victoria, crushed Masontown and reduced the mill to splinters in 1926. Fortunately, the town was completely vacant. In 1968, the Forest Service finished the job by burning the remaining cabins.

The site involves a short hike and a gain of 500 feet in elevation. The Royal Mountain trail leaves from the bike trail on the southwest side of Frisco and goes to the Masontown site.

For a map showing the site, refer to "Curtin."

Mary Ellen Gilliland, *Summit,* Alpenrose Press, Silverthorne, Colorado, 1980, pp. 181-183.

Mary Ellen Gilliland, *Frisco!,* Alpenrose Press, Silverthorne, Colorado, 1984, pp. 84-86.

Robert L. Brown, *Colorado Ghost Towns - Past and Present,* Caxton Printers, Caldwell, Idaho, 1977, pp. 179-182.

MONTEZUMA
And Its Smelly Funeral

- *Summit County, Snake River drainage*
- *Accessible via graded dirt road*
- *Town had a post office; a number of original structures remain*

Montezuma's Summit House, built in 1869, appears in this historic photograph on the far right. It was destroyed by fire in 1959. *(Colorado Historical Society F10786)*

A rather large, old bachelor prospector once lived near his mine above Decatur along Peru Creek. Occasionally, he would venture to Montezuma for supplies, then quite a long span of time went by without any of the residents seeing the old prospector. A miner stopped by his cabin in the spring only to find the old fellow dead. He had died sometime during the winter, and his body was frozen stiff. A group of Montezuma men went up to the cabin with a wagon to bring the old prospector down to town for a proper burial.

The funeral service was set up for the following day in the schoolhouse. A warm spell, however, caused a sudden acceleration in the services as the heat caused the corpse to thaw and expand in the casket. At first, there was a cracking sound as the casket planks began to separate. This was followed by a horrible stench as the gases from the corpse were released. An immediate evacuation of the school was necessary, and a handful of strong men returned to bind the casket with straps. It was quickly removed to the Montezuma cemetery for a hasty burial.

In a beautiful mountain valley surrounded by high peaks, at an elevation of 10,200 feet, sits the old mining town of Montezuma. It never quite surrendered to the full status of a ghost town, but certainly came close.

In 1863, a prospector named John Coley is credited by some historians as making the first discovery of silver ore in Colorado Territory. His discovery was located high above Montezuma on Glacier Mountain near Sts. John. Although somewhat difficult to believe given the complexity of the smelting process, Coley showed silver ingots in Georgetown and Empire he had smelted at the site of the discovery. This property was eventually purchased by the Boston Silver Mining Company at Sts. John.

In June, 1865, a party of prospective investors arrived in the wide valley below the site of Coley's discovery. Among them was D. C. Collier. He suggested a town be established and that it be named for the famous Aztec emperor, Montezuma. He blazed "Montezuma" into a tree near his tent. Also among the members of this party was Henry M. Teller who later gained fame not only in mining, but as a Colorado senator.

A correspondent for *The Central City Miner's Register*, D. C. Collier, was sent to Montezuma in June, 1865 to record what the place was like. Collier wrote that the town consisted of, "...brush cabins and tents." A survey was in progress to lay out the town's streets. According to Collier, the town voted on the name "Montezuma."

The first store was opened in 1866 and was operated by W. Webster. Oliver Milner and two other worked together to construct the town's first cabin. In 1869, Milner had the mail contract between Montezuma and Breckenridge and was paid $15 a trip. The amount was raised by private subscription.

Miners and prospectors began moving into the Montezuma area in 1868 over Loveland Pass. The town of Montezuma began to grow and gained equal footing with Beckenridge as one of Summit County's principal towns. A wagon road was constructed over 13,132 foot Argentine Pass in 1869 under the name The Georgetown and Snake River Road. A branch off this toll road from a point near Chihuahua was built to serve Montezuma. At the toll gate, a large sign was hung on supports over the road. A toll of $1 was charged for a wagon with one span, and to pass without paying commanded a fine of $100.

The Colorado Central arrived in Georgetown in 1877 and was the closest rail link to Montezuma. In 1878, a wagon road was built over Webster Pass, which connected the Snake River area with South Park. The "High Line" wagon road over Loveland Pass was completed in 1879. Then in 1883, the Denver, South Park & Pacific arrived in the Blue River Valley. This railroad built a spur up to Keystone in 1883 to serve the mining areas along Peru Creek and the Snake River. The railroad even graded an extension to Montezuma, but never laid rail on the grade.

Tom Fields did the first survey of Montezuma, which was completed in 1866. This was followed by a second survey in 1878, then the final survey in 1881. At this point, a patent for the town site was secured to withdraw the land from the public domain. The town was incorporated this same year, and the following year, the first town election was held.

The Sisapo Smelter and Sampling works were built in 1870 to process the silver ore. M. P. Felch and George Burnbull con-structed Montezuma's first hotel in 1868 while R. O. Jones built the town's second hotel a year later. By 1881, the population of Montezuma stood at 743. Its first newspaper, *The Montezuma Millrun*, appeared as a weekly in 1882. It was started by James Oliver who moved from Central City. This pioneer newspaper was published until 1888.

A look at Montezuma in 1882 shows that it had three hotels plus a boarding house, three stores, three saloons, two blacksmith shops and a shoemaker. There was also a livery stable and tin shop. By 1884, Montezuma had over 100 buildings including many homes, a

Some of Montezuma's homes have character as evidenced by this small frame building. The town dates back to 1865 and was incorporated in 1881. *(Kenneth Jessen 097B6)*

bank, school, church, post office, plus its stores, hotels, several restaurants and a number of saloons. It also had a hardware store and meat packing company. Several mining companies had offices in Montezuma. The town also had several lawyers and a justice of the peace.

The first school was called the Halfway, and it was constructed halfway between Montezuma and Sts. John in 1876 to serve both communities. Its school district also included the towns of Chihuahua and Decatur (Rathbone-Argentine). In 1880, Montezuma had risen to become the largest town in the area and at this time, constructed its own school. Later modifications included an entry and belfry. This structure still stands and is operated as a museum by the Summit Historical Society. It sits on the hillside to the east of the town center and was still an active school until 1958.

Father John Dyer held Methodist services in Montezuma during its early years. As an itinerant preacher, Dyer traveled from mining camp to mining camp preaching the Gospel. He covered a very wide area including not only Summit County, but Park County and parts of Lake County. His first trip to Montezuma was in 1865, and the *Millrun* reported twenty years later that Father Dyer was still preaching sermons in town. Dyer's first service was held out of doors, and the call to worship was given by hammering on a circular saw. Ironically, it was the Catholics who constructed the first and only church in Montezuma while the Protestants continued to use the schoolhouse.

Of special note was the 1865 Fourth of July celebration where Father Dyer preached a sermon. The Star Spangled Banner was sung led by "Commodore" Stephen Decatur. The evening closed with a gunfire salute.

Montezuma had its share of "soiled doves," but one woman was outstanding in her profession. She was known as "Dixie," but her real name was Ada Smith. She stayed with the town well beyond its glory days and aged along with its residents. She was certainly not glamorous or even good looking for that matter. In her later years, her face became wrinkled. During the boom years, she maintained a neat white cottage set back from Main Street where she kept her "girls." After Montezuma's population dwindled, she serviced her clientele alone. Dixie was always dressed in gaudy colors and wore big hats.

Montezuma's main street, sometime between 1879 and 1882. Many of these buildings were subsequently destroyed by fires. *(Colorado Historical Society F1561)*

Dixie loved baseball. She went out to see the local ball club play, and she kept to herself by sitting alone at one end of the rough grandstand made of planks. She cheered for the home team along with other residents, but realized she would never be accepted by Montezuma's "polite" society.

Dixie's purchasing habits were a little strange. She bought Columbine milk by the case, far in excess of what she could consume. She gave it to the town's stray cats and dogs. She clipped coupon labels, purchased cans of beef to get more labels, and gave the surplus beef to Montezuma's strays.

Eventually, law and order prevailed, and no "bawdy" houses or "disorderly" houses of prostitution were allowed. Fines ranged from $5 to $50, and for drunkenness, a similar range of fines were imposed. Gambling was also ruled illegal, and the faro tables were closed. Even shuffleboard was outlawed.

Fire is the number one cause of the destruction of Colorado's mining towns. Montezuma was almost wiped out in 1915 by a fire, which reduced to ashes a barn moved from Chihuahua, two saloons, the Montezuma Hotel and a number of homes before it was brought under control. Another fire in 1949 cost the town one of its historic log structures, a store and the town's third oldest structure. Some ten frame buildings were reduced to ashes in 1959, including the Summit House Hotel built in 1869. At the time, only seventy five people remained in the town. A fire in 1963 destroyed another old hotel, the Rocky Mountain House.

Montezuma is easy to reach via a paved road, which runs from the Keystone ski area up to the edge of town. At the Keystone ski area, exit U. S. 6 on the Montezuma Road, which is paved. The ski area parking lots will be off to the right. Just prior to reaching Montezuma, the Peru Creek Road to Decatur and Chihuahua will leave the paved Montezuma Road to the left.

Immediately south of Montezuma there is a cluster of log structures on the east side of the road and a mine on the west side. Some of the structures have been restored for seasonal use.

and a sign indicates that this is "Rileyville." There isn't any record of such a town or mining camp by that name, but this means little. It could have been a suburb of Montezuma.

For a map showing Montezuma's location, see "Chihuahua."

This old structure sits along Montezuma's main street with the restored schoolhouse in the background. The school, constructed in 1880, is operated by the Summit Historical Society as a museum and is open during the summers. *(Kenneth Jessen 097D10)*

Colorado Prospector, Vol. 24, No. 2.

Elizabeth Rice Roller, *Memoirs from Montezuma*, Chihuahua and Sts. John, Summit Historical Society, Breckenridge, Colorado, pp. 21-24.

Mary Ellen Gilliland, *Summit*, Alpenrose Press, Silverthorne, Colorado, 1980, pp. 67-75.

"Montezuma, Its Early History" *The Montezuma Millrun,* June 24, 1882.

The Central City Miner's Register, July 8, 1865.

The Denver Tribune, April 18, 1878.

Verna Sharp, *A History of Montezuma, Sts. John and Argentine*, Summit Historical Society, Breckenridge, Colorado, 1971, pp. 6-15.

William H. Bauer, James L. Ozment, John H. Willard, *Colorado Post Offices*, Colorado Railroad Museum, Golden, Colorado, 1990, p. 100.

NAOMI

- *Summit County, Blue River drainage*
- *Access unknown*
- *Town had a post office; one standing structure remains*

Originally called Josie, Naomi was located at the mouth of Rock Creek approximately eight miles north of the Silverthorne exit off of I-70. Discoveries of silver ore in the Gore Range to the west were made in 1881 and 1882, but no mines were developed to bring out the ore. Naomi was already established, and the miners simply added to its population. George Crofutt listed Naomi as having a population of 125 in 1885. The male population was listed at eighty in 1892.

Naomi got its own post office in 1882, under its original name Josie. The following year, however, the post office name was changed to Naomi, and it remained an active post office until 1888.

The town passed into the hands of the Gould brothers, and a store and hotel were added to its businesses. A sawmill began operation cutting ties for the Denver & Rio Grande as the railroad graded down the Blue River toward Middle Park. Rails were never laid north of Dillon, however, leaving behind an expanse of unused railroad grade.

The site is privately owned by the Rock Creek Ranch, and only the partial remains of the Naomi hotel remain standing.

George Crofutt, *Crofutt's Grip Sack Guide of Colorado 1885*, Johnson Books, Boulder, Colorado, 1966, 1981, p. 123.

Mary Ellen Gilliland, *Summit*, Alpenrose Press, Silverthorne, Colorado, 1980, p. 183.

William H. Bauer, James L. Ozment, John H. Willard, *Colorado Post Offices*, Colorado Railroad Museum, Golden, Colorado, 1990,pp. 80, 103.

PARKVILLE
County Seat, Buried

- *Summit County, Swan River drainage*
- *Accessible over graded dirt road*
- *Town had a post office; no standing structures remain*

One of the earliest mining camps in the Blue River Valley area of Colorado was Parkville, founded around 1860 shortly after rich gold deposits were discovered. The town sprang up at the mouth of Georgia Gulch on the Swan River about six miles east of Colorado 9. The gulch was named by a Georgian prospector, Highfred, who made the first discovery. By 1861, the canyon bottom at the base of Georgia Gulch was dotted with small miner's cabins erected for protection against the severe winters. The population of Parkville quickly grew to an estimated 1,800 residents.

This discovery turned out to be one of the richest in Colorado history with men panning an extraordinary $300 to $500 in gold per day at a time when a day's wages amounted to $1.50 to $2.00. A single claim worked for an entire summer season could produce upwards to $10,000 in gold dust. From 1860 to 1862, an estimated three million dollars in placer or free gold was removed from this relatively small area.

Parkville was the largest town in this entire part of Colorado and became the logical choice for the Summit County seat. At time, Summit County stretched all the way west across Colorado to the Utah line and enclosed the entire northwestern portion of the state. In 1861, Parkville lost the vote to become Colorado's territorial capitol by only 11 votes.

Feelings ran high in 1861 as the country entered the Civil War. Colorado attracted both Union and Confederate sympathizers. A Rebel and a Yankee got into a fight over the slavery issue in Parkville to the point where a duel to the death seemed to be the only way to resolve the conflict. Seconds were selected, and they carefully loaded a pair of revolvers. Other armed men stood by ready to shoot if one of the combatants cheated by firing before the count of three. The Rebel and the Yankee grabbed opposite ends of a handkerchief, and with the other hand, pointed their pistols at point blank range at each other. The expected outcome was sudden death for both men. At the command of "make ready" the men cocked their revolvers. The count was given, "one, two, three." After the deafening noise of the revolvers, the small cabin was filled with a cloud of black powder smoke.

Both of the men fell backwards to the floor with holes burned in their shirts. The local doctor hurriedly knelt over first one body then the other. He felt for a pulse and opened their shirts to determine where the entry wound was located. Each man had a red bruise, and that was all the doctor could find.

The two men managed to get to their feet amid uncon-

The remains of one of the Risdon gold dredges, which once operated along the Swan River, can be seen along the road to Parkville. This dredge began operation in 1898, and worked its way up the Swan River before it was abandoned. *(Kenneth Jessen 096C5)*

trolled laughter. The seconds had loaded the guns with wax bullets and had not let the astonished doctor in on the prank. Allegedly, the disgruntled doctor stormed out of the cabin muttering something about how his own revolver carried real bullets made of real lead.

The Union Army camped near Parkville to drum up recruits, and in the process, the first American flag was raised in the area by Lieutenant Roath. Daily drills were held by the First Regiment, Colorado Volunteers, much to the disgust of Confederate sympathizers.

Parkville was a full-fledged town complete with a drug store, meat market, saddle shop, and a brewery. The brewery, by the way, was started by Henry Weiss and produced lager beer. Weiss claimed he made as much money as those who worked the original gold deposits. There was a hotel, the Chapin House, which could seat up to fifty guests for dinner. Parkville was the site of the first Masonic Temple on the Western Slope. The temple was

dedicated by Parson John Chivington in 1861. Chivington later went down in infamy for his slaughter of unarmed women and children at Sand Creek. On the lower level of the lodge was a general store. The town had three theaters, one with a 30 x 40 foot stage. The Colorado Minstrels

An old cabin east of Parkville is all that is left of this former Summit County seat. Parkville itself was buried under tons of tailings from hydraulic mining. *(Kenneth Jessen 096C6)*

performed at the Gayosa Hall. Nightly performances by the Pioneer Theatre Company were held in a big tent. At the Georgia Hall dances were held.

The saloons included the Metropolitan and the Bed Rock. The town attracted its share of professional gamblers, and as put by one writer of the time, "...saloons, open day and night, to furnish professional sports ... and to fleece the verdant miners of their hard earned dust and highly prized nuggets."

The most unique business in Parkville was a privately run mint. Gold coins of $5 and $10 denominations were cast then stamped with dies to provide some medium of exchange other than gold dust. The only known coins from this mint are at the Smithsonian Museum, and the dies are at the Colorado State Historical Society.

Parkville lacked the proper facilities to house the county offices, and the commissioners decided on January 6, 1862, to move them to Breckenridge. The Park Hotel in Breckenridge was purchased in May for $125 for the county offices, and the Masonic Hall was rented as the courthouse. The move was gradual, and up until June, 1864, the commissioners alternated their meetings between Parkville and Breckenridge.

A more colorful version of the relocation of the county seat has some zealous Breckenridge residents taking the county records from Parkville under the cloak of darkness and hiding them. After Parkville residents had cooled off, new county offices were opened in Breckenridge.

Nothing was sacred in the early mining economy of Colorado. The hills were stripped of all their timber for the mines, for cabins and use as fuel. Hydraulic mining, using high pressure hoses, washed gravel down from the banks leaving scars still visible today. Parkville, the former county seat, was not immune. It was slowly buried under tons of tailings from hydraulic mining forcing all but one resident to leave. This last resident filed a law suit, but lost. This explains why hardly a trace of Parkville can be found today. In 1882, a *Denver Times* article related how the town was being buried. Another article during the same year told of how only the roof tops of Parkville were visible. Only the small cemetery to the east of the town was spared.

To reach the Parkville site is easy. About halfway between the Dillon Reservoir and Breckenridge take the Tiger Road up the Swan River east of Colorado 9. Parkville is reached by driving up the Tiger Road past Delaware Flats and past the site of Tiger for about 5 3/4 miles. The road swings gradually south and at the Parkville site is headed due south. Just before reaching the Parkville site, the graded dirt road splits with one road on the east side of the valley while a rougher dirt road parallels it on the west side. Take the crossover to the west side. Note the raw piles of dredge tailings that mark the Parkville site. After entering the forest beyond the tailings, a sign will indicate where the Parkville cemetery is located. A short quarter of a mile hike through the trees will lead to the Mason's marker along with a few graves.

Little else remains of Parkville, and the road continues to up Georgia Gulch but requires four-wheel drive to negotiate.

For a map showing the location of the Parkville site, see "Lincoln City."

The Mason's marker at the Parkville cemetery, noting the pioneer Mason's lodge was located in this early mining town. *(Kenneth Jessen 103C1)*

Mary Ellen Gilliland, *Summit*, Alpenrose Press, Silverthorne, Colorado, 1980, pp. 228-235.

Sandra F. Prichard, *Roadside Summit*, The Human Landscape Part II, Summit Historical Society, Breckenridge, Colorado, 1992, pp. 69-70.

Summit County Journal, April 11, 1925.

PRESTON

Picturesque

- *Summit County, Gold Run Gulch drainage*
- *Accessible via graded dirt road*
- *Town had a post office; several standing structures remain*

According to postal records, the Preston post office was moved from Delaware Flats in 1875, to Preston, located at the head of Gold Run Gulch. It closed on January 18, 1884, only to reopen less than a month later. In 1889, the post office was moved to Braddockville (or Braddock), very close to Delaware Flats. Braddockville had the advantage of a station along the Denver, South Park & Pacific. The wandering post office remained opened until 1890 at Braddockville.

One of the two cabins at Preston, not far from Breckenridge. *(Kenneth Jessen 097B11)*

477

What kept Preston alive was the Jumbo mine located close to this pretty town. Preston had a large boarding house, which stood until recent years, a sawmill, the offices of three mining companies, millinery shop, produce store, and a number of cabins where the miners lived.

Activities in Preston seemed to be dominated by John Shock who ran the produce store, the boarding house and was also the postmaster. His wife operated a millinery and dress shop, an unusual store for such a small mining town.

Not much else is know about life in Preston. It is located in one of the most picturesque settings of any Colorado mining town in a lush meadow surrounded by tall trees, which provide shade throughout the summer. To reach Preston, turn east on the Tiger Road and skirt the north side of the golf course. Take the first dirt road to the right (Forest Service 300) around the golf course and by the driving range. The road then begins to climb up Gold Run Gulch past the remains of the Jesse Mill. At the intersection of a second road coming from the west sits Preston. There are two cabins in relatively good shape and the collapsed remains of several other structures. By turning right at the top of the meadow, the road continues on to French Gulch. In dry weather, the road should be passable by car.

For a map showing the location of Preston, see "Braddockville."

Mary Ellen Gilliland, *Summit*, Alpenrose Press, Silverthorne, Colorado, 1980, pp. 183-184.
William H. Bauer, James L. Ozment, John H. Willard, *Colorado Post Offices*, Colorado Railroad Museum, Golden, Colorado, 1990, pp. 23, 116.

REXFORD

- *Summit County, North Fork of the Swan River drainage*
- *Town had a post office*
- *Accessible by four-wheel drive vehicle; several collapsed cabins remain*

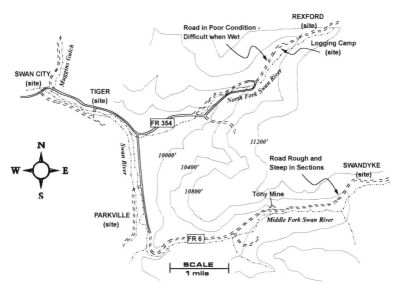

Rexford is located up the North Fork of the Swan River, and the road is relatively good until it swings across the creek. At this point, a four-wheel drive trail climbs up through the trees and through bogs to the site.

Rexford is located about three and a half miles up the North Fork of the Swan River in a relatively remote area. The road to Rexford leaves the Tiger Road before Parkville and is graded for about a mile. It then becomes a little rougher for another mile and a quarter. Where the graded road swings around to the left in a hairpin turn after crossing the creek, a single track four-wheel

479

drive road continues to the right up the canyon to Rexford. This road is quite swampy in places and continues up the creek for 1.2 miles to the Rexford site. In the process, the road passes three collapsed cabins of a more contemporary design believed to be the remains of a logging camp.

At Rexford, there are no standing buildings, but the remains of eight or more structures dot the meadow. Rexford, by the way, is located only a mile southeast of the Keystone Ski Area boundary.

Daniel Patrick discovered rich ore near the Rexford site in 1880. The mine, which was named the Rochester Queen, was developed in 1881 with a 75-foot shaft and a 325-foot drift into the lode. The town of Rexford was formed on land owned by the Rexford Mining Corporation and was located a few hundred yards below the mine. The town got its own post office in 1882, but it closed the following year. A mill was built near the mine portal.

The Rochester Queen produced $5,000 worth of ore per month during its first three months of operation. Shipments from the mine were made during 1881 and 1882 to the Argo smelter outside of Denver. The ore was complex and expensive to mill, not to mention the high cost of transportation. It contained iron, copper, galena and some gold. The ore was found in fissures six to ten inches wide.

Exactly what happened to the mine and to the town is not known, but most certainly, the town had fallen in population below that required for postal service by 1883. By 1929, the road to the town and its mine was not passable, and Rexford had long been abandoned.

In 1955, Muriel Sibell Wolle, ghost town historian, received a letter from one of her fans who said that quite a few buildings were still standing. This included several two-story structures, and the observer noted that Rexford's buildings were in a relatively high state of preservation.

Robert L. Brown describes Rexford in his 1972 book noting that the general store, with its false front and big glass windows, was still standing. A small log cabin also stood next to the store

Collapsed remains of a log structure at Rexford, located up the North Fork of the Swan River. *(Kenneth Jessen 104C10)*

and beyond the cabin, the walls of the town's only saloon were standing, but with a tall tree growing inside. By the time of Brown's visit, there was only the crumbling remains of the boarding house. It was the largest structure in Rexford. Another large structure also stood at the edge of the meadow, and all of the surface buildings at the mine were gone by this time.

Muriel Sibell Wolle, *Timberline Tailings*, Sage Books, Chicago, 1977, pp. 73-74.

Robert L. Brown, *Colorado Ghost Towns - Past and Present*, Caxton Printers, Caldwell, Idaho, 1977, pp. 219-223.

William H. Bauer, James L. Ozment, John H. Willard, *Colorado Post Offices*, Colorado Railroad Museum, Golden, Colorado, 1990, p. 122.

ROBINSON
Streets Paved With Silver

- *Summit County, Ten Mile Creek drainage*
- *Site buried*
- *Town had a post office*

An early view of Robinson looking northeast with the Robinson mill in the background. *(Colorado Historical Society F33427)*

The tailings from molybdenum mining has filled the entire upper portion of the Ten Mile Creek drainage and along with it, the towns of Carbonateville and Robinson. These towns were entirely the product of mining and they were buried by it as well. Robinson sprang up practically as an instant town based on the discovery of rich silver ore. At 10,778 feet, it was a tough place to live, but its size rivaled other towns at lower elevations.

In 1860, prospectors discovered placer gold in McNulty Gulch in upper Ten Mile Creek, but soon, the gold was exhausted

and the area forgotten. After the passage of nearly twenty years, a
Leadville merchant, George Robinson, grubstaked a couple of
prospectors. The deal he made was simple; supplies for half ownership in any discovery. The two men, Charles Jones and John
Sheddon, struck it rich and along with them, George Robinson.
Robinson wisely purchased the half owned by the two prospectors and headed East to raise development capital. With $100,000,
the Robinson Consolidated Mining Company was organized.

Once the word got out, prospectors poured into the area to
look for their own vein of silver ore. At the base of Fremont Pass,
the town of Carbonateville developed. It was a log town with sixty
businesses. One mile down the canyon, the town of Ten Mile City
was organized and would eventually be renamed Robinson.

George Robinson had a strong influence on the town and
did not want the typical haphazard growth so common among
other mining towns. The town was officially founded in 1879, but
A. J. Streeter had already constructed Robinson's first building.
Robinson himself built the Robinson Hotel and helped get a bank
going. The most prominent structure was the Robinson Smelting
Works, owned by the Robinson Consolidated Mining Company
and originally located at Carbonateville. Tall smoke stacks and
three large buildings comprised the combination mill and
smelter.

The Robinson *Tribune* made its debut in 1880. By this time,
there were four saw mills operating to fill the demand for milled
lumber and mine timbers plus stores of all sorts, a telegraph office
and a number of saloons.

George Robinson was now quite wealthy having risen from
a Leadville storekeeper to having ownership in a number of
mines, a smelter and a town. This town would soon eclipse other
towns in the area. He was elected as the state's lieutenant governor in November, 1880.

At this same time, George Robinson got into a dispute over
the ownership of the Smuggler mine, and to protect the property,
he placed an armed guard inside the portal of the mine behind its

locked door. The guard had strict orders to shoot anyone attempting to enter. Robinson heard that an army of 100 men were marching on his mine with the intent to storm it and take over its operation by force. Robinson hurried to the Smuggler to investigate and shook the door so that he could talk to the guard. The guard could not see Robinson and asked what he wanted, but failed to hear Robinson's reply. The guard did as he was instructed; he fired through the door, mortally wounding the mine owner.

By this time, nearly 1,000 people lived in Robinson. In 1881, the town's isolation was lessened by the arrival of the narrow gauge Denver & Rio Grande over Fremont Pass. Now Robinson was connected to the outside world through Leadville. This same year, a schoolhouse was constructed for sixty-six students. The Catholics built Robinson's first church the following year.

How lucky could a town get? The narrow gauge Denver, South Park & Pacific constructed its line across the Blue River Valley from Breckenridge, through Frisco, up Ten Mile Creek and reached Robinson in 1884. The route over the Denver & Rio Grande through Leadville to Denver was 294 miles and cost a passenger $13.95. The new Denver, South Park & Pacific line was only 131 miles to Denver, and its fare was $11.75.

Life was still fairly primitive. Miner's cabins sat on the steep hillside above the town. So steep was the slope that the back of these homes were flush with the soil while their fronts were supported by stilts. The only sanitation facilities were outhouses behind each dwelling. Muddy paths led down the hill into the town. Board walks were constructed in front of the businesses along the main street to reduce the mud problem. Burros, released by the miners, roamed the streets of Robinson searching for any morsel of food they could find.

Robinson continued to grow through the 1880s gaining five more hotels in addition to the Robinson House. There was also a boarding house, grocery stores, a meat market, a bakery, at least one restaurant and a number of saloons. The businesses lined the town's major streets including Main, Palmer, Ballou, and Fairfield.

Robinson was also the headquarters for four mining companies. There were assay offices, a watchmaker, blacksmith shop and a notary public. Most unusual was Robinson's Italian fruit vendor. The snow never melted completely from under the porches and sheds, and ice cream could be made any time of the year, even on the hottest summer day.

Robinson's streets were literally paved with silver or more accurately, slag containing silver from the smelter. Silver ore of the type found near Robinson must be roasted to drive off the unwanted sulphur. The process of heating the ore in the open air caused some of the silver to oxidize. When the ore was melted in a crucible, the silver oxide combined with the slag. The slag was skimmed off and discarded. The slag was crushed and used as road base for Robinson's streets.

A Mr. Primrose "mined" the silver in one of Robinson's streets, and the *Denver Republican* reported that assays on the slag ran as high as $100 per ton. Primrose went about digging up the street much to the annoyance of the town fathers and citizens trying to steer their wagons around the holes. The matter was settled when Primrose agree to give the town twenty percent of the profit from the silver recovered in the street!

This photograph was taken in 1926, well after the town of Robinson was abandoned. The site is buried under tons of tailings from the molybdenum mine at Climax. *(Colorado Historical Society F33432)*

The devaluation of silver in 1893 with the repeal of the Sherman Silver Purchase Act ended silver's artificially high price and also ended Colorado's silver mining boom. The population of Robinson dropped quickly as the mines closed, and by 1910, only 150 people remained. During the 1930s, the last remaining family to live in Robinson was observed removing the boards from the church for lumber and firewood.

The tailings from the milling process is composed of fine silt. When the silt washes into streams, it clogs the natural flow causing flooding. Polluted with tons of silt, Tenmile Creek started flooding creating a swamp at Robinson. This hastened the town's deterioration. The photograph taken by ghost town historian Robert L. Brown in his *Colorado Ghost Towns*, published in 1972, shows the Robinson site completely void of any structures. AMAX needed more room to deposit the tailings from its enormous mine at Climax on Fremont Pass and purchased the entire valley. Today, the Robinson site is under millions of tons of fine tailings from molybdenum mining.

For a map showing Robinson's location, see "Kokomo-Recen."

Mary Ellen Gilliland, *Summit,* Alpenrose Press, Silverthorne, Colorado, 1980, pp. 250-257.

Robert L. Brown, *Colorado Ghost Towns - Past and Present,* Caxton Printers, Caldwell, Idaho, 1977, pp. 224-228.

Stanley Dempsey and James E. Fell, Jr. *Mining the Summit,* University of Oklahoma Press, Norman, Oklahoma, 1986, pp. 82-102.

STS. JOHN
Named For Two Saints

- *Summit County, Saints John Creek*
- *Accessible via dirt road*
- *Town had a post office; several standing structures remain*

Sts. John when it was alive with activity. It reached a population of about two hundred during the 1880s. *(Colorado Historical Society F41729)*

In 1861, several Summit County miners were hunting deer and ran out of bullets. They found some galena ore, which looks similar to lead, and cast their bullets. Not knowing that the galena might be valuable, they continued their hunting trip. Several years later, one of the men was astonished to see some silver ore from Nevada that looked identical to the ore they used for their bullets.

One of the men wrote another miner who lived in Empire, Joseph Coley, and asked him to return to the area and stake a

The mine superintendent's home at Sts. John is one of two structures left standing. Taken in late June, this photograph illustrates how long the snow lingers in this high altitude town. *(Kenneth Jessen 097B2)*

claim. Coley did just that and also built a roasting furnace. The smokestack was constructed by placing a hollow log vertically over the furnace then covering it all the way around with rocks and clay. The rocks and clay were built up to the top of the log. Coley then burned out the log leaving a stone flue.

He was successful in casting some silver buttons, which were hauled on the backs of donkeys over the precipitous Argentine Pass to Georgetown. At a Georgetown mill, he was told that the buttons did not contain enough silver to make the transportation and milling profitable. But Coley knew the ore was rich enough to process locally.

Another version of this story says that Coley discovered the silver ore on one of his prospecting trips from his home in Empire.

By 1865, mining started at the Coley claim at the base of Glacier Mountain. The settlement was founded in 1867 and was originally called Coleyville, and the number of miners continued to increase as production rose. In the same year, the name of the town was changed to Sts. John by a group of Masons. It was named after their patron saints, St. John the Baptist and St. John the Evangelist.

The Boston Silver Mining Association hired John Collum, a Cornish mining engineer, to develop the mine and find a way to process the silver-galena-lead ore. Collum discovered that the normal smelting furnace could not heat this ore to a high enough temperature. He had a blast furnace constructed, which used forced air to increase the rate at the fuel is burned. This additional air elevated its internal temperature. Construction on this furnace began in 1869. In 1872, the original mill and smelter were replaced by a more modern structure.

It required a lot of machinery to operate a mill and smelter on any economical scale. Power for this mill came from a large stationary steam engine with thirteen inch cylinders. It developed one hundred horsepower. A pair of boilers were used to supply the steam. The fly wheel alone weighed six thousand pounds, and all of the machinery was hauled to Sts. John by wagon.

But even this new mill could not be operated profitably. The property changed hands six years later and was purchased by the Boston Mining Company. The refining process was improved and silver production climbed. Most of the structures in Sts. John were built at this time.

Smelter stack remains above the mill at Sts. John used to process silver ore. *(Kenneth Jessen 097B4)*

English investors operated the mines and mill for one season. The investors sent their own manager, Mr. Mumby, who was an advocate of physical fitness. Typical of the thinking at this time, he believed in a daily cold bath. Each morning, Mumby jogged from Sts. John down to Montezuma and plunged into a pool created by a small dam in the river. Several families in Montezuma, however, had built this dam so they could have drinking water in their homes and took a dim view of someone using it as a bathtub. Mumby, at the insistence of the families, had to look elsewhere for a bathing pool.

Sts. John reached a peak population during the 1880s of around two hundred. It had its own post office, which was started in 1876 and operated up until 1881. Sts. John also had two hotels, a company store and a two and a half story boarding house as well as a guest house. Its simple log cabins were scattered up and down the valley with some homes made of milled lumber. The assay office contained a three hundred-volume library to encourage reading instead of drinking. No saloons were allowed in Sts. John, but Montezuma was just two miles away. This is where those thirsty miners went for entertainment.

A log schoolhouse was built at the first switchback above Montezuma and served both towns until 1880 when Montezuma constructed its own school.

Sts. John and its mine remained active until about 1914. The price of silver had already taken a substantial drop, but the ore was rich enough for mining to continue. From that point on, the town site has been occupied sporadically.

The superintendent's office, still standing, was beautifully furnished. When the Boston Mining Company stopped work and

Mining stopped at Sts. John around the start of World War I, but today its two remaining structures are seasonally occupied. *(Colorado Historical Society F1542)*

There is quite a bit of track and mine equipment left at the mine at Sts. John. Silver ore was mined here beginning in the mid-1860s lasting past the turn of the century. *(Kenneth Jessen 097B5)*

withdrew from Sts. John, this structure was abandoned, furniture and all. The assay office, with its extensive library, was also abandoned.

When ghost town historian Muriel Sibell Wolle visited Sts. John during the 1940s, the large mill was still standing as well as the two-story boarding house. The mine superintendent's office and another structure are all that remain today.

Sts. John can be reached over a rough road more suitable for a truck, but negotiable by car provided the driver takes care. (The road is shown as a four-wheel drive road on most maps.) The road to Sts. John leaves the main intersection in Montezuma, runs past an old barn and begins climbing. There is a side road taking off to the left leading to a mine. At Sts. John, the two remaining structures are privately owned. The remains of the mill and its chimney can be seen above the town site.

Colorado Prospector, Vol. 24, No. 2, pp. 6-7.

"First Find in Colorado," *The Denver Republican*, July 22, 1881.

Muriel Sibell Wolle, *Stampede to Timberline*, Sage Books, Chicago, 1949, 1974, pp. 132-134.

"Our Summit County Letter," *Rocky Mountain News*, August 15, 1872.

Verna Sharp, *A History of Montezuma, Sts. John and Argentine*, Summit Historical Society, Breckenridge, Colorado, 1971, pp. 16-20.

William H. Bauer, James L. Ozment, John H. Willard, *Colorado Post Offices*, Colorado Railroad Museum, Golden, Colorado, 1990, p. 127.

SWAN CITY

- *Summit County, Swan River drainage*
- *Accessible via graded dirt road*
- *Town had a post office; no standing structures remain*

This small mining town was founded in May, 1880, and by August, had its own post office, store, hotel and saloon. Stage service was provided by Dave Braddock from the Blue River Valley. By 1885, a dozen log cabins had been added to Swan City, and its estimated population was 100.

Some of the gold ore found in the area assayed at $800 per ton, but the big money in gold was to occur many years later when gold dredges were used to recover free gold in the gravel of the Swan River. By 1890, the mines in the area were exhausted of their rich ore, and Swan City was no longer listed in the directory of mining camps in Summit County.

Dredging has totally obliterated the site, and today, nothing remains at Swan City. The site is located at the mouth of Brown's Gulch on the south and Muggins Gulch to the north.

See "Rexford" for a map locating the Swan City site.

Don and Jean Griswold, *Colorado's Century of "Cities"*, Self Published, 1958, p. 175.

Mary Ellen Gilliland, *Summit*, Alpenrose Press, Silverthorne, Colorado, 1980, p. 185.

William H. Bauer, James L. Ozment, John H. Willard, *Colorado Post Offices*, Colorado Railroad Museum, Golden, Colorado, 1990, p. 138.

SWANDYKE

Carl Fulton's Town

- *Summit County, Middle Fork of the Swan River*
- *Accessible by four-wheel drive vehicle*
- *Town had a post office; one standing structure remains*

This old two-story log building is one of the most ghostly structures at any Colorado ghost town, and it is located at Swandyke. *(Kenneth Jessen 104C6)*

Carl Fulton traveled to the West from his Ohio home to try his hand at prospecting. His problem was that he was thirty years too late, and by 1897, all of the good placer and lode claims had already been taken and mined in the Breckenridge area. Carl elected to go up the Swan River, well beyond all established mining camps, and up its Middle Fork. At elevations approaching 13,000 feet he found an abundance of gold ore. Much of it was at the surface and in the form of free milling gold, which had been oxidized.

At the base of the natural glaciated amphitheater in a small meadow, the town of Swandyke was founded either by Fulton himself or prospectors that followed. Buildings included a hotel able to accommodate 75 people, boarding house, general store, blacksmith shop, saw mill and a number of log homes. At its peak, Swandyke was estimated to have a population of 200.

The first winter endured by its residents was 1898-1899, one of the worst in Summit County history. At Swandyke, snow reached the rooftops. Carl Fulton continued to work his mine and piled the ore outside waiting for spring. An avalanche carried the ore down the mountainside and also demolished a mill.

Mining included the Swandyke Gold Mining and Milling Company, which consolidated a dozen claims and built a stamp mill using the cyanide leaching process. The mill was completed in 1899. The Carrie group of mines encountered free milling gold ore and also had its own stamp mill. A large vein of partly oxidized gold ore was mined at the Pompeii, and at other locations, ore was discovered near the surface with assay value as high as $90 per ton. An extraordinary streak of gold-bearing quartz, with gold particles large enough to see, had assay values approaching $2,000 a ton.

Robert L. Brown in his book, *Colorado Ghost Towns- Past and Present,* cites a report that speculated that enough ore existed in the Swandyke area to support a large population for many years. There was plenty of timber to fuel the boilers at the mills and for mine timbers, and an amphitheater with an abundant supply of water. The author of the report recommended Swandyke as a summer resort.

Muriel Sibell Wolle, in her 1949 book, *Stampede to Timberline*, saw a two-story structure at the entrance to Swandyke said to have served as a hotel, a cabin with lace curtains and newspapers dating back to 1901, and a barn that was partially collapsed. Robert L. Brown visited Swandyke in 1967 and saw the same three structures with the foundation of many other structures among the trees. Today, only the two-story log hotel remains, the other buildings having yielded to the forces of nature.

Swandyke is located high up the Middle Fork of the Swan River at an elevation of 11,200 feet just a mile from the Continental Divide. To the southeast of Swandyke is Whale Peak at 13,078 feet, Sheep Mountain at 12,495 feet and Glacier Peak at 12,853 feet.

To reach Swandyke, take the Swan River Road. At the North Fork, go straight ahead toward the Parkville site. This road is graded, but becomes quite rough. Do not cross over to the west (right) side of the valley just prior to the Parkville site; continue straight ahead. Beyond Parkville, the road swings sharply from the south to the east and is suitable only for a four-wheel drive vehicle. The road is narrow, rough and quite steep in places. Some driver skill is required to avoid hitting the undercarriage on large rocks, but a four-wheel drive club grades the road occasionally. After about four miles and past the Tony Mine, the only remaining structure in Swandyke will be seen sitting on the left side of the road. The collapsed remains of other buildings can be found in the small meadow above and below the road.

For a map showing Swandyke's location, see "Rexford."

Mary Ellen Gilliland, *Breckenridge!*, Alpenrose Press, Silverthorne, Colorado, 1988, pp. 23-24.

Mary Ellen Gilliland, *Summit*, Alpenrose Press, Silverthorne, Colorado, 1980, p. 185.

Robert L. Brown, *Colorado Ghost Towns - Past and Present*, Caxton Printers, Caldwell, Idaho, 1977, pp. 263-268.

William H. Bauer, James L. Ozment, John H. Willard, *Colorado Post Offices*, Colorado Railroad Museum, Golden, Colorado, 1990, p. 138.

TIGER

Burned By The Forest Service

- *Summit County, Swan River drainage*
- *Accessible via graded dirt road*
- *Town had a post office; no standing structures remain*

An undated photograph shows the ghost town of Tiger. In 1973, the Breckenridge Volunteer Fire Department, under the direction of the Forest Service and Bureau of Reclamation, burned Tiger to the ground. *(Colorado Historical Society F6077)*

There are many reasons why so little is left of Colorado's old mining towns. Some were swept away by avalanches while heavy snows and high winds destroyed others. Vandals have taken their toll on the old buildings, but accidental fires, while the towns were still occupied, has been the primary cause of destruction. With the exception of the assay office, the ghost town of Tiger was intentionally burned.

Historical accounts of when Tiger was founded vary. Robert L. Brown, in his fine book, *Colorado Ghost Towns,* dates the

discovery of the Tiger
Lode and the Tiger
Extension to 1864.
What followed was a
tent city, which gave
way to more permanent
structures and the town
of Tiger. The IXL and
Cashier mines came
along shortly after the
original discoveries.
Brown associates Tiger
with Swan City, located
a short distance away.

The Lomax Placer in Breckenridge is operated as a historic site by the Summit Historical Society and is the home of the assay building from Tiger. *(Kenneth Jessen 107C5)*

Other historians separate Swan City from Tiger saying that they were offset in time by thirty years. John Taylor examined the high producing IXL Lode after the turn of the century. This mine had been long abandoned at the time. Taylor found a pocket of rich ore and purchased the property in 1917. A modern mill was constructed near the mine on the south side of the Swan River Valley. The tunnel in the IXL was extended into the Cashier.

The town of Tiger, founded after the turn of the century, was owned by the Royal Tiger Mining Company. Its employees were provided free electricity, steam heat, running water, a good school and playground. A boarding house, bunkhouse, mine office, blacksmith shop, assay office and sawmill filled out Tiger's commercial structures. The company also provided free movies and dances to the miners and families. A physician visited the site. As posted in 1918, married miners and mill workers received $165 a month;. single men received $150 . Rent for a family in a company owned home was $10 per month while single men paid $4 for a furnished room. Tiger's population was around 250. The post office opened in 1919, and lasted until 1940, when the mine closed.

Tiger lasted longer than most Colorado mining towns and because the town was not as old as other abandoned sites, Tiger's buildings remained in good condition. Transients occupied the town during the 1960s and according to Breckenridge resident Morine Nichols, these "flower children" had permission from the mining company. It was discovered that the property actually sat on public land and the transients were warned many times to vacate the buildings. In 1973, the Breckenridge Volunteer Fire Department, under the direction of the Forest Service and Bureau of Reclamation, burned Tiger to the ground. Only the assay office was spared, and it was later moved to the Lomax Placer display on Ski Hill Road in Breckenridge. This is an outdoor museum operated by the Summit Historical Society.

From historic photographs, Tiger had a main street lined on both sides with buildings. Subsequent dredging operation obliterated the portion of Tiger closest to the Swan River. One early photograph shows a row of five buildings on the north side with a mill in the background and one structure on the south side. A photograph taken by Robert Brown in the late 1960s shows a half dozen frame structures.

Other than a wilderness outfitter on the south bank of the Swan River, there are no standing structures at the Tiger site. The ruins of the Tiger mine and mill complex are located on the far south side of the valley along with several crude seasonal buildings built well after the mine closed.

The Tiger Road leaves Colorado 9 about half way between Frisco and Breckenridge and heads east. The Tiger site is nearly five miles up this road just beyond Muggins Gulch after the road crosses from the south side of the Swan River to the north side. *See "Rexford" for a map showing Tiger's location.*

John K. Aldrich, *Ghosts of Summit County*, Centennial Graphics, Lakewood, 1986, pp. 51-52.

Mary Ellen Gilliland, *Summit*, Alpenrose Press, Silverthorne, Colorado, 1980, pp. 185-187.

Robert L. Brown, *Colorado Ghost Towns - Past and Present*, Caxton Printers, Caldwell, Idaho, 1977, pp. 277-280.

Sandra F. Prichard, *Roadside Summit, The Human Landscape Part II*, Summit Historical Society, Breckenridge, Colorado, 1992, pp. 67-68.

William H. Bauer, James L. Ozment, John H. Willard, *Colorado Post Offices*, Colorado Railroad Museum, Golden, Colorado, 1990, p. 141.

WAPITI
Name For The Elk

- *Summit County, Georgia Gulch drainage*
- *Site accessible by four-wheel drive road*
- *Town had a post office; one partially collapsed structure remains*

Wapiti was originally named Victoria until 1894 when it got its own post office, under the name Wapiti. The post office remained active until 1903. The small camp, probably consisting of no more than a half dozen structures, was located near Farncomb Hill, one of the richest mineralized areas in Colorado. Farncomb Hill was where the Wire Patch lode of pure wire gold was located.

Muriel Sibell Wolle received a letter from a fan that was later published in her book, *Timberline Tailings*, to the effect that

The combination store, living quarters and post office in Wapiti when the mines were still active. The collapsed structure remains today. *(Colorado Historical Society F8406)*

One of the remaining structures at the ghost camp of Wapiti, located above the Parkville site. It served as a store, living quarters and post office. *(Kenneth Jessen 103C5)*

Wapiti was located on the Parkville side of the divide separating French Creek from the Swan River. This individual reported that in 1957, two cabins remained at Wapiti and that they were in relatively good condition.

Today, only the partially collapsed remains of one structure remains at Wapiti and it sits right along the four-wheel drive road to the site. It was a combination mine office, living quarters and post office.

To reach Wapiti, take the Tiger Road up the Swan River past the Parkville site. The route to Wapiti crosses the dredge tailings immediately north of the Parkville site over to the west side of the Swan River then turns south for a short distance past the Parkville cemetery. The road then begins a steep climb up Georgia Gulch crossing over to American Gulch. The road has several sharp switchbacks, but takes only a few minutes to reach Wapiti from Parkville. The road continues past Wapiti, over the divide, and down to Lincoln.

For a map showing Wapiti's location, see "Lincoln City."

Mary Ellen Gilliland, *Summit*, Alpenrose Press, Silverthorne, Colorado, 1980, p. 187.

Muriel Sibell Wolle, *Stampede to Timberline*, Sage Books, Chicago, 1949, 1974, p. 71.

William H. Bauer, James L. Ozment, John H. Willard, *Colorado Post Offices*, Colorado Railroad Museum, Golden, Colorado, 1990, p. 148.

WHEELER

- *Tenmile Creek drainage; accessible by paved road*
- *Town had a post office*
- *No standing structures remain; site part of Copper Mountain Ski area*

In the flat, open area at the base of Vail Pass where West Tenmile Creek and the main fork of Tenmile Creek join is the Wheeler town site. The location today is at the intersection of I-70 and Colorado 91, and the location is now called Wheeler Junction. The Copper Mountain Ski area occupies part of the site.

Wheeler was named for Judge John S. Wheeler who had a ranch on this spot and grew hay for the numerous draft animals used in the mining industry. The area was quite swampy and was ideal for growing hay. Judge Wheeler also constructed a sawmill in 1878 to meet the demand for milled lumber for the area's towns and mines. Eventually, a half dozen sawmills were in operation in the general area, and the town of Wheeler began to grow. It had several saloons, a billiard hall, a blacksmith shop, several stores and a hotel. The town got its own post office in 1880, which remained active for fourteen years.

Swedish immigrants were attracted to the lumber industry in Wheeler, and they became the major ethnic group. Swedes were well known for their logging skills.

Wheeler was nearly obliterated in 1882 by a fire, which broke out in the upper story of a building next to the Wheeler post office. Their fire spread quickly to the general store, post office, milk house, a store room and Judge Wheeler's private office. No fire fighting equipment was available. A couple of sawmill workers combined their efforts with four Cornish miners to bring the fire under control. The Denver & Rio Grande station agent saved

Judge Wheeler's home.

The Denver & Rio Grande was first to come through the Wheeler town site and constructed a small station. In 1884, the Denver, South Park & Pacific reached Wheeler and constructed its own station along with a water tank. The South Park called its station Solitude, while the name Wheeler was used by the Denver & Rio Grande.

Today, nothing remains at the site itself. Most of the site is covered by highways while some of the site is part of the Copper Mountain golf course.

This old homestead cabin is the only original structure still standing near the Wheeler site. *(Sonje Jessen SJ025)*

Mac Poor, Denver, *South Park & Pacific*, Rocky Mountain Railroad Club, Denver, 1976, p. 447.

Mary Ellen Gilliland, *Summit*, Alpenrose Press, Silverthorne, Colorado, 1980, pp. 188-189.

William H. Bauer, James L. Ozment, John H. Willard, *Colorado Post Offices*, Colorado Railroad Museum, Golden, Colorado, 1990, p. 151.

WILD IRISHMAN

- *Summit County, Sts. John Creek drainage*
- *Accessible by four-wheel drive road*
- *Site had no post office; one standing structure and remains of several others*

Accessible over a rough four-wheel drive road in a beautiful alpine meadow at timberline on Glacier Mountain was the small mining camp of Wild Irishman. There is still one cabin, with its roof intact, plus the remains of several other cabins among the trees. Above the camp was the Wild Irishman mine, a silver producer during the silver boom in the late 1870s.

It was Irish New York City policeman Michael Dulhaney who found the silver ore and worked the mine, wearing his old policeman's hat. Colorado legend has it that when Dulhaney made his initial discovery, his hollering for joy caused a flash flood in Sts. John Creek, which wiped out three other mining camps!

Wild Irishman reached its peak in the early 1880s and after the silver crash in 1893, was probably abandoned. It was never incorporated nor did it have a post office or school.

Wild Irishman is accessible by driving to Sts. John above Montezuma and crossing the creek. The camp is approximately two miles up this road. There are several other roads branching off on both sides. In particular, a prominent road heads to the right and dead ends.

At the time Robert Brown wrote his book in the 1960s, *Jeep Trails to Colorado Ghost Towns*, there were four standing structures at the mine, which have since collapsed.

The setting for Wild Irishman is beautiful. It is located in an alpine meadow at timberline on Glacier Mountain. *(Kenneth Jessen 097D11)*

Mary Ellen Gilliland, *Summit*, Alpenrose Press, Silverthorne, Colorado, 1980, pp. 187-188.

Robert L. Brown, *Jeep Trails to Colorado Ghost Towns*, pp. 232-234.

INDEX